Social Motivation

FRONTIERS OF SOCIAL PSYCHOLOGY

Series Editors:

Arie W. Kruglanski, University of Maryland at College Park
Joseph P. Forgas, University of New South Wales

Frontiers of Social Psychology is a series of domain-specific handbooks. Each volume provides readers with an overview of the most recent theoretical, methodological, and practical developments in a substantive area of social psychology, in greater depth than is possible in general social psychology handbooks. The editors and contributors are all internationally renowned scholars whose work is at the cutting edge of research.

Scholarly, yet accessible, the volumes in the *Frontiers* series are an essential resource for senior undergraduates, postgraduates, researchers, and practitioners and are suitable as texts in advanced courses in specific subareas of social psychology.

Published Titles

Negotiation Theory and Research, Thompson
Close Relationships, Noller & Feeney
Evolution and Social Psychology, Schaller, Simpson & Kenrick
Social Psychology and the Unconscious, Bargh
Affect in Social Thinking and Behavior, Forgas
The Science of Social Influence, Pratkanis
Social Communication, Fiedler
The Self, Sedikides & Spencer
Personality and Social Behavior, Rhodewalt
Attitudes and Attitude Change, Crano & Prislin
Social Cognition, Strack & Förster
Social Psychology of Consumer Behavior, Wänke
Social Motivation, Dunning
Intergroup Conflicts and their Resolution, Bar-Tal

Forthcoming Titles

Explorations in Political Psychology, Krosnick & Chiang
Goal-directed Behavior, Aarts & Elliot
Group Processes, Levine
Social Metacognition, Briñol & DeMarree
Social Judgment and Decision Making, Krueger
Behavioral Economics, Stapel & Zeelenberg

For continually updated information about published and forthcoming titles in the *Frontiers of Social Psychology* series, please visit: www.psypress.com/frontiers

Social Motivation

Edited by
David Dunning

Ψ Psychology Press
Taylor & Francis Group

New York   London

Psychology Press
Taylor & Francis Group
711 Third Avenue,
New York, NY 10017

Psychology Press
Taylor & Francis Group
27 Church Road
Hove, East Sussex BN3 2FA

First issued in paperback 2015

Psychology Press is an imprint of the Taylor and Francis Group, an informa business

© 2011 by Taylor and Francis Group, LLC

International Standard Book Number: 978-1-138-87681-1 (pbk)
International Standard Book Number: 978-1-84169-754-3 (Hardback)

For permission to photocopy or use material electronically from this work, please access www.copyright.com (http://www.copyright.com/) or contact the Copyright Clearance Center, Inc. (CCC), 222 Rosewood Drive, Danvers, MA 01923, 978-750-8400. CCC is a not-for-profit organization that provides licenses and registration for a variety of users. For organizations that have been granted a photocopy license by the CCC, a separate system of payment has been arranged.

Library of Congress Cataloging-in-Publication Data

Social motivation / [edited by] David Dunning.
    p. cm. -- (Frontiers of social psychology)
    Includes bibliographical references and index.
    ISBN 978-1-84169-754-3 (hardcover : alk. paper)
    1. Motivation (Psychology)--Social aspects. I. Dunning, David (David A.)

BF503.S655 2011
302'.1--dc22

2010026987

Visit the Taylor & Francis Web site at
http://www.taylorandfrancis.com

and the Psychology Press Web site at
http://www.psypress.com

Contents

About the Editor

David Dunning is Professor of Psychology at Cornell University. An experimental social psychologist, Dr. Dunning is a fellow of both the American Psychological Society and the American Psychological Association. He has published nearly 100 scholarly journal articles, book chapters, and commentaries, and has also served as an associate editor of the *Journal of Personality and Social Psychology*. He is also the former Executive Officer of the Society for Personality and Social Psychology, an international organization with over 5,600 members, as well as the Foundation for Personality and Social Psychology. Much of his research has been supported financially by the National Institute of Mental Health and the National Science Foundation, and was recently reviewed in his book *Self-insight: Roadblocks and detours on the path to knowing thyself* (2005, Psychology Press).

Contributors

Nadia Ahmad
University of Kansas
Department of Psychology
Lawrence, Kansas, USA

Ashley Batts Allen
Duke University
Department of Psychology and
    Neuroscience
Durham, North Carolina, USA

C. Daniel Batson
University of Kansas
Department of Psychology
Lawrence, Kansas, USA

Abraham P. Buunk
University of Groningen and Royal
    Netherlands Academy of Arts and
    Sciences
Social and Organizational Psychology
Groningen, the Netherlands

Thai Q. Chu
University of California, Santa Barbara
Department of Psychology
Santa Barbara, California, USA

Geoffrey L. Cohen
Stanford University
School of Education and Department
    of Psychology
Stanford, California, USA

David Dunning
Cornell University
Department of Psychology
Ithaca, New York, USA

Detlef Fetchenhauer
University of Cologne
Department of Economic and Social
    Psychology
Cologne, Germany

Robert A. Josephs
University of Texas at Austin
Department of Psychology
Austin, Texas, USA

John T. Jost
New York University
Department of Psychology
New York, New York, USA

Heejung S. Kim
University of California,
    Santa Barbara
Department of Psychology
Santa Barbara, California, USA

Mark R. Leary
Duke University
Department of Psychology and
    Neuroscience
Durham, North Carolina, USA

I-Ching Lee
National Cheng-Chi University
Department of Psychology
Taipei, Taiwan

Clelia Anna Mannino
University of Minnesota
Department of Psychology
Minneapolis, Minnesota, USA

Pranjal H. Mehta
Columbia University
Graduate School of Business
New York, New York, USA

Allen M. Omoto
Claremont Graduate University
School of Behavioral and
    Organizational Sciences
Claremont, California, USA

Justin H. Park
University of Bristol
Department of Experimental
    Psychology
Bristol, UK

Eileen V. Pitpitan
University of Connecticut
Department of Psychology
Storrs, Connecticut, USA

Felicia Pratto
University of Connecticut
Department of Psychology
Storrs, Connecticut, USA

Mark Snyder
University of Minnesota
Department of Psychology
Minneapolis, Minnesota, USA

Eric L. Stocks
University of Texas at Tyler
Department of Psychology &
    Counseling
Tyler, Texas, USA

Judy Y. Tan
University of Connecticut
Department of Psychology
Storrs, Connecticut, USA

Gregory M. Walton
Stanford University
Department of Psychology
Stanford, California, USA

1

Social Motivation
Some Introductory Notes

DAVID DUNNING

The human organism is remarkably tuned in to its social world. Within 36 hours of being born, babies already show a preference for human faces, especially if those faces contain eyes gazing back at them. Within a scant 12 to 36 hours, infants prefer a video of their mother's face to a video of a stranger's (Bushnell, Sai, & Mullin, 1989). And within 70 hours, and certainly by two to three weeks, infants begin to imitate some of the facial expressions and physical actions of the adults around them (Anisfeld, 1996; Jones, 2007; Meltzoff & Moore, 1977, 1983). Within four days of birth, they become upset if an adult becomes still and stops interacting with them (Nagy, 2008). By six weeks, babies will imitate the mannerisms of a person they recognize that they have seen before, presumably as a way to confirm their recognition—a strategy that is different from the one they adopt with objects, which they shake to confirm their memory of (Meltzoff & Moore, 1994). By nine months, infants are already recognizing that other people are independent agents with minds of their own. By this time, they display and give objects to others (Bakeman & Adamson, 1984), follow the gaze of other people (Scaife & Bruner, 1975), and use other people's emotional reactions as cues about how they should react to new situations (Campos & Sternberg, 1981; Feinman & Lewis, 1983).

In a sense, the fact that the human organism is so acutely sensitive to other people is no surprise. People may live in a world of nature and objects, but it is other people who most likely determine the rewards that people covet and the punishments they fear. Throughout human evolution, people have depended on others as they grow from infant to child and then to adulthood. Any discerning observer quickly realizes that the human organism is not well suited to survive in the earth's natural environment. Our bodies are rather defenseless against the elements and even more vulnerable against possible predators. Thus, to survive,

1

people have long needed to rely on coordination and cooperation with others in their social group (Brewer & Caporael, 2006; Sober & Wilson, 1998), and it is only natural that, whether it be by selection or conditioning, people have become so attuned to the others who might compose that group.

This close tuning of people to others is also revealed in just how powerful an influence other people have on our thoughts, feelings, and behavior. Just the hint of the presence of another individual is enough to significantly alter people's behavior. For example, consider people who are asked to play a "dictator game" in the laboratory, in which they are given some amount of money and simply asked if they want to split the money with some other random, anonymous person. If the computer screen they are using to enter their response has two splotches on it that somewhat resemble human eyes, people give substantially more than they would otherwise (Haley & Fessler, 2005; Rigdon, Ishii, Watabe, & Kitayama, 2009), an effect replicated in a field setting during charity drives (Bateson, Nettle, & Roberts, 2006).

More normal, everyday levels of social pressure carry effects that can go well beyond our insight into them. People conform to the opinions of others much more than they anticipate (Douglas & Sutton, 2004, 2008) and to social groups with which they identify more than they are aware (Cohen, 2003). Women believe that they will respond to sexual harassment with assertive confrontation, yet when they experience harassment, their actions typically turn to indirect attempts of deflection (Swim & Hyers, 1999; Woodzicka & LaFrance, 2001).

Ordinary social pressures can also produce extraordinary consequences. In a review of airplane crashes between 1968 and 1994, the National Transportation Safety Board (1994) found at least 16 instances in which junior members of the crew knew of critical problems with the pilot's performance but failed to intervene before a fatal crash. Among medical professionals, a survey sponsored by the American Association of Critical-Care Nurses (Maxfield, Grenny, McMillan, Patterson, & Switzler, 2005) found that only 10% interceded when they spotted colleagues cutting corners, violating procedure, and otherwise putting patients in danger. And, of course, there is the classic Asch (1955) experiment, which showed that people are willing to dismiss the evidence of their own eyes in judgments of the physical environment, and the equally classic Milgram (1974) experiment, which showed that people, for all intents and purposes, will commit possible negligent homicide simply after being told that the "experiment requires that you continue."

A ROAD MAP FOR THIS VOLUME

Thus, the social world is a place filled with powerful forces to which people are tightly attuned. As a consequence, it is very likely that the most significant motives that people harbor are also attuned to trying to navigate their social world; thus, the focus of this volume. Within the social arena, what goals do people set? What rewards do they aim to fulfill? What punishments and costs do they strive to avoid? What drives do they struggle to satisfy?

The specific list of motives this volume concentrates on will come as no surprise to the behavioral science researcher, student, or interested layperson. In all, the volume will concentrate on three basic motives. The first will be the need to belong. The second will be the desire to help others. The last will focus on the need to gain influence and power.

But before getting to that set of motives, Park and Buunk will begin by discussing the importance of considering an evolutionary approach in any treatment of social motivation. In their chapter, Park and Buunk survey recent findings from behavioral science and describe how evolution may have selected various behavioral tendencies among our forebears to become some of the behavioral endowments we now possess in our contemporary worlds. In particular, they focus on environmental threats our ancestors most likely had to conquer and talk about how adaptations to those threats may influence social behavior today. For example, fears about disease may have led our ancestors—and thus us—to avoid individuals from different social groups or those among them who looked ill or odd. Natural selection may have also selected for those who were jealous of romantic rivals.

From this discussion of evolution, the volume moves to the motive to belong, with three chapters that focus on this motive. It is not a surprise that people might worry about whether they are valued members of their social groups, for not being in a group is significantly aversive. Social isolation has been linked to bad health and even early mortality, effects that are equivalent to the impacts of cigarette smoking on health (House, 2001). And even the slightest hint of ostracism is experienced as painful and distressing (Williams, 2007).

Leary and Allen begin the discussion on the need to belong, focusing on the tactics people use to establish their "relational value" to others. The authors focus on four characteristics people strive to establish—that they are likable, competent, supportive, and attractive—and describe the tactics people use, such as account making and sacrifice, in this pursuit.

In their chapter, Kim and Chu take a cultural perspective and point out that what it takes to be a person of value differs among cultures. To belong in a collectivist culture, a person must focus on his or her reputation and social standing among others. To be of value in an individualist culture, instead, requires somewhat of a balancing act, in that a person must fit in, yet also be something of an outsider with an outsized view of one's self. Kim and Chu describe how the differential pursuit of social belonging and its opposite, self-expression, across cultures leads to difference in thought itself, as well as how people arrange their social relationships.

In the final chapter on social belonging, Walton and Cohen turn to the consequences of social belonging. They point out the classic *social identity theory* principle that people's conceptions of the self are made up, in part, of the social groups they belong to and identify with. As a consequence, they adopt the attitudes and behaviors favored by their groups and are motivated to achieve only if other members of their group also wish to achieve. To do otherwise would be to strike out alone on a lonely and uncertain path.

The volume then turns to prosocial behavior and the motives that may underlie them. In a sense, the fact that people perform acts that benefit others rather than the self has always been a puzzle—but in some academic circles it has been a central and vexing one. Economics, for example, has gotten much theoretical mileage for over a century assuming that people are rational, self-interested actors who are interested only in their own personal material prospects. Evolutionary biology, similarly, has sustained itself for decades assuming that the creatures that adapt and survive, and thus who pass on their genes to their offspring, must be those who are squarely concerned about themselves only (and maybe, just maybe, their genetic kin). How can we reconcile the insights from these academic disciplines with the idea that the social world is replete with incontrovertible acts of selfless behavior?

Batson, Ahmad, and Stocks take up the challenge first. In their chapter, they discuss the many types of motives that might underlie acts of altruism, sorting them into four different categories—altruism to ultimately benefit the self, to ultimately benefit the other person, to benefit a group, or to uphold a moral principle. Along the way, they carefully conduct the tricky business of teasing apart altruism that ultimately serves selfish gains (e.g., I help you, compelling you to reciprocate later) from selfless altruism. In doing so, they emphasize the emotional underpinning of prosocial behavior, in particular pointing out how empathizing with another is an important precursor to generosity and self-sacrifice.

In the chapter that follows, Mannino, Snyder, and Omoto turn to selfless acts in the real world, asking why people volunteer to serve others in their community. Much like Batson et al., they carefully point out that volunteerism can be prompted by many different goals, some of which involve following personal pursuits (such as self-development), validating personal identities, and ratifying connections that people have to others and to the places in which they live.

Finally, Dunning and Fetchenhauer return us to the lab to ask why people make themselves vulnerable to others in a prosocial way, trusting anonymous strangers who have no necessary compulsion to reciprocate that trust. Their studies on economic games, perhaps, present the biggest challenge to economic approaches to prosocial behavior, in that they discover that people's willingness to trust others has little to do with the chance of reward and appears to be more about the act of trust itself rather than the potential gains and losses that might accrue from it. Like Batson, they ultimately focus on the emotions that surround the decision to trust and question the notion that trust is an analytical decision of social calculation.

The final section of the volume examines the motives attached to social hierarchy. It was the German sociologist Robert Michels who asserted nearly 100 years ago that all organizations, no matter how small or large, and no matter how democratic or autocratic, inevitably develop into oligarchies, with elites who hold more power, and influence than those lower down on the ladder of status (Michels, 1911/1915). Our last three chapters are devoted to the arrangements that people make as a consequence of this inevitability.

Mehta and Josephs concentrate on the struggle for status at the individual level and explore recent approaches that examine the biology behind human motivations. From a perspective on social endrocrinology, they concentrate on testosterone (T) and discuss how people's baseline T levels lead them to strive toward or away from status, away or toward affiliation, and how gains or losses in status drive changes in the level of T that they possess. Broad in their approach, they discuss the roles played by other hormones in other social motives, such as the part played by oxytocin in affiliation and cortisol in social approach.

Pratto, Lee, Tan, and Pitpitan follow with a discussion of power that bridges the individual and collective levels and describes why people want power in the first place, pointing out that power can provide basic needs and the social ones of acceptance and legitimacy. Along the way, they point out that people gain influence through multiple means—such as through having resources that others want, knowledge that others do not have, and force that others succumb to—discussing the degree to which these forms of power are fungible.

Jost ends, in his description of *system justification theory*, by explaining important motivational forces that leave social hierarchies in place. At the core of the chapter, Jost argues that people often strive to justify the social hierarchy that already exists, even if they hold a disadvantaged place within that hierarchy. In a scholarly approach, he compares and contrasts this perspective with Tajfel and Turner's (1979) *social identity theory* (which holds that everyone should favor their own group) and the *social dominance theory* of Sidanius and Pratto (1992) (who asserted that it is especially elite groups who strive, with some individual differences, to hold their hegemony over groups of lower power and status).

EMERGENT THEMES

A careful reader will see many themes emerge across the chapters. One theme is that a comprehensive account of social motivation will have to include analyses from many different levels and approaches. In this volume, one sees traditional laboratory methods from social psychology (such as Leary and Allen, Batson et al.), but one also sees field studies situated in the real world (Mannino et al., Walton and Cohen). One sees how the study of social motivation can profit from work on biomarkers (Mehta and Josephs), behavioral economics (Dunning and Fetchenhauer, Pratto et al.), and frameworks germinating from sociological theory (Jost). Cultural (Kim and Chu) and evolutionary analyses (Park and Buunk) also make crucial contributions to the study of social motives. The study of social motives is a big topic, and it is not a shock that a comprehensive and coherent analysis requires such multidisciplinary study.

But perhaps the most important theme that arises from the volume is that the study of social motivation requires careful and cautious thought. It is easy to see a behavior (e.g., giving clothes to a Salvation Army store) and assume that it is motivated by the most obvious consequence that follows from that behavior (e.g., other less-fortunate people benefit). But, as many of the scholars contributing to this volume point out, that assumption would be a potentially facile analysis that misses the real story.

It is, however, a type of analysis that one often sees in academic scholarship. Researchers, for example, see participants who have received a sizable sum of money in a lab experiment share that money with others who have not been so lucky and assume that people are driven by motives for fairness (Rabin, 1993) or egalitarianism (Dawes, Fowler, Johnson, McElreath, & Smirnov, 2007). But is that really what is going on? People do not react to all situations that clearly have dimensions of fairness and egalitarianism to them. In lab studies, people will not share if the person to be benefited by their largesse has yet to be identified, even if doing so would produce obviously more fair and equal results. It is only after a specific other person has been designated, or an interpersonal relationship between potential giver and recipient has been established, that people decide to give (Dunning & Fetchenhauer, this volume; Small & Loewenstein, 2003; Small, Loewenstein, & Slovic, 2007). Thus, it does not seem to be a general motive, or "taste," for fairness and egalitarianism that is at play. The most obvious consequence fails as the most likely explanation.

Assuming that behaviors are motivated by their most obvious consequences is facile for two interlocking reasons. First, single behaviors can be motivated by many different motives. As Mannino and colleagues observe, the decision to volunteer can reflect many motives. It can be spurred by a desire for altruism, to meet new people, or to express personal values, among many other possibilities. People may differ in the specific motive that produces that behavior. Alternatively, a single individual may harbor multiple motives that spur his or her decision. Or a person may decide to volunteer because of one motive (e.g., to express personal values) but over time come to stick with the decision because of another (e.g., retain a valued circle of friendships). In short, when it comes to the impact of motives on social behavior, one must be mindful of *equifinality*, the notion that the same behavior can be prompted via many different psychological means.

The second interlocking notion that one must be mindful of is that a single behavior can have many consequences, some intended and some not. As Batson et al. remind us in their chapter, an individual may give to a homeless person specifically to alleviate the distress they feel upon seeing a person less fortunate. The fact that the homeless person is now better off is a perfectly foreseeable consequence, but it is not the one that drove the person's behavior. As such, if one observes a behavior and links it to a specific consequence, one cannot be sure that it was that particular consequence that drove the behavior. One, instead, must be mindful of *multifinality*, the fact that a single cause, in this case one specific behavior, can prompt many effects. One must not be careless in identifying the specific effect that might be the most motivationally relevant.

The relevance of equifinality and multifinality to motivational analyses is made sharper by the fact the motives exist at very different levels. Park and Buunk point out, for example, that motives can be either *proximal* or *distal*. Imagine a rather youngish man, or woman, spending a good deal of time arranging his or her hair in the mirror before going out on a Saturday night. The distal cause that might prompt this behavior is the evolutionarily relevant goal of passing along one's genes to a new generation of offspring. The proximate goal might simply be to look physically attractive tonight.

At what level does social motivation take place? In any particular context, is the social motivation in play a proximate one, one that has an unintended consequence at the distal level? Or do social motivations organize themselves at the distal level? The question matters. For example, Jost notes that people tend to arrange their beliefs in ways that justify any current social hierarchy. But do they do so because they intend to achieve that distal goal, or do they serve that distal goal inadvertently in striving to achieve a more proximal goal, such as dispelling the cognitive dissonance people might feel if they believe they are disadvantaged? Answering that question may predict when the more distal goal comes into play. If people can achieve their more proximal goals in alternative ways (by, for example, deciding that they really are not socially disadvantaged), then the more distal goal will not be pursued. However, if it is the distal goal that is key, then it will be pursued regardless.

Goals also differ, as Batson et al. describe, in whether they are *instrumental* or *ultimate* goals. Instrumental goals are those that people pursue to achieve some other purpose; they are means to an end. Most people pursue employment not because a job is an end in itself but because jobs provide money and benefits. The job is the instrument to achieve those ends. Ultimate goals, in contrast, are ends in themselves. Some people choose the arts as their job because the act of self-expression is its own reward. This distinction affirms the observation that behaviors serve multiple goals and have consequences that are both intended and unintended.

Beyond this, Park and Buunk observe another reason why it may be a mistake to assume that a motivational explanation for a social behavior resides in its most obvious consequence. In a sense, behaviors that look motivated may not be purpose driven at all but instead be behavioral tendencies, or habits, that are triggered automatically by some external stimulus. In the example that opens their chapter, they discuss the fact that many birds will roll their eggs back into their nest if those eggs fall out. At first blush, this seems to be mindful, purposive behavior, but Park and Buunk point out that birds also do the same with baseballs and doorknobs. To miss the fact that apparently motivated behaviors might instead be *fixed action patterns* is to make an analytical mistake that can lead to misprediction. Assuming a fixed action pattern is instead mindfully motivated might mean to give it credit for flexibility that it does not have. It also may lead to predictions about behavioral scope that are mistaken. For example, assuming that birds mindfully herd their eggs back into their nests is to miss the specific environmental triggers (e.g., white spherical things) that are likely to elicit the behavior.

As such, the study of social motivations should necessitate a checklist of possibilities for any scholar. He or she must ask whether the behavior is motivated at all, as well as specify the motivation that really prompts the behavior under study and the scope of situations that elicit that motivation. He or she must look at any motivational phenomenon from distal and proximate levels, as well as consider instrumental and ultimate motivations. This list is not exhaustive but is offered to suggest just how challenging, but hopefully how interesting, the motivational analysis of social behavior might be.

WHAT MAY BE LEFT OUT

Of course, as snapshots of current thinking in the field, the chapters composing this volume may leave out some issues that are well worth mulling over. There is one topic missing in this book in particular that I hope someday a successor volume will take up. That issue is the mystery of social coordination. It is clear that to successfully live with others, people must shape their actions every day to ensure that those actions harmonize and dovetail with the actions of others. People must coordinate so their social interactions run smoothly—without undue effort or harm. It is important, for example, that car drivers know that they should sidle over to the right side of the road after they pull out of the driveway (or, in a few countries, to the left) to let cars going the other way pass to their left. The alternative would be a world in which drivers would have to enter an effortful, awkward, and potentially dangerous negotiation with every car coming at them. Or imagine a world in which people did not have well-learned rules about turn-taking in conversation, or who should speak first at a faculty meeting, or, among romantic couples, which way they should tilt their head for a kiss.

Thus, it is clear that making life a little less nasty, brutish, and short requires successful coordination with others. And, to date, there has been little, if any, work on whether or when people harbor a specific motivation to coordinate or the extent to which such a motive might lead to a general expertise at it.

Such study is warranted because casual observation suggests that people show a remarkable dexterity at social coordination. One need only walk down a busy midtown avenue in Manhattan to recognize that almost all people effortlessly navigate around each other without the whole crowd devolving into chaos. Schelling (1960), in his classic work on social coordination, showed that a surprising majority of Americans knew that if they had to meet a friend in New York the next day—but had no chance to arrange a specific time and place before the meeting itself—that they should just show up at the information booth at Grand Central Terminal at noon (with some tourists occasionally suggesting the front of the Empire State Building, still at noon). Studies of natural disasters and man-made ones (such as airplane crashes and war) show that everyday citizens are instantly able, with calm and bravery, to coordinate effective first responses to an emergency well before the professionals arrive (Fischhoff, 2005).

Or do they? There is another, more disturbing, portrait of social coordination that can be painted. A worrisome literature from medicine suggests that people fail at coordination even when it is a matter of life or death. One study of nearly 2,500 deadly or near-deadly incidents occurring in medical care discovered that communication failures were the root cause of roughly 70% of cases (Joint Commission, 2004). Doctors or nurses failed to speak up at critical times, or gave incomplete information, or failed to notify everyone on the medical team of critical information, or failed to explain the rationale for various procedures, or chose language with different levels of specificity or generality that other members of a medical team discounted as uninformative (Leonard, Graham, & Bonacum, 2004; Lingard et al., 2004). Often, members of a medical team failed to coordinate their actions because they had very different understandings of the situation at hand. In essence, they failed to recognize that they were not "all at the same movie," with frequently fatal results (Lingard et al., 2004). In aviation, coordination failures are so frequent, and their consequences so severe, that airlines have been driven to mandate exhaustive checklists and conversational rules to compel cockpit teams toward social coordination that does not appear to arise naturally (Helmreich, 2000).

There are many motivational questions that can be asked about social coordination. When are people motivated to coordinate with others, and when might they be less motivated? Are there other social motivations that interfere with social coordination, and what are the consequences of that interference? Does the motivation to coordinate lead to the right choices, or are there mistakes that people make that lead to social disorder even when it is not wanted?

CONCLUDING REMARK

But those are questions for another book. Herein, I think the reader will find that there are many crucial questions that psychologists are already answering with intelligence and rigor. This introduction is designed to set the table for the book, and I believe the reader will find that the meal offered at that table is already quite plentiful. It is my hope that it is also stimulating, enjoyable, and one worth savoring.

REFERENCES

Anisfeld, M. (1996). Only tongue protrusion modelling is matched by neonates. *Developmental Review, 16*, 149–161.

Asch, S. E. (1955). Opinions and social pressure. *Scientific American, 193*, 31–35.

Bakeman, R., & Adamson, L. (1984). Coordinating attention to people and objects in mother–infant and peer–infant interactions. *Child Development, 55*, 1278–1298.

Bateson, M., Nettle, D., & Roberts, G. (2006). Cues of being watched enhance cooperation in a real-world setting. *Biology Letters, 3*, 412–414.

Brewer, M. B., & Caporael, L. (2006). An evolutionary perspective on social identity: Revisiting groups. In M. Schaller, J. Simpson, & D. Kenrick (Eds.), *Evolution and social psychology* (pp. 143–161). New York: Psychology Press.

Bushnell, I. W. R., Sai, F., & Mullin, J. T. (1989). Neonatal recognition of the mother's face. *British Journal of Developmental Psychology, 7*, 3–15.

Campos, J., & Sternberg, C. (1981). Perception, appraisal, and emotion: The onset of social referencing. In M. Lamb & L. Sherrod (Eds.), *Infant social cognition: Empirical and theoretical considerations* (pp. 273–314). Hillsdale, NJ: Lawrence Erlbaum.

Cohen, G. L. (2003). Party over policy: The dominating impact of group influence on political beliefs. *Journal of Personality and Social Psychology, 85*, 808–822.

Dawes, C. T., Fowler, J. H., Johnson, T., McElreath, R., Smirnov, O. (2007). Egalitarian motives in humans. *Nature, 446*, 794–796.

Douglas, K. M., & Sutton, R. M. (2004). Right about others, wrong about ourselves? Actual and perceived self–other differences in resistance to persuasion. *British Journal of Social Psychology, 43*, 585–603.

Douglas, K. M., & Sutton, R. M. (2008). The hidden impact of conspiracy theories: Perceived and actual influence of theories surrounding the death of Princess Diana. *Journal of Social Psychology, 148*, 210–221.

Feinman, S., & Lewis, M. (1983). Social referencing at 10 months: A second order effect on infants' responses to strangers. *Child Development, 54*, 878–887.

Fischhoff, B. (2005, August 7). A hero in every aisle seat. *New York Times*, Sect. 4, p. 13.

Haley, K. J., & Fessler, D. M. T. (2005). Nobody's watching? Subtle cues affect generosity in an anonymous economic game. *Evolution and Human Behavior, 26*, 245–256.

Helmreich, R. L. (2000). On error management: Lessons from aviation. *British Journal of Medicine, 320*, 781–785.

House, J. S. (2001). Social isolation kills, but how and why? *Psychosomatic Medicine, 63*, 273–274.

Joint Commission. (2004). *Sentinel event statistics.* Retrieved from http://www.jcaho.org

Jones, S. S. (2007). Imitation in infancy: The development of mimicry. *Psychological Science*, *18*, 593–599.

Leonard, M., Graham, S., & Bonacum, D. (2004). The human factor: The critical importance of effective teamwork and communication in providing safe care. *Quality and Safety in Health Care, 13*, 85–90.

Lingard, L., et al. (2004). Communication errors in the operating room: An observational classification of recurrent types and effects. *Quality and Safety in Health Care, 13*, 330–334.

Maxfield, D., Grenny, J., McMillan, R., Patterson, K., & Switzler, A. (2005). *Silence kills: The seven crucial conversations in healthcare*. Provo, UT: Vitalsmarts. Retrieved from http://www.silencekills.com/

Meltzoff, A. N., & Moore, M. K. (1977). Imitation of facial and manual gestures by human neonates. *Science, 198*, 75–78.

Meltzoff, A. N., & Moore, M. K. (1983). Newborn infants imitate adult facial gestures. *Child Development, 54*, 702–709.

Meltzoff, A. N., & Moore, M. K. (1994). Imitation, memory, and the representations of persons. *Infant Behavior and Development, 25*, 39–61.

Michels, R. (1915). *Political parties: A sociological study of the oligarchical tendencies of modern democracy* (E. Paul & C. Paul, Trans.). New York: Free Press. (Original work published 1911)

Milgram, S. (1974). *Obedience to authority: An experimental view*. New York: HarperCollins.

Nagy, E. (2008). Innate intersubjectivity: Newborns' sensitivity to communication disturbance. *Developmental Psychology, 44*, 1779–1784.

National Transportation Safety Board (1994). *Safety study: A review of flightcrew-involved, major accidents of U.S. air carriers, 1978–1990*. Washington, DC: National Technical Information Service.

Rabin, M. (1993). Incorporating fairness into game theory and economics. *American Economic Review, 83*, 1281–1302.

Rigdon, M. L., Ishii, K., Watabe, M., & Kitayama, S. (2009). Minimal social cues in the dictator game. *Journal of Economic Psychology, 30*, 358–367.

Scaife, M., & Bruner, J. S. (1975). The capacity for visual joint attention in the infant. *Nature, 253*, 265–266.

Schelling, T. (1960). *The strategy of conflict*. Cambridge, MA: Harvard University Press.

Sidanius, J., & Pratto, F. (1992). *Social dominance: An intergroup theory of social hierarchy and oppression*. New York: Cambridge University Press.

Small, D. A., & Loewenstein, G. (2003). Helping "A" victim or helping "THE" victim: Altruism and identifiability. *Journal of Risk and Uncertainty, 26*(1), 5–16.

Small, D. A., Loewenstein, G., & Slovic, P. (2007). Sympathy and callousness: The impact of deliberative thought on donations to identifiable and statistical victims. *Organizational Behavior and Human Decision Processes, 102*, 143–153.

Sober, E., & Wilson, D. S. (1998). Unto others: The evolution and psychology of unselfish behavior. Cambridge, MA: Harvard University Press.

Swim, J. K., & Hyers, L. L. (1999). Excuse me—what did you just say?! Women's public and private responses to sexist remarks. *Journal of Experimental Social Psychology, 35*, 68–88.

Tajfel, H., & Turner, J. (1979). An integrative theory of intergroup conflict. In W. G. Austin & S. Worchel (Eds.), *The social psychology of intergroup relations* (pp. 94–109). Monterey, CA: Brooks-Cole.

Williams, K. D. (2007). Ostracism: The kiss of social death. *Social and Personality Psychology Compass, 1*, 236–247.

Woodzicka, J. A., & LaFrance, M. (2001). Real versus imagined gender harassment. *Journal of Social Issues, 57*, 15–30.

2

Interpersonal Threats and Automatic Motives

JUSTIN H. PARK and ABRAHAM P. BUUNK

Not one man in a billion, when taking his dinner, ever thinks of utility. He eats because the food tastes good and makes him want more. If you ask him *why* he should want to eat more of what tastes like that, instead of revering you as a philosopher he will probably laugh at you for a fool.

—William James (1890/1950, p. 386)

M any species of waterfowl display a fascinating behavioral sequence. Upon observation of an egg that has rolled away from its nest, the brooding animal waddles over to the egg and nudges it back to the nest with its beak (Lorenz, 1965). Repeated displacement of an egg results in repeated replacement by the animal. For human observers, it's difficult not to attribute humanlike motives—it appears as though the bird really *wants* to keep all of its eggs inside the nest. In fact, if we had observed a person engaging in the same egg-nudging behavior, the most sensible explanation would be that this person wants—is motivated—to keep the eggs inside the nest.

But appearances are deceiving. Simple experiments have revealed that these birds will also perform the same egg-nudging behavior on objects such as baseballs and doorknobs that have been placed in the vicinity of the nest (Tinbergen, 1951). Termed *fixed action patterns*, these seemingly complex behaviors are in fact simple stimulus–response reflexes. Waterfowl do not possess goal-directed motives that we are tempted to attribute—they don't really care about the welfare of their eggs, per se. Whatever "motive" underlies the egg-nudging fixed action pattern, it is manifestly distinct from the apparent function served by it (for a similar discussion, see Schaller, 2003).[1]

The discovery of fixed action patterns had profound implications for biologists' understanding of animal behavior. It provoked researchers to address several critical issues, and it led to a fruitful meta-theoretical framework for studying behavioral tendencies (Lorenz, 1965; Tinbergen, 1951). The essential aspects of the framework are as follows. First, fixed action patterns reveal a history of evolutionary *selection*. Any behavior that is part of a species' natural repertoire suggests natural selection of behavioral variants that conferred fitness benefits to predecessors (Bolles, 1970). ("Confer fitness benefits" is shorthand for saying that the trait in question increased the likelihood of survival and reproduction for the ancestral animals that possessed the trait.) Second, if fixed action patterns conferred fitness benefits, this implies that they served some adaptive *function* for the ancestral animals. One might reasonably hypothesize that the egg-nudging behavior was selected because it served—usually reliably—the fitness-enhancing function of gathering eggs that rolled away from the nest (this sort of explanation of behavior is also known as "ultimate" explanation). Finally, careful empirical investigation of fixed action patterns uncovers the specific *mechanisms* that underlie them. In the case of the egg-nudging sequence, waterfowl seem to possess a mechanism that detects superficially egglike objects and triggers the nudging behavior (this sort of explanation of behavior is also known as "proximate" explanation). Under some circumstances, such mechanisms produce functionally futile responses (in terms of fitness), which, ironically, expose the design features of the mechanisms (by observing birds collecting baseballs and doorknobs, researchers were able to infer that the birds respond mechanically to objects that look roughly like eggs instead of accurately identifying their own eggs under variable circumstances).

In this chapter, we describe lines of research in which a similar framework has been applied to the study of human motives. We begin by describing the theoretical foundations of the evolutionary approach and the ways in which this approach can generate new and testable hypotheses regarding various psychological processes. We then review research lines in various domains of interpersonal phenomena that have tested those hypotheses. Throughout this endeavor we have tried to apply the lessons learned from the humble fixed action patterns. This is not to suggest that humans exhibit behaviors that could properly be called fixed action patterns. Nonetheless, the key idea—that seemingly goal-directed motives may in fact be largely automatic programs—can be usefully applied to the study of human behavior.

Perhaps the most important lesson for psychological researchers is to refrain from attaching humanlike goal-directed motives to observed behavior, even, paradoxically, to human behavior.[2] This is because the actual motives that drive behavior may be logically independent of the apparent goal served by them, even if we are tempted—as in the case of fixed action patterns—to attribute rational, goal-directed motives. Bowlby (1969) similarly noted the need to separate "function" from "causation" when explaining instinctive behavior. For example, to say that "a bird engages in egg-nudging behavior *in order to* keep them in the nest" conflates function (the evolutionary reason for the existence of the behavior) with actual causes of the behavioral pattern (the mechanical program and the contextual triggers). As we illustrate below, the automatic nature of goal-like "motives" can be exposed given appropriate circumstances (Schaller, 2003), and, like waterfowl, people may occasionally exhibit responses that appear functionally futile to "wiser" observers (such as experimental psychologists). Indeed, instances of functionally futile behavior may be an inevitable consequence of psychological programs shaped by evolution.

Of course, the notion that various primes can automatically trigger behavior is not new (e.g., Bargh, Chen, & Burrows, 1996). Thus, many psychologists will have no difficulty accepting the argument that many behavioral reactions are reflexive and relatively unmediated. Our present thesis pertains more to motivation researchers: Goal-directed motives are constructs to be demonstrated, not assumed (cf. Pittman, 1998).

THEORETICAL FOUNDATIONS OF AN EVOLUTIONARY APPROACH TO MOTIVATION

There is a common misperception that an evolutionary approach implies that people are geared—consciously or unconsciously—toward gene propagation (Park, 2007). Perhaps this is not surprising, given the ease with which people perceive goal-directedness in behavior and in many other natural phenomena (Heider & Simmel, 1944; Keleman, 2004); gene propagation is often depicted—if only metaphorically—as the ultimate purpose of biological organisms. But as the brief discussion above makes clear, there is no need to assume that "gene propagation" is anywhere on the minds of individual animals, including humans, even while engaging in fitness-enhancing behavior. As observed by James (1890/1950), no one eats food for utility.

Then, what drives people? Among researchers adopting an evolutionary perspective, the prevailing view is that evolved motives—in both human and non-human animals—are unlikely to be devoted to abstract fitness-enhancing goals such as "survival" and "reproduction," much less to "gene propagation." Rather, it's more likely that animals possess proximate psychological mechanisms that are geared toward more specific problems within domains such as finding food, mates, and allies and avoiding disease, injury, and exclusion—mechanisms that are largely blind to the ultimate "goal" of gene propagation (e.g., Pinker, 1997; Tooby & Cosmides, 1992).[3] Another way of saying this is that ancestral individuals who happened to possess psychological tendencies that dealt better with those specific problems were more likely to pass on their genes (along with the same psychological tendencies).

As humans are a social species, a substantial portion of evolved psychological mechanisms is expected to handle problems posed by group living (Fiske, 2003; Schaller, Park, & Kenrick, 2007). Although sociality conferred considerable benefits to humans—leading to the evolution of a diverse array of psychological mechanisms that make cooperative group living possible—it also generated a large number of problems, ranging from communicable pathogens to competition for mates. Different problems call for different, functionally specialized solutions, and several research programs have made significant strides by considering those functionally specialized solutions (Schaller et al., 2007).

For various reasons, applying an evolutionary perspective to psychological questions is theoretically and methodologically complicated (e.g., Conway & Schaller,

2002). The process of evolution—natural selection of adaptive traits—operates on populations over long stretches of time. But most psychologists are interested in cognitive and emotional processes operating within individuals at much shorter time intervals and in how such processes are influenced by specific situational and individual-level variables. So how does one integrate these logically distinct levels of analysis?

One way is to begin with observed psychological dispositions (e.g., the need to belong) and speculate on the possible adaptive functions that they serve (e.g., Baumeister & Leary, 1995). In the long run, however, this inductive process is best complemented by a deductive process in which one begins with educated guesses about adaptive problems faced by humans and derives hypotheses regarding the mechanisms that are likely to have evolved in response to those problems. From the perspective of motivation research, the primary objective then is to come up with clear hypotheses concerning the specific motives that are likely to have evolved to solve various adaptive problems (keeping in mind that these "motives" need not be goal directed in any rational sense) and the ways in which these motives may operate within individual humans—hypotheses that can then be empirically tested. We provide several examples of this logical process below.

It becomes clear that the evolutionary approach, viewed from this perspective, does not—indeed, cannot—replace existing social psychological approaches to the study of human motivation. Rather, the evolutionary approach offers clues as to the ultimate origins of motives (*why* humans have the motives they have) and suggests hypotheses regarding the operation of the motivational processes.

Moreover, from an evolutionary perspective, emotional–motivational systems (which often provide the impetus for behavior) are an integral part of functionally specialized mechanisms (Ellsworth, 2007; Keltner, Haidt, & Shiota, 2006). What sorts of features might we expect evolved motivational systems to possess? There isn't a single kind of evolved motive, of course. Some are relatively broad—cutting across many social situations—and may be genuinely goal directed (e.g., the need for positive self-views, the need to understand; Dunning, 2003; Fiske, 2003). Others are activated under more specific circumstances and may produce only apparently goal-directed behavior (e.g., disgust, fear; Curtis, Aunger, & Rabie, 2004; Öhman & Mineka, 2001), operating, in many important ways, like fixed action patterns. The "motives" that we discuss in this chapter are generally of the latter category—those that are activated relatively automatically in response to specific cues and compel specific kinds of psychological and behavioral responses, regardless of whether the alleged function is actually served in the end. Indeed, as with fixed action patterns, it often happens that functionally futile responses tell us more about the underlying nature of these mechanisms.

Unlike fixed action patterns of nonhuman animals, people's psychological mechanisms—even those that are activated automatically—are characterized by a high degree of flexibility. Evolved psychological mechanisms, including functional motivational systems, are associated with specific benefits, but their operation typically entails costs as well. Thus, these mechanisms often show evidence of functional flexibility—being more strongly activated when additional regulatory information indicates that the benefits are especially likely to outweigh the costs (Haselton &

Nettle, 2006; Schaller et al., 2007). Such regulatory information may lie in individuals' external environments (e.g., threatening situations) as well as within individuals (e.g., chronically fearful personality). This, of course, makes it convenient for social and personality psychologists to locate person and situation effects (with which they are eminently familiar) within an evolutionary framework.

As a simple example from recent research, there may be a general tendency for people to seek out—and thus notice more quickly—attractive members of the opposite sex. However, consistent with functional cost–benefit considerations, this tendency is stronger among people with an unrestricted approach to mating, a pattern that is moreover limited to men (Duncan et al., 2007). In this example, the effects of two individual-difference variables (sex and sociosexuality) on visual attention have been illuminated by recognizing that attentional processes likely evolved to be functionally flexible, with specific individual-difference variables providing informational input. Below, we provide several more examples of ways in which the automatic activation of emotional–motivational systems is moderated by various contextual and individual variables.

SPECIFIC INTERPERSONAL THREATS AND EVOLVED SOCIAL MOTIVES

In this section, we illustrate the present approach by reviewing several active lines of empirical research. Specifically, we describe three classes of interpersonal threats that humans have dealt with, describe functionally specialized psychological mechanisms (including emotional–motivational systems) that likely evolved in response to those threats, and summarize empirical research documenting the consequences of these mechanisms in various social contexts. The classes of interpersonal threats that we discuss are superficially diverse—communicable disease, harmful outgroups, and romantic rivals—but they are all likely to have imposed substantial selection pressure throughout the evolutionary history of the highly social *Homo sapiens*.

As we highlight, not only have these research lines identified mechanisms that plausibly have been shaped by evolution, they have provided deeper insights into interpersonal phenomena—ranging from attraction to stigmatization—that are of perennial interest to social psychologists.

Communicable Disease

A fundamental problem for any group-living species is communicable disease. Many lethal or otherwise harmful pathogens are transmitted between individuals of the same species through various kinds of contact. In response to this problem, social animals have evolved not only complex physiological defense mechanisms but also a sort of "behavioral immune system" that allows animals to detect pathogen-carrying conspecifics and selectively avoid them (Kurzban & Leary, 2001; Loehle, 1995; Schaller & Duncan, 2007). Aversion toward and avoidance of infected conspecifics has been observed in many human and nonhuman animals (e.g., Crandall

& Moriarty, 1995; Goodall, 1986b; Kavaliers & Colwell, 1995; Kiesecker, Skelly, Beard, & Preisser, 1999).

One might be tempted to assume that there exist goal-directed motives that allow animals to efficiently and accurately avoid infected conspecifics. However, the fact that relatively simple animals (such as mice) avoid diseased others, and the fact that any scientific understanding of disease emerged only recently (and only in some societies), suggest that any evolved "motive" underlying avoidance of infected others is likely to operate mechanically and independently of any rational understanding of disease. Indeed, research indicates that what people actually respond to are various bodily cues (e.g., lesions, rashes) that are correlated with the presence of pathogens, rather than knowledge of infection itself (Duncan, 2005; Kurzban & Leary, 2001; Schaller, Park, & Faulkner, 2003).

The perception of disease-connoting cues may then trigger specific emotional responses such as disgust (e.g., Curtis et al., 2004) and the activation of disease-relevant cognitions such as appraisals of contagion and contamination (e.g., Rozin, Millman, & Nemeroff, 1986; Woody & Teachman, 2000). These appraisals are far from sophisticated: People seem to believe that "things that once have been in contact with each other may influence each other through transfer of some of their properties via an 'essence' " (Rozin et al., 1986, p. 703), which, in some cases, is perceived to have a physical basis (Nemeroff & Rozin, 1994). Developmental psychologists have found that the notion of contagion is something that children learn very quickly (Kalish, 1996; Solomon & Cassimatis, 1999); among adults, the desire to avoid diseased others is correlated with the perceived contagiousness of the disease (Bishop, 1991; Crandall & Moriarty, 1995). Moreover, historical evidence indicates that people have long possessed an understanding of disease as something that can be communicated interpersonally, though their understanding may have been rudimentary (Conrad & Wujastyk, 2000). Nearly universal aversion toward people with visually conspicuous diseases such as leprosy is a good illustration of this process in operation.

If the evolutionary perspective offered only the suggestion that it is adaptive to avoid diseased others, it would be of limited scientific value. But there are several nonobvious implications that follow from a careful consideration of how this mechanism might operate. One implication is that, much like the actual immune system, the behavioral immune system may respond overinclusively, sometimes responding to cues that signal no real threat. This is because bodily cues that signal infection are imperfectly correlated with infection, giving rise to a signal-detection problem in which some sort of detection errors are inevitable.

For pathogen-detection mechanisms, the following errors are possible: perceiving a healthy individual to be a pathogen carrier (false positive) and perceiving a pathogen carrier to be healthy (false negative). The costs associated with these two errors are asymmetrical. An adaptive approach to these errors (*error management theory*; Haselton & Buss, 2000; Haselton & Nettle, 2006) suggests that inferential mechanisms are biased toward minimizing the more costly form of error, even though this inevitably leads to an increase in the less costly form of error. In the domain of pathogen detection, false negatives impose substantially greater fitness costs than false positives; consequently, the inferential mechanisms are likely to be biased toward minimizing false negatives (Haselton & Nettle, 2006; Kurzban & Leary, 2001; Nesse, 2005). This means that people may be biased toward inferring that healthy people are diseased, rather than the reverse. An important implication is that any gross deviation from what is considered "normal" appearance or behavior in a given society (even in the absence of contagious disease) may be interpreted as evidence of infection, automatically triggering an aversive response (Kurzban & Leary, 2001; Schaller & Duncan, 2007). Not unlike a bird that mechanically nudges any roughly egglike object toward its nest, people react mechanically to various morphological abnormalities, regardless of whether the function of avoiding disease is actually served.

Importantly, people's automatic aversive responses are likely to be functionally flexible. Like physiological immune responses, behavioral responses entail costs and benefits. They should thus be activated especially strongly when the benefits of avoiding disease are high (and are likely to exceed the costs). Information concerning the benefits of avoidance behavior may be present in the environment (e.g., outbreak of disease in the local area) or within individuals (e.g., suppressed immune system). Simply put, the motivation to avoid individuals bearing disease-connoting cues is expected to be particularly powerful among people with heightened (perceived) susceptibility to pathogens (Schaller & Duncan, 2007).

These implications have led to several lines of inquiry and interesting discoveries. One set of studies investigated the degree to which physical disabilities (regardless of whether they have infectious causes) may be perceived as a heuristic cue for pathogens (Park, Faulkner, & Schaller, 2003). In one study conducted in Canada, Park et al. (2003) found that students with chronically heightened concerns about disease are less likely to have friends with physical disabilities. In another study, employing a computer-based reaction-time task, Park et al. (2003) found that the perception of physically disabled people automatically activates disease-relevant cognitions, even though perceivers were fully aware that the physical disabilities had noninfectious causes. Moreover, this effect was stronger among people with chronically or experimentally heightened concerns about disease (at least among European Canadian participants; among Asian Canadians, disgust sensitivity was a better predictor of the tendency to implicitly associate disability with disease-relevant cognitions).

Other studies have found that the perception of a facial birthmark automatically activates disease cognitions, even when perceivers are aware that no contagious disease is present (Duncan, 2005), and that features associated with old age may also activate disease-avoidance responses (Duncan & Schaller, 2009). In a recent study conducted in Canada, Duncan and Schaller (2009) found that students with both chronically and experimentally heightened concerns about disease made stronger implicit associations between old people and disease concepts but not unpleasant concepts in general (again, the effect was limited to European Canadians; among East Asian Canadians, the implicit associations were elevated regardless of concerns about disease—we revisit these cultural differences below).

A wide range of physical cues seems to trigger the disease-avoidance process. In cultures in which thin body types are considered the norm, gross obesity may be perceived as a disease cue, leading to aversive responses. In one recent study

(Klaczynski, 2008), 7-year-old and 10-year-old American and Chinese children were asked to sample drinks "created" by obese and average-weight children (the weight status of the drink maker was manipulated via photos on the package label). After sampling the drinks, children gave lower taste ratings to the drinks made by obese children; what is more telling, they believed that the drinks made by obese children were more likely to cause illness, especially among those who had, prior to sampling the drinks, read a story about an ill child who had infected other children by coughing (in the control condition, the ill child coughed, but the other children did not become ill). Consistent with the view presented in this chapter, Klaczynski (2008) noted the implicit, automatic nature of the obesity–disease link:

> The current argument is not that children have explicit beliefs that obesity is an illness or that children explicitly recognize the similarities between obesity and certain illnesses; rather, it is that children are implicitly aware that an illness-like "wrongness" characterizes obesity. It is this inexplicable sense that motivates avoidance of unfamiliar obese individuals. (p. 60)

In a study with university students, Park, Schaller, and Crandall (2007) found that those with chronically heightened concerns about disease harbor more strongly negative attitudes toward fat people. This relationship emerged especially strongly among people who had viewed images of obese people immediately prior to expressing their antifat attitudes, consistent with the idea that it is the visual perception of physical deviation that activates the behavioral immune system. In another study, employing a computer-based reaction-time task, Park et al. (2007) found that the perception of obese people automatically activates disease-relevant cognitions, especially following experimentally induced pathogen salience. In both of these studies, additional methods and analyses ruled out the possibility that the effects are due simply to nonspecific (disease-irrelevant) negativity toward obesity.

Disease-connoting cues come not only in the form of morphological deviation but also in the form of cultural outgroupness. This follows from the fact that humans have historically lived in small groups and contact with members of other groups often introduced diseases to which individuals had no immunity (Diamond, 1999). For people within any given culture, certain outgroups may appear especially foreign with respect to food preparation and hygiene practices. Because each culture has developed (via cultural evolution) its own set of practices for preventing infection, cultures with different practices—especially in the domains of food preparation and hygiene—may be perceived as posing disease threats. Thus, the perception of outgroups, particularly those that are subjectively foreign, may activate disease-avoidance responses.

Some preliminary evidence for this hypothesis came from studies showing that people attribute more threat to germs that come from a disliked peer than from a lover (Nemeroff, 1995). More direct evidence emerged from a series of studies conducted by Faulkner, Schaller, Park, and Duncan (2004). They found that Canadian participants with chronically heightened concerns about disease tend to harbor more strongly negative attitudes toward cultural outgroup members, but only those outgroup members perceived to be subjectively foreign in the disease-relevant domains (e.g., Africans, Sri Lankans); such effects were not found for outgroup members perceived to be subjectively familiar (e.g., Asians, Europeans). Faulkner et al. (2004) also found parallel effects in studies in which concerns about disease were experimentally manipulated.

Other studies, employing somewhat different methodologies, have replicated and extended these findings. One study found that chronically heightened concerns about disease are associated with both outgroup negativity and ingroup positivity, even after controlling for concerns about death (Navarrete & Fessler, 2006). Another study found that individual differences in disgust sensitivity are associated with both negativity toward outgroups and positivity toward the ingroup (Navarrete & Fessler, 2006). Yet another study examined reactions of pregnant women. In the first trimester of pregnancy, both the fetus and the mother are more susceptible to infection (because of suppressed immune responses), implying the hypothesis that women in this period may exhibit stronger disease-avoidance responses. In a cross-sectional study of pregnant women, Navarrete, Fessler, and Eng (2007) found that women in the first trimester exhibit stronger ingroup positivity and outgroup negativity.

In sum, findings from several lines of research suggest that humans possess psychological mechanisms designed to motivate avoidance of potentially diseased others. Owing to the design features of these mechanisms, aversive responses are activated automatically and overinclusively, sometimes even in the face of conflicting rational assessments of contagiousness. In most of the studies described above, the people or groups that activated the disease-avoidance response posed no real threat of infection. Thus, not unlike waterfowl nudging doorknobs, people appear to respond reflexively to disease-connoting cues, regardless of the actual health status of the target individual.

It is also important to note that these automatic responses are flexible, in a manner consistent with functional cost–benefit considerations. Most of the studies described above revealed that the aversive responses are especially pronounced among people with heightened sensitivity to disease, because of either internal or external events. By adopting an evolutionary perspective, not only have these research lines provided clues toward understanding the ultimate function of emotional–motivational responses associated with disease avoidance (e.g., disgust, desire for physical distance), they have also produced a more detailed picture of the contextual and individual variables that are involved in phenomena generally classified as "stigmatization."

Harmful Outgroups

In addition to the unintentional harm that people may inflict on each other in the form of communicable pathogens, people may sometimes be intentionally harmful. There are various instances in which people may aggress against others; we focus here on aggression resulting from clashes between members of different coalitional groups. Humans are a tribal species, and the fitness costs imposed by intergroup conflict—and the adaptive responses that evolved—are ancient (Van Vugt & Park, 2010). Not only are present-day hunter-gatherer groups highly territorial (e.g., Eibl-Eibesfeldt, 1974; Kelly, 1995), there is evidence that chimpanzees (which are also a group-living species) are highly territorial and that intergroup encounters are often hostile (Dugatkin, 1997; Goodall, 1986a; Wrangham & Peterson, 1996). Given the recurrent problem posed by potentially harmful outgroup members, there likely evolved psychological mechanisms that facilitate avoidance of such harmful encounters (Kurzban & Leary, 2001; Sidanius & Pratto, 1999). Indeed, people are highly attentive to cues suggesting coalitional alliance and quickly discriminate ingroup members from outgroup members; moreover, the perception of potentially harmful outgroup members activates cognitive and emotional responses (e.g., fear, anxiety, danger-relevant thoughts) that facilitate adaptive behavior (e.g., avoidance, caution; Kurzban & Neuberg, 2005; Schaller & Neuberg, 2008).

Like the behavioral immune system, psychological mechanisms underlying outgroup avoidance must deal with the problem of signal detection. Again, there are greater costs associated with false negatives (failing to perceive dangerous outgroup members) than with false positives (perceiving benign people as dangerous outgroup members). One consequence is that features that superficially serve as an indicator of outgroup membership may automatically activate the relevant psychological responses, regardless of whether such features actually signal coalitional alliance. In contemporary social contexts, visually conspicuous cues such as ethnicity may activate the responses, especially for groups such as African Americans that are—for various reasons—stereotyped as being hostile (indicating that substantial social learning is involved in perceiving certain social categories as harmful outgroups). As a consequence, interactions with such outgroup members may elicit psychological and physiological responses associated with fear and anxiety (e.g., Blascovich, Mendes, Hunter, Lickel, & Kowai-Bell, 2001; Phelps et al., 2000). In short, humans appear to possess motives that serve the function of avoiding dangerous outgroup members—but, again, these avoidance responses may be activated regardless of whether the function is served.

Along these lines, Kurzban, Tooby, and Cosmides (2001) hypothesized that people's tendency to quickly categorize others according to "race" is a result of racial features being erroneously perceived as a coalition cue. Kurzban et al. (2001) demonstrated that manipulating aspects of the context (emphasizing other, more valid coalition cues) can eliminate people's tendency to automatically encode the race of target individuals (however, the same procedure did not eliminate people's tendency to automatically encode the sex of target individuals, which makes sense given that efficient perception of sex is biologically relevant for other reasons).

Furthermore, the automatic activation of motives underlying outgroup avoidance is expected to be functionally flexible—activated especially strongly in the presence of information suggesting greater benefits (e.g., elevated possibility of harm, greater probability of intergroup contact). Along these lines, it's worth noting that dangerous intergroup conflicts have historically involved males more than females. This is true for chimpanzees as well as for humans (Chagnon, 1988; Goodall, 1986a). As a consequence, not only are males more likely to be perceived as harmful outgroup members, the functional psychological mechanisms that are activated in response to outgroup threat may be especially sensitized among males (Schaller & Neuberg, 2008; Van Vugt & Park, 2010). This contrasts with the threat of communicable disease discussed above, for which one expects few sex differences (except in circumscribed instances, such as during pregnancy), and it is consistent with the logic of functional flexibility.

There are many kinds of regulatory cues suggesting elevated risk of injury and/ or intergroup contact. A fundamental cue—one that nearly everyone confronts on a daily basis—is ambient darkness. A series of studies examined the effects of ambient darkness on functionally specific psychological responses. In one study, Schaller, Park, and Faulkner (2003) asked Canadian students to rate the ingroup (Canadians) and an outgroup (Iraqis) on four trait dimensions, two of which were danger relevant (hostile, trustworthy) and two of which were not (ignorant, openminded). The ratings were made in either a dark room or a well-lit room. By reverse scoring the negative items and by subtracting ratings of the outgroup from ratings of the ingroup, the researchers created a measure of ingroup favoritism. The results showed that for the traits unrelated to danger, ingroup favoritism was identical across the dark and light conditions; however, for traits connoting danger, ingroup favoritism was higher in the dark. Subsequent studies conducted by Schaller, Park, and Faulkner (2003) showed that such effects are especially pronounced among people who tend to believe that the world is a dangerous place.

Schaller, Park, and Mueller (2003) conducted similar studies employing computer-based reaction-time methodology. They found that students sitting in a dark room were more likely to implicitly associate members of an outgroup (Africans) with danger-relevant negative words (but not with danger-irrelevant negative words), and these effects were specific to participants with chronically heightened beliefs about danger.

Another regulatory cue suggesting heightened threat posed by outgroup members is being a member of a numerical minority. Indeed, there is evidence that when people are in a relatively smaller group, they are more hypervigilant to potential dangers from outside the group (Roberts, 1996; Wirtz & Wawra, 1986). But minority status is a matter of perception. Schaller and Abeysinghe (2006) observed that there often are "double minority" situations in which all members of conflicting groups perceive themselves to be in the minority. For instance, Jews outnumber Arabs within Israel, but within the Middle East more broadly, Arabs outnumber Jews. Sinhalese outnumber Tamils within Sri Lanka, but within southern Asia more broadly, Tamils outnumber Sinhalese.

In a study conducted in Sri Lanka, Schaller and Abeysinghe (2006) asked Sinhalese students to first complete a geography task that temporarily made salient either just the island nation of Sri Lanka (within which Sinhalese outnumber Tamils) or a broader region of south Asia (within which Sinhalese are outnumbered by Tamils) and then to complete measures of stereotypes and conflict-relevant attitudes. Results revealed that when participants focused on the broader geographical region (and thus perceived the ingroup as the minority), their stereotypic perceptions of Tamils were more demonizing and their conflict-relevant attitudes were less conciliatory. Thus, it appears that psychological mechanisms that evolved within the context of face-to-face intergroup conflict may, in contemporary contexts, underlie attitudes toward ethnic and national outgroups. And the evolutionary approach may aid discovery of additional variables (such as perceived ingroup/outgroup size) that importantly influence those attitudes.

In addition to attributing danger-relevant stereotypes to potentially dangerous outgroup members, another sort of functional response is to (mis)perceive aggressive intention in such people (again, inferring nonexistent aggressive intent is less costly than failing to perceive existent aggressive intent). Maner et al. (2005) termed this tendency *functional projection*, and they proposed that people may tend to perceive anger in the faces of outgroup members (especially male outgroup members), even if those people are holding neutral expressions. In two studies, Maner et al. (2005) found that experimentally heightened self-protective motive (which involved showing participants scenes from the movie *Silence of the Lambs*) increased the tendency among White American participants to perceive anger in the faces of Black men and Arab men (but not in the faces of White men or women).[4]

In sum, several lines of research indicate that humans possess a specific set of mechanisms devoted to categorizing others on the basis of coalitional group membership and perceiving them as dangerous people. Often, this highly automatic categorization process is based on superficial cues (such as race) that do not actually correspond to coalitional alliances. Unlike domain-general theories of intergroup psychology (e.g., social identity theory), the evolutionarily based theory of coalitional psychology specifies the kinds of people that are likely to be automatically categorized on the basis of group membership (categorization often occurs on the basis of visually salient cues), as well as the kinds of psychological responses that are likely to be precipitated by the perception of such people (activation of danger-relevant cognitions and perception of aggression). The logic of functional flexibility has also generated hypotheses—and new empirical results—pertaining to contextual and individual variables that may moderate responses toward coalitional outgroup members.

Romantic Rivals

Thus far, we have discussed interpersonal threats that impinge on one's physical well-being. Given the importance of survival, it is no surprise that humans possess an array of psychological mechanisms associated with avoiding injury and death. For reproductive success, however, mechanisms for survival are useless unless accompanied by mechanisms for reproduction. There is now a huge literature documenting the ways in which women and men identify, attract, and retain optimal mates (e.g., Buss, 1994; Rhodes, 2006). Following the overarching theme of this chapter, we focus here on a specific form of interpersonal threat in the realm of mating relationships—the threat posed by competitors for an existing mate—and the associated psychological mechanisms that guard against this threat.

There is indeed an emotional–motivational system that has been hypothesized to deal with this type of threat: jealousy (Buss, 2000; Daly, Wilson, & Weghorst, 1982). The activation of jealousy—which may include several more specific emotions (fear, anger)—drives one to ward off rivals and to increase both vigilance and affection. Just like the other "motives" discussed above, jealousy is triggered largely automatically in response to specific cues—information suggesting that a rival individual is interested in one's partner and/or vice versa (Buunk, Massar, & Dijkstra, 2007). And like those other threat-based motives, jealousy is on a hair-trigger, going off at the slightest suggestion of threat (Buss, 2000).

Of course, warding off rivals and increasing vigilance and affection are costly activities. Thus, the logic of functional flexibility suggests that jealousy responses (including vigilance and inference of infidelity) should be especially strong when they are most beneficial. There are several such instances. Most fundamentally, a partner's infidelity may be more costly for males than for females because of the possibility of cuckoldry; thus, jealousy responses may be functionally more beneficial for men. Indeed, Andrews et al. (2008) hypothesized—and found—that men more accurately detect their partner's infidelity; they also found that men make more false-positive errors (i.e., inferring nonexistent infidelity).

It has also been hypothesized that different types of partner infidelity—sexual versus emotional—impose different costs for females and males, with a partner's sexual infidelity being relatively more costly for males and a partner's emotional infidelity being relatively more costly for females (Buss, Larsen, Westen, & Semmelroth, 1992). Indeed, not only are men's and women's jealousy reactions differentially activated by these two types of infidelity (e.g., Buss et al., 1992; Buunk, Angleitner, Oubaid, & Buss, 1996; Schützwohl, 2007), men are particularly attentive to cues suggesting sexual infidelity, whereas women are particularly attentive to cues suggesting emotional infidelity (Schützwohl, 2006, 2008). And as indicated by the existence of false-positive errors (Andrews et al., 2008), many apparent infidelity cues are presumably inauthentic and lead to functionally futile responses. Moreover, the fact that women's fertility (probability of conception) varies across the menstrual cycle introduces another moderator to men's cost–benefit "calculations" with respect to the deployment of jealousy responses (for a discussion, see Haselton & Nettle, 2006).

Other kinds of regulatory cues may also signal greater (fitness) benefits associated with stronger jealousy. Across both sexes, some people may have lower (perceived) mate value, especially in comparison with their partner, thus requiring them to exercise greater vigilance against desertion or mate poaching. Also, certain environmental conditions (e.g., unbalanced sex ratio) may indicate that one is at greater risk of desertion. And in some cases, the rival who poses a threat may be particularly attractive. Below, we review several lines of research testing hypotheses derived from the basic premise that rivals that are especially attractive to the opposite sex may trigger especially powerful jealousy reactions (Dijkstra & Buunk, 1998). We also describe some recent empirical findings showing that certain rivals evoke jealousy among some people more strongly than others.

In the mating market, different kinds of traits are considered attractive by men and women. Relatively speaking, women pay particular attention to men's traits indicating the ability to attain fitness-enhancing resources (e.g., status, dominance) or traits indicating fitness itself (e.g., physical attractiveness, masculinity), and men pay particular attention to women's traits indicating reproductive potential (e.g., youth, physical attractiveness; Buss, 1994; Gangestad & Simpson, 2000). A straightforward hypothesis derived from this perspective is that rivals possessing traits that are attractive to the opposite sex are likely to evoke especially strong feelings of jealousy.

To test this hypothesis, Dijkstra and Buunk (2002) presented Dutch participants with a jealousy-evoking scenario and asked them to indicate the kind of person that would make them most jealous. Men were more likely than women to mention rivals' physical dominance, social status, and "smoothness" as characteristics that would make them jealous. In contrast, women were more likely than men to mention rivals' sexy appearance and slenderness as characteristics that would make them jealous. On the basis of the array of characteristics provided by participants, Dijkstra and Buunk (2002) developed a questionnaire comprising a list of characteristics and conducted additional research in which participants were asked to indicate their level of jealousy if a rival surpassed them on each of those characteristics. As expected, men indicated stronger jealousy than women when the rival was more socially or physically dominant or had a higher status than themselves; on the other hand, women indicated stronger jealousy than men when the rival was more physically attractive than themselves.

Other studies have found conceptually similar results (Buss, Shackelford, Choe, Buunk, & Dijkstra, 2000). In parallel studies conducted in Korea, the Netherlands, and the United States, Buss et al. (2000) found that across all three cultural samples, men reported greater distress than did women when a rival surpassed them on financial prospects, job prospects, and physical strength. In contrast, women in all three samples reported greater distress than did men when a rival surpassed them on facial and bodily attractiveness.

Although these findings are consistent with the hypothesis that men and women possess sex-specific functionally specialized jealousy mechanisms, it's also possible that men and women have simply learned to respond with greatest distress to rivals who happen to pose the highest threat (i.e., dominant rivals in the case of males and physically attractive rivals in the case of females). Additional research conducted with homosexual participants provided a particularly strong test of the hypothesis that these responses reflect sex-specific mechanisms, rather than socially learned responses (Buunk & Dijkstra, 2001). In this study, gay men and lesbian women were presented with jealousy-evoking scenarios in which the relevant characteristics of rivals were experimentally manipulated. Like heterosexual men, gay men especially value physical attractiveness (but not dominance) in partners (Bailey, Gaulin, Agyei, & Gladue, 1994). Consequently, a rational assessment of threat should lead gay men to be especially jealous of physically attractive rivals. However, Buunk and Dijkstra (2001) found that gay men are more jealous of dominant rivals than physically attractive rivals. Likewise, lesbian women, like heterosexual women, were more jealous of physically attractive rivals. This pattern of results parallels those of heterosexual men and women (Dijkstra & Buunk, 1998), suggesting that the sex-specific tendency for some kinds of rivals to evoke especially strong jealousy is deeply rooted and immune to rational assessments.

Additional evidence from research employing subliminal priming methodology suggests that the sex-specific effects of rivals' characteristics on jealousy are quite automatic. In one study, Massar, Buunk, and Dechesne (2009) asked Dutch participants to indicate as quickly as possible whether two neutral words presented on the computer screen were related to each other by pressing one of two colored keys on the keyboard. The words in this "association task" were neutral words such as *house* and *garden*. In between these two neutral words, participants were subliminally exposed to words of various characteristics. To ensure that participants would assign the characteristics to another individual (rather than to themselves), each word was preceded by a subliminally presented personal pronoun—*he* for male participants and *she* for female participants. The characteristics were those that were most often mentioned in a pretest when men and women were asked to generate words related to attractiveness (*pretty, beautiful, slender, sexy*) and social dominance (*tough, money, power, success*). (These are imperfect translations of Dutch words that apply equally to men and women.)

After completing the association task, participants read a jealousy-evoking scenario and indicated how jealous they would be in such a situation. The results were instructive. Women reported more jealousy following subliminal exposure to attractiveness words than to social dominance words (the effect was limited to those self-reporting high mate value; those with low mate value reported elevated jealousy across both exposure conditions). A different pattern of results was observed among men. These findings further highlight the utility of a functional perspective on illuminating sex-specific links between rivals' characteristics and jealousy.

Thus far, we have described the ways in which jealousy may be differentially activated by different kinds of rivals. Of course, a given rival may be more threatening to some people than to others. By asking participants to imagine rivals that surpassed them on certain traits, the studies described above indirectly tested the impact of participants' own characteristics. Independent of such social comparisons, however, people who are less attractive as potential mates (because of the lack of desirable traits) may be chronically more jealous than others. A few lines of research have investigated the role of people's own characteristics more directly by obtaining more objective measures.

There is evidence that fluctuating asymmetry (an indicator of developmental stability; Gangestad & Simpson, 2000) is associated with jealousy, with morphologically more asymmetrical people reporting greater jealousy (Brown & Moore, 2003). Recent studies indicate that height is also associated with jealousy and is associated differently for men and women (Buunk, Park, Zurriaga, Klavina, & Massar, 2008). Male height is linearly associated with fitness—not only are taller men considered more attractive, they have greater reproductive success (e.g., Pawlowski, Dunbar, & Lipowicz, 2000). Female height, on the other hand, is curvilinearly associated with fitness—average-height women have greater reproductive success than tall or short women (e.g., Nettle, 2002). Paralleling such fitness effects of height, Buunk et al. (2008) found preliminary evidence showing that male height is linearly associated with jealousy (with taller men reporting less jealousy), whereas female height is curvilinearly associated with jealousy (with average-height women reporting the least jealousy).

Another study examined the relationship between people's second-to-fourth digit ratio (2D:4D) and jealousy in response to rivals with various superior characteristics (Park, Wieling, Buunk, & Massar, 2008). Because 2D:4D is correlated with prenatal testosterone levels (with the result that men tend to have lower 2D:4D than women; Manning, 2002; van Anders, Vernon, & Wilbur, 2006), it can serve as a crude indicator of "masculinity" and "femininity." Because people are expected to be especially jealous of rivals who surpass them on desired trait dimensions, one possibility is that dominant rivals are especially jealousy-evoking for men with higher (more "feminine") 2D:4D, and physically attractive rivals are especially jealousy-evoking for women with lower (more "masculine") 2D:4D. A study by Park, Wieling, et al. (2008) revealed essentially this pattern of results. Although the process by which these objective indicators of mate value (e.g., height, 2D:4D) affect levels of jealousy remains unclear, a link between lower self-esteem and higher jealousy suggests that self-esteem serves as a mediator (Buunk & Dijkstra, 2006).

In sum, there is substantial evidence that jealousy is an emotional–motivational system that evolved in response to the problem posed by romantic rivals. But jealousy responses are neither invariant nor erratic. In accordance with the logic of functional flexibility, jealousy is activated by rivals who pose the greatest threat, especially among people who are—because of their lack of specific desirable traits—particularly vulnerable to that form of threat, and jealousy is not activated in a rational manner. Given the ambiguity of information regarding one's partner's infidelity, error-management considerations indicate that there are likely to be many instances of false alarms—functionally futile jealousy reactions to nonexistent threats.

IMPLICATIONS FOR THE STUDY OF MOTIVATION AND ADDITIONAL ISSUES

Regardless of theoretical perspective, most psychologists would agree that human motivation is linked to some sort of function, whether one conceptualizes function in terms of psychological goal-directedness or in terms of history of natural selection. In this chapter, we focused on emotional–motivational systems that may appear motivated in the goal-directed sense, although they actually operate more like fixed action patterns. Logically separating presumed function from actual causes of behavior is especially important when discussing tendencies that allegedly have an evolutionary basis, as it is tempting to assume that evolution has designed behavioral tendencies that "serve the goal" of survival or reproduction or whatever else that seems intuitively beneficial (Park, 2007). Once we make this logical distinction, the functional perspective offers epistemological tools not only for understanding the origins of human motives but also for uncovering their mechanistic features. There is thus no need to assume that avoidance tendencies are actually motivated by a desire to avoid disease or dangerous outgroups; there is likewise no need to assume that jealousy responses are motivated by a desire to protect one's genetic interests. We must separate function from causation (Bowlby, 1969).

Ultimately, psychologists are interested in the stuff that does occupy people's heads and causes behavior. As we have tried to show, the approach outlined here can greatly aid inquiry into actual mental events and causes of behavior. The approach reminds researchers to look beneath apparent goal-directedness; it also facilitates the articulation of more textured and fine-grained hypotheses regarding cues and specific responses to those cues. For instance, people do not react to some vague notion of infection; they react to specific tangible cues, some that actually connote infection and some that do not. Furthermore, it isn't simply a general feeling of negativity that underlies avoidance tendencies; rather, different emotional–motivational states, activated within specific people and under specific circumstances, compel specific kinds of psychological reactions that underlie phenomena often categorized under the umbrella term "prejudice" (Cottrell & Neuberg, 2005; Neuberg & Cottrell, 2006). Similarly, threats to one's relationship do not evoke simply general unpleasantness; rather, a specific emotional–motivational state is aroused, which compels specific forms of behavior and whose strength varies predictably across people and contexts (Buunk et al., 2007).

The functional perspective (and more specifically, error management theory; Haselton & Buss, 2000; Haselton & Nettle, 2006) also provides a means of understanding and predicting apparently faulty cognitions or futile motivational states. Many fundamental motives that immediately precede behavior are triggered largely reflexively in response to specific cues. The fact that these mechanisms are cue based means that there is often a signal-detection problem for which one type of error is functionally less costly than the other type of error. Whether the mechanism underlies waterfowl's detection of eggs or people's detection of unfaithful partners, there are likely to be biases toward reducing one type of error (which increases the other type of error), leading to occasional occurrences of apparently nonfunctional (or dysfunctional) responses. What is more important, the observation of such nonfunctional responses gives additional credence to the notion that many of these "motives" are not characterized by true goal-directedness.

The implications of evolved emotional–motivational systems reach beyond the immediate psychological level of analysis. The reasoning we have outlined here is fully compatible with—and usually complements—the observation that many psychological tendencies are learned and can vary across cultures (Schaller, 2007; Schaller et al., 2007). For instance, although it is clearly true that people acquire many stimulus–response associations during development, an evolutionary perspective is required to explain why people are quicker to acquire some associations, such as fear of snakes, than other associations, such as fear of flowers (Öhman & Mineka, 2001). Similarly, we know that cultural differences in psychological traits and behavior emerge either because similar psychological mechanisms are evoked differently in different regions or because different cultural norms are transmitted in different locales (Tooby & Cosmides, 1992). Our task then becomes identifying the relevant ecological variables that are responsible for the differential evocation of certain dispositions (Gangestad, Haselton, & Buss, 2006) and/or the factors—both psychological and environmental—that make some cultural variants more readily transmittable than others (Schaller, Faulkner, Park, Neuberg, & Kenrick, 2004).

Of course, this is not to say that complete answers to problems posed by learning and cultural differences are currently available or easily obtainable. In the research reviewed above, there were instances of cultural differences (different patterns of responses to heuristic disease cues among European and Asian

Canadians) that remain unexplained. It's possible that the prevalence and types of disease in the local area influence the acquisition and perception of potentially disease-connoting cues (e.g., Gangestad & Buss, 1993). It's also possible that people in different cultures conceptualize disease and the process of becoming ill differently (e.g., Nguyen & Rosengren, 2004), resulting in different patterns of aversive responses toward apparently diseased others. We simply do not know. There are also cultural differences in jealousy responses that demand additional theoretical and empirical attention (e.g., Buunk et al., 1996). Explanations of these sorts of cultural differences will likely be incomplete without an overarching framework grounded in function.

A good example of integrating evolved psychology with cultural variation comes from recent work linking pathogen prevalence with cultural variation in psychological and behavioral dispositions. Some parts of the world, for various reasons, are characterized by higher prevalence of disease-causing pathogens. According to the logic of functional flexibility, people in those regions may benefit from psychological and behavioral tendencies that lead to reduced contact with unfamiliar things, individuals, and groups. At the individual level, traits such as introversion, low openness to experience, and restricted sociosexuality tend to be associated with reduced interpersonal contact. Schaller and Murray (2008) thus hypothesized—and found—that regions that are characterized by higher prevalence of pathogens are also inhabited by people characterized by greater introversion, lower openness to experience, and more restricted sociosexuality. At the cultural level, collectivism (as opposed to individualism) is associated with more strongly defined ingroup–outgroup distinctions and reduced intergroup contact. Indeed, regions with higher pathogen prevalence also tend to have more collectivistic cultures (Fincher, Thornhill, Murray, & Schaller, 2008).

Finally, we should note that although our review focused on motives that are subjectively aversive, there are several research programs focusing on more positive motives that underlie behavior, such as altruism and cooperation (Van Vugt & Van Lange, 2006). For instance, empathy (and other related emotional states) has been found to motivate altruistic behavior (e.g., Eisenberg & Miller, 1987), and this may be explained—in part—by conceptualizing empathy as an emotional–motivational state that evolved to serve the adaptive function of kin-directed altruism (Park, Schaller, & Van Vugt, 2008; Schaller, 2003).[5] Again, the fact that kin-directed altruism has an evolutionary basis does not imply that people actually think about genetic benefits when they react positively to kin. Rather, specific cues that are typically associated with kinship may automatically activate altruistic "motives," which may mechanically engender prosocial behavior, regardless of whether the function of assisting genetic kin is actually served (Park & Schaller, 2005).

Whether we are investigating "negative" motives such as the desire to avoid disease or more "positive" motives such as the desire to help kin, the simple lessons learned from fixed action patterns apply equally. We must remember that the actual psychological state that compels a specific action—even seemingly goal-directed action—may be completely blind to the goal served by it. Only then can investigation of immediate precursors of behavior proceed fruitfully without being sidetracked by questions such as "Are people really motivated to pass on their genes?" or "Do altruistic motives really exist?" In many instances, searching for goal-directed motivational states may prove fruitless, just as it would have been fruitless to search for the motive in waterfowl to "keep eggs inside the nest."

ACKNOWLEDGMENTS

Preparation of this chapter was supported in part by the Royal Netherlands Academy of Arts and Sciences. We thank Lesley Duncan, Jessica Pass, and Mark Schaller for their helpful comments.

NOTES

1. Psychologists typically conceptualize *motive* in terms of some sort of goal-directed state. As Pittman (1998) noted in his review, "Motivationally oriented psychologists like to look inside the person for desires: what is wanted, what is strived for, what will feel satisfying or unsatisfying to the actor?" (p. 550). In this chapter, we focus on states that may *appear* goal directed but are in fact largely automatic. For simplicity we employ the term *motive* to refer to these states as well; we use quotation marks when it is necessary to clearly distinguish these automatic "motives" from the traditional conceptualization of motive.

2. Inferences of rational motives (and other mental states) are, of course, a natural product of another set of functional mechanisms, usually referred to as *theory of mind* (Saxe, Carey, & Kanwisher, 2004). Theory of mind, when functioning normally, is powerful—people readily assign motives and other human characteristics even to plain shapes moving on a screen (Heider & Simmel, 1944). Although theory of mind is interesting in its own right, psychological researchers often must override their own theory-of-mind inferences in order to gain a deeper understanding of actual causes of behavior. One might even say that a key ingredient of scientific thinking in general is the explicit rejection of superfluous anthropomorphic explanations for natural phenomena.

3. We should note that the extent to which the mind is "domain specific" or "modular" (and what it means for the mind to have such characteristics) is a matter of ongoing debate (e.g., Barrett & Kurzban, 2006; Prinz, 2006). For researchers adopting an evolutionary perspective, the most relevant insight is that the mind comprises *functionally specialized* mechanisms (Barrett, 2007).

4. Functional projection is not limited to the perception of aggression. Maner et al. (2005) also found that men with heightened mate-search goals are more likely to perceive sexual arousal in the faces of attractive women who are in fact holding neutral expressions (the reason being that missing a real mating opportunity is more costly than falsely inferring a nonexistent one).

5. Because of the high degree of genetic relatedness between kin—such as between parents and offspring and between siblings—Hamilton (1964) hypothesized that tendencies to be altruistic toward close kin could be naturally selected.

REFERENCES

Andrews, P. W., Gangestad, S. W., Miller, G. F., Haselton, M. G., Thornhill, R., & Neale, M. C. (2008). Sex differences in detecting sexual infidelity: Results of a maximum likelihood method for analyzing the sensitivity of sex differences to underreporting. *Human Nature, 19,* 347–373.

Bailey, J. M., Gaulin, S., Agyei, Y., & Gladue, B. A. (1994). Effects of gender and sexual orientation on evolutionarily relevant aspects of human mating psychology. *Journal of Personality and Social Psychology, 66,* 1081–1093.

Bargh, J. A., Chen, M., & Burrows, L. (1996). Automaticity of social behavior: Direct effects of trait construct and stereotype activation on action. *Journal of Personality and Social Psychology, 71,* 230–244.

Barrett, H. C. (2007). Modules in the flesh. In S. W. Gangestad & J. A. Simpson (Eds.), *The evolution of mind: Fundamental questions and controversies* (pp. 161–168). New York: Guilford.

Barrett, H. C., & Kurzban, R. (2006). Modularity in cognition: Framing the debate. *Psychological Review, 113,* 628–647.

Baumeister, R. F., & Leary, M. R. (1995). The need to belong: Desire for interpersonal attachments as a fundamental human motivation. *Psychological Bulletin, 117,* 497–529.

Bishop, G. D. (1991). Lay disease representations and responses to victims of disease. *Basic and Applied Social Psychology, 12,* 115–132.

Blascovich, J., Mendes, W. B., Hunter, S. B., Lickel, B., & Kowai-Bell, N. (2001). Perceiver threat in social interactions with stigmatized others. *Journal of Personality and Social Psychology, 80,* 253–267.

Bolles, R. C. (1970). Species-specific defense reactions and avoidance learning. *Psychological Review, 77,* 32–48.

Bowlby, J. (1969). *Attachment and loss: Vol. 1, Attachment.* London: Hogarth.

Brown, W. M., & Moore, C. (2003). Fluctuating asymmetry and romantic jealousy. *Evolution and Human Behavior, 24,* 113–117.

Buss, D. M. (1994). *The evolution of desire: Strategies of human mating.* New York: Basic Books.

Buss, D. M. (2000). *The dangerous passion: Why jealousy is as necessary as love and sex.* New York: Free Press.

Buss, D. M., Larsen, R. J., Westen, D., & Semmelroth, J. (1992). Sex differences in jealousy: Evolution, physiology, and psychology. *Psychological Science, 3,* 251–255.

Buss, D. M., Shackelford, T. K., Choe, J., Buunk, B. P., & Dijkstra, P. (2000). Distress about mating rivals. *Personal Relationships, 7,* 235–243.

Buunk, A. P., & Dijkstra, P. (2006). Temptations and threat: Extradyadic relations and jealousy. In A. L. Vangelisti & D. Perlman (Eds.), *The Cambridge handbook of personal relationships* (pp. 533–556). New York: Cambridge University Press.

Buunk, A. P., Massar, K., & Dijkstra, P. (2007). A social cognitive evolutionary approach to jealousy: The automatic evaluation of one's romantic rivals. In J. P. Forgas, M. G. Haselton, & W. von Hippel (Eds.), *Evolution and the social mind: Evolutionary psychology and social cognition* (pp. 213–228). New York: Psychology Press.

Buunk, A. P., Park, J. H., Zurriaga, R., Klavina, L., & Massar, K. (2008). Height predicts jealousy differently for men and women. *Evolution and Human Behavior, 29,* 133–139.

Buunk, B. P., Angleitner, A., Oubaid, V., & Buss, D. M. (1996). Sex differences in jealousy in evolutionary and cultural perspective: Tests from the Netherlands, Germany, and the United States. *Psychological Science, 7,* 359–363.

Buunk, B. P., & Dijkstra, P. (2001). Evidence from a homosexual sample for a sex-specific rival-oriented mechanism: Jealousy as a function of a rival's physical attractiveness and dominance. *Personal Relationships, 8*, 391–406.

Chagnon, N. A. (1988). Life histories, blood revenge, and warfare in a tribal population. *Science, 239*, 985–992.

Conrad, L. I., & Wujastyk, D. (2000). *Contagion: Perspectives from pre-modern societies.* Burlington, VT: Ashgate.

Conway, L. G., III, & Schaller, M. (2002). On the verifiability of evolutionary psychological theories: An analysis of the psychology of scientific persuasion. *Personality and Social Psychology Review, 6*, 152–166.

Cottrell, C. A., & Neuberg, S. L. (2005). Different emotional reactions to different groups: A sociofunctional threat-based approach to "prejudice." *Journal of Personality and Social Psychology, 88*, 770–789.

Crandall, C. S., & Moriarty, D. (1995). Physical illness stigma and social rejection. *British Journal of Social Psychology, 34*, 67–83.

Curtis, V., Aunger, R., & Rabie, T. (2004). Evidence that disgust evolved to protect from risk of disease. *Proceedings of the Royal Society of London B, 271*, S131–S133.

Daly, M., Wilson, M., & Weghorst, S. J. (1982). Male sexual jealousy. *Ethology and Sociobiology, 3*, 11–27.

Diamond, J. (1999). *Guns, germs, and steel: The fates of human societies.* New York: Norton.

Dijkstra, P., & Buunk, B. P. (1998). Jealousy as a function of rival characteristics: An evolutionary perspective. *Personality and Social Psychology Bulletin, 24*, 1158–1166.

Dijkstra, P., & Buunk, B. P. (2002). Sex differences in the jealousy-evoking effect of rival characteristics. *European Journal of Social Psychology, 32*, 829–852.

Dugatkin, L. A. (1997). *Cooperation among animals: An evolutionary perspective.* New York: Oxford University Press.

Duncan, L. A. (2005). *Heuristic cues automatically activate disease cognitions despite rational knowledge to the contrary.* Unpublished master's thesis, University of British Columbia.

Duncan, L. A., Park, J. H., Faulkner, J., Schaller, M., Neuberg, S. L., & Kenrick, D. T. (2007). Adaptive allocation of attention: Effects of sex and sociosexuality on visual attention to attractive opposite-sex faces. *Evolution and Human Behavior, 28*, 359–364.

Duncan, L. A., & Schaller, M. (2009). Prejudicial attitudes toward older adults may be exaggerated when people feel vulnerable to infectious disease: Evidence and implications. *Analyses of Social Issues and Public Policy, 9*, 97–115.

Dunning, D. (2003). The zealous self-affirmer: How and why the self lurks so pervasively behind social judgment. In S. J. Spencer, S. Fein, M. P. Zanna, & J. M. Olson (Eds.), *Motivated social perception: The Ontario Symposium* (Vol. 9, pp. 45–72). Mahwah, NJ: Lawrence Erlbaum.

Eibl-Eibesfeldt, I. (1974). The myth of the aggression-free hunter and gatherer society. In R. L. Holloway (Ed.), *Primate aggression, territoriality, and xenophobia* (pp. 435–457). New York: Academic Press.

Eisenberg, N., & Miller, P. A. (1987). The relation of empathy to prosocial and related behaviors. *Psychological Bulletin, 101*, 91–119.

Ellsworth, P. C. (2007). Appraisals, emotions, and adaptation. In J. P. Forgas, M. G. Haselton, & W. von Hippel (Eds.), *Evolution and the social mind: Evolutionary psychology and social cognition* (pp. 71–88). New York: Psychology Press.

Faulkner, J., Schaller, M., Park, J. H., & Duncan, L. A. (2004). Evolved disease-avoidance mechanisms and contemporary xenophobic attitudes. *Group Processes and Intergroup Relations, 7*, 333–353.

Fincher, C. L., Thornhill, R., Murray, D. R., & Schaller, M. (2008). Pathogen prevalence predicts human cross-cultural variability in individualism/collectivism. *Proceedings of the Royal Society B, 275*, 1279–1285.

Fiske, S. T. (2003). Five core social motives, plus or minus five. In S. J. Spencer, S. Fein, M. P. Zanna, & J. M. Olson (Eds.), *Motivated social perception: The Ontario Symposium* (Vol. 9, pp. 233–246). Mahwah, NJ: Lawrence Erlbaum.

Gangestad, S. W., & Buss, D. M. (1993). Pathogen prevalence and human mate preferences. *Ethology and Sociobiology, 14*, 89–96.

Gangestad, S. W., Haselton, M. G., & Buss, D. M. (2006). Evolutionary foundations of cultural variation: Evoked culture and mate preferences. *Psychological Inquiry, 17*, 75–95.

Gangestad, S. W., & Simpson, J. A. (2000). The evolution of human mating: Trade-offs and strategic pluralism. *Behavioral and Brain Sciences, 23*, 573–644.

Goodall, J. (1986a). *The chimpanzees of Gombe: Patterns of behavior*. Cambridge, MA: Harvard University Press.

Goodall, J. (1986b). Social rejection, exclusion, and shunning among the Gombe chimpanzees. *Ethology and Sociobiology, 7*, 227–236.

Hamilton, W. D. (1964). The genetical evolution of social behaviour: I, II. *Journal of Theoretical Biology, 7*, 1–52.

Haselton, M. G., & Buss, D. M. (2000). Error management theory: A new perspective on biases in cross-sex mind reading. *Journal of Personality and Social Psychology, 78*, 81–91.

Haselton, M. G., & Nettle, D. (2006). The paranoid optimist: An integrative evolutionary model of cognitive biases. *Personality and Social Psychology Review, 10*, 47–66.

Heider, F., & Simmel, M. (1944). An experimental study of apparent behavior. *American Journal of Psychology, 57*, 243–259.

James, W. (1950). *The principles of psychology* (Vol. 2). New York: Dover. (Original work published 1890)

Kalish, C. W. (1996). Preschoolers' understanding of germs as invisible mechanisms. *Cognitive Development, 11*, 83–106.

Kavaliers, M., & Colwell, D. D. (1995). Discrimination by female mice between the odours of parasitized and non-parasitized males. *Proceedings of the Royal Society of London B, 261*, 31–35.

Keleman, D. (2004). Are children "intuitive theists"? Reasoning about purpose and design in nature. *Psychological Science, 15*, 295–301.

Kelly, R. L. (1995). *The foraging spectrum: Diversity in hunter-gatherer lifeways*. Washington, DC: Smithsonian Institution Press.

Keltner, D., Haidt, J., & Shiota, M. N. (2006). Social functionalism and the evolution of emotions. In M. Schaller, J. A. Simpson, & D. T. Kenrick (Eds.), *Evolution and social psychology* (pp. 115–142). New York: Psychology Press.

Kiesecker, J. M., Skelly, D. K., Beard, K. H., & Preisser, E. (1999). Behavioral reduction of infection risk. *Proceedings of the National Academy of Sciences, 96*, 9165–9168.

Klaczynski, P. A. (2008). There's something about obesity: Culture, contagion, rationality, and children's responses to drinks "created" by obese children. *Journal of Experimental Child Psychology, 99*, 58–74.

Kurzban, R., & Leary, M. R. (2001). Evolutionary origins of stigmatization: The functions of social exclusion. *Psychological Bulletin, 127*, 187–208.

Kurzban, R., & Neuberg, S. (2005). Managing ingroup and outgroup relationships. In D. M. Buss (Ed.), *The handbook of evolutionary psychology* (pp. 653–675). Hoboken, NJ: Wiley.

Kurzban, R., Tooby, J., & Cosmides, L. (2001). Can race be erased? Coalitional computation and social categorization. *Proceedings of the National Academy of Sciences, 98*, 15387–15392.

Loehle, C. (1995). Social barriers to pathogen transmission in wild animal populations. *Ecology, 76*, 326–335.

Lorenz, K. Z. (1965). *Evolution and modification of behavior*. Chicago: University of Chicago Press.

Maner, J. K., Kenrick, D. T., Becker, D. V., Robertson, T. E., Hofer, B., Neuberg, S. L., Delton, A. W., Butner, J., & Schaller, M. (2005). Functional projection: How fundamental social motives can bias interpersonal perception. *Journal of Personality and Social Psychology, 88*, 63–78.

Manning, J. T. (2002). *Digit ratio: A pointer to fertility, behavior and health*. New Brunswick, NJ: Rutgers University Press.

Massar, K., Buunk, A. P., & Dechesne, M. (2009). Jealousy in the blink of an eye: Jealous reactions following subliminal exposure to rival characteristics. *European Journal of Social Psychology, 39*, 768–779.

Navarrete, C. D., & Fessler, D. M. T. (2006). Disease avoidance and ethnocentrism: The effects of disease vulnerability and disgust sensitivity on intergroup attitudes. *Evolution and Human Behavior, 27*, 270–282.

Navarrete, C. D., Fessler, D. M. T., & Eng, S. J. (2007). Elevated ethnocentrism in the first trimester of pregnancy. *Evolution and Human Behavior, 28*, 60–65.

Nemeroff, C. (1995). Magical thinking about illness virulence: Conceptions of germs from "safe" versus "dangerous" others. *Health Psychology, 14*, 147–151.

Nemeroff, C., & Rozin, P. (1994). The contagion concept in adult thinking in the United States: Transmission of germs and of interpersonal influence. *Ethos, 22*, 158–186.

Nesse, R. M. (2005). Natural selection and the regulation of defenses: A signal detection analysis of the smoke detector principle. *Evolution and Human Behavior, 26*, 88–105.

Nettle, D. (2002). Women's height, reproductive success and the evolution of sexual dimorphism in modern humans. *Proceedings of the Royal Society of London B, 269*, 1919–1923.

Neuberg, S. L., & Cottrell, C. A. (2006). Evolutionary bases of prejudice. In M. Schaller, J. A. Simpson, & D. T. Kenrick (Eds.), *Evolution and social psychology* (pp. 163–187). New York: Psychology Press.

Nguyen, S. P., & Rosengren, K. S. (2004). Causal reasoning about illness: A comparison between European- and Vietnamese-American children. *Journal of Cognition and Culture, 4*, 51–78.

Öhman, A., & Mineka, S. (2001). Fear, phobia, and preparedness: Toward an evolved module of fear and fear learning. *Psychological Review, 108*, 483–522.

Park, J. H. (2007). Persistent misunderstandings of inclusive fitness and kin selection: Their ubiquitous appearance in social psychology textbooks. *Evolutionary Psychology, 5*, 860–873.

Park, J. H., Faulkner, J., & Schaller, M. (2003). Evolved disease-avoidance processes and contemporary anti-social behavior: Prejudicial attitudes and avoidance of people with physical disabilities. *Journal of Nonverbal Behavior, 27*, 65–87.

Park, J. H., & Schaller, M. (2005). Does attitude similarity serve as a heuristic cue for kinship? Evidence of an implicit cognitive association. *Evolution and Human Behavior, 26*, 158–170.

Park, J. H., Schaller, M., & Crandall, C. S. (2007). Pathogen-avoidance mechanisms and the stigmatization of obese people. *Evolution and Human Behavior, 28*, 410–414.

Park, J. H., Schaller, M., & Van Vugt, M. (2008). Psychology of human kin recognition: Heuristic cues, erroneous inferences, and their implications. *Review of General Psychology, 12*, 215–235.

Park, J. H., Wieling, M. B., Buunk, A. P., & Massar, K. (2008). Sex-specific relationship between digit ratio (2D:4D) and romantic jealousy. *Personality and Individual Differences, 44*, 1039–1045.

Pawlowski, B., Dunbar, R. I. M., & Lipowicz, A. (2000). Tall men have more reproductive success. *Nature, 403*, 156.

Phelps, E. A., O'Connor, K. J., Cunningham, W. A., Funayama, E. S., Gatenby, J. C., Gore, J. C., & Banaji, M. R. (2000). Performance on indirect measures of race evaluation predicts amygdala activation. *Journal of Cognitive Neuroscience, 12*, 729–738.

Pinker, S. (1997). *How the mind works*. New York: Norton.

Pittman, T. S. (1998). Motivation. In D. T. Gilbert, S. T. Fiske, & G. Lindzey (Eds.), *The handbook of social psychology* (4th ed., Vol. 1, pp. 549–590). New York: McGraw-Hill.

Prinz, J. J. (2006). Is the mind really modular? In R. J. Stainton (Ed.), *Contemporary debates in cognitive science* (pp. 22–36). Malden, MA: Blackwell.

Rhodes, G. (2006). The evolutionary psychology of facial beauty. *Annual Review of Psychology, 57*, 199–226.

Roberts, G. (1996). Why individual vigilance declines as group size increases. *Animal Behaviour, 51*, 1077–1086.

Rozin, P., Millman, L., & Nemeroff, C. (1986). Operation of the laws of sympathetic magic in disgust and other domains. *Journal of Personality and Social Psychology, 50*, 703–712.

Saxe, R., Carey, S., & Kanwisher, N. (2004). Understanding other minds: Linking developmental psychology and functional neuroimaging. *Annual Review of Psychology, 55*, 87–124.

Schaller, M. (2003). Ancestral environments and motivated social perception: Goal-like blasts from the evolutionary past. In S. J. Spencer, S. Fein, M. P. Zanna, & J. M. Olson (Eds.), *Motivated social perception: The Ontario Symposium* (Vol. 9, pp. 215–231). Mahwah, NJ: Lawrence Erlbaum.

Schaller, M. (2007). Turning garbage into gold: Evolutionary universals and cross-cultural differences. In S. W. Gangestad & J. A. Simpson (Eds.), *The evolution of mind: Fundamental questions and controversies* (pp. 363–371). New York: Guilford.

Schaller, M., & Abeysinghe, A. M. N. D. (2006). Geographical frame of reference and dangerous intergroup attitudes: A double-minority study in Sri Lanka. *Political Psychology, 27*, 615–631.

Schaller, M., & Duncan, L. A. (2007). The behavioral immune system: Its evolution and social psychological implications. In J. P. Forgas, M. G. Haselton, & W. von Hippel (Eds.), *Evolution and the social mind: Evolutionary psychology and social cognition* (pp. 293–307). New York: Psychology Press.

Schaller, M., Faulkner, J., Park, J. H., Neuberg, S. L., & Kenrick, D. T. (2004). Impressions of danger influence impressions of people: An evolutionary perspective on individual and collective cognition. *Journal of Cultural and Evolutionary Psychology, 2*, 231–247.

Schaller, M., & Murray, D. R. (2008). Pathogens, personality, and culture: Disease prevalence predicts worldwide variability in sociosexuality, extraversion, and openness to experience. *Journal of Personality and Social Psychology, 95*, 212–221.

Schaller, M., & Neuberg, S. L. (2008). Intergroup prejudices and intergroup conflicts. In C. Crawford & D. L. Krebs (Eds.), *Foundations of evolutionary psychology* (pp. 399–412). Mahwah, NJ: Lawrence Erlbaum.

Schaller, M., Park, J. H., & Faulkner, J. (2003). Prehistoric dangers and contemporary prejudices. *European Review of Social Psychology, 14*, 105–137.

Schaller, M., Park, J. H., & Kenrick, D. T. (2007). Human evolution and social cognition. In R. I. M. Dunbar & L. Barrett (Eds.), *Oxford handbook of evolutionary psychology* (pp. 491–504). Oxford, UK: Oxford University Press.

Schaller, M., Park, J. H., & Mueller, A. (2003). Fear of the dark: Interactive effects of beliefs about danger and ambient darkness on ethnic stereotypes. *Personality and Social Psychology Bulletin, 29*, 637–649.

Schützwohl, A. (2006). Sex differences in jealousy: Information search and cognitive preoccupation. *Personality and Individual Differences, 40,* 285–292.

Schützwohl, A. (2007). Decision strategies in continuous ratings of jealousy feelings elicited by sexual and emotional infidelity. *Evolutionary Psychology, 5,* 815–828.

Schützwohl, A. (2008). The disengagement of attentive resources from task-irrelevant cues to sexual and emotional infidelity. *Personality and Individual Differences, 44,* 633–644.

Sidanius, J., & Pratto, F. (1999). *Social dominance: An intergroup theory of social hierarchy and oppression.* New York: Cambridge University Press.

Solomon, G. E. A., & Cassimatis, N. L. (1999). On facts and conceptual systems: Young children's integration of their understandings of germs and contagion. *Developmental Psychology, 35,* 113–126.

Tinbergen, N. (1951). *The study of instinct.* Oxford, UK: Clarendon Press.

Tooby, J., & Cosmides, L. (1992). The psychological foundations of culture. In J. H. Barkow, L. Cosmides, & J. Tooby (Eds.), *The adapted mind: Evolutionary psychology and the generation of culture* (pp. 19–136). New York: Oxford University Press.

Van Anders, S. M., Vernon, P. A., & Wilbur, C. J. (2006). Finger-length ratios show evidence of prenatal hormone-transfer between opposite sex twins. *Hormones and Behavior, 49,* 315–319.

Van Vugt, M., & Park, J. H. (2010). The tribal instinct hypothesis: Evolution and the social psychology of intergroup relations. In S. Stürmer & M. Snyder (Eds.), *The psychology of prosocial behavior: Group processes, intergroup relations, and helping,* (pp. 13–22). Chichester, UK: Wiley-Blackwell.

Van Vugt, M., & Van Lange, P. A. M. (2006). Psychological adaptations for prosocial behavior: The altruism puzzle. In M. Schaller, J. A. Simpson, & D. T. Kenrick (Eds.), *Evolution and social psychology* (pp. 237–261). New York: Psychology Press.

Wirtz, P., & Wawra, M. (1986). Vigilance and group size in *Homo sapiens. Ethology, 71,* 283–286.

Woody, S. R., & Teachman, B. A. (2000). Intersection of disgust and fear: Normative and pathological views. *Clinical Psychology: Science and Practice, 7,* 291–311.

Wrangham, R. W., & Peterson, D. (1996). *Demonic males: Apes and the origins of human violence.* Boston: Houghton Mifflin.

3

Belonging Motivation
Establishing, Maintaining, and Repairing Relational Value

MARK R. LEARY and ASHLEY BATTS ALLEN

*F*uture historians of psychology may find it ironic that social psychologists took so long to appreciate fully the role that social belonging plays in human life. Many theorists had noted that *Homo sapiens* is a more strongly social animal than many other species (Axelrod & Hamilton, 1981; Buss, 1995), but until recently, most writers viewed human sociality primarily in terms of the desire to interact or affiliate with others, with a good deal of attention devoted to topics such as affiliation motivation and sociability. However, human beings may differ from other animals most dramatically, not in terms of their tendency to affiliate or interact, but rather in their efforts to be accepted by others. Many other animals live in groups and interact with conspecifics, but none pursue the number and variety of relationships that human beings do or devote so much effort to being noticed, valued, and accepted. As Baumeister and Leary (1995) observed, "Human beings have a pervasive drive to form and maintain at least a minimum quantity of lasting, positive, and significant interpersonal relationships" (p. 497) and devote a great deal of thought, time, and energy to pursuing acceptance by other people. Their review of the literature supported the notion that the quest for belonging is a fundamental need that exerts a strong influence in virtually every domain of social behavior.

This motive has been characterized in a number of ways—as the need to belong, belongingness motivation, the motive to be accepted by others, and the desire to be relationally valued. However this motive has been labeled, previous authors have documented the potency of it and the strong reactions that occur when the need is threatened through rejection, ostracism, stigmatization, and other signs that others are disinterested in relating to the individual (for reviews, see Abrams,

Hogg, & Marques, 2005; Baumeister & Leary, 1995; Leary, 2001a; Leary & Cox, 2007; MacDonald & Leary, 2005; Williams, 2001, 2007; Williams, Forgas, & von Hippel, 2005).

This chapter begins where previous discussions of the need to belong have left off. Now that researchers have described the need to belong, its implications for behavior, and the emotional and behavioral reactions that typically accompany rejection, we will focus primarily on the maintenance of belonging—the processes by which people establish, maintain, and repair their interpersonal connections with others. As we will see, concerns with acceptance and belonging cut a broad swath across people's social lives, and much of people's interpersonal behavior appears to emerge from their deep-seated interest in being accepted by other people and belonging to social groups. Much of human behavior is enacted in the service of promoting acceptance and lowering the probability of being ignored, devalued, or rejected. The assumption that people are strongly motivated to establish and maintain connections with other people provides a starting point for explaining a wide variety of seemingly disparate interpersonal behaviors.

ESTABLISHING RELATIONAL VALUE: BASIC DIMENSIONS

Actions that promote acceptance and minimize the likelihood of rejection may be conceptualized as efforts to maintain or enhance one's *relational value*. A person's relational value reflects the degree to which other people value interacting with and having relationships with him or her (Leary, 2001b). People value their relationships with specific other people to varying degrees. People regard their relationships with certain individuals as very valuable and important, and the relational value of those individuals is quite high. People view certain other relationships as less valuable and important, and the individuals in those relationships have lower relational value to them. At the extreme, people may regard some individuals as having no relational value (i.e., they do not value having relationships with such individuals) or as even having negative relational value (i.e., they wish to avoid having connections with these individuals altogether).

Being relationally valued by other people increases one's access to a large number of desired social and material outcomes, including companionship, friendship, group memberships, romantic relationships, social and logistical support, financial and material resources, social influence, and a broad range of social, occupational, financial, recreational, and sexual opportunities. Unlike our evolutionary ancestors, who could survive only by belonging to a supportive clan, people living in a modern society can usually survive without close social bonds. However, because being inadequately accepted deprives people of both the inherent pleasure of social connections and the innumerable affordances of close relationships and group memberships, people are concerned about their relational value in other people's eyes.

A person's relational value is separate from his or her status, although having high status sometimes promotes relational value. Status has been defined in a number of ways, but for our purposes, it refers to the amount of authority or prestige that a person has relative to other people within a given social context (Stangor, 2004). People who are accorded status by others often possess attributes that also increase their relational value. For example, competence often confers higher status (and greater influence) and also makes the individual a more valued group member or relational partner. And, even when people's characteristics are unrelated to their objective contributions, as in the case of gender or race, they may nonetheless be accorded greater status and relational value. Status does not always promote relational value, however. People whose position and authority are viewed as ill-gotten or undeserved may be accorded high status but may not be valued or sought after as a relational partner or group member.

The ultimate goal for people who wish to be accepted is to establish that they have high relational value in a particular interpersonal context. To achieve this goal, they must be perceived as the kind of person who makes a desirable group member, friend, romantic partner, colleague, companion, team member, or whatever. Although people seek acceptance in a seemingly infinite number of ways, most of the actions that people take to establish, promote, and maintain their relational value fall into four basic categories that reflect the primary reasons that people are valued, accepted, and sought after versus devalued, rejected, and avoided by others. Specifically, to promote their relational value and acceptance (and to avoid rejection) in virtually any society, social group, or relationship, people try to be viewed as (a) likeable rather than unlikable, (b) competent rather than incompetent (particularly with regard to skills and tasks that other people value), (c) a good member or relationship partner in terms of supporting the group's goals and values and behaving ethically and responsibly in one's dealings with other people, and (d) more rather than less physically appealing according to local standards.

Thus, being regarded as a desirable group member or relational partner is facilitated by being perceived as likeable, competent, broadly supportive of the group or relationship, and reasonably attractive (or at least not as unattractive) relative to one's reference group. Of course, the relative importance of these sets of attributes differs as a function of the nature of the relationship and social context. For example, being physically appealing may be more relevant in romantic encounters, whereas competence is more relevant in a job interview. Even so, being perceived as decidedly unlikeable, incompetent, disloyal, or unattractive rarely promotes greater relational value and acceptance than being seen in more socially desirable ways no matter what the relationship or social context. A person who falls below some minimal criterion on any of these attributes is less likely to be sought after as a group member or relational partner than a person who passes muster on all four. And, even when one of these sets of characteristics is objectively irrelevant in a particular relational context, it can nonetheless influence other people's perceptions of the person and, thus, his or her relational value.

Because these four dimensions are central to relational value, people are motivated to foster desired images along these lines, and thus, much of what people do to establish, promote, and maintain belonging involves a strong self-presentational feature (Leary, 1995; Schlenker, 1980). When people are motivated to be accepted by others, they desire to present images of themselves that indicate that they are more, rather than less, likeable, competent, group or relationship supportive, and physically appealing. Sometimes, they may merely make verbal claims about themselves that convey these desired images, but often they must provide concrete, behavioral demonstrations that they are the kind of person with whom others will value having various social relationships.

Relational value is never established once and for all. Not only must people engage in an ongoing process of establishing connections of various kinds with new individuals, but they also must adjust their actions in response to the changing demands of established relationships. Roles and responsibilities change over time in most relationships, as when an employer expects different or better work from a long-time employee than when he or she was first hired or when the attributes valued in a marriage partner change with age, the length of the relationship, and parenthood. In addition, occasions sometimes arise in which one's value in a relationship is called into question by misbehaviors, ineptitude, disclosures of private information, or other self-presentational predicaments. Few, if any, relationships are so secure that people can afford to ignore their relational value in others' eyes or forgo efforts to maintain it. Thus, people are pervasively concerned with being seen as likeable, competent, relationship supportive (loyal, ethical, responsible), and reasonably attractive, and their efforts to make these kinds of impressions are manifested in a wide array of interpersonal behaviors.

LIKEABILITY

All other things being equal, people are more valued, accepted, and supported by others if they are liked rather than disliked. Indeed, as Dale Carnegie (1936) noted in *How to Win Friends and Influence People*, the best all-purpose way to foster acceptance by other people is to be seen as pleasant, friendly, agreeable, and generally likeable. Although disliked individuals may be tolerated if they bring other things to the table (such as being a close relative or particularly competent at an important task), the emotional costs that they exact on other people render their relational value lower overall. Not surprisingly, then, the impressions that American college students want to make on others involve characteristics that contribute to being seen as likeable, such as being perceived as friendly, fun, sincere, caring, and easy to talk to (Leary, 1995). At the same time, people do not want to be seen as boring, conceited, obnoxious, superficial, self-centered, and mean—traits that reliably lead others to dislike them.

Although research has shown that people often behave in ways that lead to liking and social approval, their ultimate goal, in our view, is not merely to be evaluated positively. Being approved of or liked typically does little to promote people's well-being unless others' positive evaluations and affective reactions toward the person convert to judgments of high relational value. Thus, what people are actually seeking when they do things to gain liking and approval are the many benefits that accrue to people who, by virtue of being liked, are relationally valued and socially accepted.

Similarity

One of the primary causes of liking is the degree to which others perceive the person to be similar to them. A great deal of research shows that people are more likely to like, interact with, befriend, and fall in love with people whom they perceive as similar to themselves (for a recent review, see AhYun, 2002). Put simply, a person's relational value is increased by his or her similarity to others.

Not surprisingly, then, people seek to identify and capitalize on areas of similarity when they interact, which may help to explain the cycles of information-gathering that occur when people first meet ("Where are you from? What do you do?"). The purpose of these exchanges is not merely to get to know the other person but also to find common ground that can be the basis for an interaction and provide clues for how to foster one's relational value in the other person's eyes. Once people learn about one another, they often mold their public images to foster impressions of similarity. For example, people may conform—in their opinions and their behavior—to increase the likelihood that others will like and ultimately accept them (Jones, 1964; Kacmar, Carlson, & Bratton, 2004; Pandey, 1986).

Research has suggested that people may even promote similarity nonconsciously. Studies by Chartrand and Bargh (1999) found that people automatically mimicked the nonverbal behaviors of an experimental confederate, shaking their feet and rubbing their faces more when the confederate shook and rubbed his. Furthermore, this effect was strongest among people who scored high in the need for affiliation (Lakin & Chartrand, 2003), a close cousin to belonging motivation. What is important is that people like those people who behaviorally mimic them in these ways more than those who do not (Chartrand & Bargh, 1999). The fact that behavioral mimicry can operate automatically and nonconsciously suggests that people may be wired to behave in ways that stimulate liking and acceptance.

Ingratiation and Favor-doing

People also increase their chances of acceptance and belonging through behaviors that convey that they like other people, such as offering flattery and praise and expressing interest in the other person (Deluga & Perry, 1994; Gordon, 1996; Stevens & Kristof, 1995; Wayne & Kacmar, 1991). Engaging in other-directed behaviors increases liking not only by the target but also by observers (Folkes & Sears, 1977). Of course, insincere flattery may backfire, although research suggests that targets tend to accept ingratiators' behavior at face value (whereas observers tend to be more skeptical) and may appreciate others' efforts to ingratiate them even if they don't believe that it is genuine (Vonk, 2002).

Similarly, doing favors increases liking. Of course, people sometimes do favors to be nice to others (particularly when the cost in time or money is low), but people also do favors to lead others to like and accept them. For example, performing favors in a work setting creates a likeable image in the eyes of one's supervisors and coworkers. Flyn (2003) showed that exchanging frequent favors is positively related to social status and individual productivity (see also Deluga & Perry, 1991). More broadly, being a "nice" person leads to greater liking and acceptance.

COMPETENCE AND SUCCESS

Many discussions of motivation draw a distinction between task-focused behaviors that are motivated by a desire for achievement, mastery, or competence and interpersonal-focused behaviors that are motivated by a desire for social rewards such as liking, status, or acceptance. Yet, it seems clear that a great deal of achievement-oriented behavior is enacted in the service of interpersonal goals, including belonging. When people seek to be competent or successful, they are often pursuing these outcomes not for their own sake but rather because excellence and achievement lead to recognition, approval, and acceptance. This is not to say that all striving for competence, achievement, and success is motivated by interpersonal rewards, but there is little doubt that people who are seen as competent and successful have higher relational value. Successful people are more likely to be sought for groups and relationships, either because their skills benefit other individuals or groups or the rewards of their achievements (such as a high salary) are desired by others or because others wish, for their own interpersonal reasons, to be associated with successful people.

Viewed in this way, much, if not most, of what people do to develop and use various talents may be motivated by the desire for acceptance or belonging. Whether we are talking about intellectual skills, artistic or musical ability, athletic prowess, or task-specific abilities (such as organizing others' activities, managing money, or problem solving), people are motivated, in part, to develop and display their skills because doing so leads others to value and accept them. Even specialized skills in cooking exotic dishes, identifying species of birds, playing Trivial Pursuit, or brewing homemade beer draw attention to oneself and are, although minor, arguably better than not having those skills.

The suggestion that achievement (and even the desire for education) is sometimes driven by a desire for acceptance and other interpersonal rewards rather than a quest for mastery or accomplishment may strike many as cynical if not downright wrong. Yet, one need only imagine what would happen to people's desire to achieve if excellence and accomplishment suddenly elicited not approbation and acceptance but disinterest, diminished respect, or ostracism instead! Recent theory and research on achievement-related goals show that interpersonal concerns with appearing competent to others, obtaining approval, and pleasing other people constitute one source of the motivation to perform well and to achieve (see Miller, Greene, Montalvo, Ravindran, & Nichols, 1996; Urdan & Mestas, 2006). We would add only that the deeper goal may be to enhance relational value, acceptance, and belonging.

Most people are eager for others to know about their accomplishments, and people who hide their successes from other people are rare. Of course, people recognize the pitfalls in advertising their competence or success too explicitly, as being seen as an egotist or braggart can undermine whatever interpersonal gains are achieved by success (Leary, Bednarski, Hammon, & Duncan, 1997). Thus, people manage their impressions in ways that convey their competence and successes while trying not to cross the line into egotism.

Although the general pattern is for people to try to project images of themselves as competent, occasions arise in which being accepted by others requires that they appear less competent than they really are. In such instances, people may "play dumb" by feigning to know less than they really do (Dean, Powers, Braito, & Bruton, 1975; Thornton, Audesse, Ryckman, & Burckle, 2006). People play dumb for a variety of reasons, but perhaps the most common is to increase their desirability to someone who might be put off by their knowledge or competence. What is interesting is that individual differences in the tendency to claim less knowledge than one has (i.e., playing dumb) and the tendency to express more knowledge than one has correlate strongly with each other, and both tendencies correlate with concerns with others' evaluations and impressions (Thornton et al., 2006).

SUPPORT FOR SHARED GOALS, NORMS, AND WAYS OF BEING

A third route to increasing social acceptance involves being viewed as the kind of person who can be counted on to be a good group member or relationship partner—a responsible and trustworthy person who supports the goals and rules of the dyad or group. This image involves a constellation of attributes involving being perceived as loyal, honest, dependable, and cooperative with respect to other members of the group or relationship in question, as well as the degree to which the person conforms to the norms, values, and tastes of the group.

In many cases, the issue is not whether the person is globally honest, dependable, or cooperative, but only whether he or she demonstrates these characteristics in the context of a particular group or relationship. We are often quite happy to consort with people who are less than fully honest and dependable in their dealings with others as long as their behaviors with respect to us are satisfactory. Even otherwise morally reprehensible groups—such as those involved in organized crime, violent street gangs, and the Ku Klux Klan—have codes of "ethical" conduct that their members are expected to obey, and such groups ostracize, if not physically harm, those who violate their codes.

Schachter's (1951) classic study showing that groups reject those who deviate from emergent group norms, even on an objectively trivial criterion, was an early demonstration of the importance of conforming to group norms in order to avoid rejection. Decades of research have subsequently shown the lengths to which people will go to maintain their acceptability in others' eyes by conforming to others' judgments, decisions, and behaviors (for a review, see Cialdini, Kallgren, & Reno, 1991) and demonstrated that people conform both to "be right" and to "be liked" (Insko, Smith, Alicke, Wade, & Taylor, 1985). Given that people often conform in the service of social acceptance, it is not surprising that conformity increases when people see others being ridiculed for nonconformity (Janes & Olson, 2000) and decreases when other nonconformists are present (Asch, 1951; Insko et al., 1985).

Many social psychological phenomena can be explained in terms of people going along with others to maintain social connections and to avoid jeopardizing their position in the group. For example, many of the symptoms of groupthink—a syndrome of faulty decision making that can befall cohesive groups—appear to arise partly from group members' efforts to maintain the cohesiveness of the group and their position in it (McCauley, 1989). Because people desire to avoid conflict and do not wish to rock the boat, they may censor their objections to the options being discussed, withhold information that might undermine group harmony or make them appear oppositional, and conform to emerging group decisions. Thus, many of the factors that undermine effective group deliberations reflect people's concerns with their acceptance by other members of the group.

Social psychological research has also shown that people's performance on various tasks is influenced by the presence of other people. For example, being observed and evaluated by others enhances performance on certain tasks (Cottrell, Wack, Sekerak, & Rittle, 1968), as does performing group tasks on which one's individual contributions can be monitored (Karau & Williams, 1995). Although social facilitation and social loafing are complex and multiply determined phenomena, enhanced performance under conditions of scrutiny, evaluation, and accountability are undoubtedly influenced by the desire for acceptance. Because higher performance makes one more relationally valued (and shirking one's duties is a basis for relational devaluation), people work harder when others are watching.

Even reciprocity, which many consider to be the foundation of any mutually satisfying interpersonal encounter (Gouldner, 1960), is enforced chiefly through the implied threat of rejection for those who fail to reciprocate (Cotterell, Eisenberger, & Speicher, 1992). Thus, a great deal of reciprocity, as well as modes of social influence that are based on reciprocity such as the reciprocal concessions technique (Cialdini et al., 1975; Hale & Laliker, 1999), are undergirded by people's concerns with being accepted by others.

Many of the rules, norms, and morals that people must follow to maintain their relational value are explicit, but people must also conform to the implicit perspectives, tastes, habits, and other ways of being that are so much a part of a particular culture that they "go without saying" for members of a particular group (what the sociologist Bourdieu [1977] called the habitus of a culture or group). Although many aspects of a group's habitus are objectively inconsequential (such as a particular way of walking or sitting or a preference for one kind of music rather than another), people whose actions, opinions, or tastes show that they have not internalized the habitus of a group may be devalued nonetheless.

PHYSICAL APPEARANCE

A good deal of research has documented that physical attractiveness leads to greater liking and social acceptance. Although exceptions exist, more attractive people are typically better liked and more highly sought as companions, friends, group members, and romantic partners than people who are unattractive. Meta-analyses show that attractive children and adults are judged and treated more positively than unattractive people, even by those who know them well (Langlois et al., 2000). Some physical features—such as facial symmetry and unblemished skin—appear to be universally regarded as attractive and, thus, lead to greater acceptance, possibly because of their role in signaling genetic fitness and an absence of pathogens and illness (Jones et al., 2001). However, other criteria for attractiveness differ across groups and social contexts so that people who wish to be accepted by a particular individual must abide by the prevailing norms regarding appearance.

Viewed in this way, virtually anything that people do to enhance their physical appeal is probably done in the service of belonging. Many people try to maintain their weight within an acceptable range (with varying degrees of success) and exercise to appear slim and fit. Not only do those who exercise regularly develop a physique that others view as more attractive, but also merely knowing that someone exercises can lead others to draw more positive inferences about a person's personal and social qualities (Martin Ginis, Lindwall, & Prapavessis, 2007). Likewise, people with light skin may strive to maintain a tan despite knowing of the health risks of excessive sun exposure because they believe (correctly, as it turns out) that being tan will enhance their attractiveness to others (Leary & Jones, 1993). The multi-billion-dollar cosmetics and personal grooming industry is based on the notion that enhancing one's appearance (and one's scent) leads to desired social outcomes.

When people believe that their appearance is undermined by fundamental flaws in their face or body, they sometimes turn to cosmetic surgery. Each year, more than two million people have nonessential cosmetic surgery to improve their appearance (Blum, 2003), presumably to gain an interpersonal edge in terms of increasing the likelihood of acceptance (Braun, 2005). Although the popularity of cosmetic surgery likely differs cross-culturally, its popularity may be raising the bar for physical appearance by leading to altered and enhanced standards of attractiveness among certain groups. For example, whereas facial wrinkles were previously acceptable because most people had wrinkles after reaching a certain age, cosmetic surgery is changing these perceptions in some societies as people see others of their age who look unwrinkled and younger. These comparisons may make people feel unattractive—and, thus, less acceptable—and motivate them to undergo cosmetic procedures in an escalating arms race of Botox and plastic surgery.

One of the most conscious and deliberate ways that people try to enhance their appearance involves the clothes that they choose to wear. People desire to wear clothing that they believe, correctly or incorrectly, enhances their appearance and that conforms to the accepted "wardrobe" of their social groups (Peluchette, Karl, & Rust, 2006). Although people's clothing preferences are influenced by an array of factors, including comfort and price, concerns with social image and, ultimately, social acceptance are undoubtedly involved (Frith & Gleeson, 2004; Simpson & Littrell, 1984).

RESTORING RELATIONAL VALUE AND REPAIRING FRACTURED BELONGING

As we have seen, efforts to establish and maintain relational value pervade much of social life. Yet, despite people's best efforts to maintain public images that will promote acceptance and belonging, events sometimes conspire to undermine the images on which people's relational value is based. When people believe that others perceive them to be less likeable, competent, relationship supportive, physically appealing, or otherwise acceptable than they desire, they typically try to repair their public images in ways that will forestall the possibility of devaluation and rejection.

Apologies

In instances in which one's acceptance is threatened by a purposeful or inadvertent misbehavior on one's part, the most obvious first remedial step involves apologizing. Although apologies have been conceptualized as tactics that repair one's social image (which is true as far as it goes; Schlenker, 1980), they may be viewed more broadly as ways of reestablishing one's relational value in the aftermath of an undesired behavior or outcome. A sincere apology conveys that one recognizes that one's behavior has violated foundational conditions of acceptance and is concerned enough about its impact and others' judgments to take steps to correct it. In contrast, the person who does not apologize after a misbehavior conveys that he or she either is unaware that the action might undermine social acceptance or, worse, simply does not care. This functional understanding of apologies appears at a young age, presumably because parents are adamant about ingraining in their children the importance of saying "I'm sorry" when they do something wrong. Children as young as three years old evaluate those who apologize for a wrongdoing more favorably than those who do not apologize (Darby & Schlenker, 1982).

When the infraction is minor—as when one clumsily steps on another's foot or accidentally belches aloud—a casual and brief apology is usually enough to repair the damage to one's image as a decent, socially acceptable individual. However, when the transgression is more serious, people typically apologize more strongly and include sincere expressions of distress and remorse. The more severe the incident, the more effortful the apology the perpetrator is expected to express before the apology should be accepted (Schlenker & Darby, 1981). Of course, in extreme cases, even strong, sincere apologies cannot repair the person's image sufficiently to induce others to accept the perpetrator. For example, a pedophile might never be fully redeemed in others' eyes no matter how much he or she apologizes.

Virtually all research has focused on the effects of apologies that are made after one has behaved in an undesired way. However, some apologies (known as *ex ante* apologies) are offered before or at the same time that the undesired outcome occurs. For example, people may apologize in advance for negative outcomes that they will create in the future ("I'm sorry, but I will be late for our meeting tomorrow") or apologize concurrently with the delivery of negative information ("I'm sorry that I have to do this, but you're fired"). Research suggests that apologies offered beforehand may have different effects than those offered afterward, with different effects on perceptions of the apologizer, judgments of fairness, and motives for revenge (Skarlicki, Folger, & Gee, 2004).

Accounts

A second way to minimize the impact of undesirable behaviors on acceptance is to offer accounts. An account is a verbal explanation for why one engaged in the unintended or unacceptable behavior (Gonzales, Pederson, Manning, & Wetter, 1990; Schlenker, 1980; Scott & Lyman, 1968). For example, a teenager who arrives home after curfew will likely provide an account for his or her actions. Previous theorists have distinguished between three primary types of accounts—refusals, excuses, and justifications (Austin, 1956; Schlenker, 1980; Turnbull, 1992). (Other, less frequently used types include concessions, requests, and disclaimers.)

The refusal account, also termed a defense of innocence, involves a straight-forward denial that the person was responsible for a wrongdoing or, often, that a wrongdoing even occurred (Leary, 1995). This "I didn't do it" account is often not well received because evidence exists that contradicts it, but when others do accept a refusal account, threats to acceptance are eliminated.

When people cannot plausibly maintain their innocence, they often offer excuses. Excuses admit that a negative behavior or outcome occurred but try to reduce one's perceived responsibility for it. For example, rather than denying that the curfew had been broken (a refusal), the late teenager might provide an excuse for being late, such as claiming he or she had lost track of the time, had to stop to help a friend, or was prevented by others from leaving the party on time. If they are accepted as truthful explanations, excuses lower the perpetrator's perceived responsibility for the behavior in question and, thus, reduce somewhat the degree to which people draw negative inferences about the person from his or her actions.

Whereas excuses minimize one's responsibility, justifications reduce the perceived negativity of the event itself (Schlenker, 1980; Scott & Lyman, 1968). Someone providing a justification accepts responsibility for the event but provides reasons why the outcome was not as bad as others believe. A teenager arriving home late could argue that being late isn't really a big deal (direct minimization), that he took some of his friends home so they wouldn't drive drunk (claimed beneficence), that his friends all had later curfews than he and he couldn't leave in the middle of what they were doing (comparative justification), or that being punctual took a backseat to a higher goal that needed to be accomplished (principled justification). These various forms of justification are all self-presentational tactics that help to protect the person's public image and relational value by lowering the perceived negativity of his or her behavior.

Nonverbal Displays

In addition to using verbal methods such as apologies, excuses, and justifications to repair one's belonging, people may repair belonging nonverbally. Nonverbal behaviors such as blushing, gaze aversion, and nervous smiling can help to repair people's images by communicating to others that they recognize that they performed an action that may result in undesired impressions and devaluation (Castelfranchi & Poggi, 1990). People who enact such behaviors after a transgression, whether intentionally or automatically, elicit more favorable reactions from observers. For example, parents whose children show nonverbal signs of embarrassment after a wrongdoing are less likely to punish their children than parents whose children do not show signs of embarrassment (Semin & Papadopoulou, 1990), and people who appear embarrassed after behaving clumsily are liked more than people who do not seem embarrassed (Semin & Manstead, 1982).

Thus, although people's first inclination may be to hide their embarrassment, they may often benefit by letting people know that they recognize their misbehavior and feel bad about it (Leary, 1995). At some level, people seem to realize that nonverbal signs of embarrassment help to repair their social images and protect belonging, because believing that others know that they are embarrassed reduces people's distress and lowers their efforts to repair their image in other ways (Leary, Landel, & Patton, 1996; Miller, 1996).

Nonverbal displays that accompany embarrassment, guilt, and shame may reflect human analogues of the appeasement behaviors that are often observed in nonhuman primates. When threatened socially, many nonhuman primates perform a set of stereotypic actions that diffuse the threat, and features of these actions resemble the nonverbal behaviors of people who have behaved in an undesired fashion. For example, the lowered gaze and appeasement grins of chimpanzees resemble the averted eyes and nervous smiling that people display after a public blunder (Leary, Britt, Cutlip, & Templeton, 1992). Although primatologists have stressed that the function of appeasement is to reduce aggression (which is true), appeasement also lowers the likelihood that the individual will be ostracized or expelled from the group—just as with human beings.

Recompensation and Sacrifice

In some instances, apologies, accounts, and other remedial behaviors successfully repair people's public images and the breaches that open in their relationship with others. In other cases, however, words are not enough. Often, a stronger means of demonstrating one's remorse and goodwill is needed, and the transgressor may be required to show some sort of compensation or penance for the wrongdoing (Bottom, Gibson, Daniels, & Murnighan, 2002). Throughout history, rituals of apology have often required some form of repayment or the presentation of a gift (Arno, 1976), and today, people must often pay a penance when they have behaved in an inappropriate manner (in terms of fines, docked salary, or jail time, for example). Offers of penance convey that the transgressor is not engaging in "cheap talk" and that he or she is willing to sacrifice something to be accepted back into the relationship (Bottom et al., 2002). Other people are more likely to forgive various misdeeds as long as people admit that they caused harm and offer to compensate for it (Schmitt, Gollwitzer, Forster, & Montada, 2004).

Offers of compensation may be particularly beneficial when they clearly involve a sacrifice on the part of the individual. People who violate expectations in a group or relationship may often ask for forgiveness and demonstrate their willingness to sacrifice their own desires for the good of the relationship. Research on close relationships shows that people's willingness to sacrifice is associated with higher partner trust, stronger relationship satisfaction, and greater commitment (Van Lange et al., 1997; Wieselquist, Rusbult, Foster, & Agnew, 1999). Sacrifice demonstrates one's commitment to the relationship and a desire to work to restore one's relational value to those who have been harmed.

COUNTEREXAMPLES

Thus far, we have seen that a great deal of people's social behavior appears to serve a fundamental desire for acceptance and belonging. Yet, numerous counterexamples come to mind in which people behave in ways that, rather than establishing and maintaining belonging, serve to distance themselves from others or overtly damage their interpersonal relationships. What are we to make of behaviors that undermine rather than promote people's relational value?

Some apparent counterexamples occur when people inadvertently mismanage social situations in ways that cause others to avoid or reject them. These cases do not actually reflect on people's efforts to establish belonging per se, but merely show that people sometimes alienate others by mistake. Similarly, other counterexamples arise because people's efforts to obtain some other goal compromise their relational value, but aside from showing that people are motivated by things other than acceptance, these counterexamples are largely irrelevant to the pursuit of belonging as well.

More interesting are examples in which people purposefully do things that anger, alienate, or drive other people away. For example, the minimal group paradigm has shown how easily and naturally members of one group will devalue, disadvantage, and reject members of other groups. People regularly mistreat members of other groups in ways that undermine the connections between them, often for no other reason than that they are members of another group (Diehl, 1990). Given that prejudice and discrimination are not likely to endear a person to the target of the mistreatment, they may appear contrary to a motive for acceptance and belonging. However, evidence suggests that, on the contrary, the rejection of outgroups may enhance people's social acceptance within their own group. Specifically, derogating and rejecting members of other groups may foster acceptance by increasing ingroup cohesion and enhancing members' attraction for one another (Pickett & Brewer, 2005).

A second set of counterexamples involves instances in which people fail to cooperate or to help others—actions that would generally undermine acceptance, because uncooperative, selfish people are usually less preferred as friends, lovers, group members, and other relational partners. Of course, as much as they might value being other-oriented and altruistic, people cannot be cooperative and helpful toward everyone without compromising their own well-being. Thus, most people are selectively helpful and cooperative, and evidence suggests that a primary determinant of when they behave prosocially is the presence of social connections with the target of their benevolence. In other words, people are most likely to behave helpfully and cooperatively when they might risk devaluation and rejection by being selfish. We have already noted, for example, that the selfishness inherent in social loafing is reduced when people's personal contributions to a group's performance can be identified (Latane, Williams, & Harkins, 1979). Similarly, people cooperate more in experimental games, such as the prisoner's dilemma, when they have met or expect to meet the other player and, thus, a budding social connection is at stake (Danheiser & Graziano, 1982; Orbell, van de Kragt, & Dawes, 1988). Along the same lines, people cooperate more with others in the common dilemma when group belonging is salient (Kramer & Brewer, 1984). Thus, cooperation and helpfulness is most likely when people's social connections might be jeopardized by selfishness.

One of the most puzzling potential counterexamples involves the fact that people sometimes respond to signs of devaluation and rejection with anger and aggression. Given that angry and aggressive behaviors naturally drive others away, why would a person who felt inadequately accepted strike out at those whose acceptance he or she presumably desires?

After a comprehensive review of research on the relationship between rejection and aggression, Leary, Twenge, and Quinlivan (2006) offered several possible explanations for the rejection–aggression link but finally concluded that the effect is probably multiply determined and that the existing data are insufficient to identify the primary causes at this time. For our purposes, some of their explanations reflect the influence of processes that undermine acceptance in the pursuit of other goals. For example, anger and aggression are particularly likely when rejected individuals believe that they have been disrespected or treated unfairly, and their bellicose response may reflect the general effect of perceived disrespect or unfairness on anger (Solomon, 1990; Vidmar, 2000). In such cases, people probably wish to be accepted, but their response is more of a reaction to disrespect or fairness than to rejection per se. Richman and Leary (2009) suggested that people's reactions to rejection episodes reflect a combination of three distinct motives—to repair belonging, to aggress, and to withdraw—and often the motive to aggress or to withdraw undermines further acceptance. We should also note that the mere fact that people respond strongly, and sometimes antisocially, to signs of devaluation and rejection shows how important they regard being valued and accepted by others.

SUMMARY AND CONCLUSIONS

We have attempted to show that a fundamental motive for belonging and acceptance lies at the root of a great deal of interpersonal behavior. We should not be misinterpreted as suggesting that belonging is the only social motive or even necessarily the most important one (although it could easily be). Rather, our goal was to show ways in which people's need to belong is manifested in their interpersonal interactions. Viewing human social behavior through the lens of belonging provides an overarching framework that integrates a number of seemingly disparate interpersonal phenomena.

We have focused here on interpersonal behaviors and dealt little with the cognitive and emotional patterns that reflect people's concerns with belonging. Yet, given that motives are usually associated with emotional concomitants that arise both when the motive is satisfied and when it is thwarted, one should expect that people's feelings would also be tied strongly to the degree to which they perceive they are valued and accepted versus devalued and rejected. Indeed, a great deal of research has demonstrated the powerful effects of low relational value on emotion, self-perceptions, self-esteem, and judgments of other people (see Leary, Koch, & Hechenbleikner, 2001). Likewise, patterns of cognition are influenced by people's concerns with acceptance (see Baumeister & Leary, 1995). For example, people who feel inadequately accepted sometimes turn to cognitive strategies to increase their sense of felt acceptance (Gardner, Pickett, & Knowles, 2005).

Many, perhaps most, interpersonal interactions and relationships are predicated on establishing at least a minimal level of mutual acceptance between the parties. Even when the primary goal of the interaction is not to establish, maintain, or repair interpersonal acceptance, people cannot afford to ignore their relational value in other people's eyes. Few interactions and relationships proceed optimally when one or more of the participants perceive that they have no relational value (or, worse, negative relational value) to other individuals. Fortunately, nature has imbued us with a strong and pervasive inclination to establish, maintain, and repair our relational value in others' eyes.

REFERENCES

Abrams, D., Hogg, M. A., & Marques, J. M. (Eds.). (2005). *The social psychology of inclusion and exclusion*. New York: Psychology Press.

AhYun, K. (2002). Similarity and attraction. In M. Allen, R. W. Preiss, B. M. Gayle, & N. A. Burrell (Eds.), *Interpersonal communication research: Advances through meta-analysis* (pp. 145–167). Mahwah, NJ: Lawrence Erlbaum.

Arno, A. (1976). Ritual of reconciliation and village conflict management in Fiji. *Oceania, XLVII*, 49–65.

Asch, S. E. (1951). Effects of group pressure upon the modification and distortion of judgment. In H. Guetzkow (Ed.) *Groups, leadership and men* (pp. 178–190). Pittsburgh, PA: Carnegie Press.

Austin, J. L. (1956). A plea for excuses. *Proceedings of the Aristotelian Society, 57*, 1–30.

Axelrod, R., & Hamilton, W. D. (1981). The evolution of cooperation. *Science, 211*(4489), 1390–1396.

Baumeister, R. F., & Leary, M. R. (1995). The need to belong: Desire for interpersonal attachments as a fundamental human motivation. *Psychological Bulletin, 117*, 497–529.

Blum, V. L. (2003). *The culture of cosmetic surgery*. Berkeley, CA: University of California Press.

Bottom, W. P., Gibson, K., Daniels, S. E., & Murnighan, J. K. (2002). When talk is not cheap: Substantive penance and expressions of intent in rebuilding cooperation. *Organization Science, 13*, 497–513.

Bourdieu, P. (1977). *Outline of a theory of practice*. New York: Cambridge University Press.

Braun, V. (2005). Just a nip and a tuck? The culture of cosmetic surgery. *Feminism and Psychology, 15*, 345–350.

Buss, D. M. (1995). Evolutionary psychology: A new paradigm for psychological science. *Psychological Inquiry, 6*, 1–30.

Carnegie, D. (1936). *How to win friends and influence people*. New York: Simon and Schuster.

Castelfranchi, C., & Poggi, I. (1990). Blushing as a discourse: Was Darwin wrong? In W. R. Crozier (Ed.), *Shyness and embarrassment: Perspectives from social psychology* (pp. 230–251). New York: Cambridge University Press.

Chartrand, T. L., & Bargh, J. A. (1999). The chameleon effect: The perception-behavior link and social interaction. *Journal of Personality and Social Psychology, 76*, 893–910.

Cialdini, R. B., Kallgren, C. A., & Reno, R. R. (1991). A focus theory of normative conduct. *Advances in Experimental Social Psychology, 24*, 201–234.

Cialdini, R., Vincent, J., Lewis, S., Catalan, J., Wheeler, D., & Darby, B. (1975). Reciprocal concessions procedure for inducing compliance: The door-in-the-face technique. *Journal of Personality and Social Psychology, 31*, 206–215.

Cotterell, N., Eisenberger, R., & Speicher, H. (1992). Inhibiting effects of reciprocation wariness on interpersonal relationships. *Journal of Personality and Social Psychology, 62*, 658–668.

Cottrell, N. B., Wack, D. L., Sekerak, G. J., & Rittle, R. H. (1968). Social facilitation of dominant responses by the presence of an audience and the mere presence of others. *Journal of Personality and Social Psychology, 9*, 245–250.

Danheiser, P. R., & Graziano, W. G. (1982). Self-monitoring and cooperation as a self-presentational strategy. *Journal of Personality and Social Psychology, 42*, 497–505.

Darby, B. W., & Schlenker, B. R. (1982). Children's reactions to apologies. *Journal of Personality and Social Psychology, 43*, 742–753.

Davison, R., & Jones, S. C. (1976). Similarity in real-life friendship pairs. *Journal of Personality and Social Psychology, 34*, 313–317.

Dean, D. G., Powers, E. A., Braito, R., & Bruton, B. (1975). Cultural contradictions and sex roles revisited: A replication and a reassessment. *Sociological Quarterly, 16*, 207–215.

Deluga, R. J., & Perry, J. T. (1991). The relationship of subordinate upward influencing behaviour, satisfaction and perceived superior effectiveness with leader-member exchanges. *Journal of Occupational Psychology, 64*, 239–252.

Deluga, R. J., & Perry, J. T. (1994). The role of subordinate performance and ingratiation in leader-member exchanges. *Group and Organization Management, 19*, 67–86.

Diehl, M. (1990). The minimal group paradigm: Theoretical explanations and empirical findings. *European Review of Social Psychology, 1*, 263–292.

Flyn, F. J. (2003). How much should I give and how often? The effects of generosity and frequency or favor exchange on social status and productivity. *Academy of Management Journal, 46*, 539–553.

Folkes, V. S., & Sears, D. O. (1977). Does everybody like a liker? *Journal of Experimental Social Psychology, 13*, 505–519.

Frith, H., & Gleeson, K. (2004). Clothing and embodiment: Men managing body image and appearance. *Psychology of Men and Masculinity, 5*, 40–48.

Gardner, W. L., Pickett, C. L., & Knowles, M. (2005). Social snacking and shielding: Using social symbols, selves, and surrogates in the service of belonging needs. In K. D. Williams, D. Kipling, J. P. Forgas, & W. von Hippel (Eds.), *The social outcast: Ostracism, social exclusion, rejection, and bullying* (pp. 227–241). New York: Psychology Press.

Gonzales, M. H., Pederson, J. H., Manning, D. J., & Wetter, D. W. (1990). Pardon my gaffe: Effects of sex, status, and consequence severity on accounts. *Journal of Personality and Social Psychology*, 58, 610–621.

Gordon, R. A. (1996). Impact of ingratiation on judgments and evaluations: A meta-analytic investigation. *Journal of Personality and Social Psychology*, 71, 54–70.

Gouldner, A. W. (1960). The norm of reciprocity: A preliminary statement. *American Sociological Review*, 25, 161–178.

Hale, J. L., & Laliker, M. (1999). Explaining the Door-in-the-Face: Is it really time to abandon reciprocal concessions? *Communication Studies*, 50, 203–211.

Insko, C. A., Smith, R. H., Alicke, M. D., Wade, J., & Taylor, S. (1985). Conformity and group size: The concern with being right and the concern with being liked. *Personality and Social Psychology Bulletin*, 11, 41–50.

Janes, L. M., & Olson, J. M. (2000). Jeer pressures: The behavioral effects of observing ridicule of others. *Personality and Social Psychology Bulletin*, 26, 474–485.

Jones, B. C., Little, A. C., Penton-Voak, I. S., Tiddeman, B. P., Burt, D. M., & Perrett, D. I. (2001). Facial symmetry and judgments of apparent health: Support for a "good genes" explanation of the attractiveness-symmetry relationship. *Evolution and Human Behavior*, 22, 417–429.

Jones, E. E. (1964). *Ingratiation.* New York: Appleton-Century-Crofts.

Kacmar, K. M., Carlson, D. S., & Bratton, V. K. (2004). Situational and dispositional factors as antecedents of ingratiatory behaviors in organizational settings. *Journal of Vocational Behavior*, 65, 309–331.

Kandel, D. B. (1978). Similarity in real-life adolescent friendship pairs. *Journal of Personality and Social Psychology*, 36, 306–312.

Karau, S. J., & Williams, K. D. (1995). Social loafing: Research findings, implications, and future directions. *Current Directions in Psychological Science*, 4, 134–140.

Kramer, R. M., & Brewer, M. B. (1984). Effects of group identity on resource use in a simulated commons dilemma. *Journal of Personality and Social Psychology*, 46, 1044–1057.

Lakin, J. L., & Chartrand, T. L. (2003). Using nonconscious behavioral mimicry to create affiliation and rapport. *Psychological Science*, 14, 334–339.

Langlois, J. H., Kalakanis, L., Rubenstein, A. J., Larson, A., Hallam, M., & Smoot, M. (2000). Maxims or myths of beauty? A meta-analytic and theoretical review. *Psychological Bulletin*, 126, 390–423.

Latane, B., Williams, K., & Harkins, S. (1979). Many hands make light the work: The causes and consequences of social loafing. *Journal of Personality and Social Psychology*, 37, 822–832.

Leary, M. R. (1995). *Self-presentation: Impression management and interpersonal behavior.* Boulder, CO: Westview.

Leary, M. R. (2001a). *Interpersonal rejection.* New York: Oxford University Press.

Leary, M. R. (2001b). Toward a conceptualization of interpersonal rejection. In M. R. Leary (Ed.), *Interpersonal rejection* (pp. 3–20). New York: Oxford University Press.

Leary, M. R., Bednarski, R., Hammon, D., & Duncan, T. (1997). Blowhards, snobs, and narcissists: Interpersonal reactions to excessive egotism. In R. M. Kowalski (Ed.), *Aversive interpersonal behaviors.* New York: Plenum.

Leary, M. R., Britt, T. W., Cutlip, W. D., & Templeton, J. L. (1992). Social blushing. *Psychological Bulletin*, 112, 446–460.

Leary, M. R., & Cox, C. (2007). Belongingness motivation: A mainspring of social action. In J. Shah & W. Gardner (Eds.), *Handbook of motivation science* (pp. 27–40). New York: Guilford.

Leary, M. R., & Jones, J. L. (1993). The social psychology of tanning and sunscreen use: Self-presentational variables as a predictor of health risk. *Journal of Applied Social Psychology, 23*, 1390–1406.

Leary, M. R., Koch, E., & Hechenbleikner, N. (2001). Emotional responses to interpersonal rejection. In M. R. Leary (Ed.), *Interpersonal rejection* (pp. 145–166). New York: Oxford University Press.

Leary, M. R., Landel, J. L., & Patton, K. M. (1996). The motivated expression of embarrassment following a self-presentational predicament. *Journal of Personality, 64*, 619–636.

Leary, M. R., Twenge, J. M., & Quinlivan, E. (2006). Interpersonal rejection as a determinant of anger and aggression. *Personality and Social Psychology Review, 10*, 111–132.

MacDonald, G., & Leary, M. R. (2005). Why does social exclusion hurt? The relationship between social and physical pain. *Psychological Bulletin, 131*, 202–223.

Martin Ginis, K. A., Lindwall, M., & Prapavessis, H. (2007). Who cares what other people think? Self-presentation in exercise and sport. In G. Tenenbaum & R. Eklund (Eds.), *Handbook of sport psychology* (3rd ed., pp. 136–157). Hoboken, NJ: John Wiley.

McCauley, C. (1989). The nature of social influence in groupthink: Compliance and internalization. *Journal of Personality and Social Psychology, 57*, 250–260.

Miller, R. B., Greene, B. A., Montalvo, G. P., Ravindran, B., & Nichols, J. D. (1996). Engagement in academic work: The role of learning goals, future consequences, pleasing others, and perceived ability. *Contemporary Educational Psychology, 21*, 388–422.

Miller, R. S. (1996). *Embarrassment: Poise and peril in everyday life*. New York: Guilford.

Orbell, J. M., van de Kragt, A. J., & Dawes, R. M. (1988). Explaining discussion-induced cooperation. *Journal of Personality and Social Psychology, 54*, 811–819.

Palmer, D. L., & Kailin, R. (1985). Dogmatic responses to belief dissimilarity in the "bogus stranger" paradigm. *Journal of Personality and Social Psychology, 48*, 171–179.

Pandey, J. (1986). Sociocultural perspectives on ingratiation. In B. Maher (Ed.), *Progress in experimental personality research* (Vol. 14, pp. 205–229). New York: Academic Press.

Peluchette, J. V., Karl, K., & Rust, K. (2006). Dressing to impress: Beliefs and attitudes regarding workplace attire. *Journal of Business and Psychology, 21*, 45–63.

Pickett, C. L., & Brewer, M. B. (2005). The role of exclusion in maintaining ingroup inclusion. In D. Abrams, M. Hogg, & J. Marques (Eds.), *The social psychology of inclusion and exclusion* (pp. 89–111). Philadelphia: Psychology Press.

Richman, L. S., & Leary, M. R. (2008). Reactions to discrimination, stigmatization, ostracism, and other forms of interpersonal rejection: A dynamic, multi-motive model. *Psychological Review, 116*, 365–383.

Schachter, S. (1951). Deviation, rejection, and communication. *Journal of Abnormal and Social Psychology, 46*, 190–207.

Schlenker, B. R. (1980). *Impression management: The self-concept, social identity, and interpersonal relations*. Monterey, CA: Brooks/Cole.

Schlenker, B. R., & Darby, B. W. (1981). The use of apologies in social predicaments. *Social Quarterly, 44*, 271–278.

Schmitt, M., Gollwitzer, M., Forster, N., & Montada, L. (2004). Effects of objective and subjective account components on forgiving. *Journal of Social Psychology, 144*, 465–485.

Scott, M. B., & Lyman, S. (1968). Accounts. *American Sociological Review, 33*, 46–62.

Semin, G. N. R., & Manstead, A. S. (1982). The social implications of embarrassment displays and restitution behaviour. *European Journal of Social Psychology, 12*, 367–377.

Semin, G. N. R., & Papadopoulou, K. (1990). The acquisition of reflexive social emotions: The transmission and reproduction of social control through joint action. In G. Duveen & B. Lloyd (Eds.), *Social representations and the development of knowledge* (pp. 107–125). New York: Cambridge University Press.

Simpson, M. M., & Littrell, M. A. (1984). Attitudes toward clothing of elderly men. *Journal of Applied Gerontology, 3*, 171–180.

Skarlicki, D. P., Folger, R., & Gee, J. (2004). When social accounts backfire: The exacerbating effects of a polite message or an apology on reactions to an unfair outcome. *Journal of Applied Social Psychology, 34*, 322–341.

Solomon, R. S. (1990). *A passion for justice: Emotions and the origins of the social contract.* Reading, MA: Addison-Wesley.

Stangor, C. (2004). *Social groups in action and interaction.* New York: Psychology Press.

Stevens, C. K., & Kristof, A. L. (1995). Making the right impression: A field study of applicant impression management during job interviews. *Journal of Applied Psychology, 80*, 587–606.

Thornton, B., Audesse, R. J., Ryckman, R. M., & Burckle, M. J. (2006). Playing dumb and knowing it all: Two sides of an impression management coin. *Individual Differences Research, 4*, 37–45.

Turnbull, W. (1992). A conversation approach to explanation, with emphasis on politeness and accounting. In M. L. McLaughlin, M. J. Cody, & S. J. Read (Eds.), *Explaining one's self to others: Reason-giving in a social context* (pp. 105–130). Hillsdale, NJ: Lawrence Erlbaum.

Urdan, T., & Mestas, M. (2006). The goals behind performance goals. *Journal of Educational Psychology, 98*, 354–365.

Van Lange, P. A. M., Rusbult, C. E., Drigotas, S. M., Arriaga, X. B., Witcher, B. S., & Cox, C. L. (1997). Willingness to sacrifice in close relationships. *Journal of Personality and Social Psychology, 72*(6), 1373–1395.

Vidmar, N. (2000). Retribution and revenge. In J. Sanders & V. L. Hamilton (Eds.), *Handbook of justice research in law.* New York: Kluwer.

Vonk, R. (2002). Self-serving interpretations of flattery: Why ingratiation works. *Journal of Personality and Social Psychology, 82*, 515–526.

Wayne, S. J., & Kacmar, K. M. (1991). The effects of impression management on the performance appraisal process. *Organizational Behavior and Human Decision Processes, 48*, 70–88.

Wieselquist, J., Rusbult, C. E., Foster, C. A., & Agnew, C. R. (1999). Commitment, pro-relationship behavior, and trust in close relationships. *Journal of Personality and Social Psychology, 77*, 942–966.

Williams, K. D. (2001). *Ostracism: The power of silence.* New York: Guilford.

Williams, K. D. (2007). Ostracism. *Annual Review of Psychology, 58*, 425–452.

Williams, K. D., Forgas, J. P., & von Hippel, W. (2005). *The social outcast: Ostracism, social exclusion, rejection, and bullying.* New York: Psychology Press.

4

Cultural Variation in the Motivation of Self-Expression

HEEJUNG S. KIM and THAI Q. CHU

From what I have seen of Americans, I think that life would not be worth living to them without this freedom of self expression.

—Albert Einstein (as shown in Updike, 2007)

Self-expression, the expression of one's own personality traits, feelings, or ideas, is a notion particularly prevalent in American culture. Central and positive in many American contexts, whether it is through speech, artistic creation, or personal choice, self-expression is constitutive of particular patterns of perceptions, actions, interactions, and institutions that foster individuals' willingness and commitment to engage in the act. Such an emphasis on expression is one of the most integral aspects of individualism (Bellah, Madsen, Sullivan, Swidler, & Tipton, 1985), as people in these cultural contexts are urged to express themselves in order to assert "a unique core of feeling and intuition" (Bellah et al., 1985, p. 334).

Although self-expression is considered fundamental in many individualistic cultural contexts, the same cultural emphasis is not found in other cultural contexts. For example, in more collectivistic cultures, the act of self-expression is in general neither central nor important, and consequently, common patterns of perceptions, actions, interaction, and institutions do not encourage or endow great meaning to self-expression. The goal of the present review is to summarize and discuss some of the cultural variations in the motivation behind and effect of self-expression. We will discuss how people from different cultures practice self-expression in their actions and interactions and the psychological implications that result from these expressions.

CULTURE AND THE DEFINITION OF THE SELF

Extensive research has shown that the dominant model of the self in more individualistic cultures, such as in the United States, is an independent self in which a person is viewed to be a unique entity that is bounded and fundamentally separate from its social surrounding. This view holds that the individual is understood, practiced, and uniquely defined as a separate or distinct entity whose behavior is determined by some amalgam of internal attributes, such as thoughts, preferences, motives, goals, attitudes, beliefs, and abilities (Fiske, Kitayama, Markus, & Nisbett, 1998). These attributes enable, guide, and constrain behavior and motivate the expression of personal thoughts and the pursuit of personal goals and well-being (Kitayama & Markus, 2000; Markus & Kitayama, 1991; Markus, Mullally, & Kitayama, 1997; Morris & Peng, 1994). In these contexts, individuals are expected to make decisions based on their own volition, rather than on external influences or social constraints (Markus & Kitayama, 1991). In addition, these assumptions also shape the model of social relationships, which are assumed to be freely chosen and carry relatively few obligations (Adams & Plaut, 2003; Miller, Bersoff, & Harwood, 1990). Thus, people view relationships to be a benevolent resource in which they can engage with relatively little caution (Adams, 2005; Kim, Sherman, Ko, & Taylor, 2006).

By contrast, in more collectivistic cultures, such as in many Asian cultures, an interdependent view of the self pervades. In these cultures, social relationships define the self, and the basic motives for a person's behaviors are sought externally, rather than internally (Markus & Kitayama, 1991; Shweder & Bourne, 1984; Triandis, 1989). Thus, a person is regarded as a flexible, connected entity who is bound to others, conforms to relational norms, and views group goals as primary and personal beliefs, needs, and goals as secondary (Kim & Markus, 1999; Kitayama & Uchida, 2005; Markus & Kitayama, 1991). In these cultures, people assume that social factors, such as norms, roles, tradition, and a sense of social obligation, guide behaviors (Fiske et al., 1998; Kitayama & Uchida, 2005). Therefore, the motivation to maintain social equilibrium, to enhance others' evaluation of oneself, and to minimize social conflict takes precedence over the enhancement and assertion of individuality (Kim & Sherman, 2007; Leung, 1987; Markus & Kitayama, 1991). The model of relationships also takes an interdependent form in which relationships with others are less voluntary but more "given" and carry greater expectation of obligations (Adams & Plaut, 2003; Miller et al., 1990). In interdependent relationships, there is a more shared sense that relationships can and do have a central impact on one's life than is assumed in independent relationships (Adams & Plaut, 2003). Therefore, one has to be relatively more cautious in this context because of the greater implications that social relationships have (Adams, 2005; Kim et al., 2006).

These different self-construals stemming from one's participation in a given cultural context can implicate a multitude of psychological processes. For instance, people from East Asian cultural contexts tend to attribute more causal explanations of social events to situational and external factors, whereas European Americans tend to attribute explanations to internal and personal factors (Morris & Peng, 1994).

People from North American cultural contexts show a stronger self-enhancement tendency—the tendency to view oneself in a positive light—compared to East Asians (Heine, Lehman, Markus, & Kitayama, 1999). Moreover, it appears that for North Americans, a sense of self-worth is more strongly tied to possessing positive abilities, psychological traits, and uniqueness, whereas for East Asians, a sense of self-worth is more strongly tied to having good relationships and maintaining face (Heine et al., 1999; Hoshino-Browne et al., 2005). Consequently, the well-being of the self depends on one's own beliefs about oneself (hence "subjective well-being") in more individualistic cultures (Diener & Diener, 1995), whereas in collectivistic cultures, judgments of one's happiness are more normatively and objectively determined, and one's beliefs about one's own happiness are less relevant (Diener & Diener, 1995; Suh, Diener, Oishi, & Triandis, 1998). Combined, these different cultural views on what constitute the core of the self and relationships influence the motivation to assert and express one's personal feelings and thoughts.

CULTURE AND SELF-EXPRESSION

The need to belong, to be accepted, and to be valued by one's relevant social groups is considered to be one of the most basic human needs (Baumeister & Leary, 1995; Leary & Baumeister, 2000). Consequently, people are motivated to become a good and valued member of their social groups and to be viewed by themselves and others as such. We argue that when people are given the goal of being accepted and valued, it is crucial for them to not only possess positive characteristics but also project and highlight one's characteristics in a manner that reflects both positively and at least somewhat accurately on the self (cf. Dunning, 2003; Kunda, 1990).

Although this motivation to be valued and accepted might be universal, studies in cultural psychology have shown that what constitutes "being a good member" varies across cultures (Heine et al., 1999; Sedikides, Gaertner, & Toguchi, 2003). For example, the ideal characteristics of a good person in individualistic cultures include uniqueness, positive self-regard, and expressiveness, whereas in collectivistic cultures they include positive social relationships, social standing, reputation, and consideration for others (Heine et al., 1999; Markus & Kitayama, 1991). This divergence in ideals implicates culturally specific ways in which people enhance their sense of self-worth and project their self-image. To be a "good person" in a collectivistic culture, one should be motivated to maintain his or her social standing and relationships. To be a "good person" in an individualistic culture, one should be motivated to convey independent viewpoints and ideas, as these are the contents of self-views one should aspire to have in each respective culture.

At the same time, differences in the content of psychological tendencies should inform and shape psychological processes as well (Shweder, 1991), resulting in cultural differences in the process by which people enhance their sense of self-worth. Thus, in cultures emphasizing independence and agency, having a dual desire both to conjoin and belong to a social group but also to appear unique as an individual seemingly poses a contradiction. To resolve this cultural paradox, the need to belong in this cultural context engenders a requisite motivation for self-expression, a form of communication with an understated notion of "others." A person is in charge of projecting one's thoughts and feelings, whether with intention of asserting one's individuality or of seeking understanding and empathy from others. Through their words and actions, people reveal their internal attributes, such as preferences, beliefs, and values considered core to a person (Kim & Markus, 2002; Kim & Sherman, 2007), and thus show their individuality and uniqueness. At the same time, in so doing, people can satisfy the other motivation of social recognition and appreciation, as these self-expressive acts enable individuals to make their private thoughts and feelings concrete, tangible, and socially recognizable to others and to themselves. Self-perception theory (Bem, 1972) suggests that people come to know their own internal states by observing their own actions and behaviors. Self-expression through words may serve as an additional avenue of insight to one's internal state. In fact, previous research conducted in the U.S. culture shows that people were more confident of and committed to their attitudes after verbally expressing them (Higgins & Rholes, 1978; Kiesler & Sakamura, 1966). This process of self-expression takes on particular importance within a culture that emphasizes internal attributes in defining the self. Essentially, self-expression is a process by which individuals assert their individuality.

However, self-expression through explicit means, such as one's words and actions, might not be as effective when one's goal is to enhance self-worth via one's possession of positive social attributes, such as social consideration and good social relationships. In cultures where these social traits are emphasized, the motivation to enhance self-worth and belongingness might take a very different form. For example, to the extent that those from more collectivistic cultures express themselves, their attributes are conveyed through actions occupying and fulfilling particular social roles and having good social standing. Moreover, acts of self-expression should be less prevalent and central, and the psychological consequences of self-expression should be less positive. Instead, the effort to enhance self-worth might take more indirect, inconspicuous, and communal forms in these cultures. In the present chapter, we shall review the empirical evidence for cultural differences in the ways in which people express and communicate themselves, focusing on a few psychological domains, namely, self-expression through speech, choice, and social support seeking.

Cultural Differences in Self-Expression Through Speech

The act of speech, perhaps the most direct form of communication and expression, carries different meanings and importance across cultures. The reasons for speaking and the values of speaking vary across cultures in how they are incorporated and practiced in everyday life. When people speak, they have assigned sufficient value to their thoughts and beliefs to be expressed and shared with others. Thus, when self-expression is intertwined with a positive opportunity to assert one's individuality, as in the American cultural context, talking is seen as a valued act and is regarded as a sign of power and control. It is an art that requires skill and practice and can also serve significant artistic, social, and entertainment functions. Even in its negative forms, talking is revered as a rare attribute—a used-car salesman is a crafty artist with words just as a shifty lawyer is a quick thinker with a sharp tongue. By contrast, in cultural contexts where expression is tied to maintaining social harmony, the power and control implicated through speech tend to carry more negative connotations. Speaking out in class, talking back to authority figures, or asking questions out of one's turn can be seen as a disruption to one's social fabric. In fact, the Vietnamese word for talkative, *nhieu-chuyen* (literally meaning "full of verse"), is synonymous with *troublemaker* (Nguyen, 1995). In these cultural contexts, silence conveys attentiveness and encouragement to the speakers and is a highly valued response.

When asked to list the primary functions of talking, European American participants are more likely to include self-expression (i.e., expression of thoughts and feelings) than Korean participants, who more often endorse social coordination and maintenance of harmony as the primary functions (Kim & Sherman, 2007). Given that the predominant function of speech in the American cultural context is to express one's mind, people tend to assume a closer connection between a person's thoughts and speech compared to those from East Asian cultural contexts. Classic studies in social psychology show that those from the U.S. cultural context tend to exhibit a robust "correspondence bias" (Jones, 1979) in which they infer that corresponding thoughts exist when people talk about their ideas, even when the situational constraints that lead to making such speech are clear. This correspondence bias is considerably weaker among East Asians, who are less likely to assume corresponding attitudes based on spoken words than European Americans (Choi & Nisbett, 1998; Miyamoto & Kitayama, 2002). Consequently, the importance of being "truthful" in conversation also differs cross-culturally. As the assumption of the correspondence between what is said and what is in mind becomes relatively weaker, deceitful communications, such as the telling of white lies and exaggerations, are more commonly practiced and condoned in collectivistic cultural contexts (Almaney & Ahwan, 1982; McLeod & Carment, 1987).

The actual effects of speech on psychological functioning also differ. One such difference can be observed in the domain of thoughts. Thoughts are often considered the core of a personhood in the Western cultural tradition (e.g., Descartes, 1637/1993). At a basic level, even thoughts that are as impersonal sounding as thought processes involving cognitive problem solving are affected by speech differently as a function of the cultural background of a speaker. Speech is more strongly linked to thoughts in Western cultural contexts, especially as a way in which one could hone and sharpen one's mind, whereas such an assumption is, by and large, absent in Eastern cultural contexts (Kim, 2002; Kim & Markus, 2002). Research on the effect of verbalization on thinking shows that people differ in how they are affected by verbalizing their thoughts as a function of their cultural background.

A series of studies (Kim, 2002) examined how verbalization of thoughts (i.e., thinking aloud) affects thinking itself (i.e., cognitive problem solving). In these studies, East Asian American and European American participants were randomly assigned either to verbalize their thoughts or to stay silent while they were working on a cognitive problem set. Results on performance (i.e., the number of items answered correctly) in the verbalization condition versus the silent condition showed that verbalization of the problem-solving process impaired performance on a reasoning test for East Asian Americans, whereas verbalization did not affect the performance for European Americans. East Asian Americans and European Americans further differ in the ways in which they respond to verbalization biologically (Kim, 2008). In this study, East Asian American and European American participants were prompted to verbalize their thought processes as they solved cognitive problems in the procedure described above while their salivary cortisol levels were being measured at different time points (i.e., baseline, stress response, and recovery). Results show that verbalization had a positive effect for European Americans in that cortisol response to the task was lower when they verbalized their thoughts than when they worked on the problems in silence. Among East Asian American participants, such a benefit was absent (Figure 4.1).

A subsequent study utilizing the methods and theory of self-affirmation research (Sherman & Cohen, 2002; Steele, 1988) tested the effect of speech on feelings of self-worth by contrasting verbal expression and silent and private reflection of one's important values. For European Americans, verbally expressing personal values made them more affirmed and more secure about themselves (i.e., less self-serving; Dunning, Leuenberger, & Sherman, 1995), but merely reflecting on their values without expressing them led to greater self-threat. In contrast, for East Asian Americans, verbalizing their values led to increases in self-threat and self-serving responses, whereas merely reflecting on their values without talking did not. In sum, the evidence gathered by contrasting these different culture groups demonstrates that the utilization, benefit, and purpose of speech greatly vary as a function of cultural ideals.

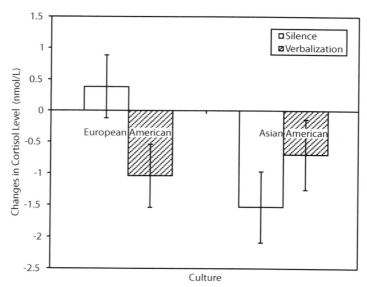

Figure 4.1 Mean cortisol level changes from baseline as a function of culture and verbalization. (From Kim, H. S., "Culture and the cognitive and neuroendocrine responses to speech," *Journal of Personality and Social Psychology*, vol. 92, pp. 32–47. Published 1999 by the American Psychological Association. Reprinted with permission.)

Cultural Differences in Self-Expression Through Choice

Another way in which individuals can express their thoughts and values is through choice. Choice making is a psychological domain in which self-expression motivation implicates its contents and processes. Americans value their freedom to choose and psychologically invest in what they choose (Iyengar & Lepper, 1999; Kim & Sherman, 2007; Snibbe & Markus, 2005; Tafarodi, Mehranvar, Panton, & Milne, 2002). This cultural emphasis stems from the fact that choice, an inherently agentic act that presumes freedom, is a way to express oneself (Kim & Drolet, 2003). Thus, it is an expression of one's free will and a reflection of one's preference, opinion, and values. Every choice one makes imparts his or her own self in this cultural context. And because choice is an observable act, it becomes an act through which a person expresses oneself for social recognition.

In the American cultural context, people are motivated to make choices that enhance their individuality and uniqueness. This motivation affects both how and what people choose. European Americans generally prefer and choose objects that represent uniqueness (Kim & Markus, 1999) and tend to respond more positively to messages that focus on uniqueness (Aaker & Schmitt, 2001; Han & Shavitt, 1994; Kim & Markus, 1999). They also show stronger tendency for variety seeking, a tendency associated with the need for uniqueness (Ariely & Levav, 2000; Drolet, 2002).

In contrast, people from collectivist cultures generally do not value the notion of standing out and highlighting their differences from others, but rather they prefer blending in and emphasizing their similarity with others. Consequently, they tend to avoid choosing objects that represent uniqueness, gravitate toward objects that represent sameness (Kim & Markus, 1999), and respond positively to messages that emphasize harmony (Aaker & Schmitt, 2001; Han & Shavitt, 1994; Kim & Markus, 1999). People from Asian cultural contexts show considerably weaker variety-seeking tendency than European Americans (Kim & Drolet, 2003).

Cultural differences in the importance of self-expression also influence how choice affects psychology. Many classic social psychological studies using the free-choice dissonance research paradigm show that people tend to increase liking for a chosen object and decrease liking for a rejected object, compared to their liking for the same objects prior to choice making (Brehm, 1956; Steele, Spencer, & Lynch, 1993). This "spreading alternatives effect," a result of self-commitment through choice (Kiesler & Sakamura, 1966), is most strongly found among those from European American cultural contexts. For people from Asian cultural contexts, the same act of choice making does not lead to the same spreading effect (Heine & Lehman, 1997; Hoshino-Browne et al., 2005; Kitayama, Snibbe, Markus, & Suzuki, 2004).

In this research paradigm, what is expressed through choice is assumed to be one's preference. For those from cultural contexts where people place emphasis on thoughts and feelings, expressing preference through choice implicates a core aspect of themselves and speaks to their character. Therefore, making a choice leads to greater investment and commitment to the chosen option and, thus, motivates people to justify their choice. In contrast, for those from cultural contexts where people do not emphasize internal attributes, what is expressed through choice does not carry much cultural importance and, therefore, does not stir up the same level of motivation to justify their choice.

Further research has aimed to address the role of expression more directly by experimentally manipulating whether one's choice gets expressed (Kim & Sherman, 2007). In these studies, East Asian American and European American participants were asked to make a choice among a variety of different pens. Half of the participants were randomly assigned to indicate their choice by writing down their pen choice, whereas the other half were instructed to make a choice without indicating their pen choice in any way (i.e., keeping it in their mind). Then, the experimenter usurped the choice and offered an alternative pen that was not chosen by participants, and participants were asked to evaluate the unchosen pen.

The results show that this manipulation of expression significantly impacted subsequent preference among European Americans, as they liked the pen given to them *less* after they expressed their choice than after they did not express their choice. In contrast, whether East Asian Americans expressed their choice or not did not have a significant impact on their liking of the pen that was given to them (Figure 4.2). Moreover, a subsequent study showed that how much a person is impacted by the expression of choice is predicted by what the person views as the core aspect of the self. That is, those who think that thoughts and feelings are the most important component of the self tend to justify their choices more. These findings suggest that self-expression, specifically the expression of internal attributes through choice, leads people from individualist cultural contexts to feel more invested in the choice as it implicates themselves, whereas the same act does not have as much psychological significance to those from collectivist cultural contexts.

However, choices not involving internal and individuating aspects of a person may be assigned different levels of importance. In cases where choice indicates

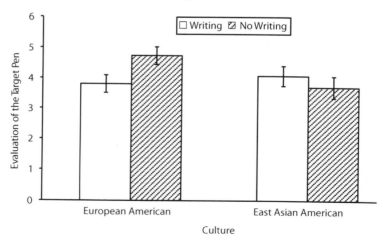

Figure 4.2   Mean (and *SE*) evaluation of the target pen as a function of culture and expression. (From Kim, H. S., & Sherman, D. K., "Express yourself": Culture and the effect of self-expression on choice. *Journal of Personality and Social Psychology, 92,* 2007. With permission.)

more external and social components of the self (i.e., social status or relationships), choice acts more as a marker of an individual's social attributes. For example, because brand-name products are generally perceived to have higher quality and higher price, they can signal higher social status. The choice of a brand-name product over a generic product indirectly conveys information that consumers who can afford higher priced products, ultimately, belong to higher social status groups.

A set of studies (Kim & Drolet, 2009) examined cultural differences in how Asian Americans and European Americans respond to choices that potentially reflect their social attributes, specifically brand-label options over generic-label options. In multiple studies, Asian Americans consistently chose brand-name options more frequently than European Americans. Furthermore, the positive relationship between self-consciousness and choice of brand-name options was found only among Asian Americans and not among European Americans. Therefore, it is inferred that Asian Americans are more concerned than European Americans about their choices if those choices reflect aspects of the self that are more culturally emphasized. This is consistent with previous findings that showed that Asian Canadians experience greater postdecision dissonance if the decision has interpersonal consequences than European Canadians (Hoshino-Browne et al., 2005) and are more motivated by choice if it is made by a close other (Iyengar & Lepper, 1999).

It is also important to note that many of these choice patterns change if alternate means to express culturally important aspects of oneself are present prior to choice making. For example, engaging in a task that allows one to express one's personal attributes (e.g., preference or values) prior to choice making reduces the tendency of variety seeking (Kim & Drolet, 2003) and individual dissonance (Hoshino-Browne et al., 2005). Similarly, engaging in a task that allows one to express one's social attributes (e.g., values or characteristics of important social groups) prior to choice making reduces the tendency of brand choice (Kim & Drolet, 2009) and interpersonal dissonance (Hoshino-Browne et al., 2005).

In sum, these reviewed studies show that there are meaningful cultural differences in the practice and effect of self-expression through speech and choice, in terms of both what people in different cultures typically express and the centrality of self-expression in their lives. So far, the reviewed findings focus on the effect of relatively intrapersonal self-expression—that is, self-expression with oneself as the primary target or with only implicit others. Yet, we view self-expression as a way in which individuals gain the sense of self-worth and ultimately seek to affirm their secure positions in social surroundings. Thus, in the next section, we turn to the psychological effect of the self-expression in more interpersonal contexts.

CULTURE AND INTERPERSONAL IMPLICATIONS OF SELF-EXPRESSION

If the motivation for and effect of self-expression differ across cultures, how do they operate in the context of relationships and interpersonal communications? Research about self-disclosure reveals the function of interpersonal communication. For those from more individualistic cultures, self-disclosure, in which people express some aspects of themselves, has positive psychological and interpersonal impacts. "Publicizing" the self in any form makes the self recognizable and observable to people, including the self, and its mostly positive effect shows the importance of self-expression in psychological processes of individuals. The speaker's act of opening up and disclosing personal information indicates a motivation to enhance interpersonal closeness in individualistic cultures (Hendrick, Hendrick, & Adler, 1988).

In contrast, for those from more collectivistic cultures, talking about one's feelings and thoughts is more often seen as irrelevant, inappropriate, and disagreeable, as it can potentially violate conversational norms or create disagreements with others (Kim & Markus, 2002). Thus, people in collectivist cultures tend to develop the habit of paying closer attention to cues from social contexts when disclosing self-relevant information, of using more implicit forms of communication such as nonverbal cues (Gudykunst & Ting-Toomey, 1988), and of relying on indirect forms of speech (Holtgraves, 1997).

Our discussion thus far has not accounted for the perceiving audience, such as "others" or society, as recognizing agents of one's attributes. The need to be accepted and valued by relevant social groups by striving to be a "good member" is probably relevant in many cultures (Baumeister & Leary, 1995; Heine et al., 1999). Clearly, how one is projected to and viewed by others (and by oneself as well) bears psychological importance, and individuals should be motivated to communicate who they are. In individualistic cultures, individuals project their "goodness" through individual expression of positive personal attributes. Regardless of the audience, the clarity and coherence of a message rests primarily on the speaker, and any misinterpretation or ambiguity that is perceived is a result of the speaker's failure to be clear and competent in expressing the thought or belief. For instance, in American cultural contexts, speakers are "held to their words" and encouraged to state intentions directly and unambiguously, for the responsibility of communication is likely to fall on the speaker, not the listener (Gudykunst, Gao, & Franklyn-Stokes, 1996; Hall, 1976).

In contrast, people in collectivistic cultures tend to rely more on the mutual recognition of one's attributes. Thus, the act of communication is an inherently interpersonal process that is mutually constructed. The success of communication hinges on successful coordination in relationships, and failed or ill-conducted communication negatively impacts relational harmony. Thus, it carries more social importance as well as costs in this cultural context. Collectivistic cultures put more emphasis on the relational function of communication than individualistic cultures, in which the informational function is more greatly emphasized (Scollon & Scollon, 1994). As a result, delivering a message is more cognitively taxing for Japanese than Americans because more cognitive resources must be allocated to tailoring the message to the recipient because of their culture's greater emphasis on relationship goals (Miyamoto & Schwarz, 2006). Thus, it is to the speaker's benefit to convey messages in a manner such that social harmony is maintained. When communication takes a more implicit, ambiguous form, there is a greater likelihood that a socially disruptive message will not be interpreted as such. Here, the burden of interpretation is more likely the responsibility of the listener (Gudykunst et al., 1996; Hall, 1976).

Indeed, research on East Asian communication processes argues that, because of the central importance of maintaining harmonious relations, the processes of face-saving and face-negotiating are recognized in some situations to be more important than honest or truthful negation (e.g., Gao, Ting-Toomey, Gudykunst, & Bond, 1996). Being open, straightforward, or assertive in public East Asian situations rarely has any of the positive connotations of honesty, power, confidence, or competence they have in many American contexts. Instead, actions of this type can threaten the cohesion of relationships and even signal the bad character of the individual involved (Tseng, 1973). What appears as passivity or critical lack of assertiveness from an American viewpoint carries with it, in many East Asian contexts, a whole palette of highly positive associations, including wisdom, flexibility, managing face, cooperativeness, caring, and maturity.

Cultural Differences in the Use of Social Support

The review above illustrates cultural differences in how much people are willing to express their thoughts in communication in general. Does this pattern of cultural difference hold true in situations in which people might disclose their thoughts and feelings in order to gain understanding and sympathy from others? Moreover, what type of psychological impacts do such disclosures and expressions have?

When an individual encounters a problem or a stressful event, one of the ways in which one can cope with it is through the use of social support. Social support is defined as information from others that one is loved and cared for, esteemed and valued, and part of a network of communication and mutual obligations (Wills, 1991). Social support may come from a spouse or companion, relatives, friends, coworkers, and community ties, such as belonging to a church or club. According to past research, social support takes the form of specific transactions involving the seeking and receiving of help through tangible assistance, informational support, or emotional support (Cohen, 1988; Wills, 1991), processes involving explicit expression of personal distress and needs. Social support has long been known to mute the experience of stress, reduce the severity of illness, and speed recovery from health disorders when they do occur (Seeman, 1996; Taylor, 2007). However, research on culture and expression suggests that there might be cultural differences in how people exercise and are affected by such an expression.

Indeed, consistent with findings on culture and expression, studies have shown that European Americans are more likely to ask for and receive social support than Asians and Asian Americans to cope with stressful events (Shin, 2002; Taylor et al., 2004). A series of studies (Taylor et al., 2004) demonstrated that Asian Americans and European Americans differ in their willingness to use social coping to deal with stressors. In the first study, European American and Korean participants provided open-ended responses regarding ways in which they coped with stressful events. Although the two groups did not differ from each other in their use of individual efforts to deal with stressors, significantly fewer Korean than American participants reported using social coping to help them cope with stress. In the second study, European American and Asian and Asian American participants were asked to describe a stressor they had recently experienced, following which they completed a scale of coping strategies in response to their stressor (the brief COPE; Carver, 1997). The two groups differed not in their individual coping (planning, positive reframing, active efforts) but in terms of their social coping (seeking informational support, seeking emotional support). Asian and Asian American students were significantly *less* likely to draw on social support for coping with stress than were the European American students, a pattern that was especially true for the Asian national and immigrant students.

At first glance, it seems contrary to expectations that an individual from a cultural context in which the self is defined by social networks and intimate relationships is less likely to draw on these very relationships for aid. However, research has identified that explicit social support is underused and discouraged among Asians and Asian Americans because they are particularly concerned about the effect that the disclosure of distress would have on their relationships, such as causing them to lose face, worrying others, and disturbing the harmony of their group (Study 3 of Taylor et al., 2004). In other words, Asians and Asian Americans are more cautious about expressing their distressed feelings and needs because of the potentially negative social implications of such acts.

Subsequent studies (Kim et al., 2006) specifically examined the effect of making close relationships salient by priming various goals (i.e., goals of the self, an ingroup, or an outgroup) on the willingness to seek social support and the eventual consequence of social support seeking. After being primed to think about their personal goals, or the goals of an outgroup with whom they do not have any meaningful relationships, Asian American participants were more willing to talk about their stressors to seek social support than after being primed with ingroup goals. In contrast, European Americans' responses were impervious to goal priming. Moreover, social support seeking in dealing with stressors was perceived to be less helpful and even harmful for Asian Americans than for European Americans, especially after the ingroup goals priming. These results show that both the decision to disclose one's distress and the expectation of its outcomes are greatly influenced by the specific nature of relationships for Asian Americans, whereas for European Americans, it is more of an individual act. That is, Asian Americans seem to weigh the potential benefits of such expressions against the potential relational costs in their decision making, whereas European Americans do not.

This idea was extended in a study that examined actual support-seeking behavior among couples in a close relationship (Sherman et al., 2010). If Asian Americans are more sensitive to the concerns of relationships, then they would be more affected by the manipulation of situational constraints on a close other who could potentially give them support. Thus, in this study, romantic couples (both of whom were either European American or Asian American) came to the lab, and one partner went through a stressful task (having to prepare and deliver a speech), whereas the other partner, the potential support provider, was given either an easy or a challenging game to play. Then, they were left alone in a room while they worked on their tasks (i.e., speech preparation for the speech giver and game for the game player), and their interactions were recorded using a hidden video camera.

Asian Americans were more sensitive to this manipulation: They sought support (i.e., explicitly asked for help and/or talked about their distress) when their partner had an easy task and, presumably, more resources to help, but they did not seek support when their partner had a more difficult task and was, presumably, more taxed. European Americans, by contrast, sought help to the same extent regardless of what their partner was doing. This study provides behavioral evidence that Asian Americans are more sensitive to the relationship concerns when considering whether to seek social support.

However, the research evidence for the benefits of social support—having a supportive social network and knowing that one is cared for by close others—in buffering individuals against stressful events remains overwhelming (Taylor, 2007). Yet, the findings on culture and social support that we reviewed so far show that Asians and Asian Americans do not utilize social support. Then, the question is whether they are deprived of this effective and crucial form of coping because of social concerns, or does social support seeking take a form that differs from the Western mode? In light of the findings on culture and self-expression, we speculated that it might be the case that the difference lies in *how* people use social support rather than *whether* people use social support. It is likely that those from more collectivistic cultures utilize social support for coping with stress in culturally appropriate ways that are different from the Western model of social support transaction, which involves explicit disclosure of one's distress. Findings from our earlier research (Kim et al., 2006; Taylor et al., 2004) suggest that Asian Americans may restrain from utilizing social support out of concern over potentially negative relational implications. Then, use of social support that does not risk one's relationships should be sought out more and should be more beneficial for those from more collectivistic cultures. In this case, social support use *without* actual disclosure of the stressor might be more culturally appropriate.

To test this idea, a study (Taylor, Welch, Kim, & Sherman, 2007) examined the effectiveness of explicit social support and implicit social support. Explicit social support is defined as "specific recruitment and use of their social networks in response to specific stressful events that involve the elicitation of advice, instrumental aid, or emotional comfort," whereas implicit social support is defined as "being in the company of close others or thinking about close others without disclosing or discussing one's problems vis à vis specific stressful events" (Kim, Sherman, & Taylor, 2008; Taylor et al., 2007). In this study, participants, both Asian Americans and European Americans, were read instructions for the Trier Social Stress Task, a stress-inducing manipulation involving a speech task and mental arithmetic task (Kirschbaum, Pirke, & Hellhammer, 1993). After the speech preparation period, but before giving the speech, participants completed one of three writing conditions. Participants in the implicit support condition were asked to think about a group that they are close to and write about the aspects of that group that are important to them, whereas participants in the explicit support condition were told to think about people to whom they are close and then to write a letter directly asking for advice and support for the upcoming tasks from one of these people. In the control condition, participants were asked to write about an unrelated topic (i.e., a campus landmark). After the writing task, participants engaged in the lab stress task under harassing conditions. Throughout the study, participants gave saliva samples to be assessed for the stress hormone cortisol. Following the laboratory stress task, participants completed a measure of post-task stress and agitation.

Asian Americans who completed the explicit support prime that invoked the thought of disclosure experienced more stress and had higher cortisol levels relative to those who completed the implicit support prime. In contrast, European Americans experienced more stress and had higher cortisol levels when they completed the implicit support prime than the explicit support prime (see Figure 4.3). Thus, the culturally congruent form of social support was more buffering during an acute stressful experience.

This pattern of cultural difference in the effect of social support was further established in a daily diary study. Korean and European American participants reported on the most stressful event they experienced on a given day, the extent to which they used implicit and explicit support to deal with that specific stressor, how supported they felt overall, and how much daily life satisfaction they felt that day (Kim et al., 2010). Controlling for the total number of people with whom they interacted on a given day, European Americans who explicitly disclosed their stressor to a greater number of people felt more satisfied with their lives that day, whereas Asian Americans did not. Furthermore, the extent to which European Americans felt socially supported and felt that they had fulfilled others' expectations on a given day was predicted only by the use of explicit social support (i.e., how much advice they had sought). For Koreans, on the other hand, the extent to

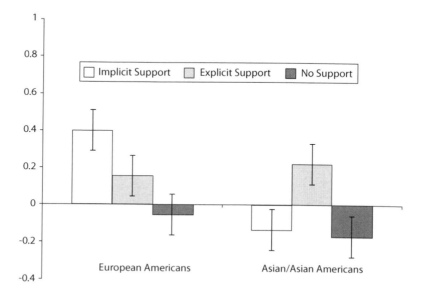

Figure 4.3   Change in cortisol levels from baseline to postchallenge as a function of culture and support condition. (From Taylor, S. E., Welch, W., Kim, H. S., & Sherman, D. K., Cultural differences in the impact of social support on psychological and biological stress responses. *Psychological Science, 18*, 2007. With permission.)

which they felt socially supported and satisfied with their lives was also predicted by how much they used implicit social support (i.e., how much they reminded themselves of those who love and care for them) and how many people with whom they spend their time without disclosing their stressor on a given day.

Taken together, these findings on culture and social support use show that for European Americans, expression of personal needs and emotional distress through direct communication leads to more positive psychological outcomes, such as more positive emotions, less stress, higher life satisfaction, and a greater sense of social support and approval. In contrast, Asians and Asian Americans consider the same expression of personal needs and emotional distress as a potential threat to social bonds. Thus, Asians and Asian Americans utilize a less direct form of social support that is unlikely to affect social relationships. Without the concern of disrupting social relationships, this implicit form of social support seems to lead to higher life satisfaction and greater sense of social approval.

Whether one desires to express his or her thoughts, feelings, and needs and how one is affected by such expressions depends on the cultural weights given to personal goals and social harmony. Whereas the motivation to be a good cultural member might be common in most cultures (Heine et al., 1999), it appears that what people do to achieve this goal greatly differs by culture, as they have to negotiate these goals within different models of social relations. By understanding cultural variation, we may better understand the nuances of communication and how people balance self-expression and social harmony.

IMPLICATIONS FOR FUTURE RESEARCH

The present review focuses on cultural differences in the willingness and motivation for individuals to express themselves and their underlying reasons and also on the actual effect of self-expression in both intrapersonal and interpersonal contexts. We speculated that the motivation for self-expression—namely, to convey intended and desired characteristics of the self—is rooted in the need for social belongingness. As social animals, humans share the necessity of others in their livelihood. Thus, we assume that the construction of the self is a collaborative process involving the communicative effort of a person and the recognition by his or her social surroundings. The motivation to communicate oneself in ways that are intended and desired by oneself, which we call the motivation of *self-communication*, is at its core a motivation for social recognition and security of belonging. In regard to self-communication, the psychological importance of being viewed by others in a way that is desirable and reflective of one's own self-view is, to be sure, relevant in cultures beyond individualistic cultures (cf. Chen, Boucher, & Tapias, 2006). But because what constitutes the core of a person differs by culture, variations in what and how people wish to communicate subsequently follow.

Self-expression might be one way to communicate one's selfhood, which is particularly prevalent in cultural contexts where the self is the actor and propagator in communicative acts. Self-expression assumes an act that is motivated and executed by an individual in the presence of passive others—an act that is inherently independent and agentic. Yet, social recognition can result from not only self-expression but also more communal and mutual forms of self-communication. In these more communal communications, others might play more active roles in the process as recognizing agents or as surrogates or intermediary communicators on behalf of a person. Thus, beyond the examination of cultural differences in the effect of self-expression, it is important to understand whether there are alternative forms of self-communication in different cultures.

Furthermore, we believe that the findings on cultural differences in the effect of expression have implications for mental and psychological health implications. Many forms of psychotherapy are built on the assumption of positive effects of self-expression, whether they are for cognitive reframing or emotional cathartic experiences. Similarly, written emotional disclosure is associated with improvements in physical health and mood (Pennebaker, Kiecolt-Glaser, & Glaser, 1988; Petrie, Booth, Pennebaker, & Davidson, 1995; Smyth, Stone, Hurewitz, & Kaell, 1999). Self-expression through music and art acts as an alternative form of catharsis and has been used in pain management and substance abuse groups as healthier outlets for inner conflicts and emotions (Adelman & Castricone, 1986; Bailey, 1986). The lack of social support seeking and the underutilization of health services are risk factors for mental health problems (Boscarino et al., 2004). In contrast, suppression of self-expression seems to be connected to mental illness, psychopathology, and negative stress responses, as well as to many physical problems such as coronary heart disease (Friedman & Booth-Kewley, 1987; Gross & Levenson, 1993; Pennebaker & Beall, 1986).

Yet, there is some empirical evidence suggesting cultural differences in the effect of expression on stress responses (e.g., Kim, 2008; Taylor et al., 2007). These findings suggest that health benefits of expression (or harms of silence) might not be universally true. Before making hasty conclusions regarding these cultural differences, it is important to recognize that the findings reviewed in the present paper do not specifically examine the effectiveness of psychotherapy or the effect of trauma writing. Thus, it will be important to investigate the effect of expression on health outcomes in broader settings.

The present review aims to contextualize the act of expression and demonstrate cultural differences in the meaning of expression. In so doing, we highlighted the psychological and biological consequences of this difference. Depending on the basic assumptions and configuration in cultural systems, self-expression could have positive or negative psychological, physical, and social impacts. These findings provide evidence for the opening observation made by Albert Einstein that to Americans, self-expression is indeed a central ingredient that gives life meaning and self-worth. Although the extent to which we understand the nature of cultural differences and similarities in the effects of self-expression is still limited, we believe that the evidence is enough to provide a framework for future research on culture and divergent effects of expression and not to take the worth and meaning of expression for granted.

ACKNOWLEDGMENTS

This research was supported by the National Science Foundation, Grant BCS-0729532.

REFERENCES

Aaker, J., & Schmitt, B. (2001). Culture-dependent assimilation and differentiation of the self: Preferences for consumption symbols in the United States and China. *Journal of Cross-Cultural Psychology, 32*, 561–576.

Adams, G. (2005). The cultural grounding of personal relationship: Enemyship in North American and West African Worlds. *Journal of Personality and Social Psychology, 88*, 948–968.

Adams, G., & Plaut, V. C. (2003). The cultural grounding of personal relationship: Friendship in North American and West African worlds. *Personal Relationships, 10*, 333–347.

Adelman, E., & Castricone, L. (1986). An expressive arts model for substance abuse group training and treatment. *Arts in Psychotherapy, 13*, 53–59.

Almaney, A., & Ahwan, A. (1982). *Communicating with the Arabs.* Prospect Heights, IL: Waveland.

Ariely, D., & Levav, J. (2000). Sequential choice in group settings: Taking the road less traveled and less enjoyed. *Journal of Consumer Research, 27*, 279–290.

Bailey, L. M. (1986). Music therapy in pain management. *Journal of Pain and Symptom Management, 1*, 25–28.

Baumeister, R. F., & Leary, M. R. (1995). The need to belong: Desire for interpersonal attachments as a fundamental human motivation. *Psychological Bulletin, 117*, 497–529.

Bellah, R. N., Madsen, R., Sullivan, W. M., Swidler, A., & Tipton, S. M. (1985). *Habits of the heart: Individualism and commitment in American life.* New York: Harper & Row.

Bem, D. J. (1972). Self-Perception Theory. In L. Berkowitz (Ed.), *Advances in Experimental Social Psychology* (Vol. 6, pp.1–62). New York: Academic Press.

Boscarino, J. A., Galea, S., Adams, R. E., Ahern, J., Resnick, H., & Vlahov, D. (2004). Mental health service and medication use in New York City after the September 11, 2001, terrorist attack. *Psychiatric Services, 55*, 274–283.

Brehm, J. W. (1956). Postdecision changes in the desirability of alternatives. *Journal of Abnormal and Social Psychology, 52*, 384–389.

Carver, C. S. (1997). You want to measure coping but your protocol's too long: Consider the Brief COPE. *International Journal of Behavioral Medicine, 4*, 92–100.

Chen, S., Boucher, H. C., & Tapias, M. P. (2006). The relational self revealed: Integrative conceptualization and implications for interpersonal life. *Psychological Bulletin, 132*, 151–179.

Choi, I., & Nisbett, R. E. (1998). Situational salience and cultural differences in the correspondence bias and actor-observer bias. *Personality and Social Psychology Bulletin, 24*, 949–960.

Cohen, S. (1988). Psychosocial models of the role of social support in the etiology of physical disease. *Health Psychology, 7*, 269–297.

Descartes, R. (1993). Discourse on method (L. J. LaFleur, Trans.). Indianapolis, IN: Bobbs-Merrill. (Original work published 1637).

Diener, E., & Diener, M. (1995). Cross-cultural correlates of life satisfaction and self-esteem. *Journal of Personality and Social Psychology, 68*(4), 653–663.

Drolet, A. (2002). Inherent rule variability in consumer choice: Changing rules for change's sake. *Journal of Consumer Research, 29*, 293–305.

Dunning, D. (2003). The zealous self-affirmer: How and why the self lurks so pervasively behind social judgment. In S. J. Spencer et al. (Eds.), *Motivated social perception: The Ontario symposium* (Vol. 9, pp. 45–72). Mahwah, NJ: Lawrence Erlbaum.

Dunning, D., Leuenberger, A., & Sherman, D. A. (1995). A new look at motivated inference: Are self-serving theories of success a product of motivational forces? *Journal of Personality and Social Psychology, 69,* 58–68.

Fiske, A. P., Kitayama, S., Markus, H. R., & Nisbett, R. A. (1998). The cultural matrix of social psychology. In D. T. Gilbert, S. T. Fiske, & G. Lindzey (Eds.), *The handbook of social psychology* (pp. 915–981). New York: Oxford University Press.

Friedman, H. S., & Booth-Kewley, S. (1987). Personality, Type A behavior, and coronary heart disease: The role of emotional expression. *Journal of Personality and Social Psychology, 53,* 783–792.

Gao, G., Ting-Toomey, S., Gudykunst, W. B., & Bond, M. H. (1996). *The handbook of Chinese psychology.* Hong Kong: Oxford University Press.

Gross, J. J., & Levenson, R. W. (1993). Emotional suppression: Physiology, self-report, and expressive behavior. *Journal of Personality and Social Psychology, 64,* 970–986.

Gudykunst, W. B., Gao, G., & Franklyn-Stokes, A. (1996). Self-monitoring and concern for social appropriateness in China and England. In J. Pandey, D. Sinha, & D. P. S. Bhawuk (Eds.), *Asian contributions to cross-cultural psychology* (pp. 255–267). Thousand Oaks, CA: Sage.

Gudykunst, W. B., & Ting-Toomey, S. (1988). Culture and affective communication. *American Behavioral Scientist, 31,* 384–400.

Hall, E. T. (1976). *Beyond culture.* New York: Doubleday.

Han, S., & Shavitt, S. (1994). Persuasion and culture: Advertising appeals in individualistic and collectivistic societies. *Journal of Experimental Social Psychology, 30,* 326–350.

Heine, S. J., & Lehman, D. R. (1997). Culture, dissonance, and self-affirmation. *Personality and Social Psychology Bulletin, 23,* 389–400.

Heine, S. J., Lehman, D. R., Markus, H. R., & Kitayama, S. (1999). Is there a universal need for positive self-regard? *Psychological Review, 106,* 766–794.

Hendrick, S. S., Hendrick, C., & Adler, N. L. (1988). Romantic relationships: Love, satisfaction, and staying together. *Journal of Personality and Social Psychology, 54,* 980–988.

Higgins, E. T., & Rholes, W. S. (1978). "Saying is believing": Effects of message modification on memory and liking for the person described. *Journal of Experimental Social Psychology, 14,* 363–378.

Holtgraves, T. (1997). Styles of language use: Individual and cultural variability in conversational indirectness. *Journal of Personality and Social Psychology, 73,* 624–637.

Hoshino-Browne, E., Zanna, A. S., Spencer, S. J., Zanna, M. P., Kitayama, S., & Lackenbauer, S. (2005). On the cultural guises of cognitive dissonance: The case of Easterners and Westerners. *Journal of Personality and Social Psychology, 89,* 294–310.

Iyengar, S. S., & Lepper, M. R. (1999). Rethinking the value of choice: A cultural perspective on intrinsic motivation. *Journal of Personality and Social Psychology, 76*(3), 349–366.

Jones, E. E. (1979). The rocky road from acts to dispositions. *American Psychologist, 34,* 107–117.

Kiesler, C. A., & Sakamura, J. (1966). A test of a model of commitment. *Journal of Personality and Social Psychology, 3,* 349–353.

Kim, H. S. (2002). We talk, therefore we think? A cultural analysis of the effect of talking on thinking. *Journal of Personality and Social Psychology, 83,* 828–842.

Kim, H. S. (2008). Culture and the cognitive and neuroendocrine responses to speech. *Journal of Personality and Social Psychology, 94,* 32–47.

Kim, H. S., & Drolet, A. (2003). Choice and self-expression: A cultural analysis of variety seeking. *Journal of Personality and Social Psychology, 85,* 373–382.

Kim, H. S., & Drolet, A. (2009). Express your social self: Cultural differences in choice of brand name versus generic product. *Personality and Social Psychology Bulletin, 35,* 1555–1566.

Kim, H. S., & Markus, H. R. (1999). Deviance or uniqueness, harmony or conformity: A cultural analysis. *Journal of Personality and Social Psychology, 77,* 785–800.

Kim, H. S., & Markus, H. R. (2002). Freedom of speech and freedom of silence: An analysis of talking as a cultural practice. In R. Shweder, M. Minow, & H. R. Markus (Eds.), *Engaging cultural differences: The multicultural challenge in liberal democracies* (pp. 432–452). New York: Russell Sage Foundation.

Kim, H. S., & Sherman, D. K. (2007). "Express yourself": Culture and the effect of self-expression on choice. *Journal of Personality and Social Psychology, 92,* 1–11.

Kim, H. S., Chu, T. Z., Sasaki, J. Y., Sherman, D. K., Knowles, E. D., Lee, E., Park, J., Suh, E. M., & Taylor, S. E. (2010). Culture and social support seeking in daily life. Unpublished manuscript, University of California, Santa Barbara.

Kim, H. S., Sherman, D. K., Ko, D., & Taylor, S. E. (2006). Pursuit of happiness and pursuit of harmony: Culture, relationships, and social support seeking. *Personality and Social Psychology Bulletin, 32,* 1595–1607.

Kim, H. S., Sherman, D. K., & Taylor, S. E. (2008). Culture and social support. *American Psychologist, 63,* 518–526.

Kirschbaum, C., Pirke, K., & Hellhammer, D. H. (1993). The "Trier Social Stress Test": A tool for investigating psychobiological stress responses in a laboratory setting. *Neuropsychobiology, 28,* 76–81.

Kitayama, S., & Markus, H. R. (2000). The pursuit of happiness and the realization of sympathy: Cultural patterns of self, social relations, and well-being. In E. Diener & E. M. Suh (Eds.), *Subjective well-being across cultures* (pp. 113–161). Cambridge, MA: MIT Press.

Kitayama, S., Snibbe, A. C., Markus, H. R., & Suzuki, T. (2004). Is there any "free" choice? Self and dissonance in two cultures. *Psychological Science, 15,* 527–533.

Kitayama, S., & Uchida, Y. (2005). Interdependent agency: An alternative system for action. In R. M. Sorrentino, D. Cohen, J. M. Olson, & M. P. Zanna (Eds.), *Cultural and social behavior: The Ontario Symposium* (Vol. 10, pp. 137–164). Mahwah, NJ: Lawrence Erlbaum.

Kunda, Z. (1990). The case for motivated reasoning. *Psychological Bulletin, 108,* 480–498.

Leary, M. R., & Baumeister, R. F. (2000). The nature and function of self-esteem: Sociometer theory. In M. Zanna (Ed.), *Advances in experimental social psychology* (Vol. 32, pp. 1–62). New York: Academic Press.

Leung, K. (1987). Some determinants of reactions to procedural models for conflict resolution: A cross-cultural study. *Journal of Personality and Social Psychology, 53,* 898–908.

Markus, H. R., & Kitayama, S. (1991). Culture and the self: Implications for cognition, emotion, and motivation. *Psychological Review, 98,* 224–253.

Markus, H. R., Mullally, P., & Kitayama, S. (1997). Selfways: Diversity in modes of cultural participation. In U. Neisser & D. Jopling (Eds.), *The conceptual self in context: Culture, experience, self-understanding* (pp. 13–61). Cambridge: Cambridge University Press.

McLeod, B. A., & Carment, D. W. (1987). *To lie or not to lie: A comparison of Canadian and Chinese attitudes towards deception.* Unpublished manuscript, McMaster University.

Miller, J. G., Bersoff, D. M., & Harwood, R. L. (1990). Perceptions of social responsibilities in India and in the United States: Moral imperatives or personal decisions. *Journal of Personality and Social Psychology, 58,* 33–47.

Miyamoto, Y., & Kitayama, S. (2002). Cultural variation in correspondence bias: The critical role of attitude diagnosticity of socially constrained behavior. *Journal of Personality and Social Psychology, 83,* 1239–1248.

Miyamoto, Y., & Schwarz, N. (2006). When conveying a message may hurt the relationship: Cultural differences in the difficulty of using an answering machine. *Journal of Experimental Social Psychology, 42,* 540–547.

Morris, M. W., & Peng, K. (1994). Culture and cause: American and Chinese attributions for social and physical events. *Journal of Personality and Social Psychology, 67,* 949–971.

Nguyen, D. H., Phan, V. G. (2006). Tuttle English-Vietnamese Dictionary. North Clarendon, VT: Tuttle Publishing.

Pennebaker, J. W., & Beall, S. K. (1986). Confronting a traumatic event: Toward an understanding of inhibition and disease. *Journal of Abnormal Psychology, 95,* 274–281.

Pennebaker, J. W., Kiecolt-Glaser, J. K., & Glaser, R. (1988). Disclosure of traumas and immune function: Health implications for psychotherapy. *Journal of Consulting and Clinical Psychology, 56,* 239–245.

Petrie, K. J., Booth, R. J., Pennebaker, J. W., & Davison, K. P. (1995). Disclosure of trauma and immune response to a hepatitis B vaccination program. *Journal of Consulting and Clinical Psychology, 63,* 787–792.

Scollon, R., & Scollon, S. W. (1994). Face parameters in East–West discourse. In S. Ting-Toomey (Ed.), *The challenge of facework: Cross-cultural and interpersonal issues* (pp. 133–157). Albany: State University of New York Press.

Sedikides, C., Gaertner, L., & Toguchi, Y. (2003). Pancultural self-enhancement. *Journal of Personality and Social Psychology, 84,* 60–79.

Seeman, T. E. (1996). Social ties and health: The benefits of social integration. *Annals of Epidemiology, 6,* 442–451.

Sherman, D. K., & Cohen, G. L. (2002). Accepting threatening information: Self-affirmation and the reduction of defensive biases. *Current Directions in Psychological Science, 11,* 119–123.

Sherman, D. K., Kim, H. S., Pearson, D. M., Kane, H., Guichard, A., & Safarjan, E. (2010). *Perceiving resources and seeking support: Culture and social support in couples.* Unpublished manuscript, University of California, Santa Barbara.

Shin, J. Y. (2002). Social support for families of children with mental retardation: Comparison between Korea and the United States. *Mental Retardation, 40,* 103–118.

Shweder, R. (1991). *Thinking through cultures: Expeditions in cultural psychology.* Cambridge, MA: Harvard University Press.

Shweder, R. A., & Bourne, E. J. (1984). Does the concept of person vary cross-culturally? In R. A. Shweder & R. A. LeVine (Eds.), *Culture theory: Essays on mind, self, and emotion* (pp. 158–199). Cambridge: Cambridge University Press.

Smyth, J. M., Stone, A. A., Hurewitz, A., & Kaell, A. (1999). Effects of writing about stressful experiences on symptom reduction in patients with asthma or rheumatoid arthritis: A randomized trial. *Journal of American Medical Association, 281,* 1304–1309.

Snibbe, A. C., & Markus, H. R. (2005). You can't always get what you want: Educational attainment, agency, and choice. *Journal of Personality and Social Psychology, 88,* 703–720.

Steele, C. M. (1988). The psychology of self-affirmation: Sustaining the integrity of the self. In L. Berkowitz (Ed.), *Advances in experimental social psychology* (Vol. 21, pp. 261–302). New York: Academic Press.

Steele, C. M., Spencer, S. J., & Lynch, M. (1993). Self-image resilience and dissonance: The role of affirmational resources. *Journal of Personality and Social Psychology, 64,* 885–896.

Suh, E., Diener, E., Oishi, S., & Triandis, H. C. (1998). The shifting basis of life satisfaction judgments across cultures: Emotions versus norms. *Journal of Personality and Social Psychology, 74,* 482–493.

Tafarodi, R. W., Mehranvar, S., Panton, R. L., & Milne, A. B. (2002). Putting oneself in the task: Choice, personalization, and confidence. *Personality and Social Psychology Bulletin, 28,* 648–658.

Taylor, S. E. (2007). Social support. In H. S. Friedman & R. C. Silver (Eds.), *Foundations of health psychology* (pp. 145–171). New York: Oxford University Press.

Taylor, S. E., Sherman, D. K., Kim, H. S., Jarcho, J., Takagi, K., & Dunagan, M. S. (2004). Culture and social support: Who seeks and why? *Journal of Personality and Social Psychology, 87,* 354–362.

Taylor, S. E., Welch, W., Kim, H. S., & Sherman, D. K. (2007). Cultural differences in the impact of social support on psychological and biological stress responses. *Psychological Science, 18,* 831–837.

Triandis, H. C. (1989). The self and social behavior in differing cultural contexts. *Psychological Review, 96,* 506–520.

Tseng, W. S. (1973). The concept of personality in Confucian thought. *Psychiatry: Journal for the Study of Interpersonal Processes, 36,* 191–202.

Updike, J. (2007, April 2). The valiant swabian. New Yorker.

Wills, T. A. (1991). Social support and interpersonal relationships. In M. S. Clark (Ed.), *Prosocial behavior* (pp. 265–289). Newbury Park, CA: Sage.

5

Sharing Motivation

GREGORY M. WALTON and GEOFFREY L. COHEN

A t the heart of social psychology lies the relationship between the individual and the group. How do other people shape a person's perceptions, thoughts, feelings, and behavior? Such questions are critical to understanding individuals and groups. They were central to classic research in social psychology. Solomon Asch's (1952) famous "line studies," for instance, compared people's perceptions when people were alone versus in a group. Asch asked participants which of several lines was the same length as a target line. The task was easy enough that when participants made judgments alone, they solved almost all the problems correctly. But when they made judgments in a group of peers, each of whom was a stooge of the experimenter and had been instructed to choose the wrong line, two thirds of participants agreed with the group on at least one trial, giving incorrect answers in seeming defiance of their senses (Asch, 1952).

Many have interpreted Asch's findings as an illustration of the weakness of the individual in the face of a unanimous group—the tendency of people to conform mindlessly to others even in contradiction to objective reality. But Asch made a more subtle and deeper point. He argued for a cognitive interdependence among people. People's individual perceptions, attitudes, and identity are constructed in conjunction with the perceptions, attitudes, and identities of others. This process begins in infancy and continues through adulthood. Asch (1952) wrote, "To be in a social relation it is necessary to stand on common ground with others and to face daily conditions with shared understanding and purpose" (p. 576). From infancy, we hold a deep-seated expectation that perceptions of physical reality will be socially shared. This expectation is evident in the tension and discomfort that Asch's participants expressed upon seeing peers disagree with their perception of reality. Indeed, given the expectation of a socially shared reality, it is reasonable for people to question their perceptions when they contradict those of a unanimous majority.

Consistent with the notion that perception originates in part in the social context, the social influence effects that Asch (1952) observed can be found even when people report their judgments anonymously, minimizing conformity pressure (Deutsch & Gerard, 1955). In addition, modern brain-imaging techniques suggest that the brain regions activated when people are said to "conform" in Asch-like experimental situations are those involved in perception. By contrast, brain regions involved in social decision making show no heightened activation (Berns et al., 2005). The results are consistent with the idea that social influence changes how people see the world (see also Nisbett & Masuda, 2003; Sherif, 1936).

Beyond perception, attitudes too are rooted in social reality (e.g., Lewin, 1952; Sinclair, Huntsinger, Skorinko, & Hardin, 2005). Infants as young as a year of age decide whether to approach or to avoid physical objects by attending to the emotional cues of caretakers (Moses, Baldwin, Rosicky, & Tidball, 2001). Adults take on attitudes from important reference groups. In one series of studies, political partisans endorsed policies proposed by their political party, writing long essays advocating such policies, even when the policy violated their deeply held liberal or conservative values (Cohen, 2003). A classic field study tracked young adults from politically conservative families who attended a liberal college. Compared with matched controls, they became more liberal, and the longer they attended the college, the more liberal they became. Even 25 years later they were more apt to vote for a liberal presidential candidate (Newcomb, Koening, Flacks, & Warwick, 1967).

One lesson from this research is that important aspects of the self—even aspects that may seem personal and unique, such as long-held attitudes—are socially transmitted and shared. They originate in the social context (see also Aron et al., 2004; Cialdini, Brown, Lewis, Luce, & Neuberg, 1997; Gardner, Gabriel, & Hochschild, 2002; Markus & Kitayama, 1991). This lesson, however, commands less attention than it ought in contemporary social psychology. Instead, a variety of lines of research portray the self as independent from, and even as opposed to, the social context (for a review, see Markus & Kitayama, 1994). In much work, the individual is conceptualized as basically good, struggling to resist the negative influence of the group (Markus & Kitayama, 1994). The group is seen as a source of irrationality (e.g., groupthink, Janis, 1972), immorality (e.g., bystander intervention, Latane & Darley, 1968), aggression (e.g., deindividuation, Haney & Zimbardo, 1998; obedience to authority, Milgram, 1974), and laziness (e.g., social loafing, Karau & Williams, 1993), which the individual must fend off to succeed and be ethical.

Similarly, much recent research conceptualizes behavior as the product of basic cognitive, motivational, and affective processes that occur in the isolated minds of individuals, as in research on automaticity (e.g., Bargh, Chen, & Burrows, 1996) and on social cognition more broadly (Kunda, 1999) and in burgeoning research on social neuroscience. In this approach, the social context is seen as providing informational inputs into basic internal processes. The mental processes constitute the key explanatory variables, not the social context. Although this research describes an important facet of human nature, social or interpersonal processes by which people develop shared beliefs, attitudes, and goals are less emphasized (cf. Aron et al., 2004). As we suggest in the present chapter, one consequence is that our understanding of the origins of human motivation is incomplete.

A SOCIAL IDENTITY APPROACH TO MOTIVATION

The focus of this chapter is on achievement motivation—the factors that impel people to persist rather than withdraw in the face of challenge and minimal external incentive. The question of motivation is a classic one in psychology (e.g., McClelland, 1961) and is relevant both to basic theories of human nature and to important social problems. Like perceptions and attitudes (Asch, 1952), we suggest that motivation originates in the social context. Indeed, motivation often arises in social settings where people work together to solve collective problems, such as athletic teams, study groups, work groups, civic organizations, and the like. We suggest that people tend to share interests and goals with others, especially with others to whom they feel socially connected. They may internalize the goals of others as their own, as well as develop new interests and goals collectively with others to whom they feel socially connected.

Our approach is informed by the notion of social identity—that aspect of people's self-definition that is based on their social groups (Tajfel & Turner, 2004). Motivation, we suggest, is often associated with whether an endeavor is tied to a person's sense of identity and their feelings of social belonging in a group associated with the endeavor.

Past research has tended to examine how people develop socially shared attitudes and other aspects of self with close relationship partners (e.g., Aron et al., 2004), valued social groups (e.g., Cohen, 2003), or people with whom a person is motivated to affiliate (e.g., Sinclair et al., 2005). By contrast, we suggest that the tendency to share interests and goals is so powerful that people can develop shared interests even with others with whom they share minimal, seemingly trivial social ties (Walton, Cohen, Cwir, & Spencer, 2010). One simple but important implication of this idea is that an activity will inspire more interest if it can be done with others rather than alone.

In addition, the idea that social belonging is critical to achievement motivation implies that students for whom this sense of belonging is threatened in school by social stigma, negative intellectual stereotypes, or numeric underrepresentation may be disadvantaged. Indeed, we suggest, processes linked to social belonging may contribute to the racial achievement gap (Walton & Cohen, 2007).

Three Reasons Why a Sense of Social Belonging Should Boost Motivation

Why would a sense of social belonging in a domain foster motivation? There are at least three reasons. First, adopting similar interests and motivations as relationship partners may affirm a positive self-image. People derive their sense of self-worth in part from being "good" or "appropriate" relationship partners and group members (Correll & Park, 2005; Leary, 2004; Sherman & Cohen, 2006; Tajfel & Turner, 2004). As a consequence, adopting interests similar to those of socially significant others may affirm people's sense of personal worth.

Second, people have a basic need to belong (Baumeister & Leary, 1995; see also Ryan & Deci, 2000). The importance of this need is underscored by research examining consequences when this need is thwarted (see Williams, 2007). Ostracism and social rejection can cause distress, even in anonymous online encounters (Williams, Cheung, & Choi, 2000). They can elicit aggression (Twenge, Baumeister, Tice, & Stucke, 2001), decrements in IQ test performance (Baumeister, Twenge, & Nuss, 2002), and decrements in self-regulation (Baumeister, DeWall, Ciarocco, & Twenge, 2005). By aligning their motivations to those of socially significant others, people may signify the integrity of their relationship. In addition, doing so may facilitate positive social interactions by creating mutually enjoyable activities in which people can participate together (see Surra, 1985).

Third, sharing motivation with others may serve important collective goals, which may be an end unto itself. A defining feature of human social life is collaborative activity, both formal and informal, which enables people to do more together than they could alone. Growing crops, raising a roof, running a business, and executing a war require teamwork and a network of people who share the same goal. Even what may be humans' most distinctive cognitive innovation—language—is at root a cooperative activity, as speakers and listeners work together to ensure that the information imparted by the speaker is relevant and appropriate to the listener's needs and understanding of the topic of conversation (Clark, 1996). A psychological mechanism by which goals and intentions become shared would offer significant advantages for individuals and the social units to which they belong (Vygotsky, 1978). If so, people may have evolved a tendency "to create shared goals to which they are jointly committed" (cf. Tomasello, Carpenter, Call, Behne, & Moll, 2005, p. 682).

Although these three processes are distinct, they share an important similarity. In each, a sense of social belonging increases motivation for a domain, not because motivation for the domain changes, but because the domain changes. The domain acquires meaning as a result of one's social connection to it, as a source of self-affirmation, as a forum for social bonding, and as a context in which to collaborate with others to accomplish shared goals. In his novel *Sons and Lovers*, the English author D. H. Lawrence captures the notion that the meaning of an activity may arise from being embedded in social relationships, writing, "Nothing had really taken place in [the children] until it was told to their mother" (1967/1973, p. 62).

A Social Identity Account as Compared to Predominant Theories of Motivation

The simple notion that motivation originates in people's social identity and sense of social belonging in an achievement domain contrasts sharply with predominant theories of motivation. Such theories posit that motivation originates in the individual self. They tend to emphasize people's perception of their competence in the domain, their sense of autonomy and free choice, and the extent to which they have met important personal goals (e.g., Bandura, 1997; Carver & Scheier, 2001; Deci & Ryan, 1985; Dweck & Leggett, 1988). The social context is seen as providing people feedback about these individualistic qualities. For example, role models can inspire people by showing that success is possible and thus boost motivation and achievement (Lockwood & Kunda, 1997; see also Aronson, Fried, & Good, 2002; Blackwell, Trzesniewski, & Dweck, 2007; Wilson, Damiani, & Shelton, 2002). Coercive incentives can lead people to attribute their participation in an activity to external pressure rather than to autonomous interest and thus undermine motivation (Deci, Koestner, & Ryan, 1999; Lepper, Greene, & Nisbett, 1973). Performance feedback can highlight a discrepancy between long-held goals and accomplishments to date and thus increase motivation (Carver & Scheier, 2001).

Taken as a whole, this literature portrays the person as informed by but disconnected from others. People's social relationships are not a central subject of analysis. One exception is self-determination theory (Ryan & Deci, 2000), which posits three needs affecting achievement motivation—needs for competence, autonomy, and relatedness. The notion of relatedness comes closest to our emphasis on social belonging. However, as the very name of the theory implies, the overriding emphasis in self-determination theory is on *self*-determination. Relationally supportive contexts are thought to allow people to feel sufficiently safe to explore and develop their natural curiosities (Ryan & Deci, 2000), an approach that draws on attachment theory (Ainsworth, Blehar, Waters, & Wall, 1978). By contrast, we suggest that people acquire their interests in transactions with socially significant others. If so, feeling socially connected to others in an achievement domain should enhance a person's motivation to achieve in that domain. If these social identity processes are powerful, then even subtle indicators of social connectedness should prove influential.

Evidence for the Role of Social Identity in Motivation

Although it differs from predominant theories, our approach, in some respects, resonates with common sense. Suppose two parents are deciding which day to send their child to an after-school program. On both days the program has small classes and skilled teachers, but, by chance, the children who go to the program on Mondays tend to be more academically engaged than the children who go on Tuesdays. As the parents know, on either day their child will interact with his or her classmates a good deal and stands to become friends with some of them. Which day should the parents choose?

Predominant theories of motivation make no clear recommendation. On both days the program offers opportunities for developing the self-concept—self-efficacy, autonomy, and goals—that underlies academic success. On the one hand, the program on Mondays might provide more role models—older children who have done well and can inspire (Lockwood & Kunda, 1997). On the other hand, the child might feel more intelligent than her classmates in the Tuesday program, boosting self-perceptions of competence (see Blanton, Buunk, Gibbons, & Kuyper, 1999). But, of course, most parents would prefer the Monday program. As parents know, peer groups matter. Make the right friends—those committed and engaged in school—and academic success is more likely. Make the wrong friends—those disengaged from school—and academic success is less likely. Children's attitudes, interests, and motivation—their very identity—are acquired in large part through peer groups (Harris, 1995, 1998). Making friends with the right crowd might be as important as receiving high-quality instruction in achieving academic success.

Consistent with this conclusion, research from disciplines outside of social psychology suggests the importance of the social context in people's development of interests and motivation. Developmental research finds that from an early age, infants exhibit a tendency to share intentions with adults (for a review, see Tomasello et al., 2005). Infants distinguish intentions from behaviors and, upon observing an adult fail to perform an act, imitate the intention, not the failed attempt (Meltzoff, 1995). In addition, infants eagerly participate in cooperative social games with adults (Ross & Lollis, 1987), even urging adult partners who have stopped participating in such games to resume (Warneken, Chen, & Tomasello, 2006).

At another level of analysis, sociological research finds that adults' preferences for movies, songs, and the like arise through social influence processes (Salganik, Dodds, & Watts, 2006). When people are ignorant of the preferences of others, there is little difference in the popularity of the most and least popular products. But when people know what peers like, the products preferred by early shoppers grow in popularity through a snowball process—they become "hip"—whereas nonpreferred products become especially unpopular. Negative behaviors, too, are the product of social influence. Binge eating among sorority women, for instance, can spread through local social norms (Crandall, 1988; see also Cohen & Prinstein, 2006; Prentice & Miller, 1993).

Other research underscores the importance of social identity in such effects. The perception that a dissimilar outgroup engages in a particular behavior can deter others from engaging in that behavior. If residents of a "nerdy" dorm wear a particular wristband or if "sketchy" graduate students are thought to drink large quantities of alcohol, undergraduates may stop wearing the wristband and drink less (Berger & Heath, 2008; Berger & Rand, 2008). It's just not what "we" do.

Likewise, research in political science suggests that social strategies are among the most potent ways to increase voter turnout. More effective than making voting convenient (e.g., by allowing people to register to vote when they apply for a driver's license) are campaign strategies that establish a social bond with voters, such as door-to-door canvassing, holding parties at the poll on election day, and the like. As Green and Gerber (2004) wrote, "Mobilizing voters is rather like inviting them to a social occasion" (p. 92). Even intellectual revolutions arise, it seems, in part through social influence. Such revolutions appear to be triggered not so much by brilliant scholars working alone but by networks of thinkers engaged in the same problem, supporting one another and egging each other on intellectually (Collins, 1998).

Overview of the Present Research

These findings suggests that an important source of people's interests, motivation, and behavior is in their social identity—their network of social relationships, the groups they affiliate with, and so forth. Consistent with this work, we suggest that people develop interests with and from others to whom they are socially connected. However, in the real world, and in many of the examples provided above, there are plausible alternative explanations for such effects. The effects could arise from social norms, conformity pressure, or just the salience of a behavior. To demonstrate the causal role of a sense of social belonging, much of our research distills the construct of belonging to its essence—to the minimal conditions needed to make people feel connected to others in an achievement domain. This approach holds constant or strips away confounding variables. In the spirit of Bob Zajonc (2001), we call this *mere belonging*. We assess its impact on motivation. In addition, our research is designed to demonstrate the intuitive significance of social belonging for motivation. We emphasize the size of the effects of intuitively small manipulations of belonging and their impact on important behaviors, such as persistence, time spent studying, and school grades.

The next section discusses our research on "mere belonging"—the impact of minimal social connections on interest and motivation. Afterward, we examine the effect on motivation and achievement when people's sense of social belonging in school is systematically threatened by negative intellectual stereotypes.

MERE BELONGING

A first set of studies tested whether a mere social link to others involved in an activity or a performance domain would boost motivation for that activity or domain (Walton et al., 2010). To provide convergent evidence for this hypothesis, the studies tested several different ways of creating a current or potential social link.

Making a Dull Activity Social

The first study tested whether motivation for a dull activity would rise merely if people had an opportunity to take part in the activity with others. This study was inspired in part by classic research on nonverbal behavior. In an elegant series of field studies, Kraut and Johnston (1979) compared people's rate of smiling in response to positive and neutral daily events when alone versus when in the company of others. They found, overwhelmingly, that people smile in the company of others but not when alone. In one study, bowlers smiled just 4% of the time after having privately observed that they had just bowled a strike or a spare but 31% of the time after having turned to face their friends waiting in the pit (regardless of the result of their bowl). Of course, this research does not resolve *why* people smile in the company of others. One reason is because smiling is a communicative act. But another reason, perhaps, is that the activity itself becomes more positive and pleasurable in the psychological company of others. Alone, bowling is simply the act of throwing a ball to knock down pins; with others it may become a forum for social interaction, bonding, and teamwork.

To test this hypothesis, we gave people a description of one of four pairs of activities. One activity in each pair was designed to be inherently appealing, and the other was dull. The pairs were (a) taste testing chocolates versus salad dressing, (b) watching movie clips versus abstract visual stimuli, (c) listening to music versus tones, and (d) bowling versus turning pegs. Each participant read a description of the two activities in one pair and saw a picture of each activity (e.g., a photograph of chocolates and one of several vials of salad dressing). They were asked to "visualize" doing the activities. In all cases, participants were led to believe that the appealing activity would be done alone. A single sentence contained the manipulation. It indicated either that the dull activity would also be done alone or that it would be completed with two or three other people. Would making the dull activity social make it more interesting?

It did. We asked participants about their preferences for the activities. When both activities would be done alone, participants strongly preferred the appealing activity to the dull one. But when the dull activity could be done with others, their preference for it rose by 40%. Why? Examination of participants' open-ended responses suggests that participants saw the dull task as being more pleasurable when done with others (e.g., "might be fun to watch with others"). They also saw it as providing opportunities for social bonding (e.g., "there would be other people so it could be a social activity"), for exchanging perspectives (e.g., "interesting to see how people differ in their perceptions"), for sharing emotions (e.g., "laughing with the people I'm testing with"), and for collaborating (e.g., "talking over a strategy with other individuals"). This change in the way participants construed the task appeared to drive the effect of condition on preferences. Controlling for them statistically mediated the condition effect on preferences.

Mere Belonging and Achievement Motivation

In the foregoing study, participants developed a shared interest for an activity they could do with others. The next set of studies extended the analysis to achievement motivation. These studies tested whether people would have greater motivation for a field of study merely as a result of having a current or potential social connection to others in that field. Previous correlational research links a sense of social connectedness in school to achievement motivation (e.g., Caprara, Barbaranelli, Pastorelli, Bandura, & Zimbardo, 2000; Furrer & Skinner, 2003; Ladd, 1990; Wentzel, 1997; see also Finn, 1989; Goodenow, 1992). In one study, participating in extracurricular activities—which facilitate students' social integration in school—nearly eliminated school dropouts among at-risk high school students (Mahoney & Cairns, 1997). In such studies, however, social belonging is confounded with many other factors. Therefore, in three experiments we manipulated *mere belonging*, the minimal conditions needed to make people feel connected to others (Walton et al., 2010). In addition, through its control conditions, each study tested whether mere belonging would increase motivation above and beyond other more individualistic factors affecting motivation, such as the inspirational effects of a positive role model (Lockwood & Kunda, 1997) or the acquisition of a personal identity in the field (Miller, Brickman, & Bolen, 1975).

The Shared-Birthday Study. In one study, undergraduates read a report ostensibly written by a graduate of the math department at their college. The report described a positive experience in the department and presented the report author as academically successful. All participants were thus exposed to a positive role model in math (see Lockwood & Kunda, 1997). We manipulated a single datum in the report—the author's birthday, embedded in a small box along with the author's name and hometown. In the same-birthday condition, the author's birthday matched the participant's birthday. In the different-birthday condition, the two birthdays differed by several months. As past research indicates, a shared birthday creates a "unit relationship" between individuals (Heider, 1958, p. 201), inducing greater cooperation (Miller, Downs, & Prentice, 1998) and liking (Jones, Pelham, Carvallo, & Mirenberg, 2004). If people adopt the goals and interests of others to whom they feel socially connected, they should be more motivated to achieve in math in the same-birthday condition than in the different-birthday condition.

They were. The primary measure of motivation was how long participants persisted on an insoluble math puzzle task. The task was completed in private, minimizing social desirability pressure, and thus provides a relatively clear index of intrinsic motivation for math. Participants in the same-birthday condition persisted 65% longer on the puzzle than did participants in the different-birthday condition. They also displayed greater motivation for math along several self-report instruments (e.g., reporting that it was "more important" for them to be good at math).

The Minimal Group Study. A second study operationalized mere belonging as membership in a minimal group, that is, a temporary group based on an arbitrary distinction. Undergraduates participated in groups of 8 or 9. Following the standard procedure for creating a minimal group (Billig & Tajfel, 1973), participants were induced to believe either that they were members of the "numbers group" or that they were the "numbers person." Both conditions thus created in participants an identity in the field of math. The manipulation varied whether that identity was socially shared (i.e., "We do math" vs. "I do math"). Notably, research finds that having a personal identity in a field fosters motivation (e.g., Miller et al., 1975). However, even relative to the condition in which they were personally labeled a "numbers person," being labeled a member of the "numbers group" led participants to persist more than twice as long on the insoluble math puzzle.

The Relational Context Study. The third study tested a different kind of social link. It manipulated the perceived *opportunity* to form social ties in the field. As in the birthday study, participants read a report about the math department ostensibly written by a former major. The manipulation involved whether the department was described as providing opportunities to cultivate skills and personal interests (the "skill-promotive context" condition) or as providing opportunities to work with others, to share experiences, and to bond socially over math (the "relational context" condition). For instance, in the former condition, one section of the report read, "[The department] sponsors several competitive exams and prizes each year … to encourage students … to develop their individual abilities." In the later condition, this section read, "Many members of the faculty are excited to work with undergraduates. … The professors encouraged us to work in groups." This comparison provides a difficult test for the mere-belonging hypothesis, as the effect of the relational context condition would have to *exceed* that of the skill-promotive context condition. It did. The relational context report produced greater persistence than the skill-promotive context report and greater self-reported motivation for math.

Mediation. We also obtained evidence for mediation. In the birthday study and the relational context study, measures assessing a sense of social connectedness to math statistically mediated the condition effect on motivation (relevant measures were not assessed in the minimal group study). In addition, we addressed a possible alternative explanation. The social links could have increased positive affect or satisfied participants' belonging needs in general, allowing them to attend to any achievement pursuit (see Ryan & Deci, 2000). If so, the manipulations should have raised motivation in general, not just for math. This was not the case. In each study, measures of motivation for the humanities yielded no condition difference; if anything, the social links decreased motivation in the humanities.

Statistical Summary. The mere-belonging effects were statistically large. To create an intuitive barometer of the size of the effect, we compared it to the effect of participants' baseline level of interest and ability in math (a composite of their SAT math score, the number of math classes they had taken in college, how personally invested they reported being in math at baseline, and whether they were or anticipated majoring in a math-related field). Pitting the mere-belonging manipulations against baseline math interest/ability and meta-analyzing across the three studies, we found the overall mere-belonging effect on math motivation (i.e., an index combining behavioral persistence and self-reported motivation) was about 70% of the size of the effect of students' baseline level of math interest/ability (ds = 0.71, 1.00, respectively; the latter effect size compares students 1 standard deviation above vs. below the mean). In addition, there was no interaction between the mere-belonging manipulations and baseline math interest/ability. Even students with the highest level of interest/ability in math were more motivated if they were socially linked to the field. One implication of the observed effect sizes is thus that students with average levels of baseline math interest/ability who were socially linked to math were more motivated, on average, than students with high levels of baseline math interest/ability who were not so linked.

SOCIAL BELONGING AND GROUP DIFFERENCES IN ACADEMIC ACHIEVEMENT

The mere-belonging studies suggest the importance of social belonging for motivation. Another way to test this effect is to examine the consequences when students' sense of belonging in school is systematically threatened. For instance, students who belong to groups that historically have been excluded from academic institutions, or whose groups are underrepresented or targeted by negative intellectual stereotypes, may reasonably wonder if others will include them in positive social relationships in school. They may be uncertain of their social belonging (Walton & Cohen, 2007; see also Mendoza-Denton, Downey, Purdie, Davis, & Pietrzak, 2002). Two sets of studies examined social belonging among students from underrepresented groups. The second set of studies then addressed the effect of uncertainty about belonging on underrepresented students' academic motivation and achievement.

Social Representations of a Field of Study and Social Belonging

The perception that there is a typical kind of person who pursues a domain is so pervasive that we sometimes overlook it (see Moscovici, 1984). Airline pilots are male, network news anchors are White, and computer whizzes are young. In part, these social representations reflect reality. But they may also perpetuate group differences. When a domain is strongly associated with a particular group, people may associate success with membership in that group, consciously or unconsciously. Even minority group members who are interested and skilled in the field may feel that they would not "fit in" there.

We tested this idea in the context of computer science. Women, Blacks, and Hispanics are each underrepresented among computer scientists (e.g., constituting 13%, 1%, and 2% of computer science faculty at research universities, respectively; Nelson, 2007). All three groups also confront stereotypes that they lack ability either in quantitative fields in particular or in intellectual endeavors in general (Steele, 1997). The social representation of the typical person who succeeds in computer science may thus be of someone who is White or Asian and male (see Cheryan, Plaut, Davies, & Steele, 2009).

In a pair of studies, we manipulated the social representation of computer science. The manipulation was designed to sever the perceived link between a specific social identity (i.e., a White or Asian male) on the one hand and belonging and success in computer science on the other. We examined the effects of this manipulation on students' sense of social belonging in computer science. The manipulation consisted of a sidebar inserted in the margin of an actual news report about the computer science department at the participants' university. In the "gender-inclusive" condition, the sidebar quoted a female computer science major, who said, "Gender doesn't really matter here. I usually don't even think about it." By contrast, in the "gender-noninclusive" condition, the quotation read, "Sometimes it's tough to make men respect you in the computer world." Participants then completed items assessing their sense of social belonging in the computer science department (e.g., their level of agreement with statements like "I belong in the Computer Science Department" and "People in the Computer Science Department are a lot like me"). In the first study, as predicted, women reported a greater sense of social belonging in the gender-inclusive condition than in the gender-noninclusive condition. Indeed, in the gender-inclusive condition, women's sense of social belonging rose to the level of men's. As expected, men's sense of belonging was unaffected by the manipulation.

We contend that the critical message communicated in this manipulation is not simply that women can belong in computer science but that the kind of people who belong are those who share an interest and commitment to the field rather than a particular group identity. If so, the manipulation should raise a sense of social belonging among students from a marginalized group different from the one targeted in the manipulation.

A second study tested this idea. It exposed Black and Hispanic men to the same gender-focused manipulation of inclusion. As predicted, they showed the same increased sense of belonging in the gender-inclusive condition that women had displayed in the first study. White and Asian men showed no effect.

If minority-group students believe that their social belonging in computer science depends not just on their level of interest in the field but also on their group identity, then the relationship between their level of interest and their sense of belonging should be relatively weak. This was the case. In control conditions, baseline interest in computer science explained 37% of the variance in majority-group students' sense of social belonging in computer science (i.e., that of White and Asian men) but only 11% of that variance among minority-group students (i.e., women, Blacks, and Hispanics). Moreover, among students with little interest in computer science, there was no difference between minority- and majority-group students in their sense of belonging in the field. A group difference emerged only among students interested in the field. The gender-inclusive message eliminated this pattern. In this condition, minority-group students reported a sense of social belonging commensurate with their level of interest in the field. The message had no effect among minority-group students low in interest, but it significantly raised a sense of belonging among students interested in computer science. In so doing, it eliminated the group difference in students' sense of belonging in the field.

Belonging Uncertainty

The research described above examined a circumstance where underrepresented and negatively stereotyped students experienced relatively low levels of social belonging in an academic discipline. But even when students experience high levels of belonging, their belonging may be uncertain or fragile (Walton & Cohen, 2007). Knowing that they could encounter both overt and subtle forms of prejudice (Dovidio & Gaertner, 2000; Harber, 1998; see also Uhlmann & Cohen, 2005), stereotyped students in mainstream school and work settings may wonder whether others will accept them and include them in positive social relationships in academic settings. In this state of *belonging uncertainty*, people may scrutinize events in their daily lives for evidence relevant to their belonging and, as a consequence, perceive in such events a more global meaning than do their nonstereotyped peers (see also Mendoza-Denton et al., 2002; Shelton & Richeson, 2005). Criticism from an instructor or social isolation among peers, for instance, may seem to signify that the stereotype is in play and that stereotyped students do not belong in the academic environment. In turn, stereotyped students' motivation may suffer. In one study, for example, Black and White college students did not differ at baseline in their interest in revising an essay they had written; after receiving critical feedback from a White instructor, however, Black students' motivation dropped in comparison to that of White students (Cohen, Steele, & Ross, 1999).

Survey Study. An initial study tested the belonging-uncertainty hypothesis using a survey methodology (Walton & Cohen, 2007). We asked participants— Black, Hispanic, and White college students—to indicate their agreement or disagreement with items assessing their absolute level of belonging in college (i.e., "I belong at [college name]") and their level of uncertainty about their belonging (e.g., "Sometimes I feel that I belong at [college name], and sometimes I feel that I don't belong"; "When something bad happens, I feel that maybe I don't belong at [college name]"). No racial group difference was observed in students' absolute level of belonging. A group difference was found only in students' level of uncertainty about their belonging. Black and Hispanic students reported greater belonging uncertainty than did White students.

Laboratory Experiment. An experimental study provided further evidence of belonging uncertainty among negatively stereotyped students (Walton & Cohen, 2007). We exposed participants to a subtle threat to their belonging in a field of study. We asked Black and White college students to list either eight friends who would fit in well in the field or two such friends. Listing eight friends is difficult, and indeed participants (both Black and White) reported greater difficulty listing eight friends than two (see Schwarz et al., 1991). The question for our participants was as follows: "What does difficulty listing these friends mean about my fit in the field?" This difficulty, we predicted, would carry a more threatening and racialized meaning to Black students than to White students. It might convey to the former that "people of my race" do not belong here. As expected, White students showed no difference by condition. But Black students reported less motivation when they were asked to list eight friends rather than two. For example, although Black students rated their potential to succeed in the field as slightly better than that of their classmates when they were asked to list two friends (i.e., their self-rating on a percentile scale was 58%), when they were asked to list eight friends, they rated themselves well below average (i.e., their self-rating was 31%). In addition, Black students seemed to interpret the difficulty they had listing friends not only as evidence that they personally did not belong in the field but also as evidence that their racial group did not. For instance, Black students asked to list eight friends were less likely than Black students in the control condition to encourage a same-race peer to major in the field (no such condition difference was found in Black students' encouragement of different-race peers).

Intervention Field Experiment. Both the survey study and the experiment suggest that adverse social events in academic contexts may carry a more global meaning to stereotyped students than to nonstereotyped students. A final study tracked students' responses to adversity in the ebb and flow of their daily lives (Walton & Cohen, 2007). Most important, the study also tested an intervention designed to protect students against belonging uncertainty and assessed its impact on their motivation and achievement in school. The intervention provided students with an alternative, nonracial, nonthreatening explanation for adversity in school. This "attributional retraining" intervention was predicted to buttress the motivation of stereotyped students in the face of adversity in school (see also Wilson et al., 2002).

We tested the intervention among Black and White first-year college students (Walton & Cohen, 2007). Students reviewed the results of an ostensible survey of upper-year students at their school. The survey results were based on the results of an actual survey but were edited to highlight critical themes. In the treatment condition, the results indicated that most students, regardless of race, doubted their belonging during the transition to college and experienced negative social events in school (e.g., felt excluded, were not invited to dinner with classmates, received critical feedback on assignments). But over time, the survey indicated, these doubts subsided, and most students came to feel at home in college. The survey thus conveyed to African American students that doubts about belonging are common at first in college, not unique to their racial group, and short-lived. This message was expected to deracialize difficulties experienced in the transition to college and help buttress African Americans' sense of belonging in school. It was expected to do so, in large part, by reducing the likelihood that African Americans would see adversity in school as evidence that the stereotype was in play.

In the control condition, participants also read the ostensible results of an upperclassmen survey, but the information was irrelevant to belonging. Instead, it indicated that students' social and political attitudes became more sophisticated over time in college.

To drive home the manipulation, both conditions incorporated dissonance tactics (see Aronson et al., 2002). Dissonance research suggests that freely advocating a message to an impressionable audience leads people to internalize that message—the "saying is believing" effect. Participants wrote an essay describing how their own experience in college illustrated the pattern of change described in the survey results. They then delivered their essay as a speech to a video camera, ostensibly to be shown to first-year students the subsequent year to help them better manage the transition to college. In total, the intervention lasted about an hour.

The intervention led to immediate and sustained benefits for stereotyped students (Walton & Cohen, 2007). In the laboratory, intervention-treated Black students reported higher levels of belonging and motivation in school as compared to peers in the control condition. When selecting courses to take from the school catalogue, they were more likely to sign up for challenging, educational classes rather than less challenging, less educational ones.

To track students' responses to adversity, we had them complete daily diary questionnaires over the week following the delivery of the treatment. Each evening students reported how much adversity they had encountered that day and their current level of academic motivation. As predicted, in the control condition there was a tight relationship between these variables for Black students: 59% of the day-to-day variance in Black students' motivation could be explained by the level of adversity they experienced each day. The treatment reduced this figure to 24%. (For White students in both conditions, there was no relationship between adversity and motivation.) Looked at another way, the treatment sustained Black students' motivation in the face of adversity. On days of low adversity, Black students in both conditions reported high levels of academic motivation. But on highly adverse days, Black students in the control condition reported relatively low levels of motivation, whereas Black students in the treatment condition continued to report relatively high levels.

The intervention also increased Black students' self-reported engagement in achievement behaviors, specifically behaviors that provide opportunities for academic enrichment but pose risks of failure and rejection. For example, the intervention increased the time Black students reported studying each day by nearly an hour and a half and boosted the number of e-mail queries they reported sending to professors threefold. White students were again unaffected by the intervention.

Finally, we examined students' grades, as assessed by official school records. Controlling for their grade point average (GPA) in the semester before the intervention, Black students' GPA in the semester after the intervention was one third of a grade point higher in the treatment condition than in the control condition. To test the robustness of this effect, we subjected it to a second comparison. We compared the GPA of students in each experimental group to the GPA of students in the same class year as participants but who had not participated in the study. Relative to Black students in this campus-wide group, Black students in the treatment condition again performed significantly better. Among White students, the treatment had no positive effect. If anything, White students tended to perform better in the control condition than in the treatment condition, but neither experimental group differed significantly from the campus-wide data for White students. Overall, the treatment was associated with a roughly 90% reduction in the racial achievement gap in the term following its administration. Given the paucity of successful interventions to close the achievement gap, these results are encouraging and await large-scale attempts at replication.

Like the mere-belonging studies, the intervention results underscore the powerful effects social belonging has on achievement motivation. An hour-long intervention to secure a sense of social belonging boosted stereotyped students' motivation and, even months later, their grades.

DISCUSSION

Commercial radio stations invariably compete over how much music they play: "60 minutes commercial free," "Fifteen songs in a row," "Two hours without a break to start your day." Such promos suggest that listeners' main concern in picking a radio station is choosing the one that plays the most music. But, peculiarly, radio stations do not maximize the amount of music they play, even holding constant ad time. They repeatedly interrupt the music with DJs, who waste seemingly precious minutes to tell silly jokes and banter back and forth. Why don't listeners revolt and migrate to other stations that focus on the music, putting DJs and the radio stations that employ them out of business?

If you have ever listened to music on the radio without a DJ, you know the answer. It's lonely. DJs create the sense that a community is listening together. You might be out doing yard work or driving alone, but if you are listening to the radio, you can hear a good DJ tell a joke and take calls from other listeners for requests, contest entries, and the like. You might feel connected to the DJ and to the radio station and to other listeners doing their errands as they listen along to the same station. And somehow as a result, the music is more captivating.

As with consumer preferences (Salganik et al., 2006), undergraduate drinking (Berger & Rand, 2008), voting (Green & Gerber, 2004), intellectual revolutions (Collins, 1998), and achievement motivation (Walton & Cohen, 2007; Walton et al., 2010), listening to the radio, it seems, is in part a social act. In each case, there is a "we" behind the "I." As the research reviewed in this chapter shows, if an activity can be done collectively or if a field offers opportunities for forming social connections, it may inspire greater interest and motivation. Even minimal social links, like a shared birthday with a peer in a field of study, can raise motivation (Walton & Cohen, 2008). The feeling that "we do it" can have effects on motivation comparable in size to the effect of individual differences in personal interest. A social connection can change the very nature of a task. What had been a boring activity to slog through—like turning pegs—becomes, when done with others, an opportunity to collaborate on a joint activity and to share perspectives and emotions. By adopting interest in such an activity, one affirms one's relationships with others engaged in the same task and facilitates positive interaction with them. In addition, analysis of the role of social belonging in motivation provides insight into the origin of racial differences in achievement, a major concern for educators and policy makers (Steele, 1997), and affords novel remedies for a portion of these differences (Walton & Cohen, 2007).

The research reviewed here underscores the collective, socially shared nature of what we usually consider to be individual attitudes, motivation, and identity. Such aspects of the personal self derive in part from relationships with others, even from relationships based on minimal ties. The social transmission of attitudes and motivations seems to be a signature characteristic of humans. More than other primates, humans are motivated to share intentions and other psychological states with others (Tomasello et al., 2005; see also Moll & Tomasello, 2007). From an early age, human infants eagerly participate in cooperative social games with adults (Ross & Lollis, 1987; Warneken et al., 2006). And cognitive neuroscience shows that humans, along with other primates, possess "mirror neurons," which activate both when a person performs a goal-directed action and when he or she observes someone else perform an action (e.g., picking up a cup; Iacoboni et al., 2005). Neurologically, in a sense your goal is my goal.

A Theoretical Paradox: Social Belonging and Individualism

Interestingly, our emphasis on socially shared aspects of self conflicts with a long tradition of Western thought, which venerates the individual and denigrates imitation. This view is reflected in common interpretations of Asch's (1952) line studies as an example of "mindless conformity." It is exemplified by Ralph Waldo Emerson's quip, "Imitation is suicide." On Emerson's view, an individual is valuable by virtue of his or her unique qualities and attributes. To imitate is to lose one's uniqueness and to be subsumed by others. Consistent with this tradition, Westerners place great value on independence and individualism (Markus & Kitayama, 1991). Their motivation for a task drops when they perceive that their autonomy or free will in choosing to engage in that task has been usurped (Iyengar & Lepper, 1999; see also Deci et al., 1999). Given these powerful cultural values, why would participants in, for instance, the mere-belonging studies, most of whom were White Americans, adopt the motivations of others?

Although future research may address this issue empirically, a possible answer involves the subtlety of the social links explored in the mere-belonging studies. People from Western cultures perform a balancing act. On the one hand, they have a genuine need to belong—to form social ties, to be connected to others, to share similar interests, and to do things together (Baumeister & Leary, 1995). On the other hand, they maintain an "independent" self-concept, seeing themselves as agentic and unique (Markus & Kitayama, 1991). Subtle social links may enable Westerners to accomplish both objectives at once. Because they are not perceived as coercive, they permit people to align their interests with the interests of others while retaining the illusion that their interests are unique and independent. This analysis leads to a prediction. In terms of cultivating people's intrinsic goals and interests, subtle social pressure ought to be more influential than overt social pressure, and subtle indicators of social belonging ought to be more influential than overt indicators—notions consistent with dissonance and self-perception theories.

Practical Lessons

For students and educators, employees and employers, the take-home lesson from this chapter is that social belonging is an important source of motivation. Linking students and workers socially to others engaged in a common endeavor can increase motivation. Even social ties that seem trivial may prove effective. Notably, the flip side of this analysis is that social connections to people who have *dis*engaged from school or work may undermine motivation, even when these social connections seem minimal.

A second important lesson is that people from groups that are underrepresented or negatively stereotyped may not experience the same sense of social belonging in school and work settings as do others. Members of different groups may see the same event in radically different ways. In addition, even when stereotyped students report a high overall sense of belonging, it may be uncertain or fragile, rising and falling in response to seemingly subtle experiences.

Importantly, this difference in construal on the part of majority- and minority-group students is not a product of bias but a normal consequence of human psychology. People invariably interpret stimuli in light of their surrounding context, a point long noted by gestalt psychologists (Asch, 1952). For people whose group is negatively stereotyped, the context includes an increased risk of social rejection and exclusion. For such individuals, a heightened sensitivity to issues of belonging may be adaptive.

The present research also shows that providing a nonthreatening, nonracial attribution for social adversity—for instance, where adversity is short-lived and shared across racial groups—can secure stereotyped students' sense of belonging and raise motivation and achievement (Walton & Cohen, 2007). Although this intervention can have positive effects, it should not be applied blindly without regard for local circumstance. For instance, in situations where prejudice is pervasive or racial barriers significant, the intervention could risk obscuring from members of the target group the bias they face.

Implications for Irrationality and Evil

Thus far we have emphasized primarily how social belonging can lead to improvements in human welfare—raise motivation and reduce group differences in academic achievement. But social belonging does not necessarily lead to positive outcomes. Indeed, social belonging may also lead to acts that could justifiably be described as evil. As noted earlier, when belonging needs are thwarted, negative outcomes may result. For instance, social rejection may increase aggressive behavior (Twenge et al., 2001). Ostracism in a school or in broader society may even contribute to school shootings or to terrorism (Williams, 2007).

Another way social belonging may produce negative outcomes is by inducing people to uncritically rally behind an ingroup—to adopt harmful attitudes, values, or behaviors modeled by group leaders or other group members. For instance, in conforming to the social norms of a valued group, people may behave aggressively, binge eat, or binge drink (Cohen & Prinstein, 2006; Crandall, 1988; Prentice & Miller, 1993). In the public sphere, people may advocate for social policies that violate their core values because their political party proposed them (Cohen, 2003). They may support politicians whom they would otherwise reject when they believe that their election is inevitable (Kay, Jimenez, & Jost, 2002).

People may even engage in genocide if they see their behaviors as defending a sacred value or ingroup from threat. Historians have documented how ordinary German citizens internalized the anti-Semitic views promoted by Hitler and other Nazi leaders before World War II. Indeed, Jews were seen as subhuman and as traitors who had conspired with the Allies to sabotage Germany after World War I. Indoctrinated with this view, ordinary German citizens—not individuals screened as especially violent or anti-Semitic—committed some of the most horrific crimes of the Holocaust. By and large, these were willing murderers; permitted to bow out without punishment, most did not (Browning, 1992; see also Goldhagen, 1997). Like Nazi Germany, terror regimes in Stalinist Russia and Mao's China used socially shared ideologies to satisfy citizens' needs for belonging and inspire popular support (Canetti, 1978; see also Bourdieu, 1977; Glick, 2002).

Belonging needs may also have contributed to undesirable political outcomes in the United States. The Vietnam War provides one example. In 1967, Harry McPherson, special counsel to the president, delivered to President Lyndon Johnson the dismal results of a fact-finding mission to Vietnam—rampant corruption in the South Vietnamese military and staunch resolve among the Viet Cong. Despite this reality, McPherson defended military escalation, telling the president, "Every aspect of our national life and our role in the world is involved in Vietnam. I feel that I am only another of those many men who have a part of their souls at stake there" (quoted in Branch, 2007, pp. 621–622). In the Cold War, the fight against Communism defined America's collective identity. This oppositional identity sustained support from politicians and from the "silent majority" of the citizenry for a war that many believe proved unwise. It took nearly eight years after McPherson's briefing, and the deaths of 58,000 American soldiers and countless Vietnamese, for the war to end—and for the material, human, and political costs of continuing the war to overtake the identity costs of ending it without victory.

CONCLUSION

Social belonging plays a key role in human motivation, but, with some notable exceptions, it has received relatively little attention in contemporary research and theory in social psychology. This lack of attention affords fruitful areas for future research. Like an alchemist who turns lead into gold, a social connection, it seems, can make a dull task interesting. A seemingly trivial social link such as one based on a shared birthday can inspire motivation. Processes linked to social belonging can cause group differences in academic achievement and provide gateways for theory-driven intervention. Individuals' interests and motivation are, in many ways, a social project.

REFERENCES

Ainsworth, M., Blehar, M., Waters, E., & Wall, S. (1978). *Patterns of attachment*. Hillsdale, NJ: Lawrence Erlbaum.

Aron, A., McLaughlin-Volpe, T., Mashek, D., Lewandowski, G., Wright, S. C., & Aron, E. N. (2004). Including others in the self. *European Review of Social Psychology, 15*, 101–132.

Aronson, J., Fried, C. B., & Good, C. (2002). Reducing the effect of stereotype threat on African American college students by shaping theories of intelligence. *Journal of Experimental Social Psychology, 38*, 113–125.

Asch, S. E. (1952). *Social psychology*. Englewood Cliffs, NJ: Prentice Hall.

Bandura, A. (1997). *Self-efficacy: The exercise of control*. New York: W. H. Freeman.

Bargh, J. A., Chen, M., & Burrows, L. (1996). Automaticity of social behavior: Direct effects of trait construct and stereotype activation on action. *Journal of Personality and Social Psychology, 71*, 230–244.

Baumeister, R. F., DeWall, C. N., Ciarocco, N. J., & Twenge, J. M. (2005). Social exclusion impairs self-regulation. *Journal of Personality and Social Psychology, 88*, 589–604.

Baumeister, R., & Leary, M. (1995). The need to belong: Desire for interpersonal attachments as a fundamental human motivation. *Psychological Bulletin, 117*, 497–529.

Baumeister, R. F., Twenge, J. M., & Nuss, C. K. (2002). Effects of social exclusion on cognitive processes: Anticipated aloneness reduces intelligent thought. *Journal of Personality and Social Psychology, 83*, 817–827.

Berger, J., & Heath, C. (2008). What drives divergence? Identity signaling, outgroup dissimilarity, and the abandonment of cultural tastes. *Journal of Personality and Social Psychology, 95*, 593–607.

Berger, J., & Rand, L. (2008). Shifting signals to help health: Using identity signaling to reduce risky health behaviors. *Journal of Consumer Research, 35*, 509–518.

Berns, G. S., Chappelow, J., Zink, C. F., Pagnoni, G., Martin-Skurski, M. E., & Richards, J. (2005). Neurobiological correlates of social conformity and independence during mental rotation. *Biological Psychiatry, 58*, 245–253.

Billig, M., & Tajfel, H. (1973). Social categorization and similarity in intergroup behaviour. *European Journal of Social Psychology, 3*, 27–52.

Blackwell, L. S., Trzesniewski, K. H., & Dweck, C. S. (2007). Implicit theories of intelligence predict achievement across an adolescent transition: A longitudinal study and an intervention. *Child Development, 78*, 246–263.

Blanton, H., Buunk, B. P., Gibbons, F. X., & Kuyper, H. (1999). When better-than-others compare upward: Choice of comparison and comparative evaluation as independent predictors of academic performance. *Journal of Personality and Social Psychology, 76*, 420–430.

Bourdieu, P. (1977). *Outline of a theory of practice*. Cambridge, UK: Cambridge University Press.

Branch, T. (2007). *At Canaan's edge: America in the King years 1965–1968*. New York: Simon & Schuster Paperbacks.

Browning, C. R. (1992). *Ordinary men: Reserve police battalion 101 and the Final Solution in Poland*. New York: HarperCollins.

Canetti, E. (1978). *Crowds and power*. New York: Seabury Press.

Caprara, G. V., Barbaranelli, C., Pastorelli, C., Bandura, A., & Zimbardo, P. G. (2000). Prosocial foundations of children's academic achievement. *Psychological Science, 11,* 302–306.

Carver, C. S., & Scheier, M. F. (2001). Optimism, pessimism, and self-regulation. In E. C. Chang (Ed.), *Optimism and pessimism: Implications for theory, research, and practice.* Washington, DC: American Psychological Association.

Cheryan, S., Plaut, V.C., Davies, P., & Steele, C.M. (2009). Ambient belonging: How stereotypical environments impact gender participation in computer science. *Journal of Personality and Social Psychology, 97,* 1045–1060.

Cialdini, R. B., Brown, S. L., Lewis, B. P., Luce, C., & Neuberg, S. L. (1997). Reinterpreting the empathy-altruism relationship: When one into one equals oneness. *Journal of Personality and Social Psychology, 73,* 481–494.

Clark, H. H. (1996). *Using language.* Cambridge, UK: Cambridge University Press.

Cohen, G. L. (2003). Party over policy: The dominating impact of group influence on political beliefs. *Journal of Personality and Social Psychology, 85,* 808–822.

Cohen, G. L., & Prinstein, M. J. (2006). Peer contagion of aggression and health-risk behavior among adolescent males: An experimental investigation of effects on public conduct and private attitudes. *Child Development, 77,* 967–983.

Cohen, G. L., Steele, C. M., & Ross, L. D. (1999). The mentor's dilemma: Providing critical feedback across the racial divide. *Personality and Social Psychology Bulletin, 25,* 1302–1318.

Collins, R. (1998). *The sociology of philosophies: A global theory of intellectual change.* Cambridge, MA: Belknap Press of Harvard University Press.

Correll, J., & Park, B. (2005). A model of the ingroup as a social resource. *Personality and Social Psychology Review, 9,* 341–359.

Crandall, C. S. (1988). Social contagion of binge eating. *Journal of Personality and Social Psychology, 55,* 588–598.

Deci, E. L., Koestner, R., & Ryan, R. M. (1999). A meta-analytic review of experiments examining the effects of extrinsic rewards on intrinsic motivation. *Psychological Bulletin, 125,* 627–668.

Deci, E. L., & Ryan, R. M. (1985). *Intrinsic motivation and self-determination in human behavior.* New York: Plenum.

Deutsch, M., & Gerard, H. B. (1955). A study of normative and informational social influence upon individual judgment. *Journal of Abnormal and Social Psychology, 51,* 629–636.

Dovidio, J. F., & Gaertner, S. L. (2000). Aversive racism and selection decisions: 1989 and 1999. *Psychological Science, 11,* 315–319.

Dweck, C. S., & Leggett, E. L. (1988). A social-cognitive approach to motivation and personality. *Psychological Review, 95,* 256–273.

Finn, J. D. (1989). Withdrawing from school. *Review of Educational Research, 59,* 117–142.

Furrer, C., & Skinner, E. (2003). Sense of relatedness as a factor in children's academic engagement and performance. *Journal of Educational Psychology, 95,* 148–162.

Gardner, W. L., Gabriel, S., & Hochschild, L. (2002). When you and I are "we," you are not threatening: The role of self-expansion in social comparison. *Journal of Personality and Social Psychology, 82,* 239–251.

Glick, P. (2002). Sacrificial lambs dressed in wolves' clothing: Envious prejudice, ideology, and the scapegoating of Jews. In L. S. Newman & R. Erber (Eds.), *Understanding genocide: The social psychology of the Holocaust* (pp. 113–142). New York: Oxford University Press.

Goldhagen, D. J. (1997). *Hitler's willing executioners: Ordinary Germans and the Holocaust.* New York: Vintage Books.

Goodenow, C. (1992). Strengthening the links between educational psychology and the study of social contexts. *Educational Psychologist, 27*, 177–196.

Green, D. P., & Gerber, A. S. (2004). *Get out the vote: How to increase voter turnout.* Washington, DC: Brookings Institution Press.

Haney, C., & Zimbardo, P. (1998). The past and future of U.S. prison policy: Twenty-five years after the Stanford Prison Experiment. *American Psychologist, 53*, 709–727.

Harber, K. D. (1998). Feedback to minorities: Evidence of a positive bias. *Journal of Personality and Social Psychology, 74*, 622–628.

Harris, J. R. (1995). Where is the child's environment? A group socialization theory of development. *Psychological Review, 102*, 458–489.

Harris, J. R. (1998). *The nurture assumption: Why children turn out the way they do.* New York: Free Press.

Heider, F. (1958). *The psychology of interpersonal relations.* Hillsdale, NJ: Lawrence Erlbaum.

Iacoboni, M., Molnar-Szakacs, I., Gallese, V., Buccino, G., Mazziotta, J. C., & Rizzolatti, G. (2005). Grasping the intentions of others with one's own mirror neuron system. *PLoS Biology, 3*, 529–535.

Iyengar, S. S., & Lepper, M. R. (1999). Rethinking the value of choice: A cultural perspective on intrinsic motivation. *Journal of Personality and Social Psychology, 76*, 349–366.

Janis, I. L. (1972). *Victims of groupthink: A psychological study of foreign-policy decisions and fiascoes.* Oxford, UK: Houghton Mifflin.

Jones, J. T., Pelham, B. W., Carvallo, M., & Mirenberg, M. C. (2004). How do I love thee? Let me count the Js: Implicit egotism and interpersonal attraction. *Journal of Personality and Social Psychology, 87*, 665–683.

Karau, S. J., & Williams, K. D. (1993). Social loafing: A meta-analytic review and theoretical integration. *Journal of Personality and Social Psychology, 65*, 681–706.

Kay, A. C., Jimenez, M. C., & Jost, J. T. (2002). Sour grapes, sweet lemons, and the anticipatory rationalization of the status quo. *Personality and Social Psychology Bulletin, 28*, 1300–1312.

Kraut, R. E., & Johnston, R. E. (1979). Social and emotional messages of smiling: An ethological approach. *Journal of Personality and Social Psychology, 37*, 1539–1553.

Kunda, Z. (1999). *Social cognition: Making sense of people.* Cambridge, MA: MIT Press.

Ladd, G. W. (1990). Having friends, keeping friends, making friends, and being liked by peers in the classroom: Predictors of children's early school adjustment? *Child Development, 61*, 1081–1100.

Latane, B., & Darley, J. M. (1968). Group inhibition of bystander intervention in emergencies. *Journal of Personality and Social Psychology, 10*, 215–221.

Lawrence, D. H. (1973). *Sons and lovers.* Scarborough, Canada: Bellhaven House Limited. (Original work published 1967)

Leary, M. R. (2004). The sociometer, self-esteem, and the regulation of interpersonal behavior. In R. F. Baumeister & K. D. Vohs (Eds.), *Handbook of self-regulation: Research, theory, and applications* (pp. 373–391). New York: Guilford.

Lepper, M. R., Greene, D., & Nisbett, R. E. (1973). Undermining children's intrinsic interest with extrinsic reward: A test of the "overjustification" hypothesis. *Journal of Personality and Social Psychology, 28*, 129–137.

Lewin, K. (1952). Group decision and social change. In T. M. Newcomb & E. L. Hartley (Eds.), *Readings in social psychology* (pp. 459–473). New York: Henry Holt.

Lockwood, P., & Kunda, Z. (1997). Superstars and me: Predicting the impact of role models on the self. *Journal of Personality and Social Psychology, 73*, 91–103.

Mahoney, J. L., & Cairns, R. B. (1997). Do extracurricular activities protect against early school dropout? *Developmental Psychology, 33*, 241–253.

Markus, H. R., & Kitayama, S. (1991). Culture and the self: Implications for cognition, emotion, and motivation. *Psychological Review, 20*, 224–253.

Markus, H. R., & Kitayama, S. (1994). A collective fear of the collective: Implications for selves and theories of selves. *Personality and Social Psychology Bulletin, 20,* 568–579.

McClelland, D. C. (1961). *The achieving society.* Princeton, NJ: Van Nostrand.

Meltzoff, A. N. (1995). Understanding the intentions of others: Re-enactment of intended acts by 18-month-old children. *Developmental Psychology, 31,* 838–850.

Mendoza-Denton, R., Downey, G., Purdie, V. J., Davis, A., & Pietrzak, J. (2002). Sensitivity to status-based rejection: Implications for African American students' college experience. *Journal of Personality and Social Psychology, 83,* 896–918.

Milgram, S. (1974). *Obedience to authority: An experimental view.* New York: Harper & Row.

Miller, D. T., Downs, J. S., & Prentice, D. A. (1998). Minimal conditions for the creation of a unit relationship: The social bond between birthday mates. *European Journal of Social Psychology, 28,* 475–481.

Miller, R. L., Brickman, P., & Bolen, D. (1975). Attribution versus persuasion as a means for modifying behavior. *Journal of Personality and Social Psychology, 31,* 430–441.

Moll, H., & Tomasello, M. (2007). Cooperation and human cognition: The Vygotskian intelligence hypothesis. *Philosophical Transactions of the Royal Society, 362,* 639–648.

Moscovici, S. (1984). The phenomenon of social representations. In R. M. Farr & S. Moscovici (Eds.), *Social representations.* New York: Cambridge University Press.

Moses, L. J., Baldwin, D. A., Rosicky, J. G., & Tidball, G. (2001). Evidence for referential understanding in the emotions domain at twelve and eighteen months. *Child Development, 72,* 718–735.

Nelson, D. J. (2007). *A national analysis of minorities in science and engineering faculties at research universities.* American Association for the Advancement of Science. Retrieved December 24, 2008, from http://cheminfo.ou.edu/~djn/diversity/Faculty_Tables_FY07/FinalReport07.html

Newcomb, T. M., Koening, K. E., Flacks, R., & Warwick, D. P. (1967). *Persistence and change: Bennington College and its students after 25 years.* New York: John Wiley.

Nisbett, R. E., & Masuda, T. (2003). Culture and point of view. *Proceedings of the National Academy of Sciences, 100,* 11163–11170.

Prentice, D. A., & Miller, D. T. (1993). Pluralistic ignorance and alcohol use on campus: Some consequences of misperceiving the social norm. *Journal of Personality and Social Psychology, 64,* 243–256.

Ross, H. S., & Lollis, S. P. (1987). Communication within infant social games. *Developmental Psychology, 23,* 241–248.

Ryan, R. M., & Deci, E. L. (2000). Self-determination theory and the facilitation of intrinsic motivation, social development, and well-being. *American Psychologist, 55,* 68–78.

Salganik, M. J., Dodds, P. S., & Watts, D. J. (2006). Experimental study of inequality and unpredictability in an artificial cultural market. *Science, 311,* 854–856.

Schwarz, N., Bless, H., Strack, F., Klumpp, G., Rittenauer-Schatka, H., & Simons, A. (1991). Ease of retrieval as information: Another look at the availability heuristic. *Journal of Personality and Social Psychology, 61,* 195–202.

Shelton, J. N., & Richeson, J. A. (2005). Intergroup contact and pluralistic ignorance. *Journal of Personality and Social Psychology, 88,* 91–107.

Sherif, M. (1936). *The psychology of social norms.* New York: Harper & Brothers.

Sherman, D. K., & Cohen, G. L. (2006). The psychology of self-defense: Self-affirmation theory. In M. P. Zanna (Ed.), *Advances in experimental social psychology* (Vol. 38, pp. 183–242). San Diego, CA: Academic Press.

Sinclair, S., Huntsinger, J., Skorinko, J., & Hardin, C. D. (2005). Social tuning of the self: Consequences for the self-evaluations of stereotype targets. *Journal of Personality and Social Psychology, 89,* 160–175.

Steele, C. M. (1997). A threat in the air: How stereotypes shape intellectual identity and performance. *American Psychologist, 52*, 613–629.

Surra, C. A. (1985). Courtship types: Variations in interdependence between partners and social networks. *Journal of Personality and Social Psychology, 49*, 357–375.

Tajfel, H., & Turner, J. C. (2004). The social identity theory of intergroup behavior. In J. T. Jost & J. Sidanius (Eds.), *Political psychology: Key readings* (pp. 276–293). New York: Psychology Press.

Tomasello, M., Carpenter, M., Call, J., Behne, T., & Moll, H. (2005). Understanding and sharing intentions: The origins of cultural cognition. *Behavioral and Brain Sciences, 28*, 675–691.

Twenge, J. M., Baumeister, R. F., Tice, D. M., & Stucke, T. S. (2001). If you can't join them, beat them: Effects of social exclusion on aggressive behavior. *Journal of Personality and Social Psychology, 81*, 1058–1069.

Uhlmann, E., & Cohen, G. L. (2005). Constructed criteria: Redefining merit to justify discrimination. *Psychological Science, 16*, 474–480.

Vygotsky, L. S. (1978). *Mind and society: The development of higher mental processes.* Cambridge, MA: Harvard University Press.

Walton, G. M., & Cohen, G. L. (2007). A question of belonging: Race, social fit, and achievement. *Journal of Personality and Social Psychology, 92*, 82–96.

Walton, G. M., Cohen, G. L., Cwir, D., & Spencer, S. J. (2010). Mere belonging: The power of social connections. Manuscript submitted for publication.

Warneken, F., Chen, F., & Tomasello, M. (2006). Cooperative activities in young children and chimpanzees. *Child Development, 77*, 640–663.

Wentzel, K. R. (1997). Student motivation in middle school: The role of perceived pedagogical caring. *Journal of Educational Psychology, 89*, 411–419.

Williams, K. D. (2007). Ostracism. *Annual Review of Psychology, 58*, 425–452.

Williams, K. D., Cheung, C. K. T., & Choi, W. (2000). Cyberostracism: Effects of being ignored over the Internet. *Journal of Personality and Social Psychology, 79*, 748–762.

Wilson, T. D., Damiani, M., & Shelton, N. (2002). Improving the academic performance of college students with brief attributional interventions. In J. Aronson (Ed.), *Improving academic achievement: Impact of psychological factors on education.* Oxford, UK: Academic Press.

Zajonc, R. B. (2001). Mere exposure: A gateway to the subliminal. *Current Directions in Psychological Science, 10*, 224–228.

6

Four Forms of Prosocial Motivation
Egoism, Altruism, Collectivism, and Principlism

C. DANIEL BATSON, NADIA AHMAD, and E. L. STOCKS

*P*eople can do spectacular things for others. Rescuers of Jews in Nazi Europe, such as Miep Gies (who helped hide Anne Frank and her parents), Oskar Schindler, and Raoul Wallenberg, risked their own lives—and the lives of loved ones—day after day for months, sometimes years. Soldiers have been known to throw themselves on grenades to protect their comrades. More than 350 firefighters and emergency rescue workers, as well as 23 police officers, died on September 11, 2001, directing others to safety after the attack on the World Trade Center. Rescue crews worked around the clock in extreme danger to free trapped victims of the Oklahoma City bombing. So did those who rescued "Baby Jessica" (18-month-old Jessica McClure) after she fell into an abandoned well in Midland, Texas. Thousands of people each year undergo discomfort and inconvenience to donate blood, and hundreds undergo painful surgery to donate bone marrow. One night, Otis Gaither, a 23-year-old construction worker, saw a mobile home ablaze. He broke down the door and dragged Larry Leroy Whitten, 44, to safety. Then he revived Whitten with mouth-to-mouth resuscitation. Gaither, who was Black, did this in spite of Whitten's white skin and prominently displayed racist symbol, the Confederate battle flag.

PROSOCIAL MOTIVATION: WHY DO WE BENEFIT OTHERS?

Such examples are heartwarming, even inspiring. They are also puzzling. Why do people do such things? Do we benefit others simply because it promotes our self-interest? Or can we also be motivated to promote the interests of others? If

103

so, which others—our immediate family, our friends, our nation, all humanity? Are people motivated to be moral? Or is our moral behavior controlled by the carrot and stick of reward and punishment? Behind these questions about prosocial motivation is an even more fundamental question about human nature. Answers to these questions can tell us something important about how truly social we humans really are—or are capable of becoming.

In the past four decades, a number of social psychologists have begun a serious attempt to answer such questions. They have drawn heavily on general theories of motivation, especially those stemming from the work of Sigmund Freud, Clark Hull, and various social learning theorists (e.g., Bandura, 1977; Dollard & Miller, 1950). But they have been most importantly influenced by the motivational theories of Kurt Lewin.

MOTIVES AS GOAL-DIRECTED FORCES

Lewin (1951) thought of motives as goal-directed forces to obtain or maintain valued states. If someone perceives a negative discrepancy between a current or an anticipated state and a valued (desired, preferred) state, then obtaining or maintaining the valued state is likely to become a goal. Lewin distinguished ultimate goals from instrumental goals and unintended consequences (also see Heider, 1958).

Ultimate Goals, Instrumental Goals, and Unintended Consequences

Ultimate goals are the valued states one seeks to obtain or maintain. "Ultimate" is not used here in a metaphysical sense; it simply refers to the state or states a person is seeking at a given time (whether consciously or unconsciously). Each ultimate goal defines a different motive. *Instrumental goals* are stepping-stones to ultimate goals. If an ultimate goal can be reached more efficiently by other means, an instrumental goal is likely to be bypassed.

To illustrate the difference between ultimate and instrumental goals, imagine that seeing a child in distress causes me distress, and I relieve the child's distress in order to relieve my own distress. In this case, relief of my own distress is an ultimate goal, and relief of the child's distress is an instrumental goal. Bernard Mandeville (1714/1732), who assumed our ultimate goals are always self-interested, portrayed this situation graphically:

> There is no merit in saving an innocent babe ready to drop into the fire. The action is neither good nor bad, and what benefit soever the infant received, we only obliged our selves, for to have seen it fall, and not strove to hinder it, would have caused a pain, which self-preservation compelled us to prevent. (p. 42)

Pursuit of a goal, whether instrumental or ultimate, often produces *unintended consequences*—effects that are not themselves a goal. Relieving the child's distress in order to relieve my distress may have led the child's mother to thank me profusely, even though receiving thanks was not one of my goals. (For further discussion of the relations between valued states, goals, and motives, see Batson [1994].)

A major implication that Lewin (1951) wished to draw from these distinctions was the importance of focusing on motives rather than on behavior or consequences, even if one's goal is to understand the occurrence of some behavior, such as helping others. Behavior is highly variable. Occurrence of a particular behavior depends on the strength of the motive or motives that might evoke that behavior, as well as on (a) the strength of competing motives if any, (b) how the behavior relates to each of these motives, and (c) other behavioral options available in the situation at the time. The more directly a behavior promotes the ultimate goal, and the more uniquely it does so among the behavioral options available, the more likely the behavior is to occur. Behavior that promotes an instrumental goal can easily change if the causal association between the instrumental and ultimate goals changes or if behavioral pathways to the ultimate goal arise that bypass the instrumental goal. Unintended consequences can also easily change as the behavioral options change, unless these consequences are a product of some behavior that directly and uniquely promotes the ultimate goal. Lewin (1951) argued that invariance—and explanatory power— is found not in behavior or consequences but in the link of a given motive to its ultimate goal.

Multiple Motives: Cooperation, Conflict, and Change

An individual can have multiple ultimate goals and multiple motives, and these motives can cooperate or conflict. Furthermore, a person's motives can change over time, often quickly. The value of some states is relatively stable, producing enduring motives (e.g., the value of air to breathe). The value of other states is more changeable; opportunities to obtain or maintain these states elicit motives only in certain situations (the value of a warm coat).

Motives as Situational Forces, Not Dispositions or Needs

Lewin's (1951) perspective on motivation can be contrasted with the perspective of another pioneer in research on motivation, Henry Murray. Lewin conceived of goals as *force fields* within the current life space of the individual, he conceived of motives as *goal-directed forces* in these fields, and he conceived of valued states as *power fields* that could, under the appropriate circumstances, activate goals and motivational forces. Motivational forces could in turn produce behavior or *movement within the life space*. In contrast, Murray (1938) and his followers treated motives as relatively stable dispositions or needs (e.g., achievement motivation), similar to valued states rather than to motives in Lewin's framework. Lewin made much of the distinction between instrumental goals, ultimate goals, and unintended consequences; Murray gave little attention to these distinctions. For Lewin, the list of potential motives is endless, as rich and varied as one's preferences. Murray and his followers attempted to identify a relatively small number of primary motives (needs).

FOUR FORMS OF PROSOCIAL MOTIVATION

Adopting a Lewinian perspective, we wish to consider four possible forms of prosocial motivation, each of which can lead a person to benefit—help—someone in need. Each form is defined by its distinct ultimate goal: self-benefit (*egoism*), benefit another individual (*altruism*), benefit a group (*collectivism*), and uphold a moral principle (*principlism*).

Egoism: Benefit Another as a Means to Benefit Oneself

Humans are clearly capable of benefiting others as an instrumental means to benefit themselves. When the ultimate goal is self-benefit, the motivation is egoistic. This is true no matter how beneficial to others or how noble the resulting behavior may be.

Many self-benefits can motivate helping. Table 6.1 lists those for which there is clear empirical evidence (see Batson, 1998, and Dovidio, Piliavin, Schroeder, & Penner, 2006, for reviews). The table is organized into three general categories, reflecting three fundamental forms of egoistic motivation: (a) gain material, social, or self-rewards; (b) avoid material, social, and self-punishments; and (c) reduce aversive arousal. In each case, benefiting another is only an instrumental means to reach the ultimate goal specified.

Gaining Rewards   Among the listed rewards in Table 6.1, only three need explanation: reciprocity credit, mood enhancement (maintenance), and empathic joy.

TABLE 6.1   Possible Self-Benefits From Benefiting Another

Receive Material, Social, and Self-Rewards

Payment	Praise
Gifts	Honor
Reciprocity credit	Enhanced self-image
Thanks	Mood enhancement (maintenance)
Esteem	Empathic joy
Heaven	

Avoid Material, Social, and Self-Punishments

Fines/imprisonment	Recrimination
Attack	Sanctions for norm violation
Censure	Shame
Guilt	Hell

Reduce Aversive Arousal

Escape a distressing situation
Escape a discrepant situation
Escape an unjust situation

Reciprocity Credit. Sociologist Alvin Gouldner (1960) spoke of the "universal norm of reciprocity"—for a benefit received, an equivalent benefit ought eventually to be returned. He believed that this norm was learned through socialization. After reviewing evidence, Gouldner concluded, "A norm of reciprocity is, I suspect, no less universal and important an element of culture than the incest taboo" (1960, p. 171). If he is right, then we can secure future benefit by providing benefit to a person in need.

Desire for reciprocity credit can even lead us to help someone we know cannot reciprocate as long as we believe in generalized reciprocity—that we get in equal measure to what we give to the world in general (Zuckerman, 1975). It can also lead us to help in order to establish a reputation as a helper if we believe that this reputation will encourage others to help us in the future because they assume we will repay them in turn (Frank, 1988; Nowak & Sigmund, 2005).

Mood Enhancement (Maintenance). Cialdini, Darby, and Vincent (1973) proposed that we are more likely to help someone when we feel bad because we know that we can self-reward for helping, which will make us feel better. Consistent with their *negative-state relief model*, Cialdini et al. (1973) found that people who felt bad because they had accidentally harmed someone—or had seen another person harm someone—were more likely to volunteer to make phone calls for a worthy cause than were people not induced to feel bad. However, when people induced to feel bad had their negative state relieved by receiving praise or a dollar before being given the chance to volunteer, they did not help more.

Helping also seems to have reward value for people in a good mood. Alice Isen and her associates (Isen, 1970; Isen & Levin, 1972) used a number of clever techniques to elevate people's mood—having them succeed at a task, giving them a cookie while they studied in the library, having them find a coin in the return slot of a public telephone. Each of these experiences increased the likelihood of these people giving help to good causes.

What is the ultimate goal of helping for people in a good mood? One possible goal is to maintain the mood. Seeing another person in need can throw a wet blanket on a good mood, so one may help in order to stay happy (Isen & Levin, 1972; Wegener & Petty, 1994). Isen (1987; Isen, Shalker, Clark, & Karp, 1978) also suggested a second possibility: People in a good mood may be after the social and self-rewards that come from helping. Their good mood may make them more likely to remember and attend to the positive, rewarding features of helping and less likely to attend to the negative features, such as the costs involved (also see Clark & Waddell, 1983; Cunningham, Shaffer, Barbee, Wolff, & Kelley, 1990).

Empathic Joy. Empathic joy is a vicarious feeling of pleasure one has at seeing a person in need experience relief. In Hoffman's (1981) words, "When the victim shows visible signs of relief or joy after being helped, the helper may actually feel empathic joy. Having experienced empathic joy, he or she may subsequently be motivated to help in order to experience it again" (p. 135). At the time Hoffman wrote, there was no empirical evidence for the existence of such a motive; now there is (Batson et al., 1991; Smith, Keating, & Stotland, 1989). Interestingly, the evidence suggests that seeking empathic joy is a motive among individuals feeling little empathic concern for the person in need, but it is not a motive among individuals feeling such concern.

Avoiding Punishments

The only punishments listed in Table 6.1 that need explanation are fines/imprisonment and sanctions for norm violation.

Fines/Imprisonment. In some countries, especially in Europe, there are Good Samaritan laws. People are liable for a fine or a jail sentence if they fail to offer aid when (a) someone else's life is in danger, (b) helping involves no serious risk of harm, and (c) no one available is better qualified to help. These laws are designed to motivate people to help in order to avoid the penalties.

Sanctions for Norm Violation. Several social norms apply to helping. They dictate that we should help—at least some people under some circumstances—lest we suffer socially administered and self-administered sanctions. We have already mentioned the norm of reciprocity. In addition to leading us to expect repayment when we help, this norm specifies that we should help those who help us. Although Gouldner (1960) believed that the norm of reciprocity was universal, he also believed that the pressure on us to reciprocate depends on the conditions under which we were helped: (a) how badly we needed help, (b) how much the other person gave relative to his or her total resources, (c) the other person's motives for helping (e.g., was it a bribe?), and (d) whether the other person helped voluntarily or was pressured into it. Research supports the importance of each of these conditions for reciprocity (e.g., Gergen, Ellsworth, Maslach, & Seipel, 1975; Pruitt, 1968; Wilke & Lanzetta, 1970). Research also indicates that failure to act in accord with the norm of reciprocity can bring punishment; indeed, people are apt to punish a failure to reciprocate even when doing so is costly to them (so-called altruistic punishment; Fehr & Gächter, 2002).

A second norm that has been applied to helping is the norm of social responsibility. This norm specifies that we should help when a person in need is dependent on us—that is, when no one else is available to help and so the person is counting specifically on us. Although such a norm does seem to exist, its effect on helping has been surprisingly difficult to demonstrate. After over a decade of research, Berkowitz (1972) concluded, "The findings do not provide any clear-cut support for the normative analysis of help-giving. ... The potency of the conjectured 'social responsibility norm' was greatly exaggerated" (pp. 68, 77).

Why has evidence that a norm of social responsibility motivates helping been so hard to find? Darley and Latané (1970) suggested that this norm may be at once too general and too specific. It may be too general in that everyone in our society adheres to it. If all adhere, then the norm cannot account for why one person helps and another does not. It may also be too specific in that along with it comes a complex pattern of exceptions. Rather than following a rule that says, "If someone is dependent on you for help, then help," people may follow a more complex rule that says, "If someone is dependent on you for help, then help, *except when* ..." Exceptions may vary for different individuals and social situations.

Other researchers have suggested that the problem with the potency of norms may lie in focus of attention. Only when attention is focused on a norm as a standard for behavior is concern about violating it likely to motivate behavior (Cialdini,

Kallgren, & Reno, 1991). Consistent with this suggestion, Gibbons and Wicklund (1982) found that when standards of helpfulness were salient, focusing on one-self increased helping. However, in the absence of salient standards, self-focus decreased helping.

Reducing Aversive Arousal   The self-benefits under aversive-arousal reduction in Table 6.1 may be less familiar than the self-benefits under rewards and punishments. Each reflects the idea that it is upsetting to see someone else suffer, and we do not want to be upset. One way to remove our upset is to relieve the other person's suffering because that is the stimulus causing us to be upset. Once again, benefit to the other is only instrumental; the ultimate goal is the self-benefit of having our upset—aversive arousal—go away. In Mandeville's (1714/1732) example of saving the innocent babe ready to drop into the fire, the motivation was to reduce aversive arousal.

Each of the three self-benefits in the third section of Table 6.1 specifies a different form of aversive arousal.

Escaping Personal Distress. Most straightforward is the motive suggested by Piliavin, Dovidio, Gaertner, and Clark (1981); Hoffman (1981); and Dovidio, Piliavin, Gaertner, Schroeder, and Clark (1991), among others. They propose that a witness's vicarious distress has much the same character as the distress of the person in need; both are aversive, and the witness is motivated to escape his or her personal distress. One way to escape is to help, because helping terminates the stimulus causing this distress. Of course, another way is to "pass by on the other side," as did the unhelpful Priest and Levite in the Parable of the Good Samaritan. Leaving the scene may enable the witness to escape just as well as helping—and at less cost.

Escaping Discrepancy. Reykowski (1982) proposed a second possibility: "The sheer discrepancy between information about the real or possible state of an object and standards of its normal or desirable state will evoke motivation" (p. 361). Reykowski applied this general psychological principle to prosocial motivation by suggesting that if a person perceives a discrepancy between the current state and the expected or ideal state of another person (i.e., perceives the other to be in need), then this will produce motivation to reduce the discrepancy. Relieving the other's need by helping is one way to reach this goal. A less prosocial way is to decide that the other's suffering is acceptable, even desirable, by blaming the victim for his or her plight (Ryan, 1971).

Escaping Injustice. Lerner's (1980) just-world hypothesis led him to propose a third possibility. If one believes in a just world—a world in which people get what they deserve and deserve what they get—then witnessing an innocent victim suffer will be upsetting because it threatens this belief. One way to remove the threat is to help the victim. Once again, however, there is an alternative. One may simply derogate the victim; if the victim is a less deserving person, then his or her suffering is more just. Consistent with Lerner's analysis, research suggests that if people can easily help relieve the suffering of an innocent victim, they are likely to do so, but if they cannot easily help, they are likely to derogate the victim (Lerner & Simmons, 1966; Mills & Egger, 1972).

Altruism: Benefit Another as an Ultimate Goal

Both for philosophers through the ages and for behavioral and social scientists today, the most intriguing and the most controversial form of prosocial motivation is altruism because, if it exists, altruism implies that we have the capacity to place intrinsic value on not only our own welfare but also the welfare of others. Is it really possible for one person to have another person's welfare as an ultimate goal rather than simply as an instrumental means of reaching the ultimate goal of some form of self-benefit?

One response to this question needs to be laid to rest at the outset. Some claim that even if it were possible for a person to be motivated to increase another's welfare, such a person would be pleased by attaining this desired goal, so this apparent altruism would actually be instrumental to egoism. Philosophers have pointed out that this argument, based on the general principle of *psychological hedonism*, involves a confusion between two different forms of hedonism. The *strong* form of psychological hedonism asserts that attainment of personal pleasure is always the goal of human action; the *weak* form asserts only that goal attainment always brings pleasure. The weak form is not inconsistent with the possibility of altruism (i.e., that one can have another's benefit as an ultimate goal); the pleasure obtained can be a consequence of reaching the goal without being the goal itself. The strong form of psychological hedonism is inconsistent with the possibility of altruism, but to affirm the strong form is simply to assert that altruism does not exist. It is an empirical assertion that may or may not be true. (See MacIntyre [1967] and Sober and Wilson [1998] for a discussion of these philosophical arguments.)

Advocates of universal egoism argue for the strong form of psychological hedonism. They assert that some self-benefit is always the ultimate goal of helping; benefiting the other is simply an instrumental goal on the way to one or another ultimately self-serving end. They remind us of all the self-benefits of helping, such as those listed in Table 6.1. Advocates of altruism argue back that simply to show that self-benefits follow from benefiting someone else does not prove that the self-benefits are ultimate goals. It is possible that the self-benefits are unintended consequences of reaching the ultimate goal of benefiting the other. If so, then the motivation is altruistic, not egoistic.

Advocates of altruism claim more than possibility, of course. They claim that altruistic motivation is an empirical reality; that at least some people, to some degree, under some circumstances, act with an ultimate goal of increasing another person's welfare. They claim that people can want another person to be happy and free of distress, not because it is upsetting to them if he or she is not (although it may be upsetting) but because they care about the other's welfare as an end in itself.

The Empathy–Altruism Hypothesis   Over the centuries, the most frequently proposed source of altruistic motivation has been an other-oriented emotional response elicited by and congruent with the perception of another person in need. Today, this emotional response is usually called *empathic concern* (Batson, 1987), *sympathy* (Wispé, 1986), or *sympathetic distress* (Hoffman, 1981). "Congruent" here refers to the valence of the emotion—positive when the perceived welfare of the other is positive, negative when the perceived welfare is negative—not to the specific content of the emotion. One might, for example, feel sad or sorry for someone who is upset and afraid. Empathic concern is "other oriented" in that it involves feelings *for* the other—feelings of sympathy, compassion, tenderness, sorrow, and the like. These other-oriented feelings appear to be a product not only of perceiving the other as in need but also of placing intrinsic value on the other's welfare (Batson, Eklund, Chermok, Hoyt, & Ortiz, 2007; Batson, Turk, Shaw, & Klein, 1995). The *empathy–altruism hypothesis* claims that empathic concern produces motivation with an ultimate goal of relieving the valued other's need—that is, altruistic motivation. Forms of this hypothesis have been offered by Thomas Aquinas, David Hume, Adam Smith, Charles Darwin, Herbert Spencer, William McDougall, and, in contemporary psychology, Hoffman (1975), Krebs (1975), and Batson (1987).

Considerable evidence supports the idea that feeling empathic concern for a person in need leads to increased helping of that person (Coke, Batson, & McDavis, 1978; Dovidio, Allen, & Schroeder, 1990; Krebs, 1975; see Batson, 1991, and Eisenberg & Miller, 1987, for reviews). But to observe an empathy–helping relationship tells us nothing about the nature of the motivation that underlies this relationship. Relieving the other person's need could be (a) an ultimate goal, producing self-benefits as unintended consequences; (b) an instrumental goal sought as a means to reach the ultimate goal of gaining one or more self-benefits; or (c) both. That is, the motivation could be altruistic, egoistic, or both.

Egoistic Alternatives to the Empathy–Altruism Hypothesis   Self-benefits in each of the three general classes listed in Table 6.1 can be gained by helping a person for whom one feels empathic concern. The empathy–altruism hypothesis does not deny that these self-benefits exist, but it claims that they are unintended consequences of acting on the altruistic motivation produced by empathy. Advocates of egoistic alternatives to the empathy–altruism hypothesis disagree; they claim that one or more of these self-benefits is the ultimate goal of prosocial motivation produced by empathy. In the past several decades, more than 30 experiments have tested various egoistic alternatives to the empathy–altruism hypothesis.

Aversive-Arousal Reduction. The most frequently proposed egoistic explanation of the empathy–helping relationship is aversive-arousal reduction. This explanation claims that feeling empathic concern is unpleasant, and the motivation it produces is directed toward benefiting oneself by eliminating these empathic feelings. Relieving the other's need is simply an instrumental means to this self-serving end.

Researchers have tested this aversive-arousal reduction explanation against the empathy–altruism hypothesis by varying the ease of escape from further exposure to the empathy-inducing need without helping. Because empathic concern is a result of witnessing the need, either terminating the need by helping or terminating exposure to it by escaping should reduce one's empathic concern. (To be effective, the escape must be not only physical but also psychological, freeing one from anticipated as well as experienced empathic concern.) Escape does not, however, enable one to reach the altruistic goal of relieving the other's need. Therefore, the aversive-arousal explanation predicts elimination of the empathy–helping relationship when escape is easy; the empathy–altruism hypothesis predicts the relationship will remain. Results of experiments testing these competing predictions have consistently supported the empathy–altruism prediction, not the aversive-arousal reduction prediction. These results cast serious doubt on this popular egoistic explanation of the motivation to help produced by empathy (see Batson, 1991, and Stocks, Lishner, & Decker, 2009, for reviews of these experiments).

Empathy-Specific Punishment. A second egoistic explanation claims that we learn through socialization that empathic concern carries with it additional obligation to help and, thus, additional shame and guilt for failure to help. As a result, when we feel empathic concern, we face impending social or self-censure beyond any general punishment associated with not helping. We say to ourselves, "What will others think—or what will I think of myself—if I don't help when I feel like this?" and we help to avoid these empathy-specific punishments. Once again, experiments designed to test this explanation have consistently failed to support it; results have supported the empathy–altruism hypothesis instead (see Batson, 1991, 1998, for reviews). Even in situations designed to eliminate the threat of social and self-censure, empathic concern still leads to increased helping (Batson et al., 1988, Studies 2–4).

Empathy-Specific Reward. The third major egoistic explanation claims that we learn through socialization that special rewards in the form of praise, honor, and pride are attendant on helping a person for whom we feel empathic concern. As a result, when we feel empathy, we think of these rewards and help out of an egoistic desire to gain them.

A general form of this explanation has been tested in several experiments and received no support (Batson et al., 1988, Studies 1 & 5; Batson & Weeks, 1996), but there are two variations for which at least some support has been claimed. Best known of these is the negative-state relief explanation proposed by Cialdini et al. (1987). Cialdini et al. suggested that empathic concern is a negative affective state—a state of temporary sadness or sorrow—and it leads one to help in order to gain mood-enhancing rewards.

At first glance, this negative-state explanation may appear to be the same as the aversive-arousal reduction explanation. Both explanations assume that empathic concern is a negative affective state. Yet, from this common starting point, they diverge. The aversive-arousal reduction explanation claims that the goal of empathy-induced helping is to eliminate the negative state; the negative-state relief explanation claims that the goal is to gain mood-enhancing self-rewards that one has learned are associated with helping.

Although the negative-state relief explanation received some initial support (Cialdini et al., 1987; Schaller & Cialdini, 1988), subsequent research revealed that this support was probably due to procedural artifacts (e.g., distraction). Experiments avoiding these artifacts have consistently supported the empathy–altruism hypothesis (Batson et al., 1989; Dovidio et al., 1990; Schroeder, Dovidio, Sibicky, Matthews, & Allen, 1988). It now seems clear that the motivation produced by empathic concern is not directed toward the egoistic goal of negative-state relief.

Smith et al. (1989) proposed a second variation on the empathy-specific reward explanation. They hypothesized that empathically concerned individuals help in order to feel vicarious joy at the needy individual's relief: "It is proposed that the prospect of empathic joy, conveyed by feedback from the help recipient, is essential to the special tendency of empathic witnesses to help. ... The empathically concerned witness to the distress of others helps in order to be happy" (Smith et al., 1989, p. 641).

Some early self-report data were supportive of this empathic-joy hypothesis, but more rigorous experimental evidence was not. Experimental results have consistently supported the empathy–altruism hypothesis (Batson et al., 1991; Smith et al., 1989). The empathic–joy hypothesis, like other versions of the empathy-specific reward explanation, seems unable to account for the empathy–helping relationship.

A Tentative Conclusion   Reviewing the empathy–altruism research, as well as recent literature in sociology, economics, political science, and biology, Piliavin and Charng (1990) concluded,

> There appears to be a "paradigm shift" away from the earlier position that behavior that appears to be altruistic must, under closer scrutiny, be revealed as reflecting egoistic motives. Rather, theory and data now being advanced are more compatible with the view that true altruism—acting with the goal of benefiting another—does exist and is a part of human nature. (p. 27)

In apparent contradiction to this conclusion, Maner et al. (2002) claimed to provide evidence that once the effects of negative affect are removed, there is no longer a positive relation between empathic concern and helping. In their research, however, they included only empathic emotions in their measure of negative affect (feeling *sympathetic, compassionate,* and *soft-hearted,* as well as three sadness items that they used in response to the need situation likely tapped sadness for the person in need—i.e., empathic concern). As a result, when controlling for negative affect, Maner et al. (2002) were actually removing the effect of empathic concern. It is not very surprising—but also not very informative—to find that once the effect of empathic concern is removed, there is no longer a relation between empathic concern and helping.

Today, almost 20 years later, the Piliavin and Charng (1990) conclusion still seems correct. Pending new evidence or a plausible new egoistic explanation of the existing evidence, the empathy–altruism hypothesis appears true.

Implications of the Empathy–Altruism Hypothesis   If the empathy–altruism hypothesis is true, the implications are wide-ranging. Universal egoism—the assumption that all human behavior is motivated by self-interest—has long dominated not only psychology but other social, behavioral, and biological sciences (Campbell, 1975; Mansbridge, 1990; Wallach & Wallach, 1983). If empathic concern can produce motivation with the ultimate goal of increasing another's welfare, then the assumption of universal egoism must be replaced by a more complex view that allows for altruism as well as egoism. Such a shift in our view of the human motivational repertoire requires, in turn, a revision of our underlying assumptions about human nature and human potential. It implies that we humans are more social than we have thought. Other people can be more to us than sources of information, stimulation, and reward as we each seek our own welfare. We have the potential to care about others for their sakes, not simply for our own.

There are more specific implications as well. First, the strong support for the empathy–altruism hypothesis begs for a better understanding of the cognitive representation of the self–other relationship when feeling empathic concern. Several representations have been proposed. Concern for another's welfare may be a product of (a) a sense of "we-ness" based on cognitive unit formation or identification with the other (Hornstein, 1982; Lerner, 1982), (b) the self expanding to incorporate aspects of the other (Aron & Aron, 1986), (c) seeing aspects of the self in the other (Cialdini, Brown, Lewis, Luce, & Neuberg, 1997), or (d) valuing the welfare of the other, who remains distinct from the self (Batson et al., 2007; Batson & Shaw, 1991; Jarymowicz, 1992).

Clearly, not all these proposals can be true, at least not at the same time. Based on research to date, it appears that neither empathic concern nor its effect on helping is a product of any of the various forms of self–other merging or overlap— we-ness, self-expansion, or self-projection (Batson, Sager, et al., 1997; Cialdini et al., 1997). Recent neuroimaging research also provides evidence that empathic concern involves self–other differentiation rather than merging (e.g., Jackson, Meltzoff, & Decety, 2005; Lamm, Batson, & Decety, 2007).

Second, the support for the empathy–altruism hypothesis forces us to face the question of why we humans have the capacity to feel empathic concern. What evolutionary function might this other-oriented emotion serve? Speculating, we believe the most plausible answer is that empathic concern evolved as part of the parental instinct among higher mammals (Bell, 2001; de Waal, 1996; Hoffman, 1981; McDougall, 1908; Zahn-Waxler & Radke-Yarrow, 1990). If parents were not intensely interested in the welfare of their very vulnerable progeny, these species would quickly die out. Empathic concern for offspring and the resulting altruistic motivation to care for them promotes the parents' reproductive potential by increasing their offspring's chance of survival.

Of course, the human capacity for empathic concern extends well beyond one's own children. People can feel empathy for a wide range of targets, including non-humans, as long as there is no preexisting antipathy (Batson, 1991; Batson et al., 2007; Batson, Lishner, Cook, & Sawyer, 2005; Shelton & Rogers, 1981). From an evolutionary perspective, this extension is usually attributed to cognitive generalization, whereby one "adopts" the target and treats him or her as offspring. Like offspring, seeing the target in need evokes empathic concern and altruistic motivation (Batson, 1987; Hoffman, 1981). Such cognitive generalization may be facilitated by two factors: (a) human cognitive capacity, including symbolic thought, and (b) lack of evolutionary advantage for strict limitation of empathic concern and parental nurturance to offspring in early human hunter-gatherer bands. In these bands, those in need were often one's children or close kin, and survival of one's genes was tightly tied to the welfare even of the nonkin (Hoffman, 1981; Sober & Wilson, 1998).

One implication of this analysis of the origin of empathy is that our empathic concern may be limited to specific individuals in need and exclude abstract collectives such as "the poor." Consistent with this possibility, in their research on the "identifiable victim effect," Kogut and Ritov (2005) found that a single child in need elicited more empathic concern and more willingness to help than did a group of needy children, even when the group included the single child (also see Slovic, 2007).

Third, might there be sources of altruistic motivation other than empathic emotion? Several have been proposed, including an "altruistic personality" (Oliner & Oliner, 1988), principled moral reasoning (Kohlberg, 1976), and internalized prosocial values (Staub, 1974). There is some evidence that each of these potential sources is associated with increased prosocial motivation, but as yet it is not clear that this motivation is altruistic. It may be, or it may be an instrumental means to the egoistic ultimate goals of maintaining one's positive self-concept or of avoiding guilt (Batson, 1991; Batson, Bolen, Cross, & Neuringer-Benefiel, 1986; Carlo, Eisenberg, Troyer, Switzer, & Speer, 1991; Eisenberg et al., 1989). More research is needed to explore these possibilities.

Finally, the empathy–altruism hypothesis may have wide-ranging practical implications (Batson, Ahmad, & Stocks, 2004). For example, people may at times wish to suppress or avoid feeling empathy. Aware of the extreme effort involved in helping, or of the impossibility of helping effectively, caseworkers in the helping professions, nurses caring for terminal patients, and pedestrians confronted by homeless persons may try to avoid feeling empathic concern in order to avoid the resulting altruistic motivation (Maslach, 1982; Shaw, Batson, & Todd, 1994; Stotland, Mathews, Sherman, Hansson, & Richardson, 1978). That is, there may be an egoistic motive to avoid altruistic motivation.

We should not expect empathy-induced altruism, once aroused, always to produce prosocial effects. Individuals may act against the collective good to benefit a person for whom empathy is felt (Batson, Ahmad, et al., 1999; Batson, Batson, et al., 1995). They may even violate their own moral principles (Batson, Klein, Highberger, & Shaw, 1995).

More positively, empathic concern has been found to direct attention to the long-term welfare of those in need, producing more sensitive care (Sibicky, Schroeder, & Dovidio, 1995). In schools, empathy-based training can increase mutual care among students, as in the Roots of Empathy project (Gordon, 2007). This empathy-based training is very different from more traditional prosocial training directed toward inhibition of egoistic impulses through shaping, modeling, and internalized guilt.

At a societal level, empathy-induced altruism may help improve attitudes toward stigmatized outgroups. Empathy inductions have been used to improve racial attitudes, as well as attitudes and action toward people with AIDS, the homeless, and even convicted murderers and drug dealers (Batson, Chang, Orr, & Rowland, 2002; Batson, Polycarpou, et al., 1997; Dovidio, Gaertner, & Johnson, 1999; Vescio, Sechrist, & Paolucci, 2003). Empathy-induced altruism also has been found to increase cooperation in a potentially competitive situation (a prisoner's dilemma) and to do so even when one knows that the target of empathic concern has acted competitively toward oneself (Batson & Ahmad, 2001; Batson & Moran, 1999).

Collectivism: Benefit Another to Benefit a Group

Collectivism is motivation to benefit a group. The ultimate goal is not to increase one's own welfare or the welfare of the specific others who are benefited but to increase the welfare of the group as a whole. Robyn Dawes and his colleagues put it succinctly: "Not me or thee but we" (Dawes, van de Kragt, & Orbell, 1988). They suggested that collectivist motivation is a product of group identity (Brewer & Kramer, 1986; Tajfel, 1981; Turner, 1987) and may be especially important in addressing social dilemmas. A social dilemma arises when (a) individuals in a group or collective have a choice about how to allocate personally held scarce resources (e.g., money, time, energy), and (b) allocation to the group provides more benefit for the group as a whole than does allocation to any single individual (e.g., oneself), but allocation to a single individual provides more benefit for that individual than does allocation to the group as a whole (Dawes, 1980). It has often been assumed that allocations to the group in a social dilemma are motivated by collectivism.

As with altruism, however, what looks like collectivism may actually be a subtle form of egoism. Attention to group welfare may simply be an instrumental means to pursue enlightened self-interest. If one recognizes that ignoring group needs in a headlong pursuit of self-interest will lead only to less self-benefit in the long run, then one may decide to benefit the group as a way to maximize long-term personal gain. Politicians and social activists often appeal to enlightened self-interest rather than to collectivism to encourage response to societal needs. They warn us of the long-term consequences for ourselves and our children of pollution and squandering natural resources; they remind us that if the plight of the poor becomes too severe, we may face revolution. Such appeals assume that collectivism is simply a form of egoism. Enlightened self-interest also underlies strategies for collective action based on (a) reciprocity (e.g., tit for tat—see Axelrod, 1984; Komorita & Parks, 1995) or (b) sanctions that punish those who seek to free ride on the contributions of other group members (Hardin, 1977; Yamagishi, 1986).

The most direct evidence that collectivism is a form of prosocial motivation independent of egoism comes from research by Dawes, van de Kragt, and Orbell (1990). They examined the responses of individuals given a choice between allocating money to themselves or allocating money to a group. Allocation to self maximized individual but not group profit, whereas allocation to the group maximized collective but not individual profit. Dawes et al. found that individuals faced with this dilemma who made their allocation after discussing it with other members of the group gave more to the group than did individuals who had no prior discussion. Moreover, this effect was specific to the ingroup with whom the discussion occurred; allocation to an outgroup was not enhanced.

On the basis of this research, Dawes et al. (1990) claimed evidence for collectivist motivation independent of egoism, arguing that their procedure ruled out the two most plausible forms of egoistic motivation: (a) enlightened self-interest and (b) avoidance of anticipated shame and guilt for violation of the norm to share.

Unfortunately, there is reason to doubt that their procedure effectively ruled out avoidance of anticipated shame and guilt. The research on norms reviewed earlier suggests that norms can be more refined than Dawes et al. assumed. The operative norm in their research may have been "share with your buddies" rather than simply "share." So, although the Dawes et al. research is important and suggestive, more and better evidence is needed to justify the conclusion that collectivist motivation is not reducible to egoism.

Principlism: Benefit Another to Uphold a Moral Principle

Western moral philosophers usually argue for the importance of a form of prosocial motivation other than egoism. Those since Kant (1724–1804) usually shun altruism and collectivism as well. Philosophers reject appeals to altruism, especially empathy-induced altruism, because feelings of empathy, sympathy, and compassion are too fickle and too circumscribed. Empathic concern is not felt for everyone in need, at least not to the same degree. Appeals to collectivism are rejected because group interest is bounded by the limits of the group. Collectivism not only permits but may even encourage doing harm to those outside the group. Given these problems with altruism and collectivism, Western moral philosophers usually advocate a fourth form of prosocial motivation, motivation with the ultimate goal of upholding a universal and impartial moral principle such as justice (Rawls, 1971). This moral motivation has been called *principlism* (Batson, 1994) or *moral integrity* (Batson, Kobrynowicz, Dinnerstein, Kampf, & Wilson, 1997).

Is acting with an ultimate goal of upholding a moral principle really possible? When Kant (1785/1889) briefly shifted from his analysis of what ought to be to what is, he admitted that even when concern for others appears to be prompted by duty to principle, it may actually be prompted by self-love (pp. 23–24). The goal of upholding a moral principle may simply be an instrumental means to reach the ultimate goal of self-benefit. If this is true, then principle-based motivation is a form of egoism.

There are conspicuous self-benefits to be gained from acting morally. One can gain the social and self-rewards of being seen and seeing oneself as a good person. One also can avoid the social and self-punishments of shame and guilt for failing to do the right thing. As Freud (1930) suggested, society may inculcate such principles in the young in order to bridle their antisocial impulses by making it in their best personal interest to act morally (also see Bandura, 1991; Campbell, 1975). Perhaps, however, through internalization (Staub, 1989) or development of moral reasoning (Gilligan, 1982; Kohlberg, 1976), principles come to be valued in their own right and not simply as instrumental means to self-serving ends.

The issue here is the same one faced with altruism and collectivism. Once again, we need to know the nature of the goal. Is upholding justice (or some other moral principle) an instrumental goal on the way to the ultimate goal of self-benefit? If so, then the motive is a subtle and sophisticated form of egoism. Alternatively, is upholding the principle an ultimate goal, with the ensuing self-benefits unintended consequences? If so, then principlism is a fourth type of prosocial motivation, independent of egoism, altruism, and collectivism.

Research suggests that people are often motivated to appear moral while, if possible, avoiding the cost of actually being moral. This motive, called *moral hypocrisy*, is a subtle form of egoism that is easily mistaken for principlism (Batson, Kobrynowicz, et al., 1997; Batson, Thompson, & Chen, 2002; Batson, Thompson, Seuferling, Whitney, & Strongman, 1999). Research also suggests that if principlism exists, it is often overpowered by self-interest. We humans are quite adept at moral rationalization (Tsang, 2002). We are good at justifying to ourselves, if not to others, why a situation that benefits us or those for whom we care does not violate our moral principles—why we have the right to a disproportionate share of the world's natural resources, why dumping our nuclear waste in someone else's backyard is fair, why attacks by our enemies are atrocities but attacks by our side are necessities. The abstractness and multiplicity of moral principles make it easy to convince ourselves that the relevant principles are those that just happen to serve our interests (Bandura, 1999; Bersoff, 1999).

Still, this may be only part of the story. Perhaps, for at least some people under some circumstances, upholding a moral principle serves as an ultimate goal, defining a form of prosocial motivation independent of egoism, altruism, and collectivism. If so, then principlism provides a motive for responding to the needs of others that transcends reliance on self-interest or on vested interest in and feeling for the welfare of certain other individuals or groups. It seems well worth conducting research to find out.

CONFLICT AND COOPERATION OF PROSOCIAL MOTIVES

To recognize four possible forms of prosocial motivation makes available more resources to those seeking to produce a more humane, caring society. At the same time, it complicates matters. Different motives, including prosocial motives, do not always work in harmony; they can undercut and compete with one another.

Conflict

Well-intentioned appeals to extended or enlightened self-interest can backfire by undermining other prosocial motives. Providing money or other incentives for showing concern may lead people to interpret their motivation as egoistic even when it is not (Batson, Coke, Jasnoski, & Hanson, 1978; Stukas, Snyder, & Clary, 1999). In this way, the assumption that there is only one answer to the question of why we act for the common good—egoism—may become a self-fulfilling prophecy (Batson, Fultz, Schoenrade, & Paduano, 1987). It may create a self-perpetuating norm of self-interest (Miller, 1999).

Nor do altruism, collectivism, and principlism always work in harmony. They can conflict with one another. For example, altruism can conflict with both collectivism and principlism. We may ignore the larger social good, or we may compromise our principles, not only to benefit ourselves but also to benefit others for whom we especially care, such as family and friends (Batson, Batson, et al., 1995;

Batson, Klein, et al., 1995). And whereas there are clear social sanctions against unbridled self-interest, there are not clear sanctions against altruism. As a result, altruism can at times pose a greater threat to the common good than does egoism (Batson, Ahmad, et al., 1999).

Cooperation

Different forms of prosocial motivation may also cooperate. Each of the four motives that we have identified has strengths. Each also has weaknesses. The potential for the greatest good may come from strategies that orchestrate these motives so that the strengths of one can overcome the weaknesses of another.

Strategies that combine appeals to either altruism or collectivism with appeals to principle seem especially promising. For example, think about the principle of justice. It is universal and impartial, but motivation to uphold justice appears to be easily co-opted and vulnerable to rationalization. Empathy-induced altruism and collectivism appear more robust, but they are limited in scope and produce partiality toward the interests of particular persons or groups. Perhaps if we can lead people to feel empathy for the victims of injustice, or to perceive themselves in a common group with them, then we can combine the unique strengths of two motives. Desire for justice may provide perspective and reason; empathy-induced altruism or collectivism may provide emotional fire and a force directed specifically toward seeing the victims' suffering end, preventing rationalization.

Something of this sort occurred, we believe, in a number of rescuers of Jews in Nazi Europe. A careful look at data collected by the Oliners and their colleagues (Oliner & Oliner, 1988) suggests that involvement in rescue activity frequently began with concern for a specific individual or individuals for whom compassion was felt—often someone known previously. This initial involvement subsequently led to further contacts and rescue activity and to a concern for justice that extended well beyond the bounds of the initial empathic concern. Something of this sort may also have been at the heart of Gandhi's and Martin Luther King's practice of non-violent protest. The TV newscast showing a small Black child being rolled down a street in Birmingham, Alabama, by water from a fire hose under the direction of local police, and the emotions it evoked, did more to arouse concern for racial equality and justice than hours of reasoned argument about civil rights.

SUMMARY AND CONCLUSION

Why do people help others, often at considerable cost to themselves? What does this behavior tell us about the human capacity to care, about the degree of interconnectedness among us, about how social we humans are? These classic philosophical questions have resurfaced in the behavioral and social sciences in recent decades. Social psychologists have begun to address the question of the nature of prosocial motivation by drawing on (a) Kurt Lewin's ideas about goal-directed motivation and the distinctions between instrumental goals, ultimate goals, and unintended consequences and (b) the experimental research methods introduced by Lewin that have become the trademark of social psychology over the past 60 years.

Specifically, social-psychological research has, first, added to and documented a long list of self-benefits that may serve as the ultimate goal of egoistic prosocial motivation. This list includes material, social, and self-rewards obtained; material, social, and self-punishments avoided; and reduction of aversive arousal.

Social-psychological research has also been used to test the claim that altruistic motivation—motivation with the ultimate goal of increasing another's welfare—exists independent of egoistic motivation. Results of over 30 experiments designed to test the empathy–altruism hypothesis against egoistic alternatives have strongly supported this hypothesis, leading to the tentative conclusion that empathic concern is a source of altruistic motivation. Other sources of altruistic motivation have also been proposed, but as yet there is not compelling research evidence to support these proposals.

Extending the analysis beyond the egoism–altruism debate, two additional forms of prosocial motivation have been identified: collectivism and principlism. Collectivism—motivation with the ultimate goal of benefiting some group or collective as a whole—has been claimed to result from group identity and to account for prosocial responses to social dilemmas. Principlism—motivation with the ultimate goal of upholding some moral principle—has long been advocated by religious teachers and moral philosophers. Whether either is a distinct form of motivation, independent of and irreducible to egoism, is not yet clear. The research done to test the empathy–altruism hypothesis against egoistic alternatives provides a useful model for future research assessing the independent status of collectivism and principlism.

More is known now than 50 years ago about why people help others. As a result, more is known about human motivation and even about human nature. These are substantial gains. Yet we need to know still more if we are to effectively use these motivational resources to build a more caring, humane society. The legacy of Lewin, which combines a rich conceptual framework for understanding motivation with the use of laboratory experiments to isolate and identify complex social motives, places social psychologists in an ideal position to learn more. A lot is riding on their ability to do so.

REFERENCES

Aron, A., & Aron, E. N. (1986). *Love and the expansion of self: Understanding attraction and satisfaction*. Washington, DC: Hemisphere.

Axelrod, R. (1984). *The evolution of cooperation*. New York: Basic Books.

Bandura, A. (1977). *Social learning theory*. Englewood Cliffs, NJ: Prentice Hall.

Bandura, A. (1991). Social cognitive theory of moral thought and action. In W. M. Kurtines & J. L. Gewirtz (Eds.), *Handbook of moral behavior and development*. Vol. 1: Theory (pp. 45–103). Hillsdale, NJ: Lawrence Erlbaum.

Bandura, A. (1999). Moral disengagement in the perpetration of inhumanities. *Personality and Social Psychology Review*, 3, 193–209.

Batson, C. D. (1987). Prosocial motivation: Is it ever truly altruistic? In L. Berkowitz (Ed.), *Advances in experimental social psychology* (Vol. 20, pp. 65–122). New York: Academic Press.

Batson, C. D. (1991). *The altruism question: Toward a social-psychological answer.* Hillsdale, NJ: Lawrence Erlbaum.

Batson, C. D. (1994). Why act for the public good? Four answers. *Personality and Social Psychology Bulletin, 20,* 603–610.

Batson, C. D. (1995). Prosocial motivation: Why do we help others? In A. Tesser (Ed.), *Advanced social psychology* (pp. 333–381). New York: McGraw-Hill.

Batson, C. D. (1998). Altruism and prosocial behavior. In D. T. Gilbert, S. T. Fiske, & G. Lindzey (Eds.), *The handbook of social psychology* (4th ed., Vol. 2, pp. 282–316). New York: McGraw-Hill.

Batson, C. D., & Ahmad, N. (2001). Empathy-induced altruism in a prisoner's dilemma II: What if the target of empathy has defected? *European Journal of Social Psychology, 31,* 25–36.

Batson, C. D., Ahmad, N., & Stocks, E. L. (2004). Benefits and liabilities of empathy-induced altruism. In A. G. Miller (Ed.), *The social psychology of good and evil* (pp. 359–385). New York: Guilford.

Batson, C. D., Ahmad, N., Yin, J., Bedell, S. J., Johnson, J. W., Templin, C. M., & Whiteside, A. (1999). Two threats to the common good: Self-interested egoism and empathy-induced altruism. *Personality and Social Psychology Bulletin, 25,* 3–16.

Batson, C. D., Batson, J. G., Griffitt, C. A., Barrientos, S., Brandt, J. R., Sprengelmeyer, P., & Bayly, M. J. (1989). Negative-state relief and the empathy–altruism hypothesis. *Journal of Personality and Social Psychology, 56,* 922–933.

Batson, C. D., Batson, J. G., Slingsby, J. K., Harrell, K. L., Peekna, H. M., & Todd, R. M. (1991). Empathic joy and the empathy–altruism hypothesis. *Journal of Personality and Social Psychology, 61,* 413–426.

Batson, C. D., Batson, J. G., Todd, R. M., Brummett, B. H., Shaw, L. L., & Aldeguer, C. M. R. (1995). Empathy and the collective good: Caring for one of the others in a social dilemma. *Journal of Personality and Social Psychology, 68,* 619–631.

Batson, C. D., Bolen, M. H., Cross, J. A., & Neuringer-Benefiel, H. E. (1986). Where is the altruism in the altruistic personality? *Journal of Personality and Social Psychology, 50,* 212–220.

Batson, C. D., Chang, J., Orr, R., & Rowland, J. (2002). Empathy, attitudes, and action: Can feeling for a member of a stigmatized group motivate one to help the group? *Personality and Social Psychology Bulletin, 28,* 1656–1666.

Batson, C. D., Coke, J. S., Jasnoski, M. L., & Hanson, M. (1978). Buying kindness: Effect of an extrinsic incentive for helping on perceived altruism. *Personality and Social Psychology Bulletin, 4,* 86–91.

Batson, C. D., Dyck, J. L., Brandt, J. R., Batson, J. G., Powell, A. L., McMaster, M. R., & Griffitt, C. (1988). Five studies testing two new egoistic alternatives to the empathy–altruism hypothesis. *Journal of Personality and Social Psychology, 55,* 52–77.

Batson, C. D., Eklund, J. H., Chermok, V. L., Hoyt, J. L., & Ortiz, B. G. (2007). An additional antecedent of empathic concern: Valuing the welfare of the person in need. *Journal of Personality and Social Psychology, 93,* 65–74.

Batson, C. D., Fultz, J., Schoenrade, P. A., & Paduano, A. (1987). Critical self-reflection and self-perceived altruism: When self-reward fails. *Journal of Personality and Social Psychology, 53,* 594–602.

Batson, C. D., Klein, T. R., Highberger, L., & Shaw, L. L. (1995). Immorality from empathy-induced altruism: When compassion and justice conflict. *Journal of Personality and Social Psychology, 68,* 1042–1054.

Batson, C. D., Kobrynowicz, D., Dinnerstein, J. L., Kampf, H. C., & Wilson, A. D. (1997). In a very different voice: Unmasking moral hypocrisy. *Journal of Personality and Social Psychology, 72,* 1335–1348.

Batson, C. D., Lishner, D. A., Cook, J., & Sawyer, S. (2005). Similarity and nurturance: Two possible sources of empathy for strangers. *Basic and Applied Social Psychology, 27,* 15–25.

Batson, C. D., & Moran, T. (1999). Empathy-induced altruism in a prisoner's dilemma. *European Journal of Social Psychology, 29,* 909–924.

Batson, C. D., Polycarpou, M. P., Harmon-Jones, E., Imhoff, H. J., Mitchener, E. C., Bednar, L. L., Klein, T. R., & Highberger, L. (1997). Empathy and attitudes: Can feeling for a member of a stigmatized group improve feelings toward the group? *Journal of Personality and Social Psychology, 72,* 105–118.

Batson, C. D., Sager, K., Garst, E., Kang, M., Rubchinsky, K., & Dawson, K. (1997). Is empathy-induced helping due to self-other merging? *Journal of Personality and Social Psychology, 73,* 495–509.

Batson, C. D., & Shaw, L. L. (1991). Evidence for altruism: Toward a pluralism of prosocial motives. *Psychological Inquiry, 2,* 107–122.

Batson, C. D., Thompson, E. R., & Chen, H. (2002). Moral hypocrisy: Addressing some alternatives. *Journal of Personality and Social Psychology, 83,* 330–339.

Batson, C. D., Thompson, E. R., Seuferling, G., Whitney, H., & Strongman, J. (1999). Moral hypocrisy: Appearing moral to oneself without being so. *Journal of Personality and Social Psychology, 77,* 525–537.

Batson, C. D., Turk, C. L., Shaw, L. L., & Klein, T. R. (1995). Information function of empathic emotion: Learning that we value the other's welfare. *Journal of Personality and Social Psychology, 68,* 300–313.

Batson, C. D., & Weeks, J. L. (1996). Mood effects of unsuccessful helping: Another test of the empathy–altruism hypothesis. *Personality and Social Psychology Bulletin, 22,* 148–157.

Bell, D. C. (2001). Evolution of parental caregiving. *Personality and Social Psychology Review, 5,* 216–229.

Berkowitz, L. (1972). Social norms, feelings, and other factors affecting helping and altruism. In L. Berkowitz (Ed.), *Advances in experimental social psychology* (Vol. 6, pp. 63–108). New York: Academic Press.

Bersoff, D. M. (1999). Why good people sometimes do bad things: Motivated reasoning and unethical behavior. *Personality and Social Psychology Bulletin, 25,* 28–39.

Brewer, M. B., & Kramer, R. M. (1986). Choice behavior in social dilemmas: Effects of social identity, group size, and decision framing. *Journal of Personality and Social Psychology, 50,* 543–549.

Campbell, D. T. (1975). On the conflicts between biological and social evolution and between psychology and moral tradition. *American Psychologist, 30,* 1103–1126.

Carlo, G., Eisenberg, N., Troyer, D., Switzer, G., & Speer, A. L. (1991). The altruistic personality: In what contexts is it apparent? *Journal of Personality and Social Psychology, 61,* 450–458.

Cialdini, R. B., Brown, S. L., Lewis, B. P., Luce, C., & Neuberg, S. L. (1997). Reinterpreting the empathy–altruism relationship: When one into one equals oneness. *Journal of Personality and Social Psychology, 73,* 481–494.

Cialdini, R. B., Darby, B. L., & Vincent, J. E. (1973). Transgression and altruism: A case for hedonism. *Journal of Experimental Social Psychology, 9,* 502–516.

Cialdini, R. B., Kallgren, C. A., & Reno, R. R. (1991). A focus theory of normative conduct: A theoretical refinement and reevaluation of the role of norms in human behavior. In M. P. Zanna (Ed.), *Advances in experimental social psychology* (Vol. 24, pp. 201–234). Orlando, FL: Academic Press.

Cialdini, R. B., Schaller, M., Houlihan, D., Arps, K., Fultz, J., & Beaman, A. L. (1987). Empathy-based helping: Is it selflessly or selfishly motivated? *Journal of Personality and Social Psychology, 52,* 749–758.

Clark, M. S., & Waddell, B. A. (1983). Effect of moods on thoughts about helping, attraction, and information acquisition. *Social Psychology Quarterly, 46*, 31–35.

Coke, J. S., Batson, C. D., & McDavis, K. (1978). Empathic mediation of helping: A two-stage model. *Journal of Personality and Social Psychology, 36*, 752–766.

Cunningham, M. R., Shaffer, D. R., Barbee, A. P., Wolff, P. L., & Kelley, D. J. (1990). Separate processes in the relation of elation and depression to helping: Social versus personal concerns. *Journal of Experimental Social Psychology, 26*, 13–33.

Darley, J. M., & Latané, B. (1970). Norms and normative behavior: Field studies of social interdependence. In J. Macaulay & L. Berkowitz (Eds.), *Altruism and helping behavior* (pp. 83–101). New York: Academic Press.

Dawes, R. M. (1980). Social dilemmas. *Annual Review of Psychology, 31*, 169–193.

Dawes, R. M., van de Kragt, A. J. C., & Orbell, J. M. (1988). Not me or thee but we: The importance of group identity in eliciting cooperation in dilemma situations; Experimental manipulations. *Acta Psychologica, 68*, 83–97.

Dawes, R. M., van de Kragt, A. J. C., & Orbell, J. M. (1990). Cooperation for the benefit of us—Not me, or my conscience. In J. J. Mansbridge (Ed.), *Beyond self-interest* (pp. 97–110). Chicago: University of Chicago Press.

de Waal, F. B. M. (1996). *Good natured: The origins of right and wrong in humans and other animals*. Cambridge, MA: Harvard University Press.

Dollard, J., & Miller, N. E. (1950). *Personality and psychotherapy*. New York: McGraw-Hill.

Dovidio, J. F., Allen, J. L., & Schroeder, D. A. (1990). The specificity of empathy-induced helping: Evidence for altruistic motivation. *Journal of Personality and Social Psychology, 59*, 249–260.

Dovidio, J. F., Gaertner, S. L., & Johnson, J. D. (1999, October). *New directions in prejudice and prejudice reduction: The role of cognitive representations and affect*. Paper presented at the annual meeting of the Society of Experimental Social Psychology, St. Louis, MO.

Dovidio, J. F., Piliavin, J. A., Gaertner, S. L., Schroeder, D. A., & Clark, R. D. III. (1991). The arousal:cost-reward model and the process of intervention: A review of the evidence. In M. S. Clark (Ed.), *Prosocial behavior* (pp. 86–118). Newbury Park, CA: Sage.

Dovidio, J. F., Piliavin, J. A., Schroeder, D. A., & Penner, L. A. (2006). *The social psychology of prosocial behavior*. Mahwah, NJ: Lawrence Erlbaum.

Eisenberg, N., & Miller, P. (1987). Empathy and prosocial behavior. *Psychological Bulletin, 101*, 91–119.

Eisenberg, N., Miller, P. A., Schaller, M., Fabes, R. A., Fultz, J., Shell, R., & Shea, C. L. (1989). The role of sympathy and altruistic personality traits in helping: A re-examination. *Journal of Personality, 57*, 41–67.

Fehr, E., & Gächter, S. (2002). Altruistic punishment in humans. *Nature, 415*, 137–140.

Frank, R. H. (1988). *Passions within reason: The strategic role of the emotions*. New York: W. W. Norton.

Freud, S. (1930). *Civilization and its discontents* (J. Riviere, Trans.). London: Hogarth Press.

Gergen, K. J., Ellsworth, P., Maslach, C., & Seipel, M. (1975). Obligation, donor resources, and reactions to aid in 3 cultures. *Journal of Personality and Social Psychology, 31*, 390–400.

Gibbons, F. X., & Wicklund, R. A. (1982). Self-focused attention and helping behavior. *Journal of Personality and Social Psychology, 43*, 462–474.

Gilligan, C. (1982). *In a different voice: Psychological theory and women's development*. Cambridge, MA: Harvard University Press.

Gordon, M. (2007). *Roots of empathy: Changing the world child by child*. Toronto: Thomas Allen.

Gouldner, A. W. (1960). The norm of reciprocity: A preliminary statement. *American Sociological Review, 25*, 161–179.

Hardin, G. (1977). *The limits of altruism: An ecologist's view of survival.* Bloomington: Indiana University Press.

Heider, F. (1958). *The psychology of interpersonal relations.* New York: Wiley.

Hoffman, M. L. (1975). Developmental synthesis of affect and cognition and its implications for altruistic motivation. *Developmental Psychology, 11,* 607–622.

Hoffman, M. L. (1981). Is altruism part of human nature? *Journal of Personality and Social Psychology, 40,* 121–137.

Hornstein, H. A. (1982). Promotive tension: Theory and research. In V. Derlega & J. Grzelak (Eds.), *Cooperation and helping behavior: Theories and research* (pp. 229–248). New York: Academic Press.

Isen, A. M. (1970). Success, failure, attention and reaction to others: The warm glow of success. *Journal of Personality and Social Psychology, 15,* 294–301.

Isen, A. M. (1987). Positive affect, cognitive organization, and social behavior. In L. Berkowitz (Ed.), *Advances in experimental social psychology* (Vol. 20, pp. 203–253). New York: Academic Press.

Isen, A. M., & Levin, P. F. (1972). Effect of feeling good on helping: Cookies and kindness. *Journal of Personality and Social Psychology, 21,* 344–348.

Isen, A. M., Shalker, T. E., Clark, M., & Karp, L. (1978). Affect, accessibility of material in memory, and behavior: A cognitive loop? *Journal of Personality and Social Psychology, 36,* 1–13.

Jackson, P. L., Meltzoff, A. N., & Decety, J. (2005). How do we perceive the pain of others? A window into the neural processes involved in empathy. *NeuroImage, 24,* 771–779.

Jarymowicz, M. (1992). Self, we, and other(s): Schemata, distinctiveness, and altruism. In P. M. Oliner, S. P. Oliner, L. Baron, L. A. Blum, D. L. Krebs, & M. Z. Smolenska (Eds.), *Embracing the other: Philosophical, psychological, and historical perspectives on altruism* (pp. 194–212). New York: New York University Press.

Kant, I. (1889). *Kant's critique of practical reason and other works on the theory of ethics* (4th ed.) (T. K. Abbott, Trans.). New York: Longmans, Green. (Original work published 1785)

Kogut, T., & Ritov, I. (2005). The singularity effect of identified victims in separate and joint evaluations. *Organizational Behavior and Human Decision Processes, 97,* 106–116.

Kohlberg, L. (1976). Moral stages and moralization: The cognitive-developmental approach. In T. Lickona (Ed.), *Moral development and behavior: Theory, research, and social issues* (pp. 31–53). New York: Holt, Rinehart & Winston.

Komorita, S. S., & Parks, C. D. (1995). Interpersonal relations: Mixed-motive interaction. *Annual Review of Psychology, 46,* 183–207.

Krebs, D. L. (1975). Empathy and altruism. *Journal of Personality and Social Psychology, 32,* 1134–1146.

Lamm, C., Batson, C. D., & Decety, J. (2007). The neural substrate of human empathy: Effects of perspective-taking and cognitive appraisal. *Journal of Cognitive Neuroscience, 19,* 1–17.

Lerner, M. J. (1980). *The belief in a just world: A fundamental delusion.* New York: Plenum Press.

Lerner, M. J. (1982). The justice motive in human relations and the economic model of man: A radical analysis of facts and fictions. In V. J. Derlega & J. Grzelak (Eds.), *Cooperation and helping behavior: Theories and research* (pp. 249–278). New York: Academic Press.

Lerner, M. J., & Simmons, C. H. (1966). Observer's reaction to the "innocent victim": Compassion or rejection? *Journal of Personality and Social Psychology, 4,* 203–210.

Lewin, K. (1951). *Field theory in social science.* New York: Harper.

MacIntyre, A. (1967). Egoism and altruism. In P. Edwards (Ed.), *The encyclopedia of philosophy* (Vol. 2, pp. 462–466). New York: Macmillan.

Mandeville, B. (1732). *The fable of the bees: Or, private vices, public benefits.* London: J. Tonson. (Original work published 1714)

Maner, J. K., Luce, C. L., Neuberg, S. L., Cialdini, R. B., Brown, S., & Sagarin, B. J. (2002). The effects of perspective taking on helping: Still no evidence for altruism. *Personality and Social Psychology Bulletin, 28,* 1601–1610.

Mansbridge, J. J. (Ed.). (1990). *Beyond self-interest.* Chicago: University of Chicago Press.

Maslach, C. (1982). *Burnout: The cost of caring.* Englewood Cliffs, NJ: Prentice Hall.

McDougall, W. (1908). *An introduction to social psychology.* London: Methuen.

Miller, D. T. (1999). The norm of self-interest. *American Psychologist, 54,* 1053–1060.

Mills, J., & Egger, R. (1972). Effect on derogation of a victim of choosing to reduce his stress. *Journal of Personality and Social Psychology, 23,* 405–408.

Murray, H. A. (1938). *Explorations in personality.* New York: Oxford University Press.

Nowak, M. A., & Sigmund, K. (2005). Evolution of indirect reciprocity. *Nature, 437,* 1291–1298.

Oliner, S. P., & Oliner, P. M. (1988). *The altruistic personality: Rescuers of Jews in Nazi Europe.* New York: Free Press.

Piliavin, J. A., & Charng, H.-W. (1990). Altruism: A review of recent theory and research. *American Sociological Review, 16,* 27–65.

Piliavin, J. A., Dovidio, J. F., Gaertner, S. L., & Clark, R. D. III. (1981). *Emergency intervention.* New York: Academic Press.

Pruitt, D. G. (1968). Reciprocity and credit building in a laboratory dyad. *Journal of Personality and Social Psychology, 8,* 143–147.

Rawls, J. (1971). *A theory of justice.* Cambridge, MA: Harvard University Press.

Reykowski, J. (1982). Motivation of prosocial behavior. In V. J. Derlega & J. Grzelak (Eds.), *Cooperation and helping behavior: Theories and research* (pp. 352–375). New York: Academic Press.

Ryan, W. (1971). *Blaming the victim.* New York: Random House.

Schaller, M., & Cialdini, R. B. (1988). The economics of empathic helping: Support for a mood-management motive. *Journal of Experimental Social Psychology, 24,* 163–181.

Schroeder, D. A., Dovidio, J. F., Sibicky, M. E., Matthews, L. L., & Allen, J. L. (1988). Empathy and helping behavior: Egoism or altruism? *Journal of Experimental Social Psychology, 24,* 333–353.

Shaw, L. L., Batson, C. D., & Todd, R. M. (1994). Empathy avoidance: Forestalling feeling for another in order to escape the motivational consequences. *Journal of Personality and Social Psychology, 67,* 879–887.

Shelton, M. L., & Rogers, R. W. (1981). Fear-arousing and empathy-arousing appeals to help: The pathos of persuasion. *Journal of Applied Social Psychology, 11,* 366–378.

Sibicky, M. E., Schroeder, D. A., & Dovidio, J. F. (1995). Empathy and helping: Considering the consequences of intervention. *Basic and Applied Social Psychology, 16,* 435–453.

Slovic, P. (2007). "If I look at the mass I will never act": Psychic numbing and genocide. *Judgment and Decision Making, 2,* 1–17.

Smith, K. D., Keating, J. P., & Stotland, E. (1989). Altruism reconsidered: The effect of denying feedback on a victim's status to empathic witnesses. *Journal of Personality and Social Psychology, 57,* 641–650.

Sober, E., & Wilson, D. S. (1998). *Unto others: The evolution and psychology of unselfish behavior.* Cambridge, MA: Harvard University Press.

Staub, E. (1974). Helping a distressed person: Social, personality, and stimulus determinants. In L. Berkowitz (Ed.), *Advances in experimental social psychology* (Vol. 7, pp. 293–341). New York: Academic Press.

Staub, E. (1989). Individual and societal (group) values in a motivational perspective and their role in benevolence and harmdoing. In N. Eisenberg, J. Reykowski, & E. Staub (Eds.), *Social and moral values: Individual and societal perspectives* (pp. 45–61). Hillsdale, NJ: Lawrence Erlbaum.

Stocks, E. L., Lishner, D. A., & Decker, S. K. (2009). Altruism or psychological escape: Why does empathy promote prosocial behavior? *European Journal of Social Psychology, 39,* 649–665.

Stotland, E., Mathews, K. E., Sherman, S. E., Hansson, R. O., & Richardson, B. Z. (1978). *Empathy, fantasy, and helping.* Beverly Hills, CA: Sage.

Stukas, A. A., Snyder, M., & Clary, E. G. (1999). The effects of "mandatory volunteerism" on intentions to volunteer. *Psychological Science, 10,* 59–64.

Tajfel, H. (1981). *Human groups and social categories: Studies in social psychology.* Cambridge, UK: Cambridge University Press.

Tsang, J. (2002). Moral rationalization and integration of situational factors and psychological processes in immoral behavior. *Review of General Psychology, 6,* 25–50.

Turner, J. C. (1987). *Rediscovering the social group: A self-categorization theory.* Oxford, UK: Basil Blackwell.

Vescio, T. K., Sechrist, G. B., & Paolucci, M. P. (2003). Perspective taking and prejudice reduction: The mediational role of empathy arousal and situational attributions. *European Journal of Social Psychology, 33,* 455–472.

Wallach, M. A., & Wallach, L. (1983). *Psychology's sanction for selfishness: The error of egoism in theory and therapy.* San Francisco: W. H. Freeman.

Wegener, D. T., & Petty, R. E. (1994). Mood management across affective states: The hedonic contingency hypothesis. *Journal of Personality and Social Psychology, 66,* 1034–1048.

Wilke, H., & Lanzetta, J. T. (1970). The obligation to help: The effects of amount of prior help on subsequent helping behavior. *Journal of Experimental Social Psychology, 6,* 483–493.

Wispé, L. (1986). The distinction between sympathy and empathy: To call forth a concept a word is needed. *Journal of Personality and Social Psychology, 50,* 314–321.

Yamagishi, T. (1986). The provision of a sanctioning system as a public good. *Journal of Personality and Social Psychology, 51,* 110–116.

Zahn-Waxler, C., & Radke-Yarrow, M. (1990). The origins of empathic concern. *Motivation and Emotion, 14,* 107–130.

Zuckerman, M. (1975). Belief in a just world and altruistic behavior. *Journal of Personality and Social Psychology, 31,* 972–976.

7

Why Do People Get Involved? Motivations for Volunteerism and Other Forms of Social Action

CLELIA ANNA MANNINO, MARK SNYDER, and ALLEN M. OMOTO

Motivations play a vital role in determining people's choices, decisions, and actions, from whom people choose to spend time with to the food they eat to decisions about which new job to accept. Motivations in the form of needs, goals, purposes, and plans can both foster and hinder future action. Consider a university student's decision to study abroad, for example. She may choose to spend a semester overseas to bolster her résumé and make herself more competitive in the job market. She may make the decision to advance her awareness and understanding of people in other countries and cultures. She may even choose *not* to study abroad because she believes that staying on her home campus will more quickly lead to graduation. As this example illustrates, motivations are important in understanding why and how people make decisions and engage in action.

Among the decisions individuals face are those concerning whether to devote time and energy to activities that help to address societal problems. Some people join recycling programs and do their part to help the environment. Others choose to spend time volunteering at a local animal shelter or connect with ongoing social movements to enact change. Still others involve themselves in political and social movements in efforts to improve the lot of groups of people or to change society. Whatever the activity, individuals engage in motivated and goal-directed activities for the benefit of others and society as a whole—a set of phenomena known collectively as social action (for a review, see Snyder & Omoto, 2006).

One type of social action that has increasingly gained interest, both in the psychological research literature and in mainstream society, is volunteerism.

Volunteerism occurs when people willingly give time or work for the good or welfare of others without expectations of compensation or reward (Omoto & Snyder, 1995; Snyder & Omoto, 2008). Volunteering can be informal, such as when neighbors help one another, or it can be formally institutionalized in organizations and agency-based programs. Across the world, individuals and groups devote large amounts of time to benefit others through volunteerism. In the United States alone, approximately 61 million Americans engaged in some form of volunteerism through or for an organization between 2006 and 2007 (U.S. Bureau of Labor Statistics, 2008). One reason volunteerism has gained such prominent status is because society views it positively. Individuals who volunteer are often regarded as altruistic, compassionate, and generous human beings.

Society also encourages volunteerism and the values that it represents. This is especially true in North America (see Curtis, Grabb, & Baer, 1992). U.S. public opinion surveys consistently reveal that the general public supports the ideals of helping others and becoming involved in community affairs to make society a better place. For example, in the case of volunteerism, Americans agree, by margins of over three to one, that "people should volunteer some of their time to help other people and thereby make the world a better place" and that "nonprofit organizations generally play a major role in their communities" (e.g., Independent Sector, 1988).

However, even though volunteerism and other prosocial activities are socially and culturally valued, they are not socially mandated. No laws dictate that people must volunteer or must join community organizations. No punishments or social reprimands exist for people who fail to donate their time as volunteers or to make contributions of goods or money to charitable organizations. Rather, individuals volunteer because they want and choose to do so. They act of their own volition, without any requirements placed on them and with full knowledge that both their time and their energy will be spent in the endeavor.

If no external forces mandate that people volunteer, what, then, prompts them to do so? What guides people's choices among different volunteer activities, and what factors sustain their involvement over time? Engaging in volunteerism is by no means easy. Barriers are often present and can be challenging to overcome. It may take great effort and substantial personal sacrifice to find volunteer opportunities and to remain committed and involved over time. In addition, in many forms of volunteerism, volunteers help people with whom they have no prior association. Unlike the helping that may occur among family members and within friendship networks, no obligatory ties or relationship bonds exist between the volunteer and the recipient of his or her services. Moreover, unlike the helping that occurs in response to emergencies, there is no pressure from immediate circumstances to offer assistance (see Omoto & Snyder, 1995).

These features that characterize volunteerism make it an intriguing phenomenon, because all of these considerations are ones that should reduce the likelihood that people volunteer. Yet, in spite of these impediments and lack of incentives, volunteering does occur in widespread and substantial ways. Apparently, then, there are some forces that lead people to volunteer in spite of the fact that it is effortful and time-consuming, involves opportunity costs, and can include offering sustained assistance to perfect strangers to whom the volunteer has no direct obligation or responsibility. Volunteerism, we propose, is a *motivated* phenomenon, propelled by motivational forces that lead individuals to seek out volunteer activities and to surmount barriers that impede their participation as well as their sustained involvement. Motivations are the guiding forces of people's decisions to volunteer, their search for appropriate volunteer opportunities, and their continuing service—in short, of their "agendas for action" (Snyder & Cantor, 1998).

This proposition that volunteerism is a motivated phenomenon is supported by diverse literatures that have considered prosocial action from a *motivational* perspective (e.g., Snyder & Omoto, 2006, 2008). Researchers have examined how motivations "dispose" people to take action, channel them into particular forms of action, guide them through their involvement, and sustain their efforts over time. The features of volunteerism, as well as other prosocial activities, are grounded in *motivated* forms of action—activities in which people freely choose to participate and to continue their involvement over extended periods of time, often despite great personal cost.

Our goals in this chapter are to address the question of why people volunteer to benefit others and larger society and, in so doing, to explicate some of the motivations behind volunteerism. In particular, we will examine three approaches to understanding volunteerism that reflect and reveal its motivational underpinnings. The first approach that we will consider addresses volunteerism from a functional perspective, exploring the purposes, needs, and goals that volunteering serves for the individual. Next, we will consider the role of identity in motivating volunteerism. Last, we will examine the potentially critical influence of connections to a community or communities in instigating and sustaining volunteerism. Moreover, we will consider each the three approaches from the perspective of two different levels of analysis—the individual and the group—thereby exploring both intrapersonal and group forces on action. These levels of analysis incorporate the idea that the impetus for volunteering can come from within the person as well as from the person's social context and that it can reflect both individual and collective considerations.

THE FUNCTIONAL ACCOUNT OF VOLUNTEERISM

In recent years, a great deal of research has examined the motivations that encourage and sustain volunteer efforts (e.g., Davis, Hall, & Meyer, 2003; Davis et al., 1999; Omoto & Snyder, 1995, 2002; Simon, Stuermer, & Steffens, 2000; Snyder, 1993; Snyder & Cantor, 1998). One useful approach to studying and understanding motivations originates from the functionalist perspective. This approach emphasizes the reasons, purposes, needs, goals, plans, and motivations that underlie and generate psychological phenomena (Snyder, 1993; Snyder & Cantor, 1998).

In the context of volunteerism, the functional approach examines the needs met, the motives fulfilled, and the functions served by volunteering. It seeks to articulate and understand what people are trying to accomplish and gain from their volunteer experiences and also how people go about accomplishing those goals. Functionalist theorizing posits that people will seek out volunteer opportunities to the extent that they believe that volunteering will fulfill certain motives or help them to meet specific goals. The motivations disposing people to volunteer are also linked to their agendas for action over the course of their service as volunteers. That is, people's initial motives are influential not only in initiating volunteer activities but also in helping to shape the nature and quality of their experiences as volunteers, including their satisfaction with their work (e.g., Omoto & Snyder, 1995; Penner & Finkelstein, 1998; Snyder, Omoto, & Lindsay, 2004). The functional approach seeks to understand how it is that people construct their agendas for action: how they identify their motivations for volunteering, seek opportunities that fulfill those motives, and sustain their involvement over time (Snyder & Omoto, 2000).

Approached from a functionalist perspective, volunteerism need not be exclusively a selfless act performed by noble and altruistic individuals. Instead, volunteerism can be performed on behalf of others (e.g., fighting the problems of poverty, helping the environment) *and* to benefit the self (e.g., to make friends, to affirm personal values). In fact, volunteerism provides a unique mechanism through which people can simultaneously help themselves, recipients of services, and others in the broader community, all while helping to alleviate larger societal problems. As such, the functionalist account of volunteerism is instructive about how motivational foundations for these actions are personal *and* social, individual *and* collective.

Functions at an Individual Level

At the personal or *individual* level, functions reflect personal and specific needs, goals, concerns, values, and agendas for action (e.g., to enhance self-esteem, make friends, acquire skills). Through their engagement in helping behavior, individual volunteers may benefit by witnessing evidence of community solidarity and spirit and the kindness and commitment that people can show toward others. In addition, volunteers may enhance their own sense of self by increasing their feelings of helpfulness, efficacy, and self-worth and also benefit from the development and practice of interpersonal and other useful skills.

Functions at a Group Level

At the collective or *group* level, functions are relatively more oriented toward others (and beyond the self) and focus on interpersonal motives and on the benefits and emotional states that derive from group membership. These concerns for others can be directed toward similar others or people who are members of an individual's own social group (i.e., ingroup members) or toward people who belong to other social groups (i.e., outgroup members). For instance, a woman may choose to volunteer on behalf of other women (e.g., at a battered women's shelter) or for an organization that promotes causes that directly impact women, such as gender parity in the workplace. That same commitment to social justice and equality may also prompt her to fight for antidiscrimination laws and equal rights for members of ethnic minority groups and other disadvantaged groups. Thus, the motivations underlying volunteer service can unite concerns for benefiting the self and for benefiting others. Volunteers can simultaneously be engaged in actions that do good both for others and for themselves.

The Functional Approach in Action

Various attempts have been made to define and map the sets of functions that are involved in volunteering, one outcome of which has been the development of several inventories for capturing and assessing the diverse motivations that individuals can and do have for volunteering. These inventories have been used in research with volunteers serving in a variety of capacities and working on behalf of a range of causes (for a review, see Snyder & Omoto, 2008). The Volunteer Functions Inventory (VFI) provides one example. On the basis of the functionalist approach, Clary and colleagues (1998) developed the VFI to assess both self-focused and other-focused reasons why people volunteer.

This 30-item instrument assesses six key motivations: values, career, understanding, esteem enhancement, protective, and social. Personal *values* and guiding beliefs, such as an altruistic concern for others or even religious convictions and beliefs, often drive volunteer efforts. Other motives are more self-focused, such as volunteering to boost network affiliations or gain *career* experience; to gain greater *understanding* of a particular group of people or a specific problem; for *esteem enhancement*, to raise self-esteem or feel needed and wanted by others; for *protective* concerns, such as distracting oneself from personal problems; and for *social* reasons, such as to meet new people and make friends or to satisfy the expectations of close others (e.g., Clary & Snyder, 1995; Clary et al., 1998; Snyder & Clary, 2004; Snyder, Clary, & Stukas, 2000; Snyder et al., 2004).

Sample items from the VFI include *values*, "I feel it is important to help others"; *understanding*, "Volunteering lets me learn through direct, hands-on experience"; *enhancement*, "Volunteering makes me feel better about myself"; *career*, "Volunteering can help me to get my foot in the door at a place where I would like to work"; *social*, "People I know share my interest in community service"; and *protective*, "Volunteering is a good escape from my own troubles" (Clary & Snyder, 1999). Research suggests that the values function is generally most strongly endorsed by volunteers, followed by the enhancement and understanding functions (Clary, Snyder, & Stukas, 1998). Other research (e.g., Omoto & Snyder, 1995; Snyder & Clary, 2004) has also identified two additional motivations of great importance: *personal development* (e.g., development of useful skills and abilities) and *community concern* (i.e., the desire to support or assist a specific community, whether or not the volunteer is a member of that community). Taken together, then, there are many possible reasons that people get involved in volunteer work, with the common denominator in the functionalist approach being that the reasons all reflect volunteers' attempts to meet different needs and goals.

The functions identified in the VFI reflect the diversity of motives that can foster volunteerism and sustained involvement. They also reflect the potential impact of volunteerism for volunteers, recipients of service, and society at large. An individual may, for instance, be driven by personal values to volunteer at a local homeless shelter. This work offers clear evidence of the person's values regarding support for and treatment of individuals who are disadvantaged. Moreover, it permits the volunteer to support the fight against homelessness and to help sustain organizations that work to keep shelters open and safe. In this way, the volunteer has helped to ensure future services for homeless individuals and also to create awareness of, if not partial solutions for, homelessness. Despite the fact that the volunteer's actions were initiated because of relatively altruistic or other-oriented motives, through the course of his or her work, the volunteer is likely to meet other local community members and to expand his or her social network. Thus, the motives that serve as initiators of action can result in benefits to the individual, to current and potential future recipients of services, and to the community at large.

Research on the motivations of AIDS volunteers provides another illustration of the motives that underlie volunteer actions. Building on functionalist theorizing, Omoto and Snyder (1995) identified a set of motivations for AIDS volunteerism using exploratory and confirmatory factor analytic techniques in multiple samples. Results indicated that some AIDS volunteers in the United States engaged in service because of their personal convictions and beliefs or out of concern for people affected by HIV disease (*values*). Another prominent motive revolved around concern about and commitment to communities most affected by HIV disease (*community concern*). Other motives were more self-focused: searching for a greater *understanding* of AIDS and how people live with the HIV disease, promoting *personal development* such as facing challenges or enlarging social networks, and fulfilling needs related to *esteem enhancement* such as promoting self-esteem and positive feelings about the self. Among AIDS volunteers in these studies, the *values* motive was endorsed most strongly, and *esteem enhancement* was endorsed the least, with the remaining motivations falling somewhere in between (Omoto & Snyder, 1995). Although these motivations were developed in the specific context of AIDS volunteerism, they reflect the general tenets of functional theorizing and closely resemble the motivations that have been identified in research with other groups of volunteers. In fact, the specific measure utilized to tap these functions can be and has been modified for use with other types of volunteers (e.g., hospice volunteers).

A second key principle guiding the functionalist perspective is that different people have different motives for volunteerism, even for the same type of volunteer work in the same organizations. Thus, volunteer acts that appear very similar on the surface may reflect strikingly different motivations and functions. Several individuals might engage in the very same volunteer activity but for quite different underlying motives and to serve different psychological functions. For instance, two people may both choose to spend time volunteering at their local library, one doing so to make friends and the other because she or he would like to develop greater interpersonal skills. Thus, even similar beliefs and behaviors can serve very different psychological functions for different individuals (Clary, Snyder, & Stukas, 1996).

Not only do motivations apply differently to different people, but they also do not operate in isolation from each other. It is not necessarily the case that individuals have one and only one motivation for volunteering. Rather, a combination of motives may be at work in initiating and sustaining volunteer efforts. For instance, one study found that 62.9% of volunteers indicated having multiple motives for volunteering (Kiviniemi, Snyder, & Omoto, 2002). Although having many motivations may be beneficial, perhaps making it more likely that an individual will volunteer in the first place, it has been demonstrated that having multiple motivations may prove problematic over time. In fact, AIDS volunteers who expressed having many important motives were also less satisfied with their volunteer experiences and encountered more stress than individuals with only one main motive for volunteering (Kiviniemi et al., 2002).

Just as motivations do not act independently, they also are not static. Motivations may change as people move through the stages of their lives or over time within particular volunteer organizations or contexts. Omoto, Snyder, and Martino (2000) examined the purposes, expectations, and outcomes of adult hospice volunteers of varying ages. They found that younger volunteers were more motivated by interpersonal relationships, whereas older volunteers were motivated more by service or community concerns. Although these findings come from cross-sectional comparisons, it may be the case that the importance and emphasis that people place on different motivations change as they move through different periods of their lives. Motivations may also change as people become more experienced volunteers. Clary et al. (1996) used cross-sectional data from the Independent Sector's 1992 national survey of giving and volunteering in the United States to examine relations between motivations and various aspects of volunteer behavior. One of their research concerns centered on whether people with different behavioral commitments to volunteering (i.e., amount of past volunteer experience) exhibited different patterns of motivations. They found that current volunteers with less past volunteer experience were more motivated by career and understanding functions as compared to current volunteers with relatively more experience (Clary et al., 1998). They also examined whether volunteers and nonvolunteers differed in motivations. In fact, volunteers and nonvolunteers did differ on five of the six motivations assessed with the VFI. Volunteers reported greater levels of values, enhancement, social, and understanding motivations, whereas nonvolunteers reported greater career motivations (Clary et al., 1998).

These different motivational considerations are related to people's agendas for action. Different motivations may play a larger or smaller role at different stages of the volunteer process (Omoto & Snyder, 1995; Snyder, Omoto, & Smith, in press). The values motive, for instance, seems to be important in prompting individuals to make the initial decision to volunteer. However, after that point, other motivations may become more influential and guide the individual to a specific volunteer activity. Still other motives may work to maintain that individual's involvement (Clary et al., 1998). Interestingly, studies (e.g., Omoto & Snyder, 1995) indicate that AIDS volunteers tend to serve longer to the extent that they report stronger and particularly self-focused motivations for volunteering. More specifically, engaging in volunteerism for reasons related to increasing understanding, personal development, or esteem enhancement predicted longer volunteer service. In contrast, relatively other-oriented motives associated with values and community concerns were not related to length of service (Omoto & Snyder, 1995; Snyder & Omoto, 2000). In short, the evidence suggests that volunteers can be motivated by one, few, or many motives; that motives can vary with life circumstance or age; and that the motives that underlie volunteerism at one point in time and in one particular organization may be unstable and dynamic, shifting over time, with experience, or with organizational context.

Finally, critical at each juncture in the volunteer process is a match between motives and experiences. The functionalist perspective posits that people will choose to volunteer if they believe the experience will fulfill their motives for volunteering. To the extent that an individual's volunteer experience satisfies his or her motivational concerns, that individual will gain greater satisfaction from his or her time spent helping others and express greater commitment to continued service as a volunteer (Snyder et al., 2000).

THE ROLE OF IDENTITY IN MOTIVATING VOLUNTEERISM

Examining the functions served by volunteering has helped shed light on the motivational dynamics underpinning helping behaviors. Research on identity has also contributed to this understanding. Issues of identity play a role in both the antecedents and the consequences of volunteerism, in leading people both to become volunteers and to continue serving over time. For some people and in some instances, volunteer efforts are driven by, as well as become a part of, identity concerns. Research and theory on the motivational impact of identity processes in volunteerism has considered both *individual identity* and *social identity*.

Identity at an Individual Level

Both personal and social identities are relevant to processes of volunteering. At the level of personal identities, individuals may act in the service of specific and important identities and roles. For example, if an individual takes pride in being altruistic, that person may participate in volunteer actions that allow him or her to maintain that self-characterization. Individuals may volunteer because they feel that their volunteer experience helps make them distinct and unique. Also, as people grow older, volunteerism may become a way for them to gain purpose and meaning in their lives, especially when work or other role-based identities are lost or diminished (e.g., Harlow & Cantor, 1996; Okun, 1994).

For other people, the longer they engage in volunteer service, the more their identities develop, and volunteering becomes a part of what defines them as a person. Piliavin and Callero (1991), and others (e.g., Callero, 1985; Callero, Howard, & Piliavin, 1987; Charng, Piliavin, & Callero, 1988; Piliavin, Grube, & Callero, 2002), have investigated the reasons why people become blood donors and especially why some people become regular and habitual blood donors. They found that for some blood donors, the role of donor merged with personal identity so that being a blood donor became a defining part of the volunteers themselves. Interestingly, this merging of role and identity is critical in maintaining donor involvement over time (e.g., Piliavin & Callero, 1991; Piliavin et al., 2002).

Identities at a Group Level

At the social or collective level, individuals may be motivated by social identities that revolve around belonging and group membership. It is also possible, and perhaps likely, that individuals come to identify more strongly with a group or collective over the course of their volunteer experience. In fact, identification with a group or collective has been linked to who participates in social movements and the extent and length of the involvement (e.g., Simon et al., 2000; Stuermer & Kampmeier, 2003; Stuermer, Simon, Loewy, & Joerger, 2003). People who identify more strongly with social groups to which they belong work harder for that group and invest more of their personal resources into it (e.g., Barreto & Ellemers, 2000, 2002; De Cremer & Van Vugt, 1999).

Importantly, motivations at this collective level seem to be partly shaped by group membership—namely, perceived ingroup and outgroup belonging. Empathy, for example, has been shown to more strongly predict helping when the helper and the recipient of assistance are from the same ingroup than when they belonged to different groups (Stuermer, Snyder, Kropp, & Siem, 2006; Stuermer, Snyder, & Omoto, 2005). Other related models of helping posit increased assistance to ingroup members, with the added element that outgroup helping occurs when people recategorize or redefine outgroup members as belonging to their ingroup (e.g., Gaertner & Dovidio, 2000). In short, then, several factors impact the roles of both personal and social identities in motivating volunteerism and in shaping people's agendas for action.

CONSIDERATIONS OF COMMUNITY AND VOLUNTEERISM

Community has often been conceived as a backdrop for volunteer activities. People typically engage in actions in and around the communities in which they live. Community is also frequently the target of volunteer efforts. Individuals may, for example, engage in actions to beautify their neighborhood or work to fight illiteracy in their towns. In fact, there are growing indications that *connections* to a larger community, including psychological sense of community (e.g., McMillan, 1996; McMillan & Chavis, 1986; Sarason, 1974), may facilitate volunteering and other prosocial activities. Accordingly, we now turn our attention to the motivational impact of connections to community in the processes and stages of volunteerism.

We begin with the concept of *place attachment*. As discussed in the literature on environmental psychology, place attachment refers to the connection that people feel to a place that, for them, elicits feelings and emotions; for example, the place where they were born or the place where they live or work (Knez, 2005). In the late 1970s, environmental psychologists began to study the related notion of place identity (Lalli, 1992) and have since examined place identity in relation to diverse realms such as the experience of desegregation (Dixon & Durrheim, 2004), attitudes toward environmental sustainability (Uzzell, Pol, & Badenas, 2002), and the development of national identity (Devine-Wright & Lyons, 1997). Theoretical foundations of place identity propose that both physical and social environments contribute to an individual's identity development. Much like children develop self-identities by distinguishing themselves from others, so too do they develop identities tied to objects, places, and settings (Proshansky, Fabian, & Kaminoff, 1983). Place identity, then, is one aspect of an individual's identity, and, similar to gender and ethnicity, it is incorporated into a broader sense of self. Thus, the physical environment helps people to create and maintain their self and self-esteem (Korpela, 1989; Krupat, 1983; Lalli, 1992; Proshansky et al., 1983).

More recently, community psychology has expanded notions of place identity by developing broader notions of community identity and the related concept of *psychological sense of community* (Colombo & Senatore, 2005), a concept first introduced by Sarason (1974). Broadly defined, psychological sense of community refers to a feeling of belonging and being able to depend on a larger community. In the literature, it is commonly thought of as including four components: (a) a sense of membership and belonging, (b) a feeling that members make a difference in the community and that the community is important to members, (c) a sense that the community can meet the needs of its members, and (d) the presence of a shared emotional connection among members, that they share experiences and a common history (Colombo, Mosso, & De Piccoli, 2001; Kim & Kaplan, 2004; McMillan, 1996; McMillan & Chavis, 1986; Peterson, Speer, & Hughey, 2006; Prezza & Costantini, 1998; Proescholdbell, Roosa, & Nemeroff, 2006; Puddifoot, 2003).

Psychological sense of community has been explored in numerous studies, some conducted in the United States and some conducted internationally (Bishop, Colquhoun, & Johnson, 2006; Hill, 1996; Kim & Kaplan, 2004; Puddifoot, 2003; Tartaglia, 2006), and has been linked to life satisfaction (Prezza & Costantini, 1998), social identification (Obst & White, 2005), personality traits (Lounsbury, Loveland, & Gibson, 2003), positive and negative outcomes for youth in disadvantaged neighborhoods (Cantillona, Davidson, & Schweitzer, 2003), and the presence of threats to communities (Loomis, Dockett, & Brodsky, 2004). However, these studies approach psychological sense of community as a geographically bounded construct, such as connected to a neighborhood or town. Largely absent is the notion that sense of community involves feelings of psychological connectedness with other people who share similar attitudes, values, or experiences and who may not be in the same physical location.

Bridging the Individual and Group Levels

This purely psychological sense of community may have important implications for motivating volunteerism. Connections to communities and social groups can have several psychological benefits, such as enhancing self-esteem (Crocker & Luhtanen, 1990) and social identity (e.g., Tajfel & Turner, 1986). A psychological sense of community can foster in individuals a greater feeling of belonging and connection to others. It can also increase people's feelings of responsibility and obligation and strengthen their beliefs that community support is available should they need assistance.

In part because of the feelings of belonging, connection, and responsibility that psychological sense of community fosters, it could be an impetus for action and involvement. In fact, research on the processes of volunteerism has illuminated recurring themes of how connections to communities draw people into volunteerism and sustain their involvement over time. Concerns about community and influences of other community members are frequently noted among the motivations of new volunteers (Omoto & Snyder, 1995; Omoto & Snyder, 2002; Stuermer & Kampmeier, 2003). In the specific case of AIDS volunteerism, for example, community has been conceptualized in terms of the community of people affected by HIV, with community in this sense including not just people infected with HIV or who are at risk, for it but also the members of their social networks and the volunteers and staff of AIDS service organizations. There has been extensive theorizing and research about the role of psychological sense of community in this form of volunteerism; this work can serve as a valuable template for future considerations of community (e.g., Omoto & Snyder, 2002).

Cross-sectional and longitudinal studies have indicated that motivations related to this conceptualization of community are important in encouraging people to become involved in AIDS volunteerism (e.g., Omoto & Snyder, 2002, 2010). Prominent in the motivations of these volunteers are sentiments that reflect and revolve around community concerns, as the following items from a measure of community motivation suggest: "Because of my concern and worry about communities affected by AIDS"; "To help members of communities affected by AIDS"; "Because of my obligation to communities affected by AIDS"; "Because I consider myself an advocate for communities affected by AIDS"; "To get to know people in communities affected by AIDS" (see Omoto & Snyder, 1995; Snyder & Omoto, 2002). These items are typically rated quite highly in studies of volunteers (e.g., Omoto & Snyder, 1993, 1995, in press), suggesting that community concerns may play an important role in individuals' decisions to volunteer.

In addition to AIDS volunteers' rated concerns about the community affected by HIV disease, these volunteers, like other types of volunteers, seem to be moved to action through the influences of other members of their communities. Thus, for example, a longitudinal study of AIDS volunteers (Omoto & Snyder, 1999) found that 51% of volunteers knew at least one other person who was doing AIDS volunteer work, 76% knew at least one other person who was doing non-AIDS volunteer work, and 67% had some volunteer activity modeled by their parents. These community influences were influential in sparking volunteers to take action. A majority of new volunteers (57%) indicated that their path to volunteering was community based, including being asked by someone they knew, knowing others who were volunteers, or participating in community events (e.g., AIDS fund-raising walk).

Economic and political characteristics of communities may also be important to consider in understanding the roles that community and psychological sense of community play in volunteerism. For example, indicators of social connectedness, such as mobility and urbanization, appear to be potentially important in influencing social action. Relatively stable communities, those with lower rates of mobility by community members, may provide members with more opportunities to develop meaningful ties with others. As a result, community strength and cohesion may be increased, making these communities ripe for volunteerism and other forms of involvement (e.g., Oishi et al., 2007).

Just as psychological sense of community and community connections can serve as motivation for volunteerism, it seems likely that a reciprocal relationship exists as well. That is, involvement in volunteerism probably serves to build and strengthen community connections, thereby fostering heightened sense of community. It is not surprising, then, that volunteers in an AIDS service organization, over the course of their service, expressed an increasing connection to the community affected by and concerned about HIV and AIDS. Relative to when these individuals started their service as AIDS volunteers, their close friendships and social networks also increasingly came to include people who were somehow connected to their volunteer experiences (see Omoto & Snyder, 2002).

More specifically, data from a longitudinal study of AIDS volunteers (Omoto & Snyder, 1999) indicated that by the time they had served for three months, 81% of volunteers indicated having at least one friend in their AIDS service organization. Over their first six months of service, 21.1% of volunteers expressed having one *close* friend at their AIDS service organization, a number that essentially doubled from their first three months of service (11.7%). Over the same time period, the proportion of each volunteer's total social network that was made up of other AIDS volunteers increased from 22.5% to 36%. As a consequence of their work, then, AIDS volunteers seem to surround themselves with more people connected to their volunteer experiences and AIDS service organization. They are also simultaneously developing and becoming part of a community affected by and concerned about HIV and AIDS.

Strengthened community ties do not benefit just volunteers. The recipients of volunteer efforts also seem to experience positive effects. For the clients of AIDS service organizations (generally people infected with HIV), a bolstered sense of community may help to ease the isolation and indifference that many feel (Omoto & Snyder, 2002). Forging connections with other community members seems to also result in a larger social network from which the clients can get and offer support.

Community, then, provides and becomes both a context and a process for volunteer efforts. Community as a process focuses on how connections to and concerns about community motivate people to volunteer and also sustain their involvement. Connections to a psychologically defined community, whether as motivation for the initiation of action or whether they result from volunteer experiences and motivate later action, may predict the extensiveness of people's prosocial actions. As people become more strongly connected to a community and perceive greater connections to a community of people with shared concerns, they should engage in more behaviors to help that community (Mashek, Cannaday, & Tangney, 2007; Omoto & Snyder, 2002, 2010).

In fact, Omoto and Snyder's (1999) longitudinal data support this speculation. Not only did volunteers in AIDS service organizations experience increased community connections over the course of their volunteer service, but they also became increasingly involved in actively participating in their community in other ways. In fact, over the first six months of their service, AIDS volunteers showed substantial increases in a range of activities that benefit the community of people affected by HIV and AIDS: more frequent donations to AIDS groups, more frequent attendance at AIDS fund-raisers, and greater involvement in AIDS activism.

Moreover, connections to and sense of community may promote other types of civic participation and social action, including other causes and movements. Thus, community members who feel a stronger sense of community may feel more obligated to participate in community events and work on behalf of the community through charitable giving, participation in several community groups and organizations, and involvement in the political process. In short, psychological sense of community may be crucial in leading individuals to take many different forms of action.

LINKS TO SOCIAL ACTION

The motivations for volunteerism have parallels in other forms of social action, such as civic and political participation, social movements, and organizational citizenship (see Snyder & Omoto, 2007). In an attempt to better understand why people become involved in civic and political causes, Verba, Schlozman, and Brady (1995) identified four categories of benefits that people may seek from civic participation. These were *selective material benefits* (e.g., furthering one's own career), *selective social gratification* (e.g., being with other people), *selective civic gratification* (e.g., making the community or nation a better place), and *collective outcomes* (e.g., influencing government policy). These outcomes reflect both specific benefits to individual activists and collective benefits for the larger society. Through interviews with political activists, Teske (1997) also identified a diverse set of motives that give rise to political participation, including growth and development as a person, increased self-esteem, good feelings derived from doing the right thing, and gaining community.

Motivations have also been the focus of attempts to understand social movement participation, or why people engage in collective attempts to change disadvantageous conditions (e.g., fighting on behalf of targets of prejudice and discrimination, for those who have limited economic and employment opportunities, and for people who have limited access to educational opportunities and health care). Klandermans (1997) proposed three classes of motivation for social movement participation, each arising from different expected costs and benefits. The *collective motive* involves the shared benefits sought from the social movement (e.g., equal rights, higher wages). The *normative motive* has to do with expectations for how significant others will react to an individual's social movement participation (e.g., Will others approve or disapprove? Offer praise or criticism?). And finally, the *reward motive* involves individual and personal costs and benefits of participation (e.g., taking time away from work, making new friends). The role of this set of motives has been documented among participants in various social movements, including most prominently in the labor and peace movements in the Netherlands (Klandermans, 1984, 1997; Klandermans & Oegema, 1987).

Organizational citizenship behavior provides yet another example of the critical role of motivation. It has been suggested that workers must engage in organizational citizenship behaviors (i.e., prosocial behaviors directed at helping others and the organization itself) for organizations and firms to operate successfully and to encourage worker satisfaction and camaraderie (Borman & Penner, 2001; Brief & Weiss, 2002; Cropanzano & Byrne, 2000; Katz, 1964; Organ, 1988). Penner, Midili, and Kegelmeyer (1997) adopted a functional approach and conceptualized organizational citizenship as prosocial behaviors, consciously chosen by individuals and engaged in to meet needs and to satisfy motives. The same acts of organizational citizenship could reflect different motives for different individuals. Among the motives that have been explored as underlying organizational citizenship behaviors are prosocial values, organizational concern, and impression management (Rioux & Penner, 2001). Prosocial values motives appear to most strongly predict organizational citizenship behaviors directed at individuals, whereas organizational concern motives seem to be most strongly associated with organizational citizenship behaviors directed at the organization (Rioux & Penner, 2001).

Thus, volunteerism is not the only domain of social action in which theorizing and empirical exploration of the role of motivation has been central in attempts to understand why, when, how, and for how long people get involved. Across diverse types of social action (volunteerism, social movement participation, organizational citizenship behavior), it appears that a variety of motives may be involved in the agendas for action that guide and direct individual and collective action. Motivations set the stage for the processes of getting involved and staying involved in social action, including individuals' choices to get involved, the experiences they have, their satisfaction with those experiences, and their ultimate decisions about whether to continue or to terminate their participation.

CONCLUSIONS

In this chapter, we have discussed the important role of motivational perspectives in understanding volunteerism and other forms of social action. We have considered the ways that psychological functions, personal and social identities, and connections to community can serve as motivational foundations for volunteering. Moreover, we have examined the processes of motivation as they operate at the level of the individual and at the level of groups or collectives. In the specific case of volunteerism, volunteers take action on behalf of others (e.g., to help people living in poverty or who have a chronic disease) and on behalf of themselves (e.g., to gain skills or to meet new people), sometimes operating in the service of identity concerns. Thus, the functions and identities served by volunteering may encompass both personal and social group considerations. We have also examined the role of community, and especially psychological sense of community, in motivating volunteerism and other forms of social action.

We suggest that an understanding of the motivations that underlie volunteerism and broader social action has several important implications. For example, by knowing why people volunteer and what encourages them to continue their involvement, communities and volunteer organizations can make better focused and targeted efforts to increase participation in volunteer activities. Arguably, such a focus can be seen as benefiting society, especially because of the important social services provided by volunteers. To the extent that promoting volunteerism is to become a societal goal, findings from research on motivations for volunteerism and social action can readily be applied (see also Snyder & Omoto, 2008).

For instance, research suggests that persuasive messages used to recruit volunteers are more effective and gain more favorable responses if they target an individual's specific motivations (e.g., Clary et al., 1998; Clary, Snyder, Ridge, Miene,

& Haugen, 1994; Smith, Omoto, & Snyder, 2001). Volunteers are also more likely to engage in tasks that they feel match their personal motives (e.g., Houle, Sagarin, & Kaplan, 2005). When volunteers engage in a motivation-matched task, moreover, they are more satisfied with their experiences and are more likely to continue volunteering (e.g., Crain, Omoto, & Snyder, 1998; O'Brien, Crain, Omoto, & Snyder, 2000; Omoto et al., 2000). Thus, matching volunteer opportunities and tasks to motives may be one way to increase volunteerism and to ensure that volunteers sustain their involvement over time. The power of matching experiences to motives potentially can be harnessed by volunteer service organizations in the design of programs to promote the development of an effective, satisfied, and long-serving volunteer workforce (for elaboration on the translation of research on the processes of volunteerism to organizational practices, see Snyder & Omoto, 2008).

Focusing on motivations may also be useful in understanding the effects of society's changing ideas about volunteerism. In the context of recent initiatives in secondary schools and universities to promote community service through service learning programs, research on the causes and consequences of volunteerism takes on added significance. For example, research (e.g., Stukas, Snyder, & Clary, 1999; Thomas, Batson, & Coke, 1981) has found that when volunteering is placed under external control, intrinsic motivations for these acts may be decreased. In particular, Stukas et al. (1999) found that among students in mandatory volunteerism programs, the links between prior histories as volunteers and future intentions to volunteer were weakened when they perceived their volunteering to be externally controlled by a mandated program of volunteer service for academic credits. By contrast, when these students felt less external control, their past experience as volunteers more strongly predicted their future interest in volunteering (Stukas et al., 1999).

In closing, we wish to underscore that an analysis of the role of motivational considerations in understanding volunteerism has potentially important implications for expanding the theoretical frameworks that have been utilized to explain prosocial action. We expect that careful theoretical and empirical examinations of motivation can and will offer a clearer lens through which to view volunteerism and other forms of social action more generally. In addition, as understanding of the role of motivations in volunteerism and social action is increased, this understanding is likely to inform and be enriched by advances in research on prosocial actions and helping. In short, by focusing on motivations, we and other investigators are exploring some of the very foundations of many forms of individual and collective action.

ACKNOWLEDGMENT

The preparation of this chapter and the conduct of the research reported in it have been supported by grants from the National Institute of Mental Health to Mark Snyder and to Allen M. Omoto.

REFERENCES

Barreto, M., & Ellemers, N. (2000). You can't always do what you want: Social identity and self-presentational determinants of the choice to work for a low-status group. *Personality and Social Psychology Bulletin, 26,* 629–639.

Barreto, M., & Ellemers, N. (2002). The impact of respect versus neglect of self identities on identification and group loyalty. *Personality and Social Psychology Bulletin, 28,* 629–639.

Bishop, B., Colquhoun, S., & Johnson, G. (2006). Psychological sense of community: An Australian Aboriginal experience. *Journal of Community Psychology, 34*(1), 1–7.

Borman, W. C., & Penner, L. A. (2001). Citizenship performance: Its nature, antecedents, and motives. In B. W. Roberts & R. Hogan (Eds.), *Personality psychology in the workplace* (pp. 45–61). Washington, DC: American Psychological Association.

Brief, A. P., & Weiss, H. M. (2002). Organizational behavior: Affect in the workplace. *Annual Review of Psychology, 53,* 279–307.

Callero, P. L. (1985). Role-identity salience. *Social Psychology Quarterly, 48,* 203–214.

Callero, P. L., Howard, J. A., & Piliavin, J. A. (1987). Helping behavior as role behavior: Disclosing social structure and history in the analysis of prosocial action. *Social Psychology Quarterly, 50,* 247–256.

Cantillona, D., Davidson, W. S., & Schweitzer, J. H. (2003). Measuring community social organization: Sense of community as a mediator in social disorganization theory. *Journal of Criminal Justice, 31*(4), 321–339.

Charng, H., Piliavin, J. A., & Callero, P. L. (1988). Role identity and reasoned action. *Social Psychology Quarterly, 51,* 303–317.

Clary, E. G., & Snyder, M. (1995). Motivations for volunteering and giving: A functional approach. In C. H. Hamilton & W. F. Ilchman (Eds.), *Cultures of giving II: How heritage, gender, wealth, and values influence philanthropy* (pp. 111–123). San Francisco: Jossey-Bass Publishers.

Clary, E. G., & Snyder, M. (1999). The motivations to volunteer: Theoretical and practical considerations. *Current Directions in Psychological Science, 8*(5), 156–159.

Clary, E. G., Snyder, M., Ridge, R. D., Copeland, J. T., Stukas, A. A., Haugen, J. A., & Miene, P. K. (1998). Understanding and assessing the motivations of volunteers: A functional approach. *Journal of Personality and Social Psychology, 74,* 1516–1530.

Clary, E. G., Snyder, M., Ridge, R. D., Miene, P. K., & Haugen, J. A. (1994). Matching messages to motives in persuasion: A functional approach to promoting volunteerism. *Journal of Applied Social Psychology, 24*(13), 1129–1149.

Clary, E. G., Snyder, M., & Stukas, A. A. (1996). Volunteers' motivations: Findings from a national survey. *Nonprofit and Voluntary Sector Quarterly, 25*(4), 485–505.

Clary, E. G., Snyder, M., & Stukas, A. A. (1998). Service-learning and psychology: Lessons from the psychology of volunteers' motivations. In R. G. Bringle & D. K. Duffy (Eds.), *With service in mind: Concepts and models for service-learning in psychology* (pp. 35–50). Washington, DC: American Association of Higher Education.

Colombo, M., Mosso, C., & De Piccoli, N. (2001). Sense of community and participation in urban contexts. *Journal of Community and Applied Social Psychology, 11*(6), 457–464.

Colombo, M., & Senatore, A. (2005). The discursive construction of community identity. *Journal of Community and Applied Social Psychology, 15*(1), 48–62.

Crain, A. L., Omoto, A. M., & Snyder, M. (1998, April). *What if you can't always get what you want? Testing a functional approach to volunteerism.* Paper presented at the annual meeting of the Midwestern Psychological Association, Chicago, IL.

Crocker, J., & Luhtanen, R. (1990). Collective self-esteem and ingroup bias. *Journal of Personality and Social Psychology, 58*, 60–67.

Cropanzano, R., & Byrne, Z. S. (2000). Workplace justice and the dilemma of organizational citizenship. In M. Van Vugt, M. Snyder, T. Tyler, & A. Biel (Eds.), *Cooperation in modern society: Promoting the welfare of communities, states, and organizations* (pp. 142–161). London: Routledge.

Curtis, J. E., Grabb, E., & Baer, D. (1992). Voluntary association membership in fifteen countries: A comparative analysis. *American Sociological Review, 57*, 139–152.

Davis, M. H., Hall, J. A., & Meyer, M. (2003). The first year: Influences on the satisfaction, involvement, and persistence of new community volunteers. *Personality and Social Psychology Bulletin, 29*, 248–260.

Davis, M. H., Mitchell, K. V., Hall, J. A., Lothert, J., Snapp, T., & Meyer, M. (1999). Empathy, expectations, and situational preferences: Personality influences on the decision to participate in volunteer helping behaviors. *Journal of Personality, 67*, 469–503.

De Cremer, D., & Van Vugt, M. (1999). Social identification effects in social dilemmas: A transformation of motives. *European Journal of Social Psychology, 29*, 871–893.

Devine-Wright, P., & Lyons, E. (1997). Remembering pasts and representing places: The construction of national identities in Ireland. *Journal of Environmental Psychology, 17*, 33–45.

Dixon, J., & Durrheim, K. (2004). Dislocating identity: Desegregation and the transformation of place. *Journal of Environmental Psychology, 24*, 455–473.

Gaertner, S. L., & Dovidio, J. F. (2000). *Reducing intergroup bias: The common ingroup identity model*. Philadelphia: Psychology Press.

Harlow, R. E., & Cantor, N. (1996). Still participating after all these years: A study of life task participation in later life. *Journal of Personality and Social Psychology, 71*, 1235–1249.

Hill, J. L. (1996). Psychological sense of community: Suggestions for future research. *Journal of Community Psychology, 24*(4), 431–438.

Houle, B. J., Sagarin, B. J., & Kaplan, M. F. (2005). A functional approach to volunteerism: Do volunteer motives predict task preference? *Basic and Applied Social Psychology, 27*, 337–344.

Independent Sector. (1988). *Giving and volunteering in the United States: Findings from a national survey*. Washington, DC: Author.

Independent Sector. (2002). *Giving and volunteering in the United States: Findings from a national survey*. Washington, DC: Author.

Katz, D. (1964). The motivational basis of organizational behavior. *Behavioral Science, 9*, 131–133.

Kim, J., & Kaplan, R. (2004). Physical and psychological factors in sense of community: New urbanist Kentlands and nearby Orchard Village. *Environment and Behavior, 36*(3), 313–340.

Kiviniemi, M. T., Snyder, M., & Omoto, A. M. (2002). Too many of a good thing? The effects of multiple motivations on stress, cost, fulfillment and satisfaction. *Personality and Social Psychology Bulletin, 28*(6), 732–743.

Klandermans, B. (1984). Mobilization and participation: Social psychological explanations of resource mobilization theory. *American Sociological Review, 49*, 583–600.

Klandermans, B. (1997). *The social psychology of protest*. Oxford, UK: Basil Blackwell.

Klandermans, B., & Oegema, D. (1987). Potentials, networks, motivations, and barriers: Steps toward participation in social movements. *American Sociological Review, 52*, 519–531.

Knez, I. (2005). Attachment and identity as related to a place and its perceived climate. *Journal of Environmental Psychology, 25*(2), 207–218.

Korpela, K. M. (1989). Place-identity as a product of environmental self-regulation. *Journal of Environmental Psychology, 9,* 241–256.

Krupat, E. (1983). A place for place identity. *Journal of Environmental Psychology, 3,* 343–344.

Lalli, M. (1992). Urban-related identity: Theory, measurement, and empirical findings. *Journal of Environmental Psychology, 12,* 285–303.

Loomis, C., Dockett, K. H., & Brodsky, A. E. (2004). Change in sense of community: An empirical finding. *Journal of Community Psychology, 32*(1), 1–8.

Lounsbury, J. W., Loveland, J. M., & Gibson, L. W. (2003). An investigation of psychological sense of community in relation to Big Five personality traits. *Journal of Community Psychology, 31*(5), 531–541.

Mashek, D., Cannaday, L. W., & Tangney, J. P. (2007). Inclusion of community in self scale: A single-item pictorial measure of community connectedness. *Journal of Community Psychology, 35*(2), 257–275.

McMillan, D. W. (1996). Sense of community. *Journal of Community Psychology, 24,* 315–325.

McMillan, D. W., & Chavis, D. M. (1986). Sense of community: A definition of theory. *Journal of Community Psychology, 14,* 6–23.

O'Brien, L. T., Crain, A. L., Omoto, A. M., & Snyder, M. (2000, May). *Matching motivations to outcomes: Implications for persistence in service.* Paper presented at the annual meeting of the Midwestern Psychological Association, Chicago, IL.

Obst, P. L., & White, K. M. (2005). An exploration of the interplay between psychological sense of community, social identification and salience. *Journal of Community and Applied Social Psychology, 15*(2), 127–135.

Oishi, S., Rothman, A. J., Snyder, M., Su, J., Zehm, K., Hertel, A., Gonzales, M. H., & Sherman, G. D. (2007). The social-ecological model of pro-community action: The benefits of residential stability. *Journal of Personality and Social Psychology, 93,* 831–844.

Okun, M. A. (1994). The relation between motives for organizational volunteering and frequency of volunteering by elders. *Journal of Applied Gerontology, 13,* 115–126.

Omoto, A. M., & Snyder, M. (1993). AIDS volunteers and their motivations: Theoretical issues and practical concerns. *Nonprofit Management and Leadership, 4,* 157–176.

Omoto, A. M., & Snyder, M. (1995). Sustained helping without obligation: Motivation, longevity of service, and perceived attitude change among AIDS volunteers. *Journal of Personality and Social Psychology, 68,* 671–686.

Omoto, A. M., & Snyder, M. (1999). [A longitudinal study of AIDS volunteers.] Unpublished raw data, University of Kansas, Lawrence.

Omoto, A. M., & Snyder, M. (2002). Considerations of community: The context and process of volunteerism. *American Behavioral Scientist, 45*(5), 846–867.

Omoto, A. M., & Snyder, M. (2010). Influences of psychological sense of community on voluntary helping and prosocial action. In S. Stuermer & M. Snyder (Eds.), *The psychology of prosocial behavior: Group processes, intergroup relations, and helping* (pp. 224–243). Oxford, UK: Blackwell.

Omoto, A. M., Snyder, M., & Martino, S. C. (2000). Volunteerism and the life course: Investigating age-related agendas for action. *Basic and Applied Social Psychology, 22,* 181–198.

Organ, D. W. (1988). *Organizational citizenship behavior: The good soldier syndrome.* Lexington, MA: Lexington Books.

Penner, L. A., & Finkelstein, M. A. (1998). Dispositional and structural determinants of volunteerism. *Journal of Personality and Social Psychology, 74,* 525–537.

Penner, L. A., Midili, A. R., & Kegelmeyer, J. (1997). Beyond job attitudes: A personality and social psychology perspective on the causes of organizational citizenship behaviors. *Human Performance, 10*, 111–132.

Peterson, N. A., Speer, P. W., & Hughey, J. (2006). Measuring sense of community: A methodological interpretation of the factor structure debate. *Journal of Community Psychology, 34*(4), 453–469.

Piliavin, J. A., & Callero, P. L. (1991). *Giving blood: The development of an altruistic identity.* Baltimore: Johns Hopkins University Press.

Piliavin, J. A., Grube, J. A., & Callero, P. L. (2002). Role as a resource for action in public service. *Journal of Social Issues, 58*, 469–485.

Prezza, M., & Costantini, S. (1998). Sense of community and life satisfaction: Investigation in three different territorial contexts. *Journal of Community and Applied Social Psychology, 8*, 181–194.

Proescholdbell, R. J., Roosa, M. W., & Nemeroff, C. J. (2006). Component measures of psychological sense of community among gay men. *Journal of Community Psychology, 34*(1), 9–24.

Proshansky, H. M., Fabian, A. K., & Kaminoff, R. (1983). Place-identity: Physical world socialization of the self. *Journal of Environmental Psychology, 3*, 57–83.

Puddifoot, J. E. (2003). Exploring "personal" and "shared" sense of community identity in Durham City, England. *Journal of Community Psychology, 31*(1), 87–106.

Rioux, S. M., & Penner, L. A. (2001). The causes of organizational citizenship behavior: A motivational analysis. *Journal of Applied Psychology, 36*, 1306–1314.

Sarason, S. B. (1974). *The psychological sense of community: Prospects for a community psychology.* San Francisco: Jossey-Bass.

Simon, B., Stuermer, S., & Steffens, K. (2000). Helping individuals or group members? The role of individual and collective identification in AIDS volunteerism. *Personality and Social Psychology Bulletin, 26*, 497–506.

Smith, D. M., Omoto, A. M., & Snyder, M. (2001, June). *Motivation matching and recruitment of volunteers: A field study.* Paper presented at the annual meeting of the American Psychological Society, Toronto, Canada.

Snyder, M. (1993). Basic research and practical problems: The promise of a "functional" personality and social psychology. *Personality and Social Psychology Bulletin, 19*, 251–264.

Snyder, M., & Cantor, N. (1998). Understanding personality and social behavior: A functionalist strategy. In D. T. Gilbert, S. T. Fiske, & G. Lindzey (Eds.), *The handbook of social psychology* (Vol. 1, 4th ed., pp. 635–679). Boston: McGraw-Hill.

Snyder, M., & Clary, E. G. (2004). Volunteerism and the generative society. In E. de St. Aubin, D. P. McAdams, & T. Kim (Eds.), *The generative society: Caring for future generations* (pp. 221–237). Washington, DC: American Psychological Association.

Snyder, M., Clary, E. G., & Stukas, A. A. (2000). The functional approach to volunteerism. In G. R. Maio & J. M. Olson (Eds.), *Why we evaluate: Functions of attitudes* (pp. 365–393). Mahwah, NJ: Lawrence Erlbaum.

Snyder, M., & Omoto, A. M. (2000). Doing good for self and society: Volunteerism and the psychology of citizen participation. In M. Van Vugt, M. Snyder, T. R. Tyler, & A. Biel (Eds.), *Cooperation in modern society: Promoting the welfare of communities, states and organizations* (pp. 127–141). New York: Routledge.

Snyder, M., & Omoto, A. M. (2007). Social action. In A. W. Kruglanski & E. T. Higgins (Eds.), *Social psychology: A handbook of basic principles* (2nd ed., pp. 940–961). New York: Guilford.

Snyder, M., & Omoto, A. M. (2008). Volunteerism: Social issues perspectives and social policy implications. *Social Issues and Policy Review, 2*, 1–36.

Snyder, M., Omoto, A. M., & Lindsay, J. J. (2004). Sacrificing time and effort for the good of others: The benefits and costs of volunteerism. In A. G. Miller (Ed.), *The social psychology of good and evil* (pp. 444–468). New York: Guilford.

Snyder, M., Omoto, A. M., & Smith, D. M. (2009). The role of persuasion strategies in motivating individual and collective action. In E. Borgida, C. Federico, & J. Sullivan (Eds.), *The political psychology of democratic citizenship* (pp. 125–150). New York: Oxford University Press.

Stuermer, S., & Kampmeier, C. (2003). Active citizenship: The role of community identification in community volunteerism and local participation. *Psychologica Belgica, 43,* 103–122.

Stuermer, S., Simon, B., Loewy, M., & Joerger, H. (2003). The dual pathway model of social movement participation: The case of the fat acceptance movement. *Social Psychology Quarterly, 66,* 71–82.

Stuermer, S., Snyder, M., Kropp, A., & Siem, B. (2006). Empathy-motivated helping: The moderating role of group membership. *Personality and Social Psychology Bulletin, 32*(7), 943–956.

Stuermer, S., Snyder, M., & Omoto, A. M. (2005). Prosocial emotions and helping: The moderating role of group membership. *Journal of Personality and Social Psychology, 88*(3), 532–546.

Stukas, A. A., Snyder, M., & Clary, E. G. (1999). The effects of "mandatory volunteerism" on intentions to volunteer. *Psychological Science, 10*(1), 59–64.

Tajfel, H., & Turner, J. C. (1986). The social identity theory of intergroup behavior. In S. Worchel & W. G. Austin (Eds.), *Psychology of intergroup relations* (pp. 7–24). Chicago: Nelson-Hall.

Tartaglia, S. (2006). A preliminary study for a new model of sense of community. *Journal of Community Psychology, 34*(1), 25–36.

Teske, N. (1997). *Political activists in America: The identity construction model of political participation.* Cambridge: Cambridge University Press.

Thomas, G. C., Batson, D. C., & Coke, J. S. (1981). Do good Samaritans discourage helpfulness? Self-perceived altruism after exposure to highly helpful others. *Journal of Personality and Social Psychology, 40*(1), 194–200.

U.S. Bureau of Labor Statistics. (2008, January 23). *Volunteering in the United States, 2007.* Retrieved from http://www.bls.gov/news.release/volun.nr0.htm

Uzzell, D., Pol, E., & Badenas, D. (2002). Place identification, social cohesion, and environmental sustainability. *Environment and Behavior, 34*(1), 26–53.

Verba, S., Schlozman, K. L., & Brady, H. E. (1995). *Voice and equality: Civic voluntarism in American politics.* Cambridge, MA: Harvard University Press.

8

Understanding the Psychology of Trust

DAVID DUNNING and DETLEF FETCHENHAUER

*I*n January 1985, at the height of the cold war, Mikhail Gorbachev, secretary of the Communist Party of the Soviet Union, sent an intriguing letter to President Ronald Reagan of the United States of America. In it, he proposed the complete elimination, within 15 years, of the thousands of nuclear missiles that the two countries had pointed at each other. Fueled somewhat by public relations motives, offers and counteroffers began flying between the two countries, but progress was so marked and potentially so real that the two sides agreed to meet for two days face-to-face in Hofdi House, a villa outside of Reykjavik, Iceland.

In two days of intense meetings, the prospect of a radical reduction in nuclear missiles came closer and closer—but stopped on at least one major sticking point. The United States had recently begun a missile defense system, dubbed "Star Wars," that President Reagan was reluctant to give up. He offered to confine Star Wars to research and testing for 10 years, sharing the results of that research with the Soviet Union, after which both sides could deploy the missile "shields" that would have been developed. Gorbachev insisted that such research be constrained to the laboratory, but the Americans disagreed.

Frustrated, the Soviets ended the talks, saying, as Soviet aide Gyorgy Arbatov noted later, that the Americans' proposal to continue Star Wars would require an exceptional level of faith in the benevolence and honesty of the United States that the Soviets were not prepared to give. Would the Americans share all the results of their missile defense research with the Soviets? Would the United States allow the Soviet Union to match the strength of the missile defense system that they proposed to build? Gorbachev, walking to his limousine at the end of the talks, asked Reagan what else he could have done. Reagan tersely responded that he could have said "yes." With that, the two sides drove off to their respective airplanes to fly back to their respective capitals surrounded by their expansive missile defenses.

The cold war and its tensions would continue for another five years, with the missiles that could have been destroyed if an agreement had been reached remaining far longer.

In the end, the question of whether those missiles would have been destroyed was not an issue of physics. Neither was it an issue of technology or of governmental expense. Instead, the question had rested squarely on a human assessment— whether the other side could be trusted to live up to its agreements. In a bold agreement to eliminate nuclear weapons, could the other side be trusted to respond to one's disarmament with reciprocal disarmament, or would it cheat?

Although the stakes are rarely as high as they were during the Reykjavik summit, this assessment of trust is one that people must make several times a day in their social lives, whether that assessment be aimed at their friends, lesser acquaintances, or total strangers. This chapter focuses on this ubiquitous human decision. When do people extend their trust to others, and when do they withhold it? What motivates a decision to give or withhold trust?

DEFINING TRUST

In focusing on trust, we acknowledge that the term has many meanings, depending on the specific context one is talking about. Trust, for example, can more specifically refer to whether people believe others will fulfill their promises, tell the truth, or live up to agreements that they have made (Hosmer, 1995; Lewicki, McAllister, & Bies, 1998; McKnight & Chervany, 2001). Trust can be defined by the beliefs people have of others, or it can be defined by the actual choices people make in their dealings with others. People can be said to trust the intentions of others, or they can be more restrictive and trust other people only when they think others have good intentions and the competence to execute those intentions. Trust and distrust can be said to be opposites of one another or be behaviors that can occur at the same time—such as when politicians give background information to a reporter and then worry that the information might be misused (Lewicki et al., 1998).

In this chapter, we define trust in the way that it is typically defined in current work in psychology and economics, focusing on elements of trust that are common across most definitions of the concept (McKnight & Chervany, 2001). Trust, under that definition, is the willingness to make one's self vulnerable to another person in order to achieve some potential benefit. It is the willingness to run the risk of exploitation by another person in the hope that the other person will honor that trust rather than abuse it (Rousseau, Sitkin, Burt, & Camerer, 1998). One can become vulnerable in many ways. One can tell another person a secret, trusting him or her not to tell others. One can invest in a business venture, trusting that the other person will honestly report back with the gains or losses that the venture achieves. A couple can swap houses with another couple from a different town, trusting that each will leave the houses in question no less worse for wear.

The importance of trust is abundantly clear in many social contexts. Its importance for international relations, as in the previous example regarding the Reykjavik summit, is obvious—as is its significance in more personal and mundane settings. It is difficult to conceive of two people carrying on a successful marriage, for example, without each partner trusting the other to handle the financial affairs in a responsible way (in addition to making sure just not to have affairs). It is equally difficult to imagine a business thriving without supervisors and employees who trust one another in their dealings (Kramer, 1998).

UNDERSTANDING TRUST

Psychologists and sociologists have long acknowledged the importance of trust for building and maintaining harmonious and beneficial social relationships (Fehr, 1988; Holmes & Rempel, 1989; Miller & Rempel, 2004; Ostrom & Walker, 2003; see Simpson, 2007, for a recent review). Morton Deutsch (1958), for example, noted that without trust, one was left in a state of suspicion—and that any conflict between two individuals would be difficult to resolve if every move was greeted with doubt and disbelief on the part of the other. Beverly Fehr (1988) counted trust as one of the 12 essential components of love (along with such qualities as caring, honesty, and respect).

We feel, however, that given its importance in social relations, trust is an action that has been surprisingly understudied and not well understood by researchers in the behavioral sciences. Recent reviewers agree:

> One might suspect that [trust] has received widespread theoretical and empir-ical attention. Though there have been significant pockets of theory ... on trust, surprisingly little is known about how trust develops, how it is main-tained, how it shapes and interacts with major interpersonal processes (e.g., the development of intimacy and closeness) and outcomes (e.g., relationship satisfaction and stability), and how it unraveled when betrayed. (Simpson, 2007, p. 587)

But we would go further than this statement. Research psychologists have yet to identify all the various ways in which trust plays an essential role in daily social life. To date, the research has been focused on the development of trust within one-on-one relationships, usually long-term and intimate ones, such as marriage or friendship. However, each day, with perfect strangers, people act on incidental instances of trust. They hand their credit card over to a server in a restaurant in order to pay for their meal. They mail off their check to a complete stranger who just offered to sell them something on eBay. They drop their car keys off at an auto mechanic they presume will complete the correct repair and then charge the appropriate price for it.

Scholars in fields adjacent to psychology have delineated just how important acts of trust—essentially between strangers or casual acquaintances—are to ensuring a society and an economy that prospers and thrives. Political theorists have pointed out that democracies flourish only to the extent that voters trust candidates to protect their interests and pursue policies that at least bear some relationship to the proposals they campaigned on (Fukuyama, 1995; Sullivan & Transue, 1999). Economies grow only to the extent that people exhibit trust in their contracts and then honor the trust that is placed in them (Putnam, 1993).

In fact, those countries whose citizens display higher levels of trust in business dealings tend to have higher economic growth rates than those countries whose citizens do not (Knack & Keefer, 1997).

OBSERVING TRUST IN ECONOMIC GAMES

In our investigations of trust, we borrowed and adapted a paradigm from economics that asks people if they wish to take a gamble on another person—making themselves vulnerable to exploitation by that person, but with the promise of potential monetary gain, depending on what the other person decides to do. The game is a simple one, although it comes in many variations, and it focuses on the decision to trust another person for whom one has no information. In the behavioral economics literature, the game is known as either the *trust* game or the *investment* game (Berg, Dickhaut, & McCabe, 1995; Camerer, 2003; Croson & Buchan, 1999; Kreps, 1990).

In our version of it, we present participants with, for example, $5 and then offer them a deal they may wish to take up. Participants can decide to keep their $5, or they can decide to give it to some randomly chosen person, whose identity they will never come to know. If a participant gives the $5 to the other person, we will add $15 to make a total of $20 and then give that amount to the other person. That other person will then have a choice: He or she can decide to keep the entire $20 or to give $10 back to the original person—whose identity is just as hidden as his or her own is. The key question is whether participants choose to make themselves vulnerable to another person by giving up their $5 in order to achieve a potential profit or to keep the $5 and play it safe. In a sense, this situation strips some aspects of trust to its core elements of vulnerability and potential gain—in doing so it suggests some tentative core conclusions about what motivates people to trust others.

The Paradox of Trust

We focus closely on the factors that motivate people to trust in this situation because of a simple paradox that becomes blatantly clear as one reviews Western intellectual thought on this matter. Trusting others is essential for the successful conduct of human relationships, but classic analyses of trust have concluded that people should not do it. If one examines the writings of several philosophers, such as Socrates and Plato, one finds that they distrusted trust. And their successors, such as, for example, Machievelli (1515/2003) in his classic *The Prince* and Hobbes (1660/1997) in his equally classic *Leviathan*, stated that trust was something one should rarely, if ever, do. These philosophers concluded that trust was a misbegotten choice because of their belief about human nature. If other people largely act out of their own material self-interest, then any decision to trust those others will be met with exploitation, loss, and betrayal. Other people, if they acted rationally, were not to be trusted—unless, of course, they could be forced to reciprocate that trust or be subject to severe penalties if they decided not to.

Neoclassical economics—focused exclusively on how people manage their material self-interest—has largely concurred with this analysis. If other people think only of themselves, one should be wary of trusting them, for they will surely exploit any trust shown to them. What should a person holding the original $5 do? The person should always keep it. This is because of the likely behavior of the second person. If the second person is given $20, he or she should keep it—in that there is no penalty for acting in a selfish way. The other person will never know who took the $5, and thus there is no risk of retribution or even loss of reputation. Thus, if the second person's self-interest will lead him or her to keep the $20, the original person should never give up the $5 in the first place.

Rates of Trust

However, studies of economic games such as this have discovered that some people do choose to hand over money to the second person, even when that second person is a complete stranger, in violation of the neoclassical analysis. Further vexing the economic analysis, people playing the role of the second person often give money back even though they are under no compulsion to do so (Berg et al., 1995; Bolle, 1998; Buchan, Croson, & Dawes, 2002; Snijders & Keren, 2001). This behavior has been observed across many cultures (Croson & Buchan, 1999), even when the stakes are high. When the amount of money the original person has in hand is nearly 5% of the average income for a person in his or her country, people on average hand over more than a third of the money they have been given (Johansson-Stenman, Mahmud, & Martinsson, 2005).

In our own studies, involving experiments conducted in New York, the Netherlands, and Germany, we have seen that trust behavior happens at a rate well above zero. In experiments in which we approach participants with $5 in the United States (or similar amounts of money in Europe), we have seen up to 70% of our participants volunteer to give the money to another person whom they do not know, with the lowest trust level we have observed hovering around 50% (Fetchenhauer & Dunning, 2009; Schlösser, Fetchenhauer, & Dunning, 2008). Clearly, whatever people are doing, they are not reaching for their calculators, plugging in some form of a Nash equilibrium equation, and then choosing whatever the calculator says. Something else is going on.

Explaining Trust: Two Possibilities

There are two possible general answers to what could be going on. The first is that people are actually being rational. To be sure, the neoclassical economic analysis may suggest that the second person, the one considering what to do with the $20, will always choose selfishly, but people know differently. They know that their peers do not always choose the strictly self-interested option. Instead, other people frequently act in altruistic and generous ways. Perhaps these expectations are accurate and high enough to justify handing over the money. In a phrase, this avenue toward trust would be, as termed by Becker (1996), the *cognitive route* to trust. That is, although economists might provide dismal estimates about the rate at which people would reciprocate trust, people might have expectations that their trust will be honored—and to the extent that people expect their trust will be honored, they will be more likely to give it.

The second avenue toward trust, according to Becker (1996), is that the decision to trust is *noncognitive* in nature. That is, whatever prompts people to give up the $5, it is not a calculation based on expectation and the worth, or utility, to the decision maker of gaining $10 rather than $5. The decision would be produced by other means—such as just an unbending habit of providing trust. To some extent, the forces that are noncognitive are quite numerous relative to those that fall on the cognitive side of the categorization. However, one noncognitive candidate, to be discussed below, likely to be influential in trust decisions is *emotion*. That is, people do not dispassionately calculate their way toward a decision to trust. Instead, their decision is inspired by the emotions they feel as they consider the decision.

TRUST AS RATIONAL

In a series of studies, we examined whether trust is a "rational" act. In this account, people know that there are others who would return money in the trust game, and they decide to trust because their expectation of reciprocity is sufficiently high to afford the gamble. There are two variations of this account. In the *strong* version, not only do people have sufficiently high expectations that others would honor their trust, but they are accurate about the rate that trust would be honored. That is, their expectations of their peers are largely accurate.

But more than that, when asked whether they will trust another person, they act in ways that are consistent with their tolerance for risk. For example, suppose that Ernie believed that there was a 55% chance that the other person would give back $10 if he gave up his original $5—and for purposes of this example, let's stipulate that this estimate is accurate. His decision to trust would be rational if he, in general, would take any 55% or lower gamble of $5 to win $10. That is, if someone gave him a lottery ticket with a 55% chance of winning (or something lower, like 50% or 40%), he would gamble on that, too. In this scenario, his decision to trust fits in his general willingness to take on risks. However, if he would not gamble on such a ticket—instead demanding that the odds on the ticket be higher before he would gamble—then he would not be rational if he decided to trust another person. His decision to trust would not "fit" the level of risk tolerance for a straightforward gamble. His decisions would not be consistent with one another.

The *weak* version of a rational, cognitive account would keep this requirement that people's decisions to trust be consistent with the level of risk tolerance they express elsewhere. However, it would relax the requirement that people accurately estimate the likelihood that their peers would honor trust. That is, people might act rationally based on what they believe—it is just that what they believe is wrong. For example, suppose Ernie, once again, believes that the chance that someone would reciprocate his trust is 55%. He finds those odds acceptable and, indeed, would gamble on a lottery just as easily as he decides to gamble on another person. This decision, given Ernie's beliefs and risk tolerance would be rational—but it would be weakly rational only if Ernie was wrong in his estimate of the rate at which people honor trust. If the true percentage of people who would give $10 back was only 40% or 20%, his decisions are rational in a sense, even if they lead to imperfect decisions—that is, decisions that differ from what Ernie would do if he knew the truth.

The Central Role of Expectations

In a sense, the rational, cognitive account of trust behavior marries together two different forms of trust, in that a person's decision to trust is predicated to a large extent on his or her expectations of peers. If people believe that peers are largely trustworthy, they will trust. If they are more wary, they will not. But the net effect is that the decision to trust is predominantly a function of their expectations about their peers.

One can see this fusing of expectation and behavior in social psychological theorizing about trust. Deutsch (1973) defined trust as the confidence that one would find what is desired in another rather than what one feared. Others have articulated similar ideas about the nature of trust, stating that trust involves, first and foremost, the belief that others will not act in self-interested ways but consider the welfare of others (Bacharach & Gambetta, 2001; Barber, 1983; Kramer & Carnevale, 2001; Pruitt & Rubin, 1986). Even the most widely used personality measure used to assess the degree to which people are trusting focuses almost exclusively on the cognitive component of expectation, with the assumption that with expectation will come the behavior. The Rotter (1967, 1971) Interpersonal Trust Scale asks, for example, whether the respondent believes that "trust is only asking for trouble" and that "other people have a vicious streak" and are "primarily interested in their own welfare" despite what they may say.

Work on intimate relationships echoes this assumption. According to theorists, people will trust their loved ones to the extent that they believe those others are committed to the relationship and will act to benefit all who are in it (Holmes & Rempel, 1989; Wieselquist, Rusbult, Foster, & Agnew, 1999). Attachment theorists also wed expectation to behavior in the production of trust. According to Mikulincer (1998b), for example, people who are brought up in households that promote secure attachments with other people leave those individuals with positive expectations about how they will be treated by others. With such optimistic beliefs in place, people are more willing to make themselves more vulnerable to others, including taking the risks associated with being close and intimate with another person.

In general, people do have some legitimate reasons to expect, and rely on, the kindness of strangers. Despite the products of economists' Nash equations, people do act in generous and other-regarding ways—and have many reasons to do so. Theorizing from evolutionary biology and economics provides the most fundamental reasons why people can expect their peers to act in selfless, prosocial ways. First, people may act in a selfless way to another individual to create an expectation that the other individual will return the favor sometime in the future, a principle known as *reciprocal altruism* (Trivers, 1971). Several species show such behavior.

Vampire bats, for example, share blood they have collected from their victims to other bats that have not collected blood in the expectation that this sharing will be reciprocated when circumstances are reversed. Of keynote is the precondition that bats (and people, as well) will punish those who fail to reciprocate.

Second, people act in prosocial ways to establish reputations as kind and generous people who are deserving of reciprocal favors. By helping another person—even one who cannot reciprocate—an individual signals to others that he or she can be trusted in mutually beneficial interactions (Nowack & Sigmund, 1998). In doing so, a person may sustain short-term costs, in that the receiver of his or her largesse cannot return any benefit at a future date, but the person gains in the long term because others, upon observing the altruistic behavior, will be more eager to assist that other person when they are in a position to do so.

Third, people live in a world of *strong reciprocity*. In most if not all human societies, people are surrounded by others who are eager to reward altruistic acts and to punish selfish ones—even if that reward or punishment comes at an irretrievable loss (Fehr, Fischbacher, & Gächter, 2002; Gintis, 2000). Theorists argue why strong reciprocity exists. Does it arise through evolution because it profits the individual, or rather the group or society the individual is in? Or does it arise through the social training people receive in childhood, but the net effect is that people live in a world that rewards selfless behavior, at least part of the time, as well as punishes self-centered behavior? Given this, it is not surprising that the rate of selfless behavior that people see in others is not the zero as proposed by Nash equations but substantively higher.

There is also ample evidence that people have rather accurate expectations about how likely their peers are to act in kind and generous ways. In a series of studies, Dunning and colleagues asked college students to estimate the percentage of their peers who will do admirable things—such as vote in an election; play nicely rather than aggressively in a laboratory economic game; volunteer for a tedious experiment so that a young girl will not have to; volunteer to read to the blind; buy a flower, baked goods, or a box of candy in a charity drive; donate blood; and stop for pedestrians when approaching a crosswalk—and found that people's predictions of their peers tend to be rather accurate, although their predictions about their *own behavior* is woefully distorted and self-serving (Balcetis & Dunning, 2008a, 2008b; Epley & Dunning, 2000, 2006). To be sure, their predictions about their peers are not exactly dead-on, but in the main people appear to have a rough sense of how the people around them will react to situations with moral overtones.

The (Lack of) Impact of Expectation

However, studies from our labs suggest that the decision to trust another person has little to do with expectations under any definition of rationality. Specifically, when we ask participants to estimate the percentage of their peers who would give money back, the typical response hovers under 50%. That is, on average, participants expect they will receive no money back from their peers. Yet, a large majority of them decide to give their $5 to a stranger.

They give that $5 even though they would not choose to risk that money if they were, instead, considering a game of chance. That is, in our studies, we present our participants with a lottery scenario. We ask them to imagine an urn filled with white and red ping-pong balls and that we will draw one ping-pong ball from the urn. If the ball is white, the participant wins $10; if it is red, they lose. We then ask them what percentage has to be white for them to gamble their $5 on a draw from the urn. Typically, participants are risk averse and require that something like 65% to 75% of the balls have to be winning ones. That is, our participants seem to be rather cautious when gambling on an urn but somewhat reckless when gambling on another person. In fact, when we look at the risk tolerance expressed by participants in the lottery scenario, we find that only 30% to 35% would accept the odds they cite as their chance of receiving money back in the trust game. The minimum chance of winning they require for the urn is lower than the chance they think they have that the second person will reciprocate their trust. For many participants who decide to trust, their decisions, instead, are inconsistent. They decide to trust the other person but would not gamble their $5 at the same odds if that other person transformed into an urn.

Other data show that people trust in ways that violate a strict definition of rationality. In one study, we gave participants $5 and asked them to make two economic decisions—one of which they would play for real. The first decision was whether they would gamble their $5 on an urn from which they had a 46% chance of winning. The second was whether they would trust another person coming from a group in which we knew there was a 46% chance that their trust would be reciprocated. The figure 46% was chosen because across many studies, that is the average estimate participants give that their trust would be honored in the $5/$20 scenario. Although the odds were the same, participants responded to each scenario quite differently. Only 28% were willing to gamble on the urn, but 56% were willing to give the money to some anonymous person in the trust game.

Five notes should be made about these results. First, it appears that the decision to trust is not merely a matter of expectation. That is, theorists are incorrect when they state that people will choose to trust if and when they possess positive expectations that others will reciprocate that trust. In our studies, we find a wide dissociation between expectation and behavior. People choose to trust another person even when they have little expectation that they will be rewarded for that trust. They accept a risk with another person that they would not accept in a simple game of chance. As a consequence, trust in action should not be assumed from trust in expectation. Even at low expectations, people seem to be willing to trust complete strangers.

To be sure, we have found across studies that positive expectations are correlated with decisions to trust—the more people believe that their trust will be reciprocated, the more they are willing to give up the $5—but that effect does not seem to be large. In the Fetchenhauer and Dunning (2009) study cited above, in which participants were asked if they would trust another person versus gamble on an urn when either had a 46% chance of reward, there was another condition in which the chance of reward was 80%. That had a large impact on participants' willingness to gamble on the urn. Whereas only 28% would gamble on an urn with a 46% chance of winning, that percentage rose to 78% when the chance of winning was 80%. However, for decisions to trust, the proportion of those choosing to trust a complete stranger rose only from 56% to 70%. In addition, across all our studies, the large effect that is most remarkable is that people are willing to trust even in situations in which they believe they are more likely to lose their $5 than to earn a profit. That is, up to 70% of participants are willing to trust, but at the same odds only 30% or so would accept a gamble on an urn.

Second, trust does not seem to be a matter of risk tolerance. One might assume that people might trust others more frequently if they tended to be risk takers, but at least two empirical findings speak against this assumption. First, decisions to trust are uncorrelated with a person's attitudes toward risk, with those avoidant of risk just as likely to trust as those tolerant of risk (Eckel & Wilson, 2004). Second, decisions to invest in another correlate with other measures of risk taking, but only if that other is a computer reaching its decisions by some random procedure. If the other is a person (even if randomly selected), decisions to trust again vary independently from the willingness to take on risks (Houser, Schunk, & Winter, 2006).

Third, trust behavior does not seem to fit either the strong or the weak definitions of rationality we described above. Whether or not people are accurate in their estimates of others, their decisions fail to fall in line with a consistent level of risk tolerance. People's decisions in the trust game are much more risk seeking than their decisions to gamble on a chance event. Thus, the decision to trust does not appear to be a rational calculation in which people gauge the likelihood that their trust will be honored and then consult whether that likelihood fits their general willingness to take a risk. When trust is involved, that calculation seems to play a minor part but hardly suffices as a primary explanation of what is going on.

Other Explanation: Do People Have a Taste for Benefiting Others?

Fourth, one plausible alternative explanation for the results described above does not seem to account for people's overall willingness to trust. One could argue that people decide to trust because they give weight to potential benefits they could give other people. That is, when gambling on the urn, only they can win. No other person is involved. However, in the trust game, someone else may gain money— people take that into account when they decide whether to trust. That is, they know that they may reduce their wealth and utility by choosing to trust, but they know that in the grand scheme of things, there will be more wealth and utility ($20 versus $5) spread out in the world—and they give that circumstance weight in their decisions.

Not only is this account plausible, but it is also pleasing to think that people may be motivated to act selflessly because they pay attention to the outcomes of other people, even if those other people are complete strangers. The fly in the ointment in this explanation, however, is that it does not fit other data that we have collected. In those data, we asked participants whether they would trust another person when the chance of receiving $10 back was 50%. A majority (64%) said they would. However, when we asked them whether they would bet their $5 on a flip of a coin, with a chance to win $10, far fewer participants (43%) were willing to do so.

Of key importance was a third condition. One can see in the coin flip scenario that participants could be influenced by only whether they themselves won or lost the coin flip. But what if we added in another person and inserted the same scheme of payoffs included in the trust game? Thus, in an "extended coin flip" scenario, we asked participants if they would be willing to gamble their $5 on a flip of a coin. We told them that if they won, not only would they receive $10 but some random unknown person would also receive $10. If they lost, that other person would receive $20. Did adding these potential benefits to another person make participants more willing to bet on the coin? The answer was a flat "no"; only 42% decided to flip the coin—a percentage almost identical to the proportion willing to flip the coin with no other person involved.

A Note About Cynicism

Fifth, we must end by noting a remarkable irony in participants' estimates of how their peers would behave. On the whole, participants were rather cynical of their peers, thinking that a slight majority of their peers would just pocket the $20 and leave them with nothing. However, in reality, we have found that roughly 80% of peers decide to give $10 back—thus usually rewarding the level of trust that has been placed in them. Thus, although participants make decisions to trust that seem to violate their expressed tolerance for risk, they tend to be rewarded for making such "irrational" decisions.

We should note that future work should focus on why participants tend to be so wrong about their peers, thinking that less than 50% will give money back when the true odds hover much higher. This undue cynicism is even more remarkable given a growing body of evidence that people tend to be rather accurate about their peers (Balcetis & Dunning, 2008a, 2008b; Epley & Dunning, 2000, 2006; see also Nisbett & Kunda, 1985). What is it about the trust situation that draws out a heavy dose of cynicism that is not evident in other contexts?

TRUST AS EMOTIONAL

Voluminous research in psychology over the past few decades has increasingly shown that people reach their decision via two very different routes (Chaiken & Trope, 1999). The route assumed by economists, and the one featured in the discussion above, is one of conscious, deliberate calculation. People consider the payoffs associated with various choices, and then note the probabilities of attaining those payoffs, before making a choice. Under this framework, the decision to trust is a product of an effortful piece of analysis. The other route, not necessarily considered by economists, is one that is much quicker and automatic. People come to a decision as a gut reaction to the choices in front of them. Very little, or no, calculation is involved. Instead, the decision just "happens to the person" in, as Becker (1996) termed it, a "non-cognitive way."

Social Decisions as Analytical Versus Emotional

Often, this quicker, more automatic route to a decision can involve emotion. Consider, as an example, two variations of a scenario receiving much attention in an emerging literature about moral decision making. A person is standing on a bridge near a trolley track and sees a trolley barreling down on a group of five people who are working on the track. It is clear that the trolley will kill these five workers unless something is done, and there is no way to warn the workers in time. However, the person happens to be standing near a switch that would direct the trolley to a different track, sparing the five workers but regrettably killing a single worker who happens to be on the other track. Does the person throw the switch? Most people, reluctantly, say that they would. Throwing the switch kills one but does save five, and the calculation, although tragic, seems to be the moral alternative to take.

But let us alter the decision in one way, removing the switch from the scenario but adding a rather large man that the person could push onto the trolley tracks to spare the five. Would people do it? Under this scenario, most people say no, and their responses appear to be emotionally based rather than based on calculation. People just have a gut revulsion to the act of pushing a person on a train track—although the calculus of the situation in terms of lives saved remains the same—and thus refuse to do it.

In a fundamental sense, the two variations of the trolley problem demonstrate the two routes to making a social decision. The first variation of the scenario pulls for conscious calculation about the consequences of one's act. The second variation pulls for a gut, emotional reaction. Neuroimaging studies affirm this. When individuals report how they would respond to the first variation of the trolley problem, more activity is seen in areas of the brain associated with deliberate and conscious thinking through the problem, such as the parietal lobes and the right middle front gyrus. When individuals are confronted with the second variation, more activity is seen in areas of the brain associated with emotion, such as the left and left angular gyrus, bilateral posterior cingulate cyrus, and bilateral medical frontal gyrus (Greene, Sommerville, Nystrom, Darley, & Cohen, 2001).

The Emotional Dimension in Decisions to Trust

Circumstantial evidence from our lab suggests that this distinction between emotional versus analytical routes to decision matter, in that trust decisions are driven more by emotion than rational calculus. Recall that raising the odds of receiving money back in one study from 46% to 80% had a dramatic impact on whether people gambled on drawing the right color of ping-pong ball from an urn but did not have such an impact on decisions to trust. This lack of impact on trust decisions is consistent with a decision based on emotion. In several studies, Hsee and colleagues have shown that decisions that elicit emotion are less sensitive to the odds of winning or losing than are decisions devoid of emotion. For example, Rottenstreich and Hsee (2001) were asked how much they would pay to avoid a loss of $20, a rather pallid event. The amount they would pay depended greatly on the size of the risk. However, when considering electric shock, participants paid roughly the same amount of money to avoid it regardless of the odds associated with the event. In a similar vein, when participants were considering how much to pay for a chance to win a $500 discount on their tuition, their prices once again varied greatly depending on the chances of winning. However, when the prize was a $500 coupon toward a dream vacation to Paris, the amount participants offered was relatively insensitive to the chances of winning.

Hypothetical Decisions Versus Real Decisions

Other evidence from our lab circumstantially implicates emotion in the decision to trust. A growing body of evidence suggests that people do not feel emotions full-bore until they are placed in a situation that calls for an actual decision. When the decision is hypothetical, their decisions are left relatively unswayed by emotion. For example, Van Boven and colleagues asked college students whether they would—hypothetically—dance in front of their psychology class to the classic funk tune "Sex Machine" by James Brown for $5. When the question was hypothetical, a full third of the class indicated that they would volunteer. However, when the decision was posed as an actual opportunity, less than 10% of the class volunteered, citing fear of embarrassment as the reason for their reluctance (Van Boven, Loewenstein, & Dunning, 2005).

We have found similarly that the hypothetical nature versus the actual nature of a decision to trust also influences people's choices. In one study, we asked participants to consider a hypothetical decision to trust another person with €7.50 that they had earned by taking part in an experiment, with a chance that the other person would return €15 back. In contrast to all our other studies, only roughly 30% of participants indicated they would trust the other person. However, in a condition in which participants knew they may have to act on their decisions to trust, participants opted to give their €7.50 to the other person over 50% of the time.

Curiously, and in contrast to much other work, people were opting to act in a more generous and prosocial way when the decision was a real one rather than a theoretical one. In all other work to date that we know of, the usual result is the opposite—people say they will act in a prosocial way when asked hypothetically, but their real behavior rarely rises to the lofty level their hypothetical forecasts indicate (e.g., Balcetis & Dunning, 2008a, 2008b; Epley & Dunning, 2000, 2006). Even more curiously, they trust more when making actual decisions even though at the same time they become significantly more risk-averse about betting on an urn, relative to what they state they will do when considering a merely hypothetical gamble.

This counterintuitive pattern of results is explicable if we assume that the decision to trust contains important emotional components, components that kick in only when the decision is a real one with actual consequences. When merely hypothetical, people do not feel the emotions that typically surround the decision to trust, and as a consequence they are more likely to make different choices. But this pattern is merely circumstantial—it suggests emotion without specifying what the emotion is or how it induces decisions to trust. Might there be more direct evidence that the decision to trust is emotional in nature?

Implicating Emotion in Trust

In more recent work in our lab, we have found such direct evidence for the potential role of emotion in trust behavior. If expectations predict trust only weakly, emotional variables provide much stronger predictions about who will trust. In one study, we presented participants with our usual trust game, telling them there was a 50% chance that their trust would be reciprocated. But before participants chose whether to trust, we asked them how they *felt* about the decision.

We actually did more than that, asking about two different layers of emotion that might have an influence on their decision to trust, following a distinction outlined by Loewenstein and others (Loewenstein, Weber, Hsee, & Welch, 2001). The first layer was the one that economists would most likely claim to have an impact on trust and involves the emotions people *anticipate* they will feel at the conclusion of the trust game, after they have made their decision and have discovered the return decision of the person they were paired with. These emotions are not immediate emotions felt at the time of the decision but rather the emotions that people forecast that they will feel after all is said and done. In all, we asked participants to anticipate how they would feel under four different scenarios: one in which they gave up their money and got money back, one where they gave up their money and received nothing back, one in which they kept the money but found out they would have received money back, and one in which they kept the money and found that the other person would have returned no money back. Participants rated how they would feel along three dimensions: pleasantness versus unpleasantness, calm versus aroused, and in control versus out of control.

We asked participants to describe their anticipated emotions because those emotions should be influential, according to many economic theories. That is, in part of the calculation that economists suggest that people do, people give weight to the emotional consequences of their decisions. They know they will derive utility from whether they feel happy, relieved, sad, guilty, or betrayed, for example, once their transaction with their trust game partner is done, and thus they factor the impact of these emotions into their decision (Mellers, Schwartz, Ho, & Ritov, 1997; Mellers, Schwartz, & Ritov, 1999). Economic theory has often emphasized the importance of these anticipated emotions, in particular highlighting the potential role played by regret (Bell, 1982; Loomes & Sugden, 1982) and disappointment (Bell, 1985; Loomes & Sugden, 1986).

The other layer of emotion is quite obvious and is the *immediate* emotion people feel at the moment they reach a decision. How do they viscerally feel about checking off that they want to keep the money? How do they feel about ticking the box indicating that they are going to give the money up? In our study, we asked participants to rate how they felt about these two actions along the pleasantness, arousal, and control dimensions described above.

Did either anticipated or immediate emotions predict who trusted and who did not? A close scrutiny of the data provided a clear answer. Immediate emotions mattered a great deal. After performing a cluster analysis, we found that participants' feelings about keeping versus giving their money fell into two neat groups for each action. In regard to keeping the money, some participants felt positive, relatively calm, and in control, whereas others felt neutral at best, aroused, and less in control. In regard to giving the money, two similar clusters emerged. The way cluster participants felt went a long way toward predicting who would trust and who would not. Those who felt positive about giving the money but more agitated about keeping it decided to trust 91% of the time. Those who felt positive about keeping the money and agitated about giving it trusted only 35% of the time. Those in the middle (feeling positive about either action or agitated about either choice) gave their money up 65% of the time (Schlösser et al., 2008).

In short, how people felt about their choices at the moment they considered them went a long way toward predicting what they would do. But what about their anticipated emotions? What role did these emotional forecasts play? The answer appeared to be that these anticipated emotions played no role at all. There was no correlation between how people projected they would feel and what decision they ultimately chose. This was true even though people were quite accurate in their projections about how they would feel. When the trust game was concluded, and participants found out how their trust partner had responded, the emotions they felt matched the predictions they had made about how they would feel.

Corroborating Neurophysiological Evidence

Other streams of research corroborate the assertion that the decision to trust is non-cognitive in nature and, more specifically, one involving emotion. Neurochemical evidence supports the notion of trust as an emotional act. Consider oxytocin, a hormone found in mammals—including humans—that often acts as a neurotransmitter in the brain. Oxytocin is associated with emotions that tend to facilitate social behavior and bonding. It is released when people touch or hug others, as well as during sexual activity (Carmichael, Warburton, Dixon, & Davidson, 1994). Oxytocin appears to facilitate the emotions surrounding positive social interaction, including love (Carter, 1998; Uvnas-Moberg, 1998), and promotes social attachment (Insel & Young, 2001). In sum, oxytocin appears to facilitate the tendency in people to approach others in a positive way, dispelling tendencies toward social anxiety and avoidance.

With this as background, it is fascinating to note that oxytocin has been implicated in trust behavior. People who are trusted often experience a surge in oxytocin, leading them to reciprocate trust at a higher rate (Zak, Kurzban, & Matzner, 2005). People who have a dose of oxytocin spritzed up their nose show higher rates of trust than those given a placebo (Kosfeld, Heinrichs, Zak, Fischbacher, & Fehr, 2005). Importantly, these doses of oxytocin do not cause people to take risks in general. Instead, their willingness to gamble on another person is specific to other people, not to the world in general. In a similar vein, people given oxytocin are also more generous with their peers in "ultimatum games," an economic game in which participants suggest a split of money to a partner that the partner can reject if he or she wishes (Zak, Stanton, & Ahmadi, 2007).

IMPLICATIONS AND NEW DIRECTIONS

The notion that trust decisions are not a matter of calculation but rather a matter of noncognitive factors, such as emotion, suggests several avenues for future research. The first avenue begins with the fact that our research, to date, as well as that of other researchers investigating the trust game, has focused on one-off, anonymous exchanges between strangers. How does trust behavior change if one changes this situation? How does trust arise when the interaction involves individuals who bear a longer-term relationship with each other? Let us consider each of these questions in turn.

Situational Context

In work to date, researchers have avoided providing any descriptive context surrounding the decisions that participants make, examining instead what context the participants themselves will bring to inform their decisions. But what if researchers stirred some context into the decision? A researcher could easily provide some context by describing the other person as a business associate, or explicitly as a fellow student, or as one's "partner." Each of these labels suggests different norms for appropriate behavior. Calling the other person a "business associate" likely suggests that the decision is just business and nothing personal and that the participant should choose the course of behavior that best profits them economically above all else. Terming the other person as a fellow student or partner suggests a personal context and likely pulls for considering the welfare of the other person rather than making a purely economic decision.

This speculation on context does rest on some data, in that how people approach the prisoner's dilemma game depends significantly on how it is labeled. The prisoner's dilemma game is much like the trust game, in that it is an economic game usually played with strangers that requires participants to choose whether to cooperate with that stranger or to "defect," that is, choose an option that may reward the participant greatly while punishing the stranger (Rapoport & Chammah, 1965). Whether participants choose to cooperate or defect depends on whether the game is labeled as a "community game," which pulls for cooperation, versus an "investment game," which pulls for more selfish choices based on economics (Kay & Ross, 2003; Liberman, Samuels, & Ross, 2004).

Labeling an economic game as a community game versus an investment game likely influences participants' behavior through several routes, such as suggesting different norms about what is the most appropriate behavior to pursue in the game (Kay & Ross, 2003; Liberman et al., 2004). However, given our work, it is interesting to speculate whether these norms have their impact because they change expectations about how another person in the game will react or because they change the emotional reactions that people have to the options laid before them. For example, giving a prisoner's dilemma the label of "community game" may cause people to believe that their partner is more likely to cooperate. Or it might make the act of cooperation more pleasant emotionally or the choice of defecting more unpleasant. Future work could explore both possibilities.

Such work, we think, would be important for other reasons. It is very likely that the decision to trust does depend on the specific context in which it takes place. Whether people trust, and what they base that trust on, may change significantly according to whether the choice takes place in the context of a romantic relationship, among friends, in a business partnership, between political allies or rivals, or within one's own group or between members of different groups—such as negotiators coming from different countries. Exploring the norms, expectations, and emotions that arise in each of these contexts may go a long way to help explicate the psychology behind trust.

The Minimal Connection Effect

With these notions of context in mind, we should mention one circumstance that we have discovered has an important impact on whether our participants decide to trust. That circumstance is whether participants have been bound into a relationship—no matter how anonymous, fleeting, or minimal—with the person they play the trust game with, a phenomenon we term the *minimal connection effect*. It appears that people approach the trust game differently when they as of yet have not been paired up to play the game with another individual than when that pairing has already taken place. If participants are asked for their decision knowing that their interaction partner has yet to be assigned, they decide to trust much less than if they are told that the assignment has already taken place. The power of being paired, or connected, with another individual is striking given that people will decide to trust that person even if they are further told that the other person does not know about the game and will not be informed if the participants decide to keep the $5. That is, even though the decision can be a purely private one that one's partner need not know about, a majority of participants still decide to hand over the $5. In a similar fashion, if the trust game is described as an interaction between the experimenter and the participant rather than as between the participant and another individual, participants again decide to trust much less (Fetchenhauer & Dunning, 2008b).

Other work on economic games provide related evidence that people approach their dealings with a single other individual differently than they do multiple ones. Camerer and Fehr (2006), for example, examined how participants approached the ultimatum game when they had been paired with a single individual versus when they confronted five individuals, one of whom was yet to be chosen as one's interaction partner. When only a single other individual was involved, participants opted to split the money they had equally, presumably because they were concerned about the norm of fairness. However, when participants knew that their interaction partner would come from a group of five, they treated the decision much more as a business one and offered much less to the interaction partner yet to be chosen.

The minimal connection effect makes sense if one construes the decision to trust as one involving more emotion than calculation. Whether one has been paired up with another individual already should not change expectations about whether a person will trust, and our data suggest that expectations do not change when another person is assigned to the participant (Fetchenhauer & Dunning, 2008b).

However, being paired up with another person may very well change the emotional profile of the decision. If one is considering a hypothetical decision that does not yet involve another person, it is likely that the emotions associated with that decision are not greatly stirred. However, once another person is involved, emotion can matter more—in that one can now imagine the other person and simulate how he or she might respond (Hsee & Weber, 1997).

Other work shows more directly that pairing someone with a single other individual moves the decision more squarely into the realm of emotion. Work on the *identifiable victim effect* shows that people are much more likely, because of sympathy, to help a single other individual once that person has been specified. In one example, researchers asked participants in the laboratory if they would be willing to give up some money they possessed to another participant who had lost his or her money. In one condition, that other was described as a person in another room who had yet to be randomly chosen, whereas in a second condition that person had already been chosen and the participant was shown that person's identification number. In that second condition, participants were much more willing to give money than they were the first. And in a follow-up experiment, participants were more likely to donate to Habitat to Humanity if the family their contribution would go to had already been assigned rather than if the family had yet to be assigned (Small & Loewenstein, 2003). These choices to donate more once a victim has been identified has been linked to expressions of sympathy, an emotion that does not arise as much if the specific victim to be helped remains as of yet unknown (Small, Loewenstein, & Slovic, 2007).

Trust in Intimate Relationships

Another important avenue for future research would be to cross the divide from studying trust between strangers to studying trust among intimates. Trust in interpersonal relationships, such as in marriage and other romantic relationships, is a topic about which much has been written (for a review, see Simpson, 2007). For example, major theoretical models of adult attachment all emphasize the central role played by trust in people's dealings with others (Bartholomew & Horowitz, 1991; Hazan & Shaver, 1987). People who are secure in their relationships with others tend to approach other people with faith for positive expectations. In contrast, people who are anxious or preoccupied in their interpersonal attachments tend to be uncomfortable and distrustful in their relationships, even though they tend to become overly dependent on their attachments. Fearful and avoidant individuals tend to avoid trusting others at all, preferring to be aloof so that they need not depend on others.

Might our work on trust between strangers say something about trust among intimates? We think there are two major observations from our work that might be useful to consider as researchers investigate attachment processes in interpersonal relations. The first observation centers on the lack of a strong role played by expectations in producing trust. Recall that previous researchers have tended to equate trust behavior with people's expectations about others. People trust to the extent that they expect that this trust will be reciprocated (Bacharach & Gambetta, 2001;

Barber, 1983; Deutsch, 1973; Kramer & Carnevale, 2001; Pruitt & Rubin, 1986; Rotter, 1967, 1971; Simpson, 2007). Our work, however, suggests that the decision to make one's self vulnerable to another person can be disconnected from beliefs that the other person will reward that decision. In many of our experiments, people chose to give $5 to a total stranger while fully expecting, on average, that they will receive nothing back.

We wonder if such dissociations between expectation and behavior also exist in interpersonal relationships. For example, might people who are preoccupied and anxious in their attachments still choose to trust other people yet be wary of whether that trust will be honored? Might avoidant people decline to trust even when they expect their trust will be reciprocated? From looking at the attachment literature, it appears that theorists tend to think that differential trust rates follow as a function of expectation. For example, avoidant people evade trust because they are pessimistic about the generosity of others. But perhaps that is not the case, and thus the behavior people pursue in their intimate relationships—and the emotions that surround that behavior—are better understood if researchers assess *both* expectation and behavior to see whether both align and to see how people react when they do not. For example, might the stress felt by individuals with a preoccupied or anxious attachment style be driven by the fact that these individuals choose to trust others yet fear that their trust will be exploited at a substantial rate?

The second observation from our research centers on the surprisingly strong role played by emotion in predicting who will trust. Does emotion in interpersonal relationships play a stronger role in trust behavior than expectation? Work on attachment, again, reveals just how central a role emotions play in intimate relationships. Avoidant individuals disengage from others in order to reduce stress. Preoccupied individuals work to reduce stress by eliciting signs of love and compassion from their intimate partners. Secure individuals, by contrast, appear to be able to withstand distress and, thus, are more willing to take chances with others (Mikulincer, 1998a). Perhaps trust behavior by people with different attachment styles arises not because of expectation but because of the emotions they wrap around their dealings with others. If a dominant emotion is distress when making oneself vulnerable to others, perhaps avoidant individuals will decide not to trust. If the emotions associated with positive interactions are more available to secure individuals, perhaps this will lead them to be more likely to trust others.

To date, we know of no research in the attachment tradition that has simultaneously looked at expectations, emotion, and trust behavior in people with different attachment styles. To be sure, research does show that securely attached individuals report more trusting relationships with their partners and more memories of trusting over the past three-week periods (Mikulincer, 1998b). Is this greater comfort and familiarity to trust produced by expectation or emotion? To what extent are both expectation and emotion involved? Future work on this topic may prove to be quite profitable.

CONCLUDING REMARKS

In 1986, President Ronald Reagan of the United States and Soviet General Secretary Mikhail Gorbachev walked away from a potentially historic agreement that would have eliminated the threat of mutual annihilation of each other's country, as well as the world as we know it. They did so out of a matter of trust.

In this chapter, we have reviewed work in our lab, and elsewhere, about the psychology of trust—at least as how it exists between two strangers considering a monetary transaction in an anonymous laboratory. This work has proved to reveal a few surprises. Trust need not be rational, in that it follows from an analytical calculation of the odds and payoffs present in a situation. Instead, trust appears to follow from noncognitive variables, such as emotion, that stand outside the usual scholarship and thinking about the topic. But we hasten to add that we construe our work, and that of others, as mere first steps toward an understanding of trust behavior. Given the surprises we have found already, we can trust that future research will reveal at least a few more. We look forward to that future work— both with expectation and with pleasure.

REFERENCES

Bacharach, M., & Gambetta, D. (2001). Trust in signs. In K. Cook (Ed.), *Trust in society* (Vol. 2, pp. 148–184). New York: Russell Sage Foundation.

Balcetis, E., & Dunning, D. (2008a). A mile in moccasins: How situational experience reduces dispositionism in social judgment. *Personality and Social Psychology Bulletin*, *34*, 102–114.

Balcetis, E., & Dunning, D. (2008b). *On the generality of the "holier than thou" phenomenon*. Unpublished manuscript, Ohio University.

Barber, B. (1983). *The logic and limits of trust*. New Brunswick, NJ: Rutgers University Press.

Bartholomew, K., & Horowitz, L. M. (1991). Attachment styles among young adults: A test of a four-category model. *Journal of Personality and Social Psychology*, *61*, 226–244.

Becker, L. C. (1996). Trust as noncognitive security about motives. *Ethics*, *107*, 43–61.

Bell, D. E. (1982). Regret in decision making under uncertainty. *Operations Research*, *30*, 961–981.

Bell, D. E. (1985). Disappointment in decision making under uncertainty. *Operations Research*, *33*, 1–27.

Berg, J., Dickhaut, J., & McCabe, K. (1995). Trust, reciprocity, and social history. *Games and Economic Behavior*, *10*, 122–142.

Bolle, F. (1998). Rewarding trust: An experimental study. *Theory and Decision*, *45*, 83–98.

Buchan, N. R., Croson, R. T. A., & Dawes, R. M. (2002). Swift neighbors and persistent strangers: A cross-cultural investigation of trust and reciprocity in social exchange. *American Journal of Sociology*, *108*, 168–206.

Camerer, C. F. (2003). *Behavioral game theory: Experiments on strategic interaction*. Princeton, NJ: Princeton University Press.

Camerer, C. F., & Fehr, E. (2006). When does "economic man" dominate social behavior? *Science*, *311*, 47–52.

Carmichael, M.S., Warburton, V.L., Dixen, J., & Davidson, J.M. (1994). Relationships among cardiovascular, muscular, and oxytocin responses during human sexual activity. *Archives of Sexual Behavior*, *23*, 59–79.

Carter, C. S. (1998). Neuroendocrine perspectives on social attachment and love. *Psychoneuroendocrinology, 23,* 779–818.

Chaiken, S., & Trope, Y. (Eds.). (1999). *Dual process theories in social psychology.* New York: Guilford.

Croson, R. T. A., & Buchan, N. R. (1999). Gender and culture: International experimental evidence from trust games. *American Economic Review, 89,* 386–391.

Deutsch, M. (1958). Trust and suspicion. *Conflict Resolution, 2,* 265–279.

Deutsch, M. (1973). *The resolution of conflict: Constructive and destructive processes.* New Haven, CT: Yale University Press.

Eckel, C., & Wilson, R. (2004). Is trust a risky decision? *Journal of Economic Behavior and Organization, 55,* 447–465.

Epley, N., & Dunning, D. (2000). Feeling "holier than thou": Are self-serving assessments produced by errors in self or social prediction? *Journal of Personality and Social Psychology, 79,* 861–875.

Epley, N., & Dunning, D. (2006). The mixed blessings of self-knowledge in behavioral prediction: Enhanced discrimination but exacerbated bias. *Personality and Social Psychology Bulletin, 32,* 641–655.

Fehr, B. (1988). Prototype analysis of the concepts of love and commitment. *Journal of Personality and Social Psychology, 4,* 557–579.

Fehr, E., Fischbacher, U., & Gächter, S. (2002). Strong reciprocity, human cooperation, and the enforcement of social norms. *Human Nature, 13,* 1–25.

Fetchenhauer, D., & Dunning, D. (2008a). *Betrayal aversion versus principled trustfulness: How to explain risk avoidance and risky choices in trust games.* Manuscript submitted for publication, University of Cologne.

Fetchenhauer, D., & Dunning, D. (2008b). *The minimal connection effect in decisions to trust.* Unpublished manuscript, University of Cologne.

Fetchenhauer, D., & Dunning, D. (2009). Do people trust too much or too little? *Journal of Economic Psychology, 30,* 263–276.

Fukuyama, F. (1995). *Trust: The social virtues and the creation of prosperity.* New York: Free Press.

Gintis, H. (2000). Strong reciprocity and human sociality. *Journal of Theoretical Biology, 206,* 169–179.

Greene, J. D., Sommerville, R. B., Nystrom, L. E., Darley, J. M., & Cohen, J. D. (2001). An fMRI investigation of emotional engagement in moral judgment. *Science, 293,* 2105–2108.

Hazan, C., & Shaver, P. (1987). Romantic love conceptualized as an attachment process. *Journal of Personality and Social Psychology, 52,* 511–524.

Hobbes, T. (1997). *The leviathan.* New York: Touchstone Press. (Original work published 1660)

Holmes, J. G., & Rempel, J. K. (1989). Trust in close relationships. In C. Hendrick (Ed.), *Review of personality and social psychology: Close relationships* (Vol. 10, pp. 187–219). Newbury Park, CA: Sage.

Hosmer, L. T. (1995). Trust: The connecting link between organizational theory and philosophical ethics. *Academy of Management Review, 20,* 379–403.

Houser, D., Schunk, D., & Winter, J. (2006). *Trust games measure trust.* Unpublished manuscript, University of Munich.

Hsee, C. K., & Rottenstreich, Y. (2004). Music, pandas and muggers: On the affective psychology of value. *Journal of Experimental Psychology: General, 133,* 23–30.

Hsee, C. K., & Weber, E. U. (1997). A fundamental prediction error: Self-other discrepancies in risk preference. *Journal of Experimental Psychology: General, 126,* 45–53.

Insel, T. R., & Young, L. J. (2001). The neurobiology of attachment. *Nature Reviews Neuroscience, 2,* 129–136.

Johansson-Stenman, O., Mahmud, M., & Martinsson, P. (2005). Does stake size matter in trust games? *Economic Letters, 88,* 365–369.

Kay, A. C., & Ross, L. (2003). The perceptual push: The interplay of implicit cues and explicit situational construals on behavioral intentions in the prisoner's dilemma. *Journal of Experimental Social Psychology, 39,* 634–643.

Knack, S., & Keefer, P. (1997). Does social capital have an economic payoff? A cross-country investigation. *The Quarterly Journal of Economics, 112,* 1251–1288.

Kosfeld, M., Heinrichs, M., Zak, P. J., Fischbacher, U., & Fehr, E. (2005). Oxytocin increases trust in humans. *Nature, 435,* 673–676.

Kramer, R. M. (1998). Paranoid cognition in social systems: Thinking and acting in the shadow of doubt. *Personality and Social Psychology Review, 2,* 251–275.

Kramer, R. M., & Carnevale, P. J. (2001). Trust and intergroup negotiation. In R. Brown & S. Gaertner (Eds.), *Blackwell handbook of social psychology, Vol 4: Intergroup relations* (pp. 431–450). Oxford, UK: Blackwell.

Kreps, D. M. (1990). Corporate culture and economic theory. In J. Alt & K. Shepsle (Eds.), *Perspectives on positive political economy* (pp. 90–143). Cambridge, UK: Cambridge University Press.

Lewicki, R. J., McAllister, D. J., & Bies, R. J. (1998). Trust and distrust: New relationships and realities. *Academy of Management Review, 23,* 438–458.

Liberman, V., Samuels, S. M., & Ross, L. (2004). The name of the game: Predictive power of reputations versus situational labels in determining prisoner's dilemma game moves. *Personality and Social Psychology, 30,* 1175–1185.

Loewenstein, G. F., Weber, E. U., Hsee, C. K., & Welch, N. (2001). Risk as feelings. *Psychological Bulletin, 127,* 267–286.

Loomes, G., & Sugden, R. (1982). Regret theory: An alternative theory of rational choice under uncertainty. *Economic Journal, 92,* 805–824.

Loomes, G., & Sugden, R. (1986). Disappointment and dynamic consistency in choice under uncertainty. *Review of Economic Studies, 53,* 271–282.

Machievelli, N. (2003). *The prince* (R. Goodwin, Trans.). Wellesley, MA: Dante University Press. (Original work published 1515)

McKnight, D., & Chervany, N. (2001). Trust and distrust definitions: One bite at a time. In R. Falcone, M. Singh, & Y.-H. Tan (Eds.), *Trust in cyber-societies: Integrating the human and artificial perspectives* (pp. 27–54). Berlin: Springer-Verlag.

Mellers, B. A., Schwartz, A., Ho, K., & Ritov, I. (1997). Decision affect theory: How we feel about risky options. *Psychological Science, 8,* 423–429.

Mellers, B. A., Schwartz, A., & Ritov, I. (1999). Emotion-based choice. *Journal of Experimental Psychology: General, 128,* 1–14.

Mikulincer, M. (1998a). Adult attachment style and affect regulation: Strategic variations in self-appraisals. *Journal of Personality and Social Psychology, 75,* 420–435.

Mikulincer, M. (1998b). Attachment working models and the sense of trust: An exploration of interaction goals and affect regulation. *Journal of Personality and Social Psychology, 74,* 1209–1224.

Mikulincer, M., Shaver, P. R., & Pereg, D. (2003). Attachment theory and affect regulation: The dynamics, development, and cognitive consequences of attachment-related strategies. *Motivation and Emotion, 27,* 77–102.

Miller, P. J. E., & Rempel, J. K. (2004). Trust and partner-enhancing attributions in close relationships. *Personality and Social Psychology Bulletin, 30,* 695–705.

Nisbett, R. E., & Kunda, Z. (1985). Perception of social distributions. *Journal of Personality and Social Psychology, 48,* 297–311.

Nowack, M. A., & Sigmund, K. (1998). Evolution of indirect reciprocity by image scoring. *Nature, 393,* 573–577.

Ostrom, E., & Walker, J. (Eds.). (2003). *Trust and reciprocity: Interdisciplinary lessons from experimental research.* New York: Russell Sage Foundation.

Pruitt, D. G., & Rubin, J. Z. (1986). *Social conflict: Escalation, stalemate, and settlement.* New York: McGraw-Hill.

Putnam, R. D., (1993). *Making democracy work: Civic traditions in modern Italy.* Princeton: Princeton University Press.

Rapoport, A., & Chammah, A. M. (1965). *Prisoner's dilemma.* Ann Arbor: University of Michigan Press.

Rottenstreich, Y., & Hsee, C. K. (2001). Money, kisses, and electric shocks: An affective psychology of risk. *Psychological Science, 12,* 185–190.

Rotter, J. B. (1967). A new scale for the measurement of interpersonal trust. *Journal of Personality, 35,* 651–665.

Rotter, J. B. (1971). Generalized expectancies of interpersonal trust. *American Psychologist, 26,* 443–452.

Rousseau, D. M., Sitkin, S. B., Burt, R., & Camerer, C. (1998). Not so different after all: A cross-discipline view of trust. *Academy of Management Review, 23,* 393–404.

Schlösser, T., Fetchenhauer, D., & Dunning, D. (2008). *Emotional dimensions of trust behavior: Immediate versus anticipated emotions.* Unpublished manuscript, University of Cologne.

Simpson, J. A. (2007). Foundations of interpersonal trust. In A. W. Kruglanski & E. T. Higgins (Eds.), *Social psychology: Handbook of basic principles* (2nd ed., pp. 587–607). New York: Guilford.

Simpson, J. A., Rholes, W. S., & Nelligan, J. S. (1992). Support seeking and support giving within couples in an anxiety-provoking situation: The role of attachment styles. *Journal of Personality and Social Psychology, 62,* 434–446.

Small, D. A., & Loewenstein, G. (2003). Helping "A" victim or helping "THE" victim: Altruism and identifiability. *Journal of Risk and Uncertainty, 26*(1), 5–16.

Small, D. A., Loewenstein, G., & Slovic, P. (2007). Sympathy and callousness: The impact of deliberative thought on donations to identifiable and statistical victims. *Organizational Behavior and Human Decision Processes, 102,* 143–153.

Snijders, C., & Keren, G. (2001). Do you trust? Whom do you trust? When do you trust? *Advances in Group Processes, 18,* 129–160.

Sullivan, J. L., & Transue, J. E. (1999). The psychological underpinnings of democracy: A selective review of research on political tolerance, interpersonal trust, and social capital. *Annual Review of Psychology, 50,* 625–650.

Trivers, R. L. (1971). The evolution of reciprocal altruism. *Quarterly Review of Biology, 46,* 25–57.

Uvnas-Moberg, K. (1998). Oxytocin may mediate the benefits of positive social interaction and emotions. *Psychoneuroendocrinology, 23,* 819–835.

Van Boven, L., Loewenstein, G., & Dunning, D. (2005). The illusion of courage in social prediction: Underestimating the impact of fear of embarrassment on other people. *Organizational Behavior and Human Decision Processes, 96,* 130–141.

Wieselquist, J., Rusbult, C. E., Foster, C. A., & Agnew, C. R. (1999). Commitment, pro-relationship behavior, and trust in close relationships. *Journal of Personality and Social Psychology, 77,* 942–966.

Zak, P. J., Kurzban, R., & Matzner, W. T. (2005). Oxytocin is associated with human trustworthiness. *Hormones and Behavior, 48,* 522–527.

Zak, P. J., Stanton, A. A., & Ahmadi, S. (2007). Oxytocin increases generosity in humans. *PLoS ONE, 2,* e1128.

9

Social Endocrinology
Hormones and Social Motivation

PRANJAL H. MEHTA and ROBERT A. JOSEPHS

P sychologists have long understood that research on the biological systems of social behavior is critical to our understanding of human social functioning. In his 1967 book titled *The Biological Basis of Personality*, for example, Hans Eysenck reviewed the extant research on personality and physiology and called for continued research on the topic. Despite the importance that Eysenck placed on biology, biological processes were largely ignored by social and personality psychologists in the following several decades. In recent years, however, psychologists have begun to examine links between biology, personality, and social behavior. As a result, new discoveries about personality and social processes are emerging that could not have emerged with traditional social psychology methods alone. Along with advances in molecular genetics, social neuroscience, and behavioral endocrinology, the potential contributions of biological research to social psychology are greater than they've ever been.

Social endocrinology is an emerging interdisciplinary field that bridges behavioral endocrinology (the study of the interaction between hormones and behavior) with social and personality psychology. Over a century of animal research has shown that variation in hormone levels influences a variety of social behaviors. For example, testosterone increases aggression and dominance behavior in many species (Giammanco, Tabacchi, Giammanco, Di Majo, & La Guardia, 2005). Testosterone levels also rise during periods of high competition such as the mating season (Wingfield, Hegner, Dufty, & Ball, 1990), and these testosterone rises promote further dominance (Trainor, Bird, & Marler, 2004). Other animal studies show that oxytocin and progesterone promote affiliative behavior, such as parental care, social bonding, and monogamy (Bartz & Hollander, 2006). It has also been well established that glucocorticoids increase during periods of physical and psychological stress, which prepares the animal to deal with the stressor (Tsigos & Chrousos, 2002).

Although animal studies have contributed greatly to the field of behavioral endocrinology, only recently have researchers begun to examine the relationships between hormones and social behavior in humans. The past five years in particular have shown incredible growth in social endocrinology research, as more social-personality psychologists incorporate endogenous hormone measurement or exogenous hormone administration into their experiments. This new wave of research in social endocrinology has yielded unique insights into a broad array of social psychological processes, including the neuroendocrine systems that regulate social motivation and the effects of hormone–environment interactions on social behavior.

This chapter provides an overview of recent social endocrinology research on the role of hormones in human social motivation. We focus on findings from our laboratory on naturally occurring testosterone and cortisol, but we touch on research from other labs as well, including studies of oxytocin and progesterone. We start by discussing research on testosterone and status-seeking motivation. Next, we highlight recent findings on the roles of oxytocin, progesterone, and testosterone in affiliation and cooperation motivation. Third, we review studies on cortisol and social approach/inhibition. Finally, we discuss recent findings on hormone–hormone interactions and social behavior.

TESTOSTERONE AND STATUS-SEEKING MOTIVATION

Testosterone (T) is a steroid hormone derived from cholesterol. It is produced and released primarily by the testes in men and by the ovaries and adrenal cortex in women. T belongs to a class of hormones called androgens, which are those hormones that are responsible for the development and maintenance of masculine characteristics. In addition to supporting basic physical development, T is also critically involved in regulating social behavior. For example, a large amount of animal literature indicates that T levels are associated with dominance—behavior intended to gain or maintain high status (Mazur & Booth, 1998). Both naturally occurring and experimentally elevated levels of T are positively associated with social rank and dominant behaviors in a variety of species (lemurs, Cavigelli & Pereira, 2000; squirrel monkeys, Coe, Mendoza, & Levine, 1979; sifakas, Kraus, Heistermann, & Kappeler, 1999; chimpanzees, Anestis, 2006; Muller & Wrangham, 2004; baboons, Sapolsky, 1991; birds, Collias, Barfield, & Tarvyd, 2002; fish, Oliveira, Almada, & Canario, 1996; lambs, Ruiz-de-la-Torre & Manteca, 1999). This relationship between T and dominance tends to emerge most strongly during periods of social instability. Sapolsky (1991), in his research on wild baboons, for example, demonstrated that T predicted status-related behaviors when the status hierarchy was unstable (after the alpha male was crippled in fighting and social competition broke out). When the hierarchy was stable, however, T and behavior were unrelated. This basic pattern of results has been found in several other species (fish, Oliveira et al., 1996; lambs, Ruiz-de-la-Torre & Manteca, 1999; birds, Wingfield et al., 1990). Taken together, the animal literature suggests that when social status is uncertain, high T levels motivate individuals to seek out higher status.

The association between higher T and dominance has also been extended to humans. For instance, people high in basal T tend to be more aggressive and more socially dominant than individuals low in basal T (Archer, 2006; Archer, Birring, & Wu, 1998; Cashdan, 1995; Grant & France, 2001; Jones & Josephs, 2006; Josephs, Newman, Brown, & Beer, 2003; Josephs, Sellers, Newman, & Mehta, 2006; Mazur & Booth, 1998; Newman, Sellers, & Josephs, 2005; Sellers, Mehl, & Josephs, 2007; Tremblay et al., 1998). T also increases vigilance toward dominance cues such as angry, threatening faces (van Honk et al., 1999; Wirth & Schultheiss, 2007) and decreases vigilance toward submissive cues such as fearful faces (van Honk, Peper, & Schutter, 2005). These effects of T on attention seem to be strongest when dominance–submission cues are presented outside conscious awareness (e.g., van Honk et al., 2005; Wirth & Schultheiss, 2007), suggesting that the relationship between T and dominant behaviors may be mediated, at least in part, by subconscious motivational and attentional processes.

The Basal Testosterone × Status Interaction

The findings reviewed above are consistent with the hypothesis that T levels influence status-seeking motivation. However, to provide more direct tests of this hypothesis, we conducted several studies in which we experimentally manipulated social status (Jones & Josephs, 2006; Josephs et al., 2003, 2006; Mehta, Jones, & Josephs, 2008; Newman et al., 2005). In eight different studies, we measured basal T in saliva before a status manipulation, and we measured various affective, cognitive, physiological, and behavioral outcomes after the manipulation. The designs of these studies and a summary of the results are presented in Table 9.1. Figure 9.1 depicts results from Study 1 of Josephs et al. (2006). In all of the studies, the interaction between basal T and status predicted the outcomes under investigation. For example, Josephs et al. (2006) found that high T individuals paid more attention to status cues, became dysphoric, and performed poorly on complex cognitive tasks after losing status, but paid less attention to status cues, showed no evidence of dysphoria, and performed well on complex cognitive tasks after gaining status. Mehta et al. (2008) further showed that high T individuals rose in cortisol (a physiological marker of psychological stress) after losing status, but dropped in cortisol (a physiological marker of psychological relaxation) after gaining status. Taken together, this literature suggests that high T individuals are driven to rise in status; when they achieve high status, high T individuals experience relaxation (e.g., drop in cortisol, low negative affect) and adaptive functioning (e.g., good cognitive performance), but when they fail to achieve high status, high T individuals experience psychological distress (e.g., negative affect, rise in cortisol) and maladaptive functioning (e.g., poor cognitive performance).

Across these same studies, low T individuals reacted very differently to changes in status. In some of the studies, low T individuals' reactions to high and low status were similar to those in control conditions (Josephs et al., 2003; Newman et al., 2005), suggesting that low T individuals do not have the same strong drive for status that high T individuals have. However, in other studies low T individuals reacted more negatively to high status than to low status. Specifically, low T

TABLE 9.1   Studies Demonstrating a Basal Testosterone × Status Interaction

Study	Status Manipulation	Dependent Variable(s)	Participant Sample	Primary Results
Josephs et al., 2003, Study 1	Negative stereotype prime (stereotype threat)	Math performance	Women	High T women performed poorly after negative stereotype prime.
Josephs et al., 2003, Study 2	Positive stereotype prime (stereotype lift)	Math performance	Men	High T men excelled in performance after positive stereotype prime.
Newman et al., 2005	Leader/ follower	Mental rotation performance Verbal performance Cardiovascular arousal	Men and women	High T participants performed poorly in a low-status position. High T participants dropped in diastolic blood pressure in a high-status position.
Josephs et al., 2006, Study 1	Competitive victory/defeat	Analytical performance Positive and negative affect Implicit attention to status	Men and women	High T participants performed poorly, had higher negative affect, and were more attentive to status cues after losing status. Low T participants showed this pattern after gaining status.
Josephs et al., 2006, Study 2	Skilled versus unskilled opponent	Math performance Cardiovascular arousal	Men and women	High T participants performed poorly and had higher heart rate in a low-status position. Low T participants showed this pattern in a high-status position.
Jones & Josephs, 2006	Competitive victory/defeat	Affiliative behavior Aggressive behavior	Men	High T men were less affiliative and more aggressive after losing status.
Mehta et al., 2008, Study 1	Competitive victory/defeat	Change in cortisol	Men	High T men rose in cortisol after losing status but dropped in cortisol after gaining status.
Mehta et al., 2008, Study 2	Competitive victory/defeat	Change in cortisol Approach- avoidance behavior	Women	High T women rose in cortisol and showed avoidant behavior after losing status. High T women dropped in cortisol and showed approach behavior after gaining status.

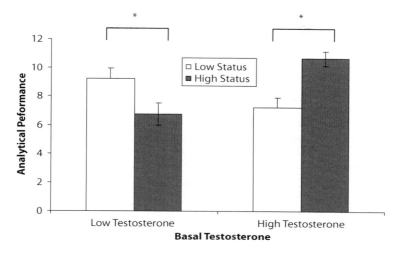

Figure 9.1   Mean Graduate Record Exam (GRE)–Analytical performance (number of items correct out of 20 questions) as a function of basal testosterone and social status. Low testosterone = men and women in bottom third of basal testosterone distribution relative to other individuals of the same sex. High testosterone = top third of basal testosterone distribution relative to other individuals of the same sex. Error bars represent 1 standard error. °p < .01. (Adapted from Josephs, R. A., Sellers, J. G., Newman, M. L., & Mehta, P. H., The mismatch effect: When testosterone and status are at odds. *Journal of Personality and Social Psychology, 90*(6), 2006, Study 1.)

participants were hypervigilant to status cues, showed elevated cardiovascular arousal, and performed poorly on complex cognitive tasks in a high-status position but not in a low-status position (Josephs et al., 2006; see Figure 9.1). These latter findings suggest that low T individuals might actually prefer low status and actively avoid high status. As Josephs and colleagues (2006) argued, low T individuals "might shun high status positions … because they lack a strong power motive … they lack a dominating, aggressive personality … and they may not believe they have what it takes physically to maintain such positions" (p. 1001). Thus, when low T individuals are thrust into a high-status position, they may experience arousal and maladaptive functioning out of a desire to return to a more comfortable and safer position of low status.

There were no sex differences in the predictive power of basal T on reactions to changes in status. Men and women high in T relative to other individuals of the same sex reacted negatively to a drop in status (Josephs et al., 2003, 2006; Mehta et al., 2008; Newman et al., 2005). Men and women low in T relative to other individuals of the same sex showed neutral (Josephs et al., 2003; Mehta et al., 2008; Newman et al., 2005) or negative reactions (Josephs et al., 2006) to a rise in status. These findings suggest that basal T is a biological marker of chronic status-seeking motivation in both men and women.

Testosterone Fluctuations and Status-Seeking Motivation

The studies reported above examined basal T as a stable trait and implied that T levels directly influence social motivation and behavior. However, not only does T influence behavior, but behavior and the social environment also influence T levels. Specifically, it seems that T levels fluctuate around basal levels in status-relevant social settings. According to the reciprocal model of T and status (Mazur & Booth, 1998), T levels should decrease when status drops but increase when status rises. These changes in T levels are expected to produce a reciprocal effect by influencing subsequent status-seeking behaviors. Specifically, there has been speculation that T increases may encourage further attempts at gaining status, whereas T decreases may lead individuals to flee the situation to avoid any further loss of status.

Empirical support for this reciprocal model comes from research in real-world sports competitions and rigged laboratory competitions. Several studies have shown that winners increase in T relative to losers for a few hours following a competition (Elias, 1981; Gladue, Boechler, & McCaul, 1989; Mazur, Booth, & Dabbs, 1992; Mazur & Lamb, 1980; McCaul, Gladue, & Joppa, 1992). However, other studies have not found this overall win–lose effect (Gonzalez-Bono, Salvador, Serrano, & Ricarte, 1999; Mazur, Susman, & Edelbrock, 1997; Schultheiss et al., 2005) but instead shown that T changes after changes in status depend on psychological factors, such as personality. For example, Schultheiss et al. (2005) found that individual differences in implicit power motive moderated the effects of victory and defeat on T changes. Specifically, high-power individuals rose in T after victory, but these same individuals dropped in T after defeat. Low-power individuals showed the opposite pattern of T changes. Jones and Josephs (2006) showed that basal T was also a moderator of the effects of victory and defeat on changes in T. High T individuals also rose in T after victory and dropped in T after defeat. Low T individuals showed the opposite pattern. Presumably, people high in power motive or high in basal T are chronically motivated to gain status. Thus, when their status drops, these individuals react strongly by dropping in T. However, when their status rises, they react strongly by rising in T.

Although this literature has uncovered several important variables that predict T changes after changes in status, researchers have simply assumed that status-induced changes in T influence subsequent status-seeking behaviors. We conducted the first study in humans that examined the relationship between postcompetition fluctuations in T and subsequent social behavior (Mehta & Josephs, 2006). We experimentally manipulated status with a rigged competition and collected saliva samples before and after the competition to measure changes in T (Mehta & Josephs, 2006). After participants provided the second saliva sample, they chose whether they wanted to (a) rechallenge their opponent to a second competition or (b) complete an alternative noncompetitive task. The results showed that changes in T after losing predicted who wanted to compete again in a second competition. Losers who rose in T were more likely to choose to rechallenge their opponent (73%) than losers who dropped in T (22%). These findings are consistent with the reciprocal model and suggest that a rise in T after a drop in status motivates further attempts at gaining status, whereas a drop in T after a drop in status motivates individuals to avoid any further loss of status.

Taken together, research on T and status suggests that basal T taps into a person's chronic status-seeking motivation, analogous to a personality trait, whereas short-term changes in T tap into a person's status-seeking motivation, analogous to mood (cf. Mehta et al., 2008).

THE SOCIAL ENDOCRINOLOGY OF AFFILIATION AND COOPERATION MOTIVATION

Research on the social endocrinology of affiliation and cooperation motivation in humans has concentrated on the roles of oxytocin and, to a lesser extent, progesterone. However, recent research implicates testosterone in social cooperation as well. In this section, we review some recent findings from these literatures.

Oxytocin and Affiliation/Cooperation Motivation

Oxytocin is a peptide hormone that is released in the brain and acts like a neurotransmitter. Oxytocin has been studied extensively across mammalian species and is critically involved in the regulation of maternal behavior and social bonding (Campbell, 2008). The animal and human literatures on oxytocin and social motivation are discussed in depth in a recent review article (Campbell, 2008). Here we highlight some recent human studies from this extensive literature.

Human studies show that oxytocin regulates affiliation and social bonding in males and females. For example, Kosfeld, Heinrichs, Zak, Fischbacher, and Fehr (2005) found that intranasal administration of oxytocin in men increased trust behavior in an economic investment game. A recent comprehensive study of pregnant mothers showed that plasma levels of oxytocin in mothers during pregnancy and in the postpartum period were positively associated thoughts, feelings, and behaviors related to mother–infant bonding (Feldman, Weller, Zagoory-Sharon, & Levine, 2007). These findings suggest that oxytocin increases affiliation motivation, which may promote maternal care during and immediately after pregnancy. Another study showed that oxytocin interacts with social support to influence affective and neuroendocrine responses to social stress (Heinrichs, Baumgartner, Kirschbaum, & Ehlert, 2003). In this study, male participants were randomly given social support (the presence of a best friend) or no support and were administrated either intranasal oxytocin or a placebo. All participants were exposed to a standardized laboratory psychosocial stressor (Trier Social Stress Test), and neuroendocrine and affective responses to the stressor were measured (Heinrichs et al., 2003). The social support and oxytocin manipulations showed an interactive effect such that a combination of social support and oxytocin treatment resulted in a blunted stress response. These findings suggest that the effect of social support on the stress response depends on oxytocin (Heinrichs et al., 2003). The results of this study are generally consistent with the "tend-and-befriend" theory, which suggests that stress promotes affiliation and social contact, particularly in women, via regulation of peptide hormones such as oxytocin (Taylor, 2006).

One mechanism by which oxytocin may promote affiliation and social cooperation is through an increased ability to recognize emotions and infer mental states in others. Consistent with this idea, Domes and colleagues (Domes, Heinrichs, Michel et al., 2007) demonstrated that oxytocin administration increased emotion recognition ability as indicated by better performance on the Reading the Mind in the Eyes Test. This test was designed to measure people's ability to infer mental states from the eye region, an area of the face important for emotional detection and social communication. Another study showed that oxytocin administration increased attention to the eye region in neutral faces (Guastella, Mitchell, & Dadds, 2008), suggesting that the positive effect of oxytocin on emotion recognition may be mediated by increased attention to the eyes.

Another mechanism by which oxytocin may promote affiliation is by making positive social cues more memorable. A recent study provided support for this hypothesis by showing that oxytocin administration improved memory for happy faces but not for angry or neutral faces (Guastella, Mitchell, & Mathews, 2008).

Other research shows that oxytocin influences neural reactivity to emotional stimuli, regardless of the valence of the stimuli. Specifically, oxytocin administration reduced amygdala reactivity to happy, angry, and fearful faces (Domes, Heinrichs, Gläscher, et al., 2007). On the basis of these findings, the authors speculated that oxytocin may reduce uncertainty about the predictive value of positive and negative social stimuli, leading to social approach and affiliation behavior.

Progesterone and Affiliation Motivation

Progesterone is a steroid hormone released primarily by the ovaries in women and by the adrenal glands in men. It plays an important role in the female menstrual cycle and pregnancy. Animal research suggests that progesterone levels during female pregnancy are involved in the regulation of maternal behavior (e.g., Pryce, Dobeli, & Martin, 1993; Rosenblatt, 2002). Some recent studies have shown that progesterone levels are also associated with affiliation motivation in humans. Schultheiss, Dargel, and Rohde (2003) demonstrated that progesterone levels were positively associated with implicit affiliation motivation in normally cycling women but not in women taking oral contraceptives.

Additional experimental studies showed that arousing affiliation motivation through movie clips led to changes in progesterone levels (Schultheiss, Wirth, & Stanton, 2004; Wirth & Schultheiss, 2006). In one study, male and female participants were shown a 30-minute clip from the film *Bridges of Madison County* depicting scenes of affiliation and intimacy. Progesterone increased from before to after the film clip. In a second study, participants were shown a 30-minute clip from the film *A.I.* depicting scenes with social rejection and maternal separation themes. Progesterone and cortisol levels increased from before to after the film clip in men and women. On the basis of these latter findings, the authors speculated that increased progesterone during social stress may facilitate social bonding with other conspecifics. This interpretation is consistent with the tend-and-befriend theory (Taylor, 2006), which posits that oxytocin release during social stress promotes social contact, especially in women.

Testosterone and Affiliation/Cooperation Motivation

Animal evidence suggests that T suppresses affiliation and social bonding (Wingfield et al., 1990). A growing human literature also demonstrates that T is negatively associated with affiliation. Across several studies, it has been shown that social bonding is inversely related to T levels. For example, correlational studies show that married men have lower T levels than unmarried men (e.g., Gray et al., 2004), and unmarried men in committed romantic relationships have lower T levels than single men (Burnham et al., 2003). McIntyre and colleagues (2006) further showed that the association between relationship status and T levels is moderated by extrapair sexual interest; extrapair sexual interest was positively associated with T in paired men but not in single men. Additional studies show that T levels are lower in men who have recently become fathers (e.g., Berg & Wynne-Edwards, 2001). In a longitudinal study, Mazur and Michalek (1998) found that men who were divorced dropped in T if they remarried, suggesting that social bonding leads to T suppression. Other studies have extended the relationship between social bonding and T to women, showing that partnered women have lower T levels than single women (van Anders & Watson, 2007) and that polygamous women have higher T levels than single and partnered women (van Anders, Hamilton, & Watson, 2007). Overall, then, these data support the hypothesis that social bonding causes T levels to drop, which in turn leads to further bonding and social cooperation. Alternatively, perhaps individuals low in basal T are more likely to enter and remain in committed, romantic relationships than individuals high in basal T. Additional longitudinal studies are needed to test between these two hypotheses.

We recently conducted a study to examine the relationship between basal T and cooperation motivation (Mehta, Wuehrmann, & Josephs, 2009). In this study, same-sex participants reported to the lab and provided a saliva sample, which was later analyzed for basal T levels. Participants were then brought into the same room and told that the study was investigating analytic reasoning and that they would be completing a test of analytic reasoning. After that, participants were randomly assigned to a competitive or cooperative social environment. In the competition condition, participants were told, "As an incentive, we've decided to take the higher scoring person of the two of you and enter you into a drawing for a prize: $25 cash. So if you do better (score higher) than the other person does, you'll be entered into the drawing." But in the cooperation condition, participants were told, "As an incentive, we've decided to add your scores together, and if you score higher than the next group that comes in, you'll both be entered into a drawing for $25 cash for each of you." Participants then completed 15 questions from the former Graduate Record Exam (GRE)–Analytical subsection. The questions selected were of medium difficulty. Participants worked independently on the problems and were not able to communicate with each other. The participants had 20 minutes to complete as many of the questions as possible.

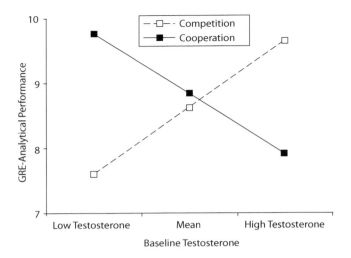

Figure 9.2   Graduate Record Exam (GRE)–Analytical performance (number of items correct out of 15) as a function of competition/cooperation condition and testosterone level (log transformed and standardized within sex). Low testosterone = 1 standard deviation below mean, high testosterone = 1 standard deviation above mean. Standardized betas: competition, $\beta = .37; p < .05$; cooperation, $\beta = -.48, p < .01$. (Adapted from Mehta, P. H., Wuehrmann, E. V., & Josephs, R. A., "When Are Low Testosterone Levels Advantageous? The Moderating Role of Individual Versus Intergroup Competition." *Hormones and Behavior*, vol. 56, pp. 158–162. Published 2009 by Elsevier. Adapted with permission.)

Results from this study are shown in Figure 9.2. Basal T moderated the effect of the social environment on performance. Specifically, basal T was positively related to performance in the competitive environment, but basal T was negatively related to performance in the cooperative environment. The positive relationship between basal T and performance in competition is consistent with previous research on basal T and status-seeking motivation. Presumably, high T individuals performed well when competing out of a strong desire to gain high status, but low T individuals performed poorly when competing out of a desire to avoid high status. This interpretation is consistent with past research demonstrating the differential effects of high and low status on high and low T individuals (Josephs et al., 2003, 2006; Mehta et al., 2008; Newman et al., 2005).

The results from the cooperation condition suggest that basal T is negatively associated with cooperation motivation. Presumably, low T individuals performed well in a cooperation setting because these individuals were motivated to affiliate and bond with others. In contrast, high T individuals may have performed poorly in the cooperation condition because T may suppress cooperation motivation. This interpretation is consistent with animal research linking high T to suppressed social bonding and high levels of social competition (Wingfield et al., 1990). The results of this study, combined with previous research linking lower T to social bonding, suggest that T, in addition to regulating status-seeking motivation, also plays an important role in influencing affiliation/cooperation motivation.

Studies in which T levels are exogenously administered provide additional evidence that T suppresses affiliation motivation. For example, one study showed that sublingual T administration in women impaired performance on an emotion recognition task (van Honk, 2008). Because inferring mental states and emotions in others is important for facilitating social bonding, an impaired ability to recognize emotions in others suggests that T may suppress the motivation to affiliate with others. An additional study showed that T administration led to lower rates of cooperation than placebo treatment in a cooperative social setting. The T administration group did not show behavioral differences from placebo administration in a competitive social setting (van Honk, 2008). Together, these studies implicate a causal role of T in suppressing affiliation/cooperation motivation.

Cortisol and Social Approach/Inhibition

Glucocorticoids are a class of hormones that are released by the adrenal glands during physical and psychological stress. The primary glucocorticoid in humans is cortisol. Most research on cortisol has focused on the dispositional and situational variables that cause acute changes in cortisol (e.g., Dickerson & Kemeny, 2004), but some research implicates cortisol in social approach/inhibition motivation. For example, animal studies show that elevated glucocorticoids during stress are associated with freezing behaviors (rats, Nunez, Ferre, Escorihuela, Tobena, & Fernandez-Teruel, 1996; primates, Kalin, Shelton, Rickman, & Davidson, 1998), a response style that is thought to be an extreme form of behavioral inhibition. Additional studies in humans demonstrate that elevated cortisol is associated with social avoidance and inhibition, including anxiety and defensiveness (Brown et al., 1996) and social inhibition and internalizing behaviors (Kagan, Reznick, & Snidman, 1987; Smider et al., 2002). Conversely, low basal cortisol has linked to social approach and aggression (Shoal, Giancola, & Kirillova, 2003; Virgin & Sapolsky, 1997). In one longitudinal study of 314 boys, low basal cortisol levels during preadolescence (age 10 to 12 years) predicted low harm avoidance, low self-control, and more aggressive behaviors 5 years later (Shoal et al., 2003). Further analyses suggested that low self-control mediated the relationship between low cortisol and aggression. Other studies show that basal cortisol is negatively correlated with extraversion (Mehta, 2007) and memory for happy faces (van Honk et al., 2003). Overall, the research suggests that high cortisol is associated with social inhibition and avoidance, whereas low cortisol is associated with social approach.

HORMONE–HORMONE INTERACTIONS AND SOCIAL BEHAVIOR

Social endocrinology research typically examines independent effects of hormones on behavior. In most of the studies reported above, a single hormone was manipulated or measured and its effects on behavior were observed. This approach has certainly been useful in identifying several important relationships between hormones and social behavior. At the same time, many studies using this approach have failed to demonstrate consistent hormone-behavior associations. For example, findings linking testosterone to aggression in humans are mixed, with many studies showing null effects (Archer et al., 1998). One explanation for such inconsistencies is that hormones may not independently channel social behavior as has been previously assumed. Instead, multiple hormones may work together to channel social behavior.

The possibility that hormone–hormone interactions may drive behavior is supported by studies demonstrating powerful interactions between androgens and glucocorticoids on neuroendocrine and neural responses to threat (Hermans, Ramsey, & van Honk, 2008; Viau, 2002). These findings suggest that androgens and glucocorticoids may also interact to influence social behavior. Consistent with this idea, two studies found that the interaction between testosterone and cortisol was associated with aggression. In one study of male delinquent adolescents (age 12 to 14 years), testosterone was positively related to overt aggression among individuals low in basal cortisol, but testosterone and overt aggression were unrelated among individuals high in basal cortisol (Popma et al., 2007). This study conceptually replicated a previous study of 17- to 18-year-old male offenders (Dabbs, Jurkovic, & Frady, 1991), which also found that high testosterone coupled with low cortisol was predictive of aggressive behaviors. These findings suggest that neuroendocrine systems associated with status-seeking motivation (testosterone) and social approach avoidance (cortisol) interact to influence the expression of aggressive behavior.

In a recent study, we tested the hypothesis that testosterone and cortisol would jointly channel fight-or-flight behavioral responses to social threat in males (Mehta & Josephs, 2010). We studied 64 men who participated in a one-on-one dominance contest in which social defeat and victory were experimentally manipulated. Before the competition, basal testosterone and basal cortisol were measured in saliva. After the competition, the men decided whether to rechallenge their opponent to a second competition (*fight*) or avoid a second competition (*flight*). Neither testosterone nor cortisol alone predicted the behavioral response to social defeat, but the testosterone–cortisol interaction did (see Figure 9.3). High testosterone + low cortisol men chose to fight (rechallenge their opponent) after defeat, whereas high testosterone + high cortisol men chose to flee (avoid a second competition). Testosterone and cortisol were unrelated to fight-or-flight behavior after victory. These findings suggest that when social status is threatened, cortisol modulates the behavioral expression of status-seeking motivation. When cortisol is low, status-seeking motivation—as indicated by high testosterone—is expressed in the form of behavioral approach, or a *fight* response. However, when cortisol is high, status-seeking motivation is expressed in the form of behavioral avoidance, or a *flight* response. This interpretation is consistent with previous research demonstrating that testosterone regulates the drive for status, whereas cortisol regulates social approach avoidance.

In another study, we examined whether the interaction between testosterone and cortisol would predict leadership behavior (Mehta & Josephs, 2010). Same-sex pairs reported to the lab and provided a saliva sample, which was analyzed for basal T and cortisol levels. Participants were randomly assigned to the

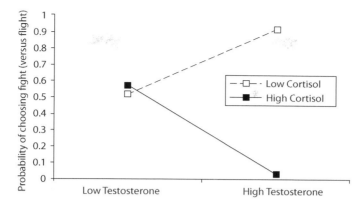

Figure 9.3   Fight-or-flight behavior following social defeat as a function of testosterone and cortisol levels. Low and high values indicate 1 standard deviation above and below the means, respectively, on the testosterone and cortisol distributions. (Adapted from Mehta, P. H., & Josephs, R. A., *Dual-Hormone Regulation of Dominance Behavior*, manuscript submitted for publication, 2010.)

role of leader or follower. Each leader–follower dyad completed a cognitive task together. Then, the participants switched leader–follower roles and completed another version of the cognitive task. The leader–follower interactions were videotaped. Seven judges later watched the videotapes and rated the leaders on 19 different social behaviors (e.g., engaged, gave clear instructions, directive, leaderlike, confident, nervous, uncomfortable). All 19 behaviors loaded on to a single factor, and thus, an overall leadership score was created for each participant. There were no main effects of basal T or basal cortisol on leadership, but there was a statistically significant T × Cortisol interaction (Mehta, 2007). Figure 9.4 depicts the pattern of the interaction. Consistent with the results of the studies reported above (e.g., Mehta & Josephs, 2010), high T + low cortisol individuals showed higher leadership scores than did high T + high cortisol individuals. These findings suggest that a pattern of high status-seeking motivation (high T) and social approach (low cortisol) leads to good leadership, whereas a pattern of high status-seeking motivation (high T) and social inhibition (high cortisol) leads to poorer leadership.

Although these findings clearly demonstrate interactions between testosterone and cortisol on aggression, fight-or-flight behavior, and leadership, additional research that incorporates affective, cognitive measures and other physiological measures (e.g., neural activity, hormone fluctuations) into social endocrinology studies will help clarify the mechanisms that underlie these interactions. Preliminary evidence suggests that high testosterone + high cortisol individuals respond to social stress with a short-term drop in testosterone (a marker of social submission) and an increase in negative affect compared to high testosterone + low cortisol individuals. Thus, it seems that high testosterone + high cortisol individuals may experience a social stressor as a threat, whereas high testosterone + low cortisol

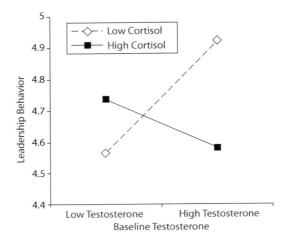

Figure 9.4   Leadership behavior as a function of basal testosterone and basal cortisol. Low testosterone = 1 standard deviation below mean on basal testosterone distribution standardized within sex, high testosterone = 1 standard deviation above mean of basal testosterone distribution standardized within sex, low cortisol = 1 standard deviation below mean, high cortisol = 1 standard deviation above mean. (Adapted from Mehta, P. H., *"Dual-Hormone Regulation of Dominance Behavior,"* manuscript submitted for publication.)

individuals may experience the same stressor as a challenge. These findings are preliminary, and more evidence is needed to support this line of reasoning.

CONCLUSIONS

Despite several decades in which the study of biology was largely ignored by social and personality psychology, biological research in the study of personality and social behavior is now on the comeback. Social endocrinology research in particular has grown tremendously in recent years, as researchers capitalize on its advantages for addressing questions in social psychology that are difficult or impossible to address with traditional self-report and behavioral methods alone. This chapter highlights the contribution of social endocrinology to research on social motivation. However, we anticipate that in the coming years, social endocrinology will make substantial contributions to many areas of social psychology, ranging from the study of emotion, social perception, and stereotyping/prejudice to culture, political psychology, and judgment and decision making.

ACKNOWLEDGMENTS

We are grateful to Sam Gosling, whose work inspired our approach to this chapter. We also thank our collaborators Matthew Newman, Jennifer Sellers, and Elizabeth Wuehrmann.

REFERENCES

Anestis, S. F. (2006). Testosterone in juvenile and adolescent male chimpanzees (*Pan troglo-dytes*): Effects of dominance rank, aggression, and behavioral style. *American Journal of Physical Anthropology, 130*(4), 536–545.

Archer, J. (2006). Testosterone and human aggression: An evaluation of the challenge hypothesis. *Neuroscience and Biobehavioral Reviews, 30*(3), 319–345.

Archer, J., Birring, S. S., & Wu, F. C. W. (1998). The association between testosterone and aggression in young men: Empirical findings and a meta-analysis. *Aggressive Behavior, 24*(6), 411–420.

Bartz, J., & Hollander, E. (2006). The neuroscience of affiliation: Forging links between basic and clinical research on neuropeptides and social behavior. *Hormones and Behavior, 50*(4), 518–528.

Berg, S. J., & Wynne-Edwards, K. E. (2001). Changes in testosterone, cortisol, and estradiol levels in men becoming fathers. *Mayo Clinic Proceedings, 76*, 582–592.

Brown, L., Tomarken, A., Orth, D., Loosen, P., Kalin, N., & Davidson, R. (1996). Individual differences in repressive-defensiveness predict basal salivary cortisol levels. *Journal of Personality and Social Psychology, 70*(2), 362–371.

Burnham, T., Chapman, J., Gray, P., McIntyre, M., Lipson, S., & Ellison, P. (2003). Men in committed, romantic relationships have lower testosterone. *Hormones and Behavior, 44*(2), 119–122.

Campbell, A. (2008). Attachment, aggression, and affiliation: The role of oxytocin in female social behavior. *Biological Psychology, 77*(1), 1–10.

Cashdan, E. (1995). Hormones, sex, and status in women. *Hormones and Behavior, 29*(3), 354–366.

Cavigelli, S. A., & Pereira, M. E. (2000). Mating season aggression and fecal testosterone levels in male ring-tailed lemurs (*Lemur catta*). *Hormones and Behavior, 37*(3), 246–255.

Coe, C. L., Mendoza, S. P., & Levine, S. (1979). Social status constrains the stress response in the squirrel monkey. *Physiology and Behavior, 23*(4), 633–638.

Collias, N. E., Barfield, R. J., & Tarvyd, E. S. (2002). Testosterone versus psychological castration in the expression of dominance, territoriality and breeding behavior by male village weavers (*Ploceus cucullatus*). *Behavioural Brain Research, 139*(6), 801–824.

Dabbs, J., Jurkovic, G., & Frady, R. (1991). Salivary testosterone and cortisol among late adolescent male offenders. *Journal of Abnormal Child Psychology, 19*(4), 469–478.

Dickerson, S. S., & Kemeny, M. E. (2004). Acute stressors and cortisol responses: A theoretical integration and synthesis of laboratory research. *Psychological Bulletin, 130*(3), 355–391.

Domes, G., Heinrichs, M., Gläscher, J., Büchel, C., Braus, D., & Herpertz, S. (2007). Oxytocin attenuates amygdala responses to emotional faces regardless of valence. *Biological Psychiatry, 62*(10), 1187–1190.

Domes, G., Heinrichs, M., Michel, A., Berger, C., & Herpertz, S. (2007). Oxytocin improves "mind-reading" in humans. *Biological Psychiatry, 61*(6), 731–733.

Elias, M. (1981). Serum cortisol, testosterone, and testosterone-binding globulin responses to competitive fighting in human males. *Aggressive Behavior, 7*(3), 215–224.

Eysenck, H. (1967). *The biological basis of personality*. Springfield, IL: Thomas.

Feldman, R., Weller, A., Zagoory-Sharon, O., & Levine, A. (2007). Evidence for a neuroendocrinological foundation of human affiliation: Plasma oxytocin levels across pregnancy and the postpartum period predict mother–infant bonding. *Psychological Science, 18*(11), 965–970.

Giammanco, M., Tabacchi, G., Giammanco, S., Di Majo, D., & La Guardia, M. (2005). Testosterone and aggressiveness. *Medical Science Monitor, 11*(4), RA136–145.

Gladue, B. A., Boechler, M., & McCaul, K. D. (1989). Hormonal response to competition in human males. *Aggressive Behavior, 15*(6), 409–422.

Gonzalez-Bono, E., Salvador, A., Serrano, M. A., & Ricarte, J. (1999). Testosterone, cortisol, and mood in a sports team competition. *Hormones and Behavior, 35*, 55–62.

Grant, V. J., & France, J. T. (2001). Dominance and testosterone in women. *Biological Psychology, 58*(1), 41–47.

Gray, P., Chapman, J., Burnham, T., McIntyre, M., Lipson, S., & Ellison, P. (2004). Human male pair bonding and testosterone. *Human Nature, 15*(2), 119–131.

Guastella, A., Mitchell, P., & Dadds, M. (2008). Oxytocin increases gaze to the eye region of human faces. *Biological Psychiatry, 63*(1), 3–5.

Guastella, A. J., Mitchell, P. B., & Mathews, F. (2008). Oxytocin enhances the encoding of positive social memories in humans. *Biological Psychiatry, 64*(3), 256–258.

Heinrichs, M., Baumgartner, T., Kirschbaum, C., & Ehlert, U. (2003, December). Social support and oxytocin interact to suppress cortisol and subjective responses to psycho-social stress. *Biological Psychiatry, 54*(12), 1389–1398.

Hermans, E. J., Ramsey, N. F., & van Honk, J. (2008). Exogenous testosterone attenuates the integrated central stress response in healthy young women. *Biological Psychiatry, 32*, 1052–1061.

Jones, A. C., & Josephs, R. A. (2006). Interspecies hormonal interactions between man and the domestic dog (*Canis familiaris*). *Hormones and Behavior, 50*(3), 393–400.

Josephs, R. A., Newman, M. L., Brown, R. P., & Beer, J. M. (2003). Status, testosterone, and human intellectual performance: Stereotype threat as status concern. *Psychological Science, 14*(2), 158–163.

Josephs, R. A., Sellers, J. G., Newman, M. L., & Mehta, P. H. (2006). The mismatch effect: When testosterone and status are at odds. *Journal of Personality and Social Psychology, 90*(6), 999–1013.

Kagan, J., Reznick, J., & Snidman, N. (1987). The physiology and psychology of behavioral inhibition in children. *Child Development, 58*(6), 1459–1473.

Kalin, N. H., Shelton, S. E., Rickman, M., & Davidson, R. J. (1998). Individual differences in freezing and cortisol in infant and mother rhesus monkeys. *Behavioral Neuroscience, 112*, 251–254.

Kosfeld, M., Heinrichs, M., Zak, P., Fischbacher, U., & Fehr, E. (2005). Oxytocin increases trust in humans. *Nature, 435*(7042), 673–676.

Kraus, C., Heistermann, M., & Kappeler, P. M. (1999). Physiological suppression of sexual function of subordinate males: A subtle form of intrasexual competition among male sifakas (*Propithecus verreauxi*)? *Physiology and Behavior, 66*(5), 855–861.

Mazur, A., & Booth, A. (1998). Testosterone and dominance in men. *Behavioral and Brain Sciences, 21*(3), 353–397.

Mazur, A., Booth, A., & Dabbs, J. M. (1992). Testosterone and chess competition. *Social Psychology Quarterly, 55*(1), 70–77.

Mazur, A., & Lamb, T. A. (1980). Testosterone, status, and mood in human males. *Hormones and Behavior, 14*(3), 236–246.

Mazur, A., & Michalek, J. (1998). Marriage, divorce, and male testosterone. *Social Forces, 77*(1), 315–330.

Mazur, A., Susman, E., & Edelbrock, S. (1997). Sex difference in testosterone response to a video game contest. *Evolution and Human Behavior, 18*(5), 317–326.

McCaul, K. D., Gladue, B. A., & Joppa, M. (1992). Winning, losing, mood, and testosterone. *Hormones and Behavior, 26*(4), 486–504.

McIntyre, M., Gangestad, S. W., Gray, P. B., Chapman, J. F., Burnham, T. C., O'Rourke, M. T., et al. (2006). Romantic involvement often reduces men's testosterone levels—but not always: The moderating role of extrapair sexual interest. *Journal of Personality and Social Psychology, 91*(4), 642–651

Mehta, P. H. (2007). *The endocrinology of personality, leadership, and economic decision-making.* Unpublished doctoral dissertation.

Mehta, P. H., Jones, A. C., & Josephs, R. A. (2008). The social endocrinology of dominance: Basal testosterone predicts cortisol changes and behavior following victory and defeat. *Journal of Personality and Social Psychology, 94*, 1078–1093.

Mehta, P. H., & Josephs, R. A. (2006). Testosterone change after losing predicts the decision to compete again. *Hormones and Behavior, 50*, 684–692.

Mehta, P., & Josephs, R. (2010). *Dual-hormone regulation of dominance behavior.* Manuscript under review, University of Texas.

Mehta, P., Wuehrmann, E., & Josephs, R. (2009). When are low testosterone levels advantageous? The moderating role of individual versus intergroup competition. *Hormones and Behavior, 56*, 185–162.

Muller, M. N., & Wrangham, R. W. (2004). Dominance, cortisol, and stress in wild chimpanzees (*Pan troglodytes schweinfurthii*). *Behavioral Ecology and Sociobiology, 55*(4), 332–340.

Newman, M. L., Sellers, J. G., & Josephs, R. A. (2005). Testosterone, cognition, and social status. *Hormones and Behavior, 47*(2), 205–211.

Nunez, J. F., Ferre, P., Escorihuela, R. M., Tobena, A., & Fernandez-Teruel, A. (1996). Effects of postnatal handling of rats on emotional, HPA-axis, and prolactin reactivity to novelty and conflict. *Physiology and Behavior, 60*(5), 1355–1359.

Oliveira, R. F., Almada, V. C., & Canario, A. V. (1996). Social modulation of sex steroid concentrations in the urine of male cichlid fish *Oreochromis mossambicus*. *Hormones and Behavior, 30*(1), 2–12.

Popma, A., Vermeiren, R., Geluk, C., Rinne, T., van den Brink, W., Knol, D., et al. (2007). Cortisol moderates the relationship between testosterone and aggression in delinquent male adolescents. *Biological Psychiatry, 61*(3), 405–411.

Pryce, C. R., Dobeli, M., & Martin, R. D. (1993). Effects of sex steroids on maternal motivation in the common marmoset (*Callithrix jacchus*): Development and application of an operant system with maternal reinforcement. *Journal of Comparative Psychology, 107*(1), 99–115.

Rosenblatt, J. S. (2002). Hormone–behavior relations in the regulation of parental behavior. In J. B. Becker, S. M. Breedlove, & D. Crews (Eds.), *Behavioral endocrinology* (2nd ed., pp. 219–260). Cambridge, MA: MIT Press.

Ruiz-de-la-Torre, J. L., & Manteca, X. (1999). Effects of testosterone on aggressive behaviour after social mixing in male lambs. *Physiology and Behavior, 68*, 109–113.

Sapolsky, R. M. (1991). Testicular function, social rank, and personality among wild baboons. *Psychoneuroendocrinology, 16*, 281–293.

Schultheiss, O., Dargel, A., & Rohde, W. (2003). Implicit motives and gonadal steroid hormones: Effects of menstrual cycle phase, oral contraceptive use, and relationship status. *Hormones and Behavior, 43*(2), 293–301.

Schultheiss, O., Wirth, M., & Stanton, S. (2004). Effects of affiliation and power motivation arousal on salivary progesterone and testosterone. *Hormones and Behavior, 46*(5), 592–599.

Schultheiss, O. C., Wirth, M. M., Torges, C. M., Pang, J. S., Villacorta, M. A., & Welsh, K. M. (2005). Effects of implicit power motivation on men's and women's implicit learning and testosterone changes after social victory or defeat. *Journal of Personality and Social Psychology, 88*(1), 174–188.

Sellers, J. G., Mehl, M. R., & Josephs, R. A. (2007). Hormones and personality: Testosterone as a marker of individual differences. *Journal of Research in Personality, 41,* 126–138.

Shoal, G., Giancola, P., & Kirillova, G. (2003). Salivary cortisol, personality, and aggressive behavior in adolescent boys: A 5-year longitudinal study. *Journal of the American Academy of Child and Adolescent Psychiatry, 42*(9), 1101–1107.

Smider, N., Essex, M., Kalin, N., Buss, K., Klein, M., Davidson, R., et al. (2002). Salivary cortisol as a predictor of socioemotional adjustment during kindergarten: A prospective study. *Child Development, 73*(1), 75–92.

Taylor, S. (2006, December). Tend and befriend: Biobehavioral bases of affiliation under stress. *Current Directions in Psychological Science, 15*(6), 273–277.

Trainor, B. C., Bird, I. M., & Marler, C. A. (2004). Opposing hormonal mechanisms of aggression revealed through short-lived testosterone manipulations and multiple winning experiences. *Hormones and Behavior, 45,* 115–121.

Tremblay, R. E., Schaal, B., Boulerice, B., Arseneault, L., Soussignan, R. G., Paquette, D., et al. (1998). Testosterone, physical aggression, dominance, and physical development in early adolescence. *International Journal of Behavioral Development, 22*(4), 753–777.

Tsigos, C., & Chrousos, G. P. (2002). Hypothalamic-pituitary-adrenal axis, neuroendocrine factors and stress. *Journal of Psychosomatic Research, 53*(4), 865–871.

Van Anders, S., Hamilton, L., & Watson, N. (2007). Multiple partners are associated with higher testosterone in North American men and women. *Hormones and Behavior, 51*(3), 454–459.

Van Anders, S., & Watson, N. (2007). Testosterone levels in women and men who are single, in long-distance relationships, or same-city relationships. *Hormones and Behavior, 51*(2), 286–291.

Van Honk, J. (2008, February). *Fear, love, and aggression: The gonads rule.* Paper presented at the annual meeting of the Society for Personality and Social Psychology, Albuquerque, NM.

Van Honk, J., Kessels, R., Putman, P., Jager, G., Koppeschaar, H., & Postma, A. (2003). Attentionally modulated effects of cortisol and mood on memory for emotional faces in healthy young males. *Psychoneuroendocrinology, 28*(7), 941–948.

Van Honk, J., Peper, J., & Schutter, D. (2005). Testosterone reduces unconscious fear but not consciously experienced anxiety: Implications for the disorders of fear and anxiety. *Biological Psychiatry, 58*(3), 218–225.

Van Honk, J., Tuiten, A., Verbaten, R., van den Hout, M., Koppeschaar, H., Thijssen, J., et al. (1999). Correlations among salivary testosterone, mood, and selective attention to threat in humans. *Hormones and Behavior, 36*(1), 17–24.

Viau, V. (2002). Functional cross-talk between the hypothalamic-pituitary-gonadal and -adrenal axes. *Journal of Neuroendocrinology, 14,* 506–513.

Virgin, C. E., & Sapolsky, R. M. (1997). Styles of male social behavior and their endocrine correlates among low-ranking baboons. *American Journal of Primatology, 42*(1), 25–39.

Wingfield, J. C., Hegner, R. E., Dufty, A. M., Jr., & Ball, G. F. (1990). The "challenge hypothesis": Theoretical implications for patterns of testosterone secretion, mating systems, and breeding strategies. *American Naturalist, 136,* 829–846.

Wirth, M., & Schultheiss, O. (2006). Effects of affiliation arousal (hope of closeness) and affiliation stress (fear of rejection) on progesterone and cortisol. *Hormones and Behavior, 50*(5), 786–795.

Wirth, M. M., & Schultheiss, O. C. (2007). Basal testosterone moderates responses to anger faces in humans. *Physiology and Behavior, 90*, 496–505.

10

Power Basis Theory
A Psychoecological Approach to Power

FELICIA PRATTO, I-CHING LEE,
JUDY Y. TAN, and EILEEN V. PITPITAN

Why do people want power? One answer to this question focuses on the
peculiar motivations of power-hungry and powerful people (e.g., Fodor,
1985; McClelland, 1975; Winter, 1973). Another answer is that power
enables people to get what they want (Boulding, 1989). As absolute control is rare,
many social psychologists define power as the potential to influence others, which
makes it relational (e.g., Fiske & Berdahl, 2007). Raven's (e.g., 1965) seminal interpersonal power–interaction model describes six methods of interpersonal influence: (a) coercion, (b) reward, (c) legitimacy, (d) expertise, (e) information, and (f)
referent (i.e., affiliation). Although these approaches have shown *how* power motivations and social influence work, they do not address *why* power is a recurrent
feature of life and for all people. They also do not explain why structural inequality,
a by-product of stable power and coalitions, is typical of societies.

For these reasons, our approach is rather different. The ecological theory we
introduce here explains that humans must use power to survive and thrive in the
context of environmental constraints and affordances. Power Basis Theory argues
that the ontological necessity of power arises from the requirements humans have
for survival (their basic needs). Power motivations are what encourage action to
meet those needs and are prompted by the psychological apparatus humans have
for detecting those needs (sensibilities). Thus, instead of focusing on idiosyncratic
power motivations, our theory harnesses ordinary motivations that stem from real
and normal needs. Hence, we define power with respect to survival needs in the
ecological system rather than with respect to relationships.

According to Power Basis Theory, the kinds of power and desires that recur in human life do so because those kinds of power and motivations address particular basic needs. The universalism of these needs and desires allows people to provide for or anticipate other people's, which creates the possibility of social influence. This possibility allows people to transform one means of meeting a need into another. This *fungibility* among different types of power is what makes power dynamic and interactive with both the physical and the social environment. By understanding the social ecology of fungibility, one can understand power dynamics and stable inequality. Moreover, our ecological analysis presumes that when desires are calibrated with true survival needs and with the ecology, the system is functional, but the inability to meet needs, confusion of desires with needs, and miscalibration between living organisms and the environment can be dysfunctional for both people and their ecology.

We first address what power is and what its relation to needs is, and we then describe the sensation and motivational systems that, when working well, calibrate the needs of the organism to the local ecology. By understanding what people's basic needs are, we are able to predict what forms of power will recur in human life, what the likely sites of power conflict will be and the power tactics and strategies individuals and groups can use, what kinds of moral and ethical issues are likely to arise concerning power, and the implications of our theory for social inequality and power dynamics. We also present new data examining implications of our theory for ethics, power dynamics, group stereotypes, and person perception. The discussion revisits how our theory differs from other theories of power and suggests avenues for research.

WHAT IS POWER?

There is no consensual definition of *power*, but several conceptions are common in social theory and social science. Social power has been defined as *control over others*—that is, forcing others to do one's will (e.g., Dahl, 1957); as *social influence* or the ability to effect change in others (e.g., Weber, 1946); and, conversely, as *freedom* or having personal *agency* (Russell, 1938). Feminist theory spotlighted *transformative power* as the ability to help others develop (Wartenberg, 1990). Theorists who consider collectives such as groups and governments define power as the means of sustaining intergroup oppression (e.g., Mills, 1956). The relational and collective views of power emphasize the importance of considering the field or context in which power is exerted or that sustains power inequality itself.

None of these definitions of power seems wrong, but because they are incompatible, we must consider what power is more broadly in order to develop a definition of power that encompasses these conceptions. Let us start with observations about power and everyday life.

The amount of stable power one has corresponds to one's quality of life. The most powerful people on earth can choose to live luxuriously; their food, clothing, housing, and medical care are not only adequate but often superior. They enjoy companionship and popularity; freedom; safety and security; access to beauty, pleasure, and information; and the ability to ensure that they and their progeny maintain a social presence far beyond the locations they inhabit and even after they die. In contrast, the least powerful people on earth often go without food, housing, good health, and other necessities; are ignored or viewed with suspicion, fear, and hostility; often suffer from violence; have few options and little knowledge that can help them; and are often overlooked or forgotten even before they die.

This association between power and life quality is no coincidence. *Power is,* according to our definition, *the means to meet survival needs or to create deficits in needs.* However, power is not situated in the person or group as agency, because the means of meeting survival requirements depends jointly on needs, the environment, and human capacities. From the perspective of the needy person, power used to meet needs is *constructive,* and power used to create need deficits or prevent needs from being met is *destructive.* Because power enables people to meet their requirements for survival, power is pertinent to everyday living and survival not only for elites or the very destitute but for everyone. In fact, we argue that the reason that power dynamics recur in all human lives and societies is that power is how people meet their basic needs. Hence, the basis of power is needs.

To complete our ecological grounding of power, we must consider not only the basic needs people have but also how their environment and people's ways of interacting with the environment afford the meeting of each need. Typically, people have the ability to detect whether their needs are currently met, through their sensibilities. Some people (e.g., adults more than children) can anticipate needs arising. Detection of need or of the relevant sensation motivates the individual to return to a state in which needs are met through action, as hunger motivates the desire to eat. The motivated action then usually satiates the need, at least temporarily.

Figure 10.1 provides an overview of the sensibility and motivation processes we propose. The top two rows denote conditions of the relevant local ecology and the person. People have a set of recurrent basic needs and typically are equipped with sensibilities to detect those needs. Their environment may afford the meeting of those needs and behaviors that meet those needs to greater or lesser degrees. For example, people need nutrition and calories from food; their needs are signaled by hunger and food cravings. However, some environments have more abundant and more ready-to-eat food than others.

The bottom row of Figure 10.1 denotes the current state of the person. At times, particular needs become increased or even acute. As this occurs, a person's sensibilities are alerted, and motivation becomes active. Motivation combines with the behavioral skill repertoire and environmental affordances to influence what actions the person might take to follow the motivation and succor the need. For example, both the environment and one's behavioral repertoire influence whether one cries, begs, hunts, buys, cooks, forages, gardens, steals, or undertakes a different action in order to eat, and both the environment and the action jointly determine how successful the action is at succoring nutritional needs. Particular behaviors may in turn feed back into the system by changing the behavioral repertoire, by changing the environment, and by satisfying needs and reducing motivation (reducing paths shown with dashed lines in Figure 10.1). In extreme cases, to be discussed later, actions can even change the sensibilities for needs, just as turning up the volume on headphones to hear better can result in deafness.

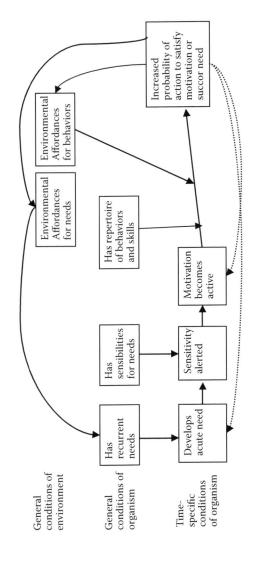

Figure 10.1   The Sensitivity/Motivation System mediating needs the environmental affordances.

Although motivation influences the likelihood of the person performing particular behaviors, motivation does not *determine* behavior. This is because people can choose among skills and behaviors and can set priorities that allow them to change the importance of a given motivation or sensibility. For example, despite a chronically operating hunger-satiation system and particular eating desires, people can learn to modify their eating habits, to fast on purpose, or to prioritize eating for health or politeness over eating to feel full. People's freedom of choice in our theory is determined by the breadth of their behavioral repertoires, by the range of behaviors in their repertoires that work within the given context, and by their ability to ignore, tame, postpone, or mutate their motivations and desires.

In Power Basis Theory, the motivational system connects the person's internal state to the environment, and its primary purpose is to alert the person to needs and to motivate actions to succor needs. To the extent that sensibilities and motivations are well calibrated and the environment affords needs being met, the system works well. However, because people are overly sensitive to losses (e.g., Kahneman, Knetsch, & Thaler, 1990), potential losses may decouple persons' motivations from their objective needs. When motivations are not to meet needs, they function as *desires*—strong wants that may feel necessary to survival but are not. Wanton desires, such as insatiable appetites for designer clothes or sweets, may result in other needs being neglected. In other words, the motivational system can take on a dysfunctional life of its own when it is not calibrated to actual survival needs.

Environmental affordances can constrain whether needs can be met, regardless of the operation of the sensibility–motivation system. For example, even if one shivers and wears a coat, a very cold environment can cause death from hypothermia. In environments that do not readily afford succoring needs, people may adapt their behaviors to meet needs, and these adaptations may or may not succor needs without creating new deficits. For example, people have responded to single-sex environments such as prisons and the military with adaptations such as prison "homosexuality" and prostitution outside all military bases, but these adaptations create other survival problems such as murder and AIDS. Hence, survival and thriving are jointly contingent on the local environment and on motivations and actions.

NEEDS AND THE BASIC FORMS OF POWER

To this point, we have stated that power motivation originates from basic needs, with the caveat that the motivational system also produces desires that are deleterious to meeting needs. An important second layer to this foundation is that people have *particular* needs that are not simply alternative forms of each other. Rather, each need must be met by need-specific forms of power. Specifying what needs are universal and chronic will tell us what kinds of power one can expect to be universal and recurrent. Our reading about human power relations and considerations of the ecology, physical conditions, and psychological states of human beings has led us to identify a small set of fundamental needs—that is, requirements for survival. In this section we describe each category of basic need, the form of power that corresponds to it, the sensibilities that signal how acute a need is or whether it is met, and the motivations that lead people to take action to succor their needs. Table 10.1 summarizes these ideas. Table 10.1 also indicates what interpersonal influence tactic from Raven's (1965) model seems to fit each type of power.

Wholeness, Violence, and Healing. The most obvious need a human has for surviving is to maintain bodily and psychological functioning. Failures of many bodily and psychological functions, including those due to severe injury and illness, certain memory deficits, and self-disregard (e.g., anorexia and depression), can cause incapacitation and death. As people chronically need wholeness of self in mind and body, the possibility of maiming or killing the body or causing extreme psychological harm implies that violence and its threat will always be forms of destructive power. Conversely, the ability to help others heal through medicinal practice, enabling rest, nursing, psychological therapy, support for self-healing, and the like, will always be potential forms of constructive power.

People generally sense their physical and emotional well-being and can also sense discomfort and pain and feel fear when their well-being is endangered. Because of these sensibilities, one can also wield power by threatening injury or death and by causing physical or psychological pain, especially if one promises relief from such pain. Such methods are called coercion and torture, respectively. Two main motivations that generally help maintain wholeness are to avoid pain and to shelter oneself from danger.

Resources and Their Control. To survive, people regularly need certain nutrients, calories, fresh water, and shelter from exposure. These direct material needs can produce indirect needs in terms of the means of production of physical necessities, such as tools for farming, housing, and making clothes. Our universal, chronic need for material resources implies that control of resources and the means to obtain, store, and use them will always be a basis of power (Marx, 1904). Because one's neighbors often have important information about how to acquire resources and how much to acquire, people often use social comparison to gauge their resource needs. In the presence of wealth, these standards may supersede needs. When people overconsume resources because they anticipate their neighbors' consumption from a common pool, or because standards are too high, they can deplete their ecological resources.

Need to Interact Competently With One's Environment and Knowledge. Interacting competently with one's environment, including with other people, is a requirement for survival (e.g., Elliot & Dweck, 2005). Knowledge enables the competence to avoid dangers and to obtain necessities. The environment determines what knowledge is required. Individuals have many kinds of knowledge, including useful habits, implicit expectations and assumptions, skills, declarative knowledge, and methods of gaining more knowledge (e.g., research). The sensations of novelty-attention and confusion motivate curiosity and mastery-striving, which in turn motivate behaviors that increase knowledge. Expectancy violations, surprises, and failures also motivate knowledge change or acquisition. Humans store knowledge not only individually but also collectively. Cultural patterns of behavior and creations implicitly store such knowledge as how to build buildings, how to worship, how to make cloth, and what is important to us. Humans also know

TABLE 10.1   Type of Power, Sensibilities, and Motivations
Corresponding to Basic Needs

Basic Need	Type of Power	Sensibilities	Motivations	IPIM Influence Method
Wholeness (healthy functioning of body and psyche)	Harm and its threat; Ability to inflict pain or give pleasure	Sense of well-being; Fear, anticipation of pain; Pain, discomfort	Drive for self-integrity and well-being; Pain avoidance and pleasure seeking	Coercion
Consume resources	Control of resources	Hunger; Thirst; Feeling cold; Upward comparison	Envy; Acquisitiveness; Greed; Desire for physical comfort	Reward
To interact competently with one's environment	Knowledge	Confusion; Surprise; Aversion to failure; Pleasure of success	Curiosity; Mastery-striving; Desire for efficacy; Pride over competency	Expertise; Information
Care from other people	Commitments from others	Empathy; Attachment; Pity; Trust and mistrust	Sense of obligation; Equity; Norm to reciprocate; Loneliness; Desire for companionship	Referent
To be respected and accepted by a community	Legitimacy	Feeling excluded; Feeling stigmatized or devalued; Feeling of recognition or appreciation; Social anxiety	Desire for social approval; Pursuit for positive self-regard	Legitimacy
To reproduce	Sexual attractiveness; Symbolic transcendence; Self-expansion	Awe; Sexual arousal; Mortality salience	Sexual desire; Desire for transcendence; Desire to lose or alter self-awareness; Hope	

Note: IPIM indicates Interpersonal Power/Interaction Model (e.g., Raven, 1965).

how to communicate in a wide variety of ways. These ways of acquiring, storing, and accessing knowledge are constructive.

Knowledge can also be destructive. Personal and cultural habits that are believed to meet needs but that in fact do not meet needs (i.e., superstitions) and may produce deficits (e.g., the belief that one will get rich by gambling) are one form of destructive knowledge. A second form of destructive knowledge is misinformation, including lies, deceptions, and withheld information, because these can lead other people to be incompetent in their environments.

Care From Others and Obligations. To survive infancy, all humans require at least three years of intensive physical and emotional care. In addition, nearly everyone needs the care of others during severe illness and extreme old age. Such care includes bodily work, such as providing food, hygiene, clothing, shelter, places to rest, and emotional work to help with psychological challenges of having needs and physical infirmity. To provide such care, most of which must be provided in person, humans usually establish social systems of obligations through families and generational roles in which adults provide care for infants and children and in which younger people care for older people and the infirm.

People's infantile desire for attachment helps us develop the more learned sensibilities that enable caring relationships (e.g., Bowlby, 1973). Through close relationship socialization, we learn empathy, which helps us to imagine others' needs and care about their well-being (e.g., Davis, 1983); pity for those in need, which can motivate a desire to help (e.g., Cialdini et al., 1987; Hendriks & Vingerhoets, 2006); jealousy, which motivates wanting care and commitment (e.g., Desteno & Salovey, 1996; Sharpsteen & Kirkpatrick, 1997); and trust, which motivates us to rely on others (e.g., Rempel, Holmes, & Zanna, 1985). These emotions all motivate caregiving. Two other socialized norms motivate obligations to care: the norms of reciprocity (e.g., Homans, 1961) and paternalism (e.g., Pratto & Walker, 2000).

Belonging to a Community and Legitimacy. Belonging to a community aids survival and is adaptive (e.g., Caporael, 1995). As people have a fundamental psychological need to belong (Baumeister & Leary, 1995; McClelland, 1975), welcoming communities are also essential to survival. Several social sensibilities signal whether one is accepted by a particular community: People notice when they are recognized and acknowledged, or they may feel left out, stigmatized, or devalued. People gauge their relative social standing or status fairly accurately (Anderson, Srivastava, Beer, Spataro, & Chatman, 2006). People are motivated to belong because being ostracized is distressful and painful (e.g., Williams, 2007). People desire social approval and especially after praise from others whom they respect or care about, and when they feel devalued, they try to change their community or membership in communities (Baumeister & Leary, 1995). Likewise, people who feel ashamed and humiliated are motivated to repair their social acceptability with behavior that connotes apology, respect for others, and deference.

Reproduction, Sexual Attractiveness, and Self-Transcendence. Reproduction is not necessary for a given person's survival unless made so by social conditions (e.g., societies in which women must bear children in order to receive material resources), but for a species, reproduction is necessary for survival. The sensibility of sexual arousal, and the motivations of lust, and desire for children encourage people to produce babies. However, these are not the only sensibilities and motivations necessary for our species to reproduce. In addition to having material needs, children require decades to mature and must be socialized to their cultures, so reproduction requires that adults succor their children's needs as well as their own. Quite often, adults must be willing to forgo their own needs to attend to those of their children. In short, human reproduction requires that adults be willing to labor for purposes other than their own desires and needs. The motivation to do this is the human desire for self-transcendence.

By self-transcendence, we mean a sensation of existing beyond oneself. This sensation can be induced in many ways: by intense sensory experiences, by greatly expanding one's perspective, and by identifying with other people and ideas. The pleasure of self-transcendent experiences, including athletic activity (Jackson, Kimiecik, Ford, & Marsh, 1998), mysticism (Graef, 1965), considering universal truths (Maslow, 1964), falling in love (Aron, Paris, & Aron, 1995), and creative activities (Arndt, Greenberg, Solomon, Pyszczynski, & Schimel, 1999), is highly motivating (e.g., Csikszentmihalyi & LeFevre, 1989; Keltner & Haidt, 2003). Escapism, or forgetting one's self, is appealing for similar reasons but may become detrimental, as with alcoholism (Steele & Josephs, 1988).

MISCALIBRATION IN THE SENSITIVITY AND MOTIVATIONAL SYSTEMS

Although human sensibility and motivation systems are largely functional and often correct themselves, we can use Figure 10.1 as a heuristic to predict ways that the systems might malfunction in the long term. People who do not notice or who deny their own needs are unlikely to have appropriate needs met. Another malfunction is to misinterpret one need for another. People may be over- or undersensitive to particular sensibilities or may lack connection between a sensibility and its concomitant motivation. People may not have learned or may have mislearned what behaviors should follow from particular motivations and can lack overall motivation. Finally, people may become insensitive to feedback such that the motivations or sensibilities do not vary with internal states. To provide examples of such miscalibrations, we describe cases within each of the six basic needs.

The Need for Wholeness of Body and Psyche. A sense of well-being indicates the fulfillment of wholeness. People with hypochondriasis misinterpret bodily symptoms as possessing a serious disease although medically they are well (American Psychiatric Association, 2000). Conversely, some people are unaware or deny that they are ill. For instance, alcoholics may deny their alcohol abuse, and autistic children and schizophrenics believe their hallucinations reflect reality (Beitman & Nair, 2005). The pain–pleasure aspect of the motivational system can make substances that stimulate pleasure not only appealing but addicting: Substances such as opiates relieve pain temporarily, followed by even more pain and discomfort, which motivates pain relief via another dose (e.g., Goodman, 1990).

The Need to Consume Resource. The hunger–satiation feedback loop is one of our most specialized sensibility systems. For example, people are sensitized to their nutritional needs not only by hunger and thirst but by more specialized cravings for foods that meet current nutrient deficits (e.g., Coelho, Polivy, & Herman, 2006). However, people with diabetes overdetect hunger, and people with Prader-Willi syndrome fail to detect satiation. Fortunately, people with either disease can use artificial sensibilities such as habits, glucose monitors, and appetite suppressants to calibrate their eating with bodily needs (Cox et al., 2006; Malerbi & Matos, 2001; University of Maryland Medical Center, 2006).

Interact Competently With One's Environment. A host of sensory and cognitive challenges, from deafness to learning disabilities, can diminish knowledge acquisition, especially without appropriate and intensive stimulation and teaching. Neurological damage can also hamper people's sensibilities and skill sets. Most tragically, children who are extremely neglected or raised with little human contact acquire almost none of the language, social, emotional, and other knowledge necessary for competence, and their motivational systems may also be permanently damaged.

The Need for Care From Others. Receiving care from and providing care to others are integral to any close relationship. Infant attachment orients people to receiving and providing care in adulthood (e.g., Bowlby, 1973). Securely attached people give and receive affection to experience happiness and satisfaction in their close relationships. In contrast, insecurely attached people may not detect care, cannot gauge others' intentions, suppress affective reactions, or even avoid intimacy (e.g., Bartholomew & Horowitz, 1991; Mikulincer & Orbach, 1995).

The Need for Social Approval. Social cues communicate whether people belong to a certain group or community, which is gauged by self-esteem (Leary & Baumeister, 2000). Those who are constantly being disapproved of may suffer from low self-esteem and develop depression symptoms (Roberts, Gotlib, & Kassel, 1996), experience less positive emotions, or become pessimistic (e.g., Twenge, Baumeister, Tice, & Stucke, 2001), which in turn makes them shy away from social interactions (Pickett & Gardner, 2005). In fact, people who are constantly rejected may behave destructively, such as by acting aggressively (Twenge et al., 2001), which would usually be sanctioned by one's social group.

The Need for Reproduction. Species and cultures need reproduction to survive, but the sensibilities and motivations that increase reproduction occur within individuals. Social conditions such as poverty and use of child labor, pronatal cultural beliefs, and limited access to artificial birth control encourage people to become parents early and often. The world's population is increasing exponentially (e.g., Ehrlich & Ehrlich, 1991), to the point that it precipitates environmental catastrophes. As a result, the sensibilities producing human life are ruining the ecology that must sustain it. Having many children is easy and may benefit individuals, but because overpopulation impoverishes the earth, a common resource, reproduction is both a social trap and a common dilemma. To stop overpopulation from destroying environmental sustainability, we must change the timescale of feedback to individuals so that short-term motivations align with long-term need sustainability (e.g., Oskamp, 2006).

Problems With the Ecology. Living persons can be miscalibrated with their ecology if the ecology gives feedback on a timescale for which people are not sensitive or if people's senses cannot detect important ecological changes. For example, human industrialization began to warm surface and water temperatures of the earth by 1750, but such anthropomorphic ecological changes predated the development of scientific means of measuring global temperatures directly by 100 years (Intergovernmental Panel on Climate Change, 2007, p. 8). Another significant kind of miscalibration results from people holding the wrong assumptions about how broad their ecology is. For example, nuclear fallout and global warming demonstrate that because of our shared and moving atmosphere, claims to sovereignty over land and water areas are insufficient for understanding what aspects of the physical environment "belong" to which groups of people. People's wrong assumptions about who is in their community can also lead to miscalibrations. For example, the reciprocation norm usually limits people taking resources from a common pool, but people are greedy among strangers (Yamagishi & Sato, 1986). Natural resources do not know or care if they are being depleted by "friends" or "strangers." There are both natural and human reasons that the human–natural ecologies may be miscalibrated in terms of their timescales for feedback, locality or scope of influence, and understanding of their functioning.

STRESS AND SURVIVAL

There is one other major pervasive possibility of malfunction in the sensibility–feedback system—namely, the stress response. The fight-or-flight stress response allows people to escape from immediate physical danger (e.g., Mason, 1968) and is regulated by the hypothalamic-pituitary-adrenal (HPA) axis. However, prolonged stress from sustained exposure to danger (e.g., constant local assault) can lead to dysregulation of the HPA axis (e.g., Yehuda, Giller, Southwick, & Lowy, 1991).

Chronic stress may result when environmental affordances do not allow a person's actions to succor needs. For example, social discrimination diminishes belonging (e.g., Mays, Cochran, & Barnes, 2007) and may produce deficits in other needs, such as wholeness and resource acquisition. Discrimination may also, depending on the individual's repertoire of skills and behaviors, trigger coping responses such as hostility and overeating that do not attenuate stress and may create new deficits (e.g., Clark, Anderson, Clark, & Williams, 1999). Over time, stress responses can lead to chronic psychological problems (e.g., helplessness, depression, paranoia) and threaten bodily wholeness by compromising the immune, neuroendrocrine, and cardiovascular systems (Cacioppo, 1994; Herbert & Cohen, 1993; Merritt, Bennett, Williams, Edwards, & Sollers, 2006). Social support buffers the negative effects of stress through HPA-axis deactivation (e.g., DeVries, Craft, Glasper, Neigh, & Alexander, 2007). Dissociative states (e.g., amnesia, depersonalization, decreased arousal) may serve as a temporary escape for victims of past trauma (Simeon et al., 2007) by providing another escape or rest from chronic stress. Eliminating chronic stressors such as institutional discrimination and exposure to danger are equally important in reducing the deleterious effects of stress.

These examples illustrate some difficulties in meeting basic needs when the sensibility, motivation, feedback, or environment of a system is miscalibrated. Such problems in a minority of cases do not imply that our analysis of the power–needs system is wrong any more than a refrigerator with a broken temperature gauge fails to be a refrigerator. The most acute problems concern how short-term motivations and responses produce behaviors that are detrimental in the long term.

NEEDS ARE SPECIFIC; BEHAVIORS ARE NOT

People have several distinct basic needs that must be met through concomitant forms of power. This specificity of needs has an important implication: Having a particular need met (e.g., one has enough material resources) does not make one powerful with respect to any other specific needs (e.g., one may still be ostracized). Even within the categories of needs we specified, certain means of fulfilling needs do not substitute for others. For example, fuel that provides warmth to people often cannot be used as food (e.g., coal). Likewise, a strong sense of belonging with one particular person often cannot be completely substituted for attachment with another person. Hence, there are real limits to each kind of power to the extent that one cannot be substituted or traded for another.

Behaviors, however, do not always have the same specificity as needs. Perhaps for efficiency, people have invented a number of behavioral patterns that fulfill many needs at once. For example, sharing a meal can not only provide nutrition but also affirm one's legitimacy and sense of affiliation and provide knowledge or a chance to verify knowledge, elicit care, and expand oneself. This implies that for a given person, several needs may be met by engaging in one behavior. In our learning histories, then, we may learn to misassociate behaviors that meet one need with a different need. For example, if we grow up sharing meals that provide food and a sense of belonging, we could come to presume that eating is what one does when one is lonely. However, eating alone when one is lonely will not fulfill the need to belong and could produce additional problems (e.g., weight gain) as well. The multipurpose efficiency of certain behaviors may miseducate people about what their needs are or how they can be met.

The fact that a given behavior can meet different needs also implies that different people may perform the behavior to meet different needs. For example, one person may participate in a dinner party to learn from the expertise of other guests, another to forge a social alliance, another to feel respected, and another to pave the way for a sexual encounter. Because a person may meet several needs with one action, and different individuals can meet different needs by one action, one cannot deduce from performance of a particular behavior what power motive or needs are driving it.

THE SOCIAL DYNAMICS OF POWER

Power Basis Theory outlines two major forms of social power dynamics. First, because needs are universal and can sometimes be detected or assumed for others, people can anticipate others' needs and desires. Therefore, people can influence others by creating need deficits and desires in others, by offering to meet needs and desires, and by enabling others to meet or preventing others from meeting their needs. This is social influence. Second, people determine what kinds of power become fungible with other kinds through their willingness to engage in transactions that transfer power from one kind or party to another and by allowing particular power transactions. This is economics. Although laws and cultural mores may prohibit particular transactions that use one form of power to gain another form (e.g., sex for money), it takes only two participating parties to establish fungibility between kinds of power. Adults from a wide variety of occupations and nationalities have provided us with examples of how people use each of the kinds of power to gain another kind of power (see Table 10.2). High fungibility implies that anyone with one form of power can become advantaged in other forms. Therefore, another means of governing power is to influence fungibility for particular parties or kinds of power. This is government.

We know of no general theories that explain how fungible different kinds of power are or what the conditions are that influence how fungible kinds of power are. Nonetheless, men's domains of power—force, legitimacy, and resources—appear to be much more fungible than women's domains of power—obligations to others and sexual access—which are less fungible because they are largely personal. Pratto and Walker (2004) postulated that the reason that relationships among men are more volatile and lethal than relationships among women, and the reason that gender inequality is relatively stable, is these differences in fungibility in gendered domains of power.

INEQUALITY

Fungibility is also the key to understanding structural inequality. Naturally, any party that has access to more than one form of power has more options and more potential for advantage. But groups and individuals who are advantaged in highly fungible kinds of power have even more behavioral options. So long as they are willing to engage in the behaviors that would enable a form of power they possess to gain more power (e.g., to use force, to sell assets, to endorse politicians), they can retain their relative advantage. Maintenance of such power is not a given, as other parties may also be attempting to meet needs and perhaps gain advantages as well. Rather, power maintenance depends on the ability and willingness to exercise power on one's own behalf, sometimes by limiting competitor's power. We can expect structural inequality to often be group based because the need to belong and self-transcendence motivate group formation and social categories, and coalitions extend the reach of power across actors.

A fungibility advantage can create an upward power spiral. U.S. history provides a good example. The colonial powers smoothed the way for the United States by reducing competition from eastern Native Americans and Atlantic pirates. The American revolutionaries were able and willing to use violence to gain control of abundant natural resources and establish legal legitimacy (in some eyes). Americans gained knowledge from immigrants and through innovation and theft (e.g., the cotton gin) to become even more economically productive via industrialization. The United States has used war and the threat of violence to maintain advantaged economic relations with many other nations but has rarely entered into colonial relations, which would give the United States greater obligations. U.S. power has generally increased up to now.

TABLE 10.2 Examples of How an Individual or Group Could Use the Form of Power in the Rows to Gain the Form of Power in the Columns

	Knowledge	Force	Legitimacy	Resources	Asymmetric Obligations	Sexuality
Knowledge		Speed traps; Develop weapons; Terror alerts; Using intimidation knowledge to hurt others	Using "intelligence" to justify foreign policy; Investigative journalism; Scientific publications to increase reputation	Insider stock trading; Identity theft; Patent expert; Hacking computers; Winning at Jeopardy game	Blackmail	Use personal knowledge to persuade someone into sexual actions or relationships
Force	Torture; Police interrogation		U.S. invasion of Iraq to promote democracy; Boxer winning title; Honor killing	Colonization; U.S. wars of expansion; Robbery	Conscription; Domestic violence to keep spouse in marriage	Rape
Legitimacy	9/11 Commission; Legacy admissions to college; Management access to knowledge	Police harassment; Liberation movements; Israeli–Palestinian violence; Marital rape; Parents physically punishing their children		De Beers "fair trade" diamonds; President rolls back environmental laws to help his friend's mine; TV evangelists soliciting contributions; Politicians receiving contributions	Elders' positions in their villages; John Gotti in the "family"; Cult members' dominance of women	Use high status to entice sexual relationship

Resources	Buying a computer or Internet access; Paying tuition for college; Pay experts	Scabs during a labor strike; Hiring private security guards	Teenagers' buying popular clothing; The rich get on boards of corporations; Political contributions		Government controls water and makes people buy it; Saudis' control of oil gets influence over United States	Prostitution; Cosmetic surgery; Spas
Asymmetric obligations	Patriot Act; Retired police officers get the police to run license numbers through their system; False friends	Winners of wars ask losers of wars to disarm	Nonviolent protests by oppressed people to draw sympathy to their cause; Nepotism; Vote for your friend	Labor strikes for wages; A couple's in-laws move in with them; Alimony; Bill Clinton asked Vernon Jordan to get Monica Lewinsky a job		Posturing indifference to a relationship to gain sexual access; A surviving brother taking his deceased brother's wife
Sexuality	Use intimate relationship to get disclosure of state or corporate secrets	Making two rivals fight for sexual favors	Women marrying "up" to increase their social status	Prostitution; Being a "kept" mistress	Prostitutes using wages to care for their children or parents	

Limited fungibility can also produce a downward spiral of power, and such spirals show how tenuous disadvantaged people are. The role of women in nearly all societies obliges them to provide care to family members and sexual access only to their husbands, neither of which is very fungible to other parties or for other kinds of power. Press reports from Iraq after the U.S.-led 2003 invasion show how tenuous this makes women's positions and those of their dependents. When invaders or locals kill women's husbands, these women not only lose the family breadwinner but may no longer be seen as legitimate family members entitled to family assets by their in-laws. Because women are not allowed to work, some have turned to illicit prostitution to support their families, for which they could easily suffer murder as punishment for violation of local religious and cultural customs. The relationships among people and their needs are what give fungibility these dynamic ripple effects.

SOME IMPLICATIONS OF POWER BASIS THEORY

Social Judgments to Aid Survival: Power and Trust

With its fundamentally ecological view of how people interact with others and the natural environment, Power Basis Theory implies that people's social perceptions should help them navigate meeting their own needs and avoiding destructive power. In fact, we believe that most people know that power can be both destructive and constructive, and so people are concerned about not only who has or lacks power but whether others are likely to behave constructively or destructively toward others (e.g., Peeters & Czapinski, 1990). One's sense of whether another person or group would use power only for its own benefit, or to benefit one or harm one, is *trust*. In fact, in scores of psychological studies, two dimensions of social judgment recur: power and trust. Although power is sometimes more specifically called status, agency, competence, dominance, or self-profitability, and trust is sometimes called warmth, communion, evaluation, likability, morality, or other-profitability, these two basic dimensions can be found in group stereotypes (Eagly & Steffen, 1984; Fiske, Cuddy, Glick, & Xu, 2002; Leach, Ellemers, & Barreto, 2007), semantic meaning (Nier, Gaertner, & Gorcheva, 2006; Osgood, Suci, & Tannenbaum, 1957), trait judgments (e.g., Peeters & Czapinski, 1990), interpersonal perception (e.g., Wiggins, 1979), and implicit personality theory (e.g., Vonk, 1993).

Societal Governance of Power

Our ecological perspective points out that the context of individual and group power is not just interpersonal but can include societies and even international relations. In fact, because the ways power is used and distributed impact whole societies, societies are confronted with the problem of how to govern the use of power. One could use the parameters of Power Basis Theory to analyze politics and governments. For example, one might analyze how governments restrain particular forms of power (e.g., violence) and enable or constrain fungibility of different kinds of power. Comparative politics could reveal how well political processes allow political actors to monopolize the means of meeting needs, to concentrate power, or to prevent concentrations of power. Obviously such a study is beyond our scope here, but studying perceptions of political individuals and groups in the context of whose needs are met and political procedures may prove a fruitful way to understand political processes.

In addition to formal governance, societies have ethical systems, which provide self-guides, social standards, and emotions to help govern how people use power. The elements of Power Basis Theory can also be used to delineate forms of formal ethical systems and cultural mores. One means of deciding whether a particular use of power is ethical is to refer to a value system that prioritizes whose needs should be met or what kinds of needs are most important. Another form of power ethics concerns what kinds of parties are entitled to exercise what kinds of power and on whose behalf. For example, domestic and international political debates have concerned whether women or governments are obliged to care for others or should be free from such encumbrances. Some such prescriptions are relational. For example, some ethics proscribe that more powerful people should not use their power against the less powerful (e.g., "No bullying!") or are obliged to use power to benefit less powerful people (e.g., charity). Some ethical systems mandate the exercise of particular kinds of power (e.g., capitalism prioritizes exchange of material resources), and others prohibit the exercise of particular kinds of power (e.g., pacifism prohibits using violence) or concern what forms of power are acceptably traded for other forms (e.g., is a cash gift an appropriate way to get one's child admitted to a hospital or school?). A fourth form of power ethics concerns the purpose of using power. Different ideologies emphasize that power should be used to bring about good, to maximize economic output, to maintain social harmony, or for personal gain. Power Basis Theory easily allows for these varieties of cultural or more formal ethical systems.

Forms of Power and Sites of Conflict

Power Basis Theory predicts that conflicts will arise among individuals and between groups and societies regarding the types of power that are concomitant to basic needs. One kind of evidence that the basic forms of power are sites of conflict is in the use of violence over each form of power. A huge number of wars could be said to concern who is the *legitimate* ruler (e.g., the war of the Roses, Pope Julius's wars against French and Venetian independence) or which groups have legitimate political control over an area (e.g., the Northern Irish conflict, most civil wars, wars of national liberation, ethnic conflicts). Another large set of conflicts have engaged the force of law, extralegal uses of force, or military action over *resource control*, including imperial wars, piracy, protection or control of trade routes, material and intellectual property rights, patents, and so forth. Force is also used to control or to suppress *knowledge*, as in Galileo's house arrest by the Pope, the Soviet Gulag, the Chinese Cultural Revolution, and the mass murder of educated people by Pol Pot. Access to *pleasure-giving substances* has also provoked wars and other violent conflicts: U.S. prohibition on alcohol led to gang warfare over control of illicit distribution, and Britain went to war with China several times over forced importation of opium and exportation of tea. The British colonized India to maintain access to tea. Whether the Trojan War over the sexually attractive Helen is apocryphal, a large number of men murder other men around the globe over *sexual jealousy* (Daly & Wilson, 1988). When individuals, groups, or nations are not satisfied with the current balance of power, or in their desires, they engage in conflict over at least one of the basic forms of power.

Strategies and Tactics in Power Struggles

Our view of power suggests several strategies for maintaining relative power over others. Parties can exercise forms of power against or on behalf of others, can try to prevent other parties from gaining or exercising forms of power, can restrict others' access to power or use of power, can influence other parties to use power to sustain themselves rather than to use it against others, and can try to restrict fungibility of different forms of power for others while maintaining high fungibility for themselves.

The basic forms of power suggest basic tactics that can be used in power struggles. We have no space to exhaustively list them all but provide a few examples of constructive and destructive tactics associated with each form of power, which can be used either by individuals or by collectives such as institutions and societies.

Wholeness-maintaining tactics include provision of medical care, rest, psychological care, and defensive apparatuses (e.g., bulletproof jackets), whereas wholeness-destroying tactics include torture, maiming, spread of disease and addictive substances, and use of weapons. As governmental sovereignty largely concerns monopolizing force, it is no surprise that governments try to control weapons, pleasure-giving drugs, the military, the police, and the justice system and other institutions of force and to credentialize healers.

Legitimacy can be conferred or removed by stigmatization or awards, through stereotypes and reputation spreading (e.g., gossip, recommendations), and by applying ideologies about who is admirable or despicable. Although legitimacy can be communicated interpersonally, the mass media, charitable organizations, religious institutions, and governments can also confer or deny legitimacy.

Commitments, obligations, and reneging on obligations can be communicated interpersonally through words and deeds, but these are often given meaning through cultural symbols, rituals, role prescriptions, and ideologies. Family members cajole, request, and argue about their commitments, but the law and religious institutions also help to define and enforce obligations through marriage customs and laws, recognition of social contracts, and enforcing or teaching obligatory roles (e.g., parental obligations or duty to country). Individuals can labor or steal to gain material resources, but collectives and governments have a wide variety of devices to control material resources, including imposing import and export taxes, engaging in collective bargaining, creating mutual aid societies, building trade routes or relationships, enforcing property laws, and providing or restricting access to water and land.

During conflict, theft of knowledge that produces resources (e.g., identity theft), pillaging, and destroying cropland are tactics aimed at increasing one's own resource control at the expense of others'. Knowledge is communicated in numerous obvious ways. Control of knowledge power can come by restricting access to education or information, lying, withholding information, developing new knowledge, or disseminating successful practices. Throughout history, an important social control device has been to prohibit literacy and education to slaves and women. During several cultural conflicts, dominators have all but destroyed the cultural knowledge of the conquered. For example, Canadians suppressed most of the rituals of the Kwakiutl, and Christians burned all the books of the Islamic library in Granada when they extirpated Muslims in 1492.

Sexual attractiveness can be enhanced with numerous beauty devices and practices, but sexual behavior can be at least partly controlled interpersonally and through social customs (e.g., killing adulteresses, sex segregation) and the law. To restrict self-transcendence and the reproduction of one's generation, groups and individuals have desecrated or hidden graves, destroyed monuments, repressed religious practices, forced sterilizations, and separated families. However, it is far harder to restrict self-transcendence than any other form of power because of the variety of means by which it can be achieved.

NEW RESEARCH ON POWER BASIS THEORY

The breadth of Power Basis Theory is reflected in the variety of research it is beginning to generate. This section shows how Power Basis Theory can be used to examine cultural ethics, power dynamics in an experimental game, the contents of group stereotypes, and person perception.

Ethical Cultural Teachings About Wants and the Use of Power

As unfettered desires and destructive power can seriously damage societies, we expect cultures to develop ways to try to curb insatiable power appetites and to sanction using power in ways that damage the community or relationships. For this reason, we expect cultural ethical and moral precepts to invoke elements of Power Basis Theory. Ethical teachings could focus on desires and motivations, on when power should be used selfishly or altruistically, and on what forms of power should be fungible with other forms of power. We illustrate this prediction by using three predominant ethical bases of culture: Buddhism, Confucianism, and the Abrahamic family of religions. Table 10.3 lists a number of moral precepts from, respectively, the five precepts from the Buddhist Sila, or ways that laypeople are to live; the six virtues promoted in Confucianism; and the Ten Commandments, which are said to be God's instructions or law for people given to Moses about 4,000 years ago. These precepts do not represent each belief system completely, but these teachings about "right living" are foundational for each ethical or moral system and also have been foundational for many of the world's modern civilizations. This brief study will show that each ethical or moral body of teachings does address central elements of our theory, including all the power bases we have discussed, their corresponding motivations and desires, or whether power is used on one's own behalf or on behalf of others.

TABLE 10.3 Examples of Common Ethical Precepts and Their Relation to Power Bases

Precept	Relation to Power Bases and Motivations or Desires
Precept 1. To refrain from taking life.	Admonition against violating wholeness.
Precept 2. To refrain from taking that which is not given.	Admonition against controlling others' resources.
Precept 3. To refrain from sensual misconduct (abstinence from immoral sexual behavior)	Prohibition against misuse of sexuality and extravagance.
Precept 4. To refrain from lying.	Prohibition against creating false knowledge.
Precept 5. To refrain from intoxicants that lead to loss of mindfulness (refrain from using drugs or alcohol).	Admonishment to maintain a state in which knowledge can be used and not confused.
Virtue: Xiao or Hsaio (Filial piety)	Obligation of children to parents (and parents to children).
Virtue: Xin (Integrity, Honesty, Trustworthiness).	Admonition to create knowledge and not create misinformation.
Virtue: Li (Propriety). Use patience and courtesy, follow rituals, act properly.	These practices demonstrate a person's legitimacy and trustworthiness.
Virtue: Yi (Righteousness). Privilege action that is right and moral.	This virtue emphasizes being trustworthy and altruistic in use of power.
Virtue: Ren (Benevolence). In deciding on actions, choose what is best for all involved rather than only what is best for oneself. Employ compassion, empathy, and understanding.	This virtue emphasizes considering the other's view and being trustworthy in relation to power.
Virtue: Chung (Loyalty). Offer help whenever possible to one's family, community, and nation.	Use one's power to help and protect oneself and others.
Confucian virtue: Shu (Forgiveness). Consider that people are all enmeshed in relation to one another before determining one's actions.	This virtue admonishes people to consider how their own power behavior affects others.
Commandment 1. You shall have no other God before me.	Admonishment to obligation.
Commandment 2. You shall create no graven images.	Admonishment to obligation.
Commandment 3. You shall not swear falsely.	Prohibition against deception (false knowledge) by using God's name to speak of trivial points such as swearing in frustration.
Commandment 4. Honor your father and mother.	Admonishment to obligation.
Commandment 5. You shall not kill.	Prohibits violating wholeness.
Commandment 6. Do not commit adultery.	Prohibits using sexuality without obligation.
Commandment 7. Do not steal or kidnap.	Prohibits taking resources and restricting others' freedom.
Commandment 8. Do not bear false witness against your neighbors.	Prohibits using false knowledge to delegitimize others.
Commandment 9. Do not covet your neighbor's wife or lust after women.	Admonition against male lust for women (sexuality).

TABLE 10.3   Examples of Common Ethical Precepts and Their Relation to Power Bases (Continued)

Precept	Relation to Power Bases and Motivations or Desires
Commandment 10. Do not covet your neighbor's house or goods.	Admonition against greed (desire for material resources).

Note: The precepts are from the Buddhist Sila for laypeople, actions deliberately taken as the right way to live. The six Confucian virtues are the most important general aspects of self-criticism and striving in Confucianism. The commandments are from the Ten Commandments, common to Judaism, Islam, and Christianity. The wording here reflects a variety of interpretations among different sects.

Buddhism. Prince Siddhartha Gautama, the Buddha, who lived about 500 BCE, renounced the luxuries of his own social position to seek and teach the right way to live. He taught that everyone suffers in life and that the cause of suffering is desire. Many of Buddha's teachings concern how to rid oneself of various desires so that one can become happy, including curbing what our theory calls power motives (e.g., greed for resources, lust for sex, envy of other's resources, deception and self-deception rather than knowledge). In other words, Buddhism prescribes happiness not by fulfilling desires suggested by need-based motivations but rather by *freeing oneself of such desires.* Several of the admonitions to the 10 perfections or virtues within Buddhism appear to be ways to prevent antisocial uses of power. For example, *generosity* should curb control of resources, as should *renunciation*; *truthfulness* should curb deception; and *sympathetic joy* should curb envy of other's resources. The general admonition of *loving kindness toward others* pertains to using any form of power in a constructive trustworthy manner. On the whole, Buddhist ethics center on relinquishing power for oneself but using some forms of power to benefit others. The five lay precepts in Table 10.3 address forms of power relating to the needs for resource control (not taking, living with what the ecology provides), wholeness (no use of violence and mood-altering drugs), reproduction and obligation (chaste sexuality), and knowledge (truth telling).

Confucianism. The Chinese sage Confucius promoted an ethical prescription of social behavior beginning about 500 BCE, which was further developed by Mencius. Confucianism has formed the basis of cultures and governmental systems throughout East Asia. Confucianism emphasizes humanism in thought and practice in its central concept of *Jen*, the expression of one's humanity in conscientiousness and altruism (Chan, 1963). Confucianism promotes harmonious social relations through individual development and cultivation (Chan, 1963; Hall & Ames, 1987), as shown in its veneration of scholars (*Ru*), who are accorded more respect than religious bodies or political authorities.

Confucianism's focus on social harmony seems to be antithetical to extreme power imbalances and especially to power abuse, as exemplified in the central edict "What you do not wish for yourself, do not do to others" (Chan, 1963). But Confucianism emphasizes not equality per se but that all persons in superior positions (e.g., parents, bosses, teachers) should be beneficent and caring toward their juniors (e.g., children, employees, and students) and that juniors owe service and reverence for their seniors (Hall & Ames, 1987). According to Confucianism, the higher in power a ruler is, the more he is obligated to those under his rule and the more exemplary he must be in order to become a man of *Jen* (Chan, 1963). In our view, Confucianism emphasizes obligation within unequal power relations, especially that those with more power should use that power to benefit others rather than themselves.

Confucianism explicitly prescribes that social influence should be performed through virtuous example and rules of propriety, or *li*, rather than by law, punishment, or force. Thus, its precepts are ideals, not laws. The six Confucian virtues listed in Table 10.3 emphasize that people should consider the intertwined nature of human relations in using power. These virtues emphasize the need to be trustworthy in using any form of power—for example, by considering what impact power use has on others, that others cannot be influenced without affecting the self, and that selfishness in general is to be eschewed in favor of maintaining good relationships. Many more particular Confucian teachings admonish against particular desires (e.g., greed, lust) and motivated temptations (e.g., lying) that do address each basic form of power.

Abrahamic Religions. Despite differences among sects, Judaism, Christianity, and Islam share the belief that humans were created by one God, which makes all humans kin and implies that God should be loved, respected, and worshiped above all. In these religions, then, all obligation is owed to the most powerful being. This ideal relation between humans and God, and with which humans are understood to struggle, is sometimes upheld as a model of an asymmetric obligatory power relationship between parents and children, rulers and subjects, and husbands and wives. All three religions also recognize the equality of each person, a stumbling block for abuse of power, and a human obligation to discern right from wrong.

Jewish tradition includes an extensive exploration of the ethical meaning of the hundreds of Jewish laws and how they prescribe that people live. Judaism prioritizes the eternal covenant between people and God and the dignity and well-being of individuals (e.g., Sacks, 2000). For example, it is acceptable not to fast for health reasons. Jewish practices also nurture the community—for example, in prioritizing family life and in welcoming the stranger. Likewise, Jewish principles such as honesty, peace, justice, and charity reveal ethics encouraging constructive power and prohibiting destructive power.

In Catholicism, the teachings of St. John (1999) Cassian, and Pope Gregory, popularized in frescos and in Dante's *Inferno*, admonish against giving in to desires. The Eight Temptations, which in Catholic doctrine become Deadly Sins or Cardinal Vices when given in to, can be said to be unfettered desires for forms of power we have addressed (despair for wholeness, greed, gluttony, sloth, envy for resources, lust for reproduction, infidelity for asymmetric obligations, pride for legitimacy, ire for violence), whereas the corresponding Catholic virtues, like Buddhism, admonish people to renounce such desires (e.g., chastity) or, like Confucianism, to use power on behalf of others (e.g., charity). The gospel of Matthew promises heaven to those who provide for the needs, including food, clothing, comfort, and companionship, of the "least" among them.

Like Judaism, Islam also has a strong tradition of both legal prohibitions of power abuse and admonitions to virtue and of enacting equality within and strengthening communities. Islam prohibits the use of alcohol, a mood-altering drug, and Sha'ria law prescribes punishments for sins such as stealing and adultery. Among the five pillars of Islam are charity, which prioritizes others' needs, and fasting, which focuses one on the needs of the poor and helps one learn to curb one's desires.

In addition to several admonitions to obligation in the Ten Commandments, the commandments collectively address every form of power addressed here: violence, sexuality (especially in the absence of obligatory relationship, namely, marriage), control of resources, knowledge, restricting freedom, and legitimacy (see Table 10.3). Ritual practices within each religion (e.g., circumcision, baptism, the hajj) may be seen as affirming one's legitimate identity as a member of the religion.

Summary. This sampling of three very rich ethical or moral traditions demonstrates that they all presume that people have fairly chronic desires and power motives that may disrupt social relationships and should be governed either by self-striving and ethical guidance or by law and custom, or both. All the moral or ethical traditions considered here have ways of addressing both the higher level aspects of our theory, such as power fungibility, interdependence, trust, and power balance, and the lower level motivations, desires, and prescriptions concerning particular needs and their corresponding types of power. Differences in how ethical principles are communicated, particularly in whether they admonish people to take particular actions or strive for particular virtues or prohibit particular actions and condemn desires, and whether these are considered "law," demonstrate that there are many ways that ethical systems can promote more prosocial and less selfish uses of power. All three traditions use stories or parables as well as abstract statements, symbols, and rituals as reminders of the ethics they proscribe. The fact that all three culturally independent systems speak against the use of particular forms of power to damage other people and selfishness demonstrates that the needs, motivations, and desires in our theory are common social-psychological problems that societies and people must address.

Experimental Games Examining Relations Among Power Fungibility, Inequality, and Survival

Power Basis Theory posits that distinct kinds of power may be fungible, depending on how people use power to meet needs or prevent deficits. To examine power dynamics among multiple, different forms of power in multiple-party interactions over time, we invented an experimental game called the In Game (see Pratto, Pearson, Lee, & Saguy, 2008). Sessions of four to six players sit around a table for a study of "how people behave in dynamic situations." We postulated that people could infer what different kinds of power (e.g., resources, force, legitimacy, obligations) are by what they enable one to do (or prevent one from doing). Thus, in the game, different kinds of power were represented not by labels but by different colored tokens and the rules about what players could do or have to do with each color token. Players who had more red tokens (force) than others could take other players' tokens without their consent. Blue tokens, representing legitimacy, could be gained by a majority vote of the players and be taken away by the same procedure. Players who had given yellow tokens (obligations) to other players had to provide those players with green tokens (resources) regularly. Each player revealed an "event card" on his or her turn, which provided choices or requirements about color tokens (power). For example, event cards gave out resource tokens from the experimenter's pool of tokens or required players to pay them to the pool. Certain event cards required that players obtain different color tokens (i.e., obligations or force) from other players. Players had to decide how to accomplish these requirements, often trying several negotiations with other players to do so. The game was not competitive in that players could not "win" it, but they could "lose" by having too few resource tokens to "survive" or stay in the game. The only goal we provided was to stay in the game. Both open- and closed-ended tests showed that players could make real-life analogies to the types of power instantiated in the game by colored tokens.

Fungibility Creates Inequality, and Inequality Contributes to Stress and Mortality

In our initial instantiations of the In Game, we wanted to test whether players would use the different forms of power fungibly and whether the possibility of using each type of power to gain other types of power creates inequality. In fact, in both versions of the game we conducted, every player began with the same number of each color of token, and each player was provided with the same constraints and options throughout the game by the event cards. In other words, the game was egalitarian, although this fact was not told to the participants. Players could decide how to make any kind of power fungible. A player could lend force tokens in exchange for resource tokens, could ask for resource tokens from players who owed obligation tokens, could be conferred legitimacy tokens if he or she played in ways that other players approved, could form coalitions to use force tokens to take tokens from other players as ways of acquiring different kinds of power.

If it is the case that people use one kind of power to gain other kinds, then one would expect the amount of each type of power that players accumulated by the end of the game to become positively correlated rather than uncorrelated, even if the amounts distributed at the beginning and throughout the game by the event cards were orthogonal. This indeed occurred, providing evidence that people will make the types of power fungible and, in doing so, create inequality.

We also tested whether inequality contributed to low "survival" (not having enough resources to remain in the game). In both experiments, we found that the more unequal the distribution of power tokens among the players was, the more players were eliminated from the game because of lack of resources, even controlling for the mean number of power tokens in the session (Pratto et al., 2008). In other words, nonsurvival was related not just to the absolute level of power in the session, but rather to how unequally power was distributed among players. This result is remarkable for two reasons. First, it was not only inequality in kind of tokens invoking nonsurvival (namely, resources) that was associated with greater rates of players being eliminated. Rather, inequality in *all* kinds of power was associated with more players being eliminated. Second, it shows that power fungibility can have mortality effects, demonstrating that power is used to meet survival needs. Finally, consistent with our notion that power struggles produce stress, we found that the more total power in a game session, the more inequality there was among players and the more instability ("stress") in their subjective well-being.

Stereotype Contents and Perceptions of Individuals Correspond to Basic Forms of Power

An important implication of our ecological view of power and its relation to basic needs is that, for people to be able to negotiate life, they should be able to perceive not only the amount of power but also the *kinds* of power that other people and groups have or lack. Such perceptions may be crucial in helping people decide how to behave toward others given their own power situation.

We tested this hypothesis in two ways. First, after playing the In Game, participants read descriptions of fictitious prior players whom we described in terms of two game actions and the number of each color of token they had at the end of the game. This indicated how these fictitious players used each type of power or had it used against them during the game. As expected, those fictitious players who accumulated more rather than fewer red (force) tokens were rated higher on a scale including *forceful, strong, threatening,* and *destructive.* Those who accumulated advantage in obligatory relations (others' yellow tokens) to other players were rated lower on a trait scale including *exploited, obedient,* and *dutiful* than players who were disadvantaged in obligatory tokens. Players who accumulated more green (resources) tokens than other players were rated higher on *wealthy* and *well-off* and lower on *poor* than players with few resource tokens, and players who accumulated more legitimacy tokens were rated more *respectable* and *admirable* and less *unpopular* than players low in legitimacy tokens. These results indicate that people can observe power in use and make in-kind trait inferences about the user without labels for the kinds of power.

Second, in a separate study from the In Game, we examined whether trait stereotypes of many groups correspond to the type of power such groups wield or lack. Pratto and Lee (2005) showed that groups could be distinguished along trait dimensions that corresponded to the form of power we believed they wield or lack. For example, groups high on violence, such as terrorists, were rated substantially higher on trait scales reflecting forcefulness (e.g., violent, abusive) than groups low on violence, such as nuns. Groups high on resource control, such as politicians, could be distinguished from groups with few resources, such as the working poor, on dimensions reflecting wealth (e.g., frugal, thrifty). Groups high on legitimacy, such as soldiers, were rated higher on dimensions reflecting respectability (e.g., respectable, dishonorable) than other groups, such as welfare recipients. Finally, groups advantaged versus disadvantaged in obligatory relationships (white collar criminals vs. housewives) were rated higher on traits reflecting dominance (e.g., obliging and dependent, both reverse coded).

We also hypothesized that judgments of trust hinge on whether others can be expected to use power to fulfill their own needs. Those judged untrustworthy may be either those who use destructive power against others or those who use constructive power only to benefit themselves. One way we tested these hypotheses was in examining stereotypes of groups that were selected to characterize a particular power-trait dimension. We expected groups that use their power to fulfill others' needs to be rated more trustworthy than groups that use power to create needs or only for their own benefit. Between 47 and 52 undergraduate participants rated one of two sets of 20 groups. We expected some groups within a set to be rated high on a particular power-trait dimension and some to be rated low on that dimension. Our measure of perceived trustworthiness was the mean of ratings of *ethical, trustworthy, corrupt* (reversed scored), and *devious* (reverse scored; α = .84). Our measure of perceived general power was the mean of ratings of *powerful, influential, unimportant* (reversed scored), and *submissive* (reverse scored; α = .72).

Within each kind of need, we compared the groups on trustworthiness, covarying their general power scores, and in each case, substantial and statistically reliable differences were found, even controlling for general power ratings (see Table 10.4). For example, many Americans know that soldiers and gang members use violence but would expect soldiers to defend them and gang

TABLE 10.4   Mean Ratings of Power and Trust for Groups That Can Fulfill or Create Needs and Effect Sizes for Group Comparisons Within Form of Power

Basic Need	Group Fulfilling Need	Group Creating Need Deficit	η^2 Trust	η^2 Power
Wholeness	Soldiers	Gang leaders	.84	.01
Mean trust	4.07	1.46		
Mean power	4.22	4.10		
Consume resources	Philanthropists	Welfare cheats	.69	.51
Mean trust	3.64	1.48		
Mean power	3.91	2.51		
Belong to a community	Judges	Pedophiles	.82	.62
Mean trust	3.72	1.17		
Mean power	4.48	2.87		
Care from others	Parents	Spoiled brats	.78	.48
Mean trust	4.18	2.00		
Mean power	4.34	3.20		

Note: Approximately 50 participants rated each group on traits from 1 (*very uncharacteristic*) to 5 (*very characteristic*). Across all groups, including those not shown here, the mean trustworthiness and general power ratings correlated slightly, $r = .22, p < .001$.

members to attack them. Consistent with this reasoning, participants rated gang members as similar in power than soldiers, $\eta^2 = .01$, $p = .33$, but as substantially less trustworthy than soldiers, $\eta^2 = .84$, $p < .001$ (see Table 10.4 for means and effect sizes). Likewise, philanthropists, who provide material resources to others, were rated not only as more powerful than welfare cheats, who take others' resources, $\eta^2 = .51$, but as substantially more trustworthy, $\eta^2 = .69$. Judges, who help maintain the integrity of a community by isolating those who violate social rules, were judged more powerful than pedophiles, $\eta^2 = .62$, whose abusive behavior tears at the integrity of communities, but were perceived to be substantially more trustworthy than pedophiles, $p < .001$. Finally, parents and spoiled brats were not judged to differ in general power, $p = .14$, but parents, who fulfill obligations to others, were judged much higher on trustworthiness than spoiled brats, who demand obligations from others, $p < .001$. Even when we set a conservative p value for these four tests together, the expected group differences in trust judgments were all reliable. More important, the effect sizes for group differences in trustworthiness were larger than the effect sizes for general power.

Another way that we tested the hypothesis that people would trust those who use power on behalf of others rather than only for their own benefit was done within the context of the In Game, described above. After playing the game, participants judged fictitious prior players who were described in terms of the number of each color of power token they ended the game with and how they described their main goal in the game. We expected those participants with prosocial goals, as indicated by the statement "I tried to help other players as much as I could," to be rated as more trustworthy than those with the selfish goal of "Getting as many tokens as I could." Regardless of whether they were high or low on four types of power, players who had prosocial goals were rated as more trustworthy ($M = 4.65$ on a 1 to 7 scale) than players with selfish goals ($M = 3.87$), $\eta^2 = .10$, $p < .001$. Taken together, our results show that group stereotypes and judgments of individuals fall along trait dimensions that correspond to particular forms of power, as well as to general power and trust. Such perceptions are, we posit, important for navigating life.

GENERAL DISCUSSION

Power Basis Theory argues that particular forms of power recur in human life because they are the means to meet particular universal and recurrent needs. We identified a small set of distinct needs and kinds of power that are reflected in large literatures in psychology, sociology, anthropology, political science, and human history. Recognizing these needs and types of power allows us to make sense of many conflicts, the ethics of power, and dimensions of social judgment. Moreover, we saw that our theory has specific places for the many ways power has been defined in social theory and social science, including coercion and oppression, transformative power (using power to help others develop), social influence, agency, and liquidity.

Our theory differs from other motivation and power theories. First, we have been very careful not to assume that every motivation reflects a real need. Although this assumption is common in social and clinical psychology, we have conceptually distinguished between needs—that is, requirements for survival—and desires. Failing to make this distinction implies that all motivations and actions they drive are both functional and ethical because their purpose is to meet basic needs. As we have seen, motivated behavior is not always functional, it does not always meet needs, and cultures and people differ in what motivations and actions they deem ethical. Second, because our theory explicitly states that the local ecology is part of the system for meeting needs, it points attention toward the long-term sustainability of the natural, cultural, and local social environment. Theories that focus on needs and motivations without addressing ecological conditions and behavioral repertoires are too myopic to consider either long-term issues or other means of meeting needs. Third, many psychological theories of motivation and needs consider only *psychological* needs, not the other needs (e.g., resources) essential to the human condition. This makes such theories nearly impossible to relate to politics, economics, international relations, intergroup relations, or culture (except through leadership), which is where many important power dynamics occur. Fourth, by defining power in relation to needs rather than in relation to other parties, we decoupled well-being from power relations. This is important because people's well-being is relative to their own needs rather than relative to others; a person who has been maimed less than another person is not necessarily well. In fact, Power Basis Theory predicts that using other people as the standard for whether one has enough power could cause serious problems for both individuals and collectives. Finally, our theory allows power to take several forms other than influence: We address power as exercised in behavior, as a potential, and as relative both to others and to survival requirements.

This new approach to understanding power suggests new avenues for research. As fungibility of different kinds of power is essential to the stability or volatility of relationships and well-being, learning more about what social conditions make which kinds of power more or less fungible would be useful. In particular, more effective interventions in organizations and governments may depend on constraining fungibility and correcting the timescales of feedback loops. Further research on ethical systems might indicate what forms of ethical systems are effective in curbing power problems such as drastic inequality and corruption. Likewise, learning the conditions in which particular power fungibility is judged ethical could expand our understanding of implicit justice theories. By providing more detailed dimensions of social perception than of power and trust, Power Basis Theory can improve understanding of interpersonal relationships and group stereotypes. Most important, Power Basis Theory allows us to incorporate not only the motives of powerful people but also the needs and motives of less powerful people so that their relationships can be dynamically understood.

ACKNOWLEDGMENTS

Our thanks to George Levinger, David A. Dunning, and the Wednesday afternoon lab group for comments on a previous draft. Please address correspondence to

Felicia Pratto, Department of Psychology, University of Connecticut, Storrs, CT 06269–1020 or felicia.pratto@uconn.edu.

REFERENCES

American Psychiatric Association. (2000). *Diagnostic and statistical manual of mental disorders (4th ed., text revision)*. Washington, DC: Author.

Anderson, C., Srivastava, S., Beer, J. S., Spataro, S. E., & Chatman, J. A. (2006). Knowing your place: Self-perceptions of status in social groups. *Journal of Personality and Social Psychology, 91,* 1094–1110.

Arndt, J., Greenberg, J., Solomon, S., Pyszczynski, T., & Schimel, J. (1999). Creativity and terror management: Evidence that activity increases guilt and social projection following mortality salience. *Journal of Personality and Social Psychology, 77,* 19–32.

Aron, A., Paris, M., & Aron, E. N. (1995). Falling in love: Prospective studies of self-concept change. *Journal of Personality and Social Psychology, 69,* 1102–1112.

Bartholomew, K., & Horowitz, L. M. (1991). Attachment styles among young adults: A test of a four-category model. *Journal of Personality and Social Psychology, 61,* 226–244.

Baumeister, R. F., & Leary, M. R. (1995). The need to belong: Desire for interpersonal attachments as a fundamental human motivation. *Psychological Bulletin, 117,* 497–529.

Beitman, B. D., & Nair, J. (2005). *Self-awareness deficits in psychiatric patients: Assessment and treatment*. New York: W. W. Norton.

Boulding, K. E. (1989). *The three faces of power.* Thousand Oaks, CA: Sage.

Bowlby, J. (1973). *Attachment and loss: Separation: Anxiety and anger* (Vol. 2). New York: Basic Books.

Cacioppo, J. (1994). Social neuroscience: Autonomic, neuroendocrine, and immune responses to stress. *Psychophysiology, 31,* 113–128.

Caporael, L. R. (1995). Sociality: Coordinating bodies, minds, and groups. *Psycoloquy.* Retrieved from FTP: Princeton.edu; directory: cogsci.ecs.soton.ac.uk/pub/harnad/Psycoloquy/1995/volume.6; file: psych.95.6.01.group-selection.1.caporael.

Cassian, J. (1999). *The monastic institutes: On the training of a monk and the eight deadly sins* (Jerome Bertram, Trans.). London: Saint Austin Press.

Chan, W. T. (1963). *A source book in Chinese philosophy*. Princeton, NJ: Princeton University Press.

Cialdini, R., Schaller, M., Houlihan, D., Arps, K., Fultz, J., & Beaman, A. (1987). Empathy-based helping: Is it selflessly or selfishly motivated? *Journal of Personality and Social Psychology, 52,* 749–758.

Clark, R., Anderson, N., Clark, V., & Williams, D. (1999). Racism as a stressor for African Americans: A biopsychosocial model. *American Psychologist, 54,* 805–816.

Coelho, J. S., Polivy, J., & Herman, C. P. (2006). Selective carbohydrate or protein restriction: Effects on subsequent food intake and cravings. *Appetite, 47,* 352–360.

Cox, D. J., Gonder-Frederick, L., Ritterband, L., Patel, K., Schachinger, H., Fehm-Wolfsdorf, G., Hermanns, N., Snoke, F., Zrebiec, J., Polonsky, W., Schlundt, D., Kovatchev, B., & Clarke, W. (2006). Blood glucose awareness training: What is it, where is it and where is it going? *Diabetes Spectrum, 19,* 43–49.

Csikszentmihalyi, M., & LeFevre, J. (1989). Optimal experience in work and leisure. *Journal of Personality and Social Psychology, 56,* 815–822.

Dahl, R. (1957). The concept of power. *Behavioral Science, 2,* 201–215.

Daly, M., & Wilson, M. (1988). *Homicide*. New York: Aldine de Gruyter.

Davis, M. R. (1983). Measuring individual differences in empathy: Evidence for a multi-dimensional approach. *Journal of Personality and Social Psychology, 44*, 113–126.

Desteno, D. A., & Salovey, P. (1996). Jealousy and the characteristics of one's rival: A self-evaluation maintenance perspective. *Personality and Social Psychology Bulletin, 22*, 920–932.

DeVries, A., Craft, T., Glasper, E., Neigh, G., & Alexander, J. (2006). Social influences on stress responses and health. *Psychoneuroendocrinology, 32*, 587–603.

Eagly, A., & Steffen, V. J. (1984). Gender stereotypes stem from the distribution of men and women into roles. *Journal of Personality and Social Psychology, 46*, 735–754.

Ehrlich, P. R., & Ehrlich, A. H. (1991). *The population explosion.* New York: Simon and Schuster.

Elliot, A. J., & Dweck, C. S. (Eds.). (2005). *Handbook of competence and motivation.* New York: Guilford.

Fiske, S. T., & Berdahl, J. (2007). Social power. In A. W. Kruglanski & E. T. Higgins (Eds.), *Social psychology: Handbook of basic principles* (2nd ed., pp. 678–692). New York: Guilford.

Fiske, S. T., Cuddy, A. J. C., Glick, P., & Xu, J. (2002). A model of (often mixed) stereotype content: Competence and warmth respectively follow from perceived status and competition. *Journal of Personality and Social Psychology, 82*, 878–902.

Fodor, E. M. (1985). The power motive, group conflict, and physiological arousal. *Journal of Personality and Social Psychology, 49*, 1408–1415.

Goodman, A. (1990). Addiction: Definition and implications. *British Journal of Addiction, 85*, 1403–1408.

Graef, H. (1965). *The story of mysticism.* London: Peter Davies.

Hall, D. L., & Ames, R. T. (1987). *Thinking through Confucius.* Albany: State University of New York Press.

Hendriks, M., & Vingerhoets, A. (2006). Social messages of crying faces: Their influence on anticipated person perception, emotions and behavioural responses. *Cognition and Emotion, 20*, 878–886.

Herbert, T., & Cohen, S. (1993). Stress and immunity in humans: A meta-analytic review. *Psychosomatic Medicine, 55*, 364–379.

Homans, G. C. (1961). *Social behavior: Its elementary forms.* New York: Harcourt Brace.

Intergovernmental Panel on Climate Change. (2007). *Climate change 2007: Synthesis report.* Retrieved January 19, 2008, from http://www.ipcc.ch/pdf/assessment-report/ar4/syr/ar4_syr.pdf

Jackson, S. A., Kimiecik, J. C., Ford, S. K., & Marsh, H. W. (1998). Psychological correlates of flow in sports. *Journal of Sport and Exercise Psychology, 20*, 358–378.

Kahneman, D., Knetsch, J. D., & Thaler, R. (1990). Experimental tests of the endowment effect and the Coase theorem. *Journal of Political Economy, 98*, 1325–1340.

Keltner, D., & Haidt, J. (2003). Approaching awe: A moral, spiritual, and aesthetic emotion. *Cognition and Emotion, 17*, 297–314.

Leach, C., Ellemers, N., & Barreto, M. (2007). Group virtue: The importance of morality (vs. competence and sociability) in the positive evaluation of in-groups. *Journal of Personality and Social Psychology, 93*, 234–249.

Leary, M. R., & Baumeister, R. F. (2000). The nature and function of self-esteem: Sociometer theory. In M. P. Zanna (Ed.), *Advances in experimental social psychology.* San Diego, CA: Academic Press.

Malerbi, F. E. K., & Matos, M. A. (2001). Blood glucose discrimination training: The role of internal and external cues. *Journal of Health Psychology, 6*, 229–240.

Marx, K. (1904). *A contribution to a critique of political economy.* New York: International Publishers.

Maslow, A. H. (1964). *Religions, values, and peak-experiences.* New York: Viking Press.

Mason, J. (1968). A review of psychoendocrine research on the sympathetic adrenal medullary system. *Psychosomatic Medicine, 30,* 631–653.

Mays, V., Cochran, S., & Barnes, N. (2007). Race, race-based discrimination, and health outcomes among African Americans. *Annual Review of Psychology, 58,* 201–225.

McClelland, D. C. (1975). *Power: The inner experience.* Oxford, UK: Irvington.

Merritt, M., Bennett, G., Williams, R., Edwards, C., & Sollers, J. (2006). Perceived racism and cardio-vascular reactivity and recovery to personally relevant stress. *Health Psychology, 25,* 364–369.

Mikulincer, M., & Orbach, I. (1995). Attachment styles and repressive defensiveness: The accessibility and architecture of affective memories. *Journal of Personality and Social Psychology, 68,* 917–925.

Mills, C. W. (1956). *The power elite.* Oxford, UK: Oxford University Press.

Nier, J. A., Gaertner, S. L., & Gorcheva, R. S. (2006). Examining the dynamism dimension of intergroup beliefs. In D. Chadee & J. Young (Eds.), *Current themes in social psychology* (pp. 145–161). Kingston, Jamaica: University of West Indies Press.

Osgood, C. E., Suci, G. J., & Tannenbaum, P. H. (1957). *The measurement of meaning.* Urbana: University of Illinois Press.

Oskamp, S. (2006). Psychological contributions to achieving an ecologically sustainable future for humanity. *Journal of Social Issues, 56,* 373–390.

Peeters, G., & Czapinski, J. (1990). Positive–negative asymmetry in evaluations: The distinction between affective and informational negativity effects. In W. Stroebe & M. Hewstone (Eds.), *European review of social psychology* (Vol. 1, pp. 33–60). Chichester, UK: Wiley.

Pickett, C. L., & Gardner, W. L. (2005). The social monitoring system: Enhanced sensitivity to social cues and information as an adaptive response to social exclusion and belonging need. In K. D. Williams, J. P. Forgas, & W. von Hippel (Eds.), *The social outcast: Ostracism, social exclusion, rejection, and bullying* (pp. 213–226). New York: Psychology Press.

Pratto, F., & Lee, I. (2005, July). *Experimental evidence that how power is used determines the contents of stereotypes.* Paper presented at the symposium of the European Association of Social Psychology, Würzberg, Germany.

Pratto, F., Pearson, A. R., Lee, I., & Saguy, T. (2008). Power dynamics in an experimental game. *Social Justice Research, 21,* 377–407.

Pratto, F., & Walker, A. (2000). Dominance in disguise: Power, beneficence, and exploitation in personal relationships. In A. Lee-Chai & J. A. Bargh (Eds.), *The use and abuse of power: Multiple perspectives on the causes of corruption* (pp. 93–114). Philadelphia: Psychology Press.

Pratto, F., & Walker, A. (2004). The bases of gendered power. In A. H. Eagly, A. Beall, & R. Sternberg (Eds.), *The psychology of gender* (2nd ed., pp. 242–268). New York: Guilford.

Raven, B. H. (1965). Social influence and power. In I. D. Steiner & M. Fishbeing (Eds.), *Current studies in social psychology* (pp. 371–382). New York: Holt, Rinehart, Winston.

Rempel, J., Holmes, J., & Zanna, M. (1985). Trust in close relationships. *Journal of Personality and Social Psychology, 49,* 95–112.

Roberts, J., Gotlib, I. H., & Kassel, J. D. (1996). Adult attachment security and symptoms of depression: The mediating roles of dysfunctional attitudes and low self-esteem. *Journal of Personality and Social Psychology, 70,* 310–320.

Russell, B. (1938). *Power: A new social analysis.* New York: Norton.

Sacks, J. (2000). *A letter in the scroll.* New York: Free Press.

Sharpsteen, D., & Kirkpatrick, L. (1997). Romantic jealousy and adult romantic attachment. *Journal of Personality and Social Psychology, 72,* 627–640.

Simeon, D., Knutelska, M., Yehuda, R., Putnam, F., Schmeidler, J., & Smith, L. (2007). Hypothalamic-pituitary-adrenal axis function in dissociative disorders, post-traumatic stress disorder, and healthy volunteers. *Biological Psychiatry, 61,* 966–973.

Steele, C. M., & Josephs, R. A. (1988). Drinking your troubles away II: An attention-allocation model of alcohol's effects. *Journal of Abnormal Psychology*, 97, 196–205.

Twenge, J. M., Baumeister, R. F., Tice, D. M., & Stucke, T. S. (2001). If you can't join them, beat them: Effects of social exclusion on aggressive behavior. *Journal of Personality and Social Psychology*, 81, 1058–1069.

University of Maryland Medical Center. (2006). *Prader-Willi syndrome*. Retrieved July 24, 2006, from http://www.umm.edu/ency/article/001605.htm

Vonk, R. (1993). Individual differences and common dimensions in Implicit Personality Theory. *British Journal of Social Psychology*, 32, 209–226.

Wartenberg, T. E. (1990). *The forms of power*. Philadelphia: Temple University Press.

Weber, M. (1946). *Essays in sociology* (H. H. Gerth & C. Wright Mills, Trans.). New York: Oxford University Press.

Wiggins, J. S. (1979). A psychological taxonomy of trait-descriptive terms: The interpersonal domain. *Journal of Personality and Social Psychology*, 37, 395–412.

Williams, K. D. (2007). Ostracism. *Annual Review of Psychology*, 58, 425–452.

Winter, D. G. (1973). *The power motive*. New York: Free Press.

Yamagishi, T., & Sato, K. (1986). Motivational bases of public goods problems. *Journal of Personality and Social Psychology*, 50, 67–73.

Yehuda, R., Giller, E., Southwick, S., & Lowy, M. (1991). Hypothalamic-pituitary-adrenal dysfunction in posttraumatic stress disorder. *Biological Psychiatry*, 30, 1031–1048.

11

System Justification Theory as Compliment, Complement, and Corrective to Theories of Social Identification and Social Dominance

JOHN T. JOST

The status quo sits on society like fat on cold chicken soup and it's quite content to be what it is. Unless someone comes along to stir things up there just won't be change.

—Abbie Hoffman (1989, p. 395)

[Everyone] in his own way is both a victim and a supporter of the system. What we understand by the system is not, therefore, a social order imposed by one group upon another, but rather something which permeates an entire society and is a factor in shaping it.

—Vaclav Havel (1991, p. 144)

The task of legitimating the established order does not fall exclusively to the mechanisms traditionally regarded as belonging to the order of ideology, such as law. ... The most successful ideological effects are those which have no need of words, and ask no more than complicitous silence.

—Pierre Bourdieu (1977/1986, p. 188)

S ystem justification theory—as initially proposed by Jost and Banaji (1994) and recently updated, revised, and revisited by Jost, Banaji, and Nosek (2004); Jost and Hunyady (2002, 2005); and Kay et al. (2007)—has two major goals. The first is to understand *how* and *why* people provide cognitive and ideological support for the societal status quo, even when their support appears to conflict with personal and group interests (e.g., Haines & Jost, 2000; Jost, 1997, 2001; Jost & Kay, 2005; Jost, Pelham, & Carvallo, 2002; Kay, Jimenez, & Jost, 2002; Kay & Jost, 2003; Kay, Jost, & Young, 2005). Thomas Frank (2004) declared this "the preeminent question of our times" (p. 1) in his provocative best seller *What's the Matter With Kansas?*

Specifically, Frank sought to dissect "a working-class movement that has done incalculable, historic harm to working-class people;" that is, to explain why citizens in the poorest regions of the United States have been the most enthusiastic supporters of "conservative" right-wing political candidates and policies that have "smashed the welfare state, reduced the tax burden on corporations and the wealthy, and generally facilitated the country's return to a nineteenth-century pattern of wealth distribution" (p. 6). Political scientists such as Bartels (2006) and Gelman (2008) have disputed many specifics of Frank's historical account, but the central phenomenon—which provides considerable grist for the mill of a system justification theorist—remains puzzling and real: Why do members of the working class so often embrace conservative ideas that serve to perpetuate their state of disadvantage?

The second goal of system justification theory is to analyze the social and psychological consequences of supporting and defending what Bourdieu (1977/1986) referred to as "the established order." That is, what are the psychological benefits of buying into the notion that existing social, economic, and political arrangements are good, fair, legitimate, and desirable (Jost & Hunyady, 2002; Napier & Jost, 2008b)? Is it easier or more emotionally satisfying to accept the way things are than to try— most likely in vain—to change the system (Jost, Wakslak, & Tyler, 2008; Wakslak, Jost, Tyler, & Chen, 2007)? And what are the costs of embracing the societal status quo, especially for members of disadvantaged groups—that is, for society's "losers" (Jost & Burgess, 2000; Jost & Thompson, 2000; O'Brien & Major, 2005)?[1]

This chapter is not intended as a comprehensive review of empirical progress on system justification theory (for reviews, see Blasi & Jost, 2006; Jost, Banaji, & Nosek, 2004; Jost & Hunyady, 2002, 2005; Kay et al., 2007). Rather the goal here is to distinguish it from two other theoretical perspectives, namely social identity theory and social dominance theory (see also Jost & Hunyady, 2002; Rubin & Hewstone, 2004; Sidanius, Pratto, van Laar, & Levin, 2004). Whereas social identity theory emphasizes processes of group categorization and social comparison that lead people to develop distinctive and more or less satisfying conceptions of themselves and the groups to which they belong (Tajfel, 1978, 1981; Tajfel & Turner, 1979/1986), social dominance theory emphasizes the dynamics of power struggles between members of dominant and subordinate groups—that is, hegemonic conflicts that are assumed to be as old as the human species itself (Sidanius & Pratto, 1993, 1999). System justification theory, we suggest, is a compliment, a complement, and in some ways also a corrective to its two renowned influential predecessors. Clarifying the conceptual relations between the three theories seems worthwhile, especially given the apparent difficulty that some commentators have in telling social dominance and system justification theories apart (e.g., Désert & Leyens, 2006; Reicher, 2004; Turner, 2006).

System justification theory is a compliment to social identity theory and social dominance theory because it has so obviously been inspired and influenced by them. The theoretical richness, interdisciplinary scholarship, and practical relevance of social identity and social dominance theories, we think, raised the standards for the field of social psychology, and we have sought to follow their illustrious examples (see also Jost & Major, 2001). A system justification perspective is a good complement to theories of social identification and social dominance because it devotes further (and novel) theoretical and empirical attention to some of their key concepts, including social status, power, perceived legitimacy, system stability, hierarchy enhancement, legitimizing myths, ideological consensus, and the presence or absence of cognitive alternatives to the status quo (e.g., see Sidanius & Pratto, 1999; Tajfel, 1981).

Finally, and most ambitiously, we argue here that system justification theory provides a useful corrective to theories of social identification and social dominance by conceptualizing the social order not merely as something that is imposed by one group on another but rather as a *collaborative process by which existing structures of inequality are accommodated, justified, and rationalized by nearly everyone in society*, including those who are most disadvantaged by the status quo. This collaboration is part of the reason why it is so difficult to accomplish social change (e.g., Jost, 1995; Jost, Banaji, & Nosek, 2004; Jost, Glaser, Kruglanski, & Sulloway, 2003; Wakslak et al., 2007), as such diverse commentators as Abbie Hoffman (1989), Vaclav Havel (1991), and Pierre Bourdieu (1977/1986) have noted. By attending to the legitimation needs of the social system itself, system justification theory strives to go beyond purely individual and group levels of analysis, which are the only levels addressed comprehensively by social identity theorists (see also Stangor & Jost, 1997). Although social dominance theorists embrace societal, institutional, and organizational levels of analysis, we question some of the evolutionary assumptions concerning the inevitability of inequality that underpin this theory.

In what follows, I begin by tracing the theoretical and empirical origins of the system justification perspective, paying appropriate tribute to theorists of social identification and social dominance, among others (see also Jost & van der Toorn, 2011). In laying out what is distinctive about a system justification approach, we argue that these other theories underestimate the strength of system justification motives and, relatedly, the power of *false consciousness* to lead people to endorse system-serving beliefs that are contrary to their own social and political interests (see Jost, 1995; Jost & Banaji, 1994; Jost & Jost, 2007). In our view, theorists who dismiss the notion of false consciousness in favor of a more self-interested conception of human behavior underestimate the degree to which inequality in society is *internalized* by individuals and therefore consistently overestimate the likelihood of rebellion (e.g., Gurr, 1970; Jackman, 1994; Scott, 1990; Simon & Klandermans, 2001; Turner, 2006).

In the remainder of this chapter, I summarize evidence that members of disadvantaged groups are sometimes even more likely than members of advantaged groups to support the social order and its authorities; this evidence is consistent with a strong form of the system justification hypothesis that emphasizes processes of *rationalization* and the reduction of *ideological dissonance* on behalf of the system, but it is inconsistent with theories of social identification and social dominance. I then discuss several general areas of agreement and disagreement between a system justification perspective and each of the other two theories, before closing with a few concluding remarks.

ORIGINS OF THE SYSTEM JUSTIFICATION PERSPECTIVE

System justification theory originated in an explicit attempt to integrate and expand upon three existing bodies of substantive theoretical and empirical work: social identity theory, social justice research, and Marxist–feminist theories of ideology (see Jost & Hunyady, 2002; Jost & van der Toorn, 2011). In addition, we drew on Festinger's (1957) cognitive dissonance theory—especially concepts of justification and rationalization—and McGuire's (1983, 1989, 1997) perspectivist philosophy of social science, which assumes that "all knowledge—including scientific knowledge—is contextualized or situated, that is, it is knowledge *from some perspective,* [and] the task of the researcher is to creatively generate and critically assess multiple hypotheses, each of which presumably has some domain of truthful application" (Jost, Banaji, & Prentice, 2004, p. 3). Thus, I do not argue that system justification theory is right and the other theories are wrong. Rather, the goal of the perspectivist is to create epistemic value by appreciating and (if possible) integrating distinctive, even seemingly opposing, theoretical insights (Jost & Hardin, in press). In this way, system justification theory is self-consciously pluralistic, even promiscuous, in its approach to theorizing about social and political behavior, as is social dominance theory, which draws explicitly on diverse intellectual traditions associated with Machiavelli, Marx, Mosca, Pareto, Gramsci, and evolutionary biology, to name just some of its influences (see Sidanius, Levin, Federico, & Pratto, 2001; Sidanius & Pratto, 1999).

The first major substantive influence on the development of system justification theory was that of social identity theory, especially the writings of Tajfel (1978, 1981, 1982) and his many students, collaborators, and admirers (Brown, 1988; Ellemers, Wilke, & van Knippenberg, 1993; Hewstone, 1989; Hinkle & Brown, 1990; Hogg & Abrams, 1988; Reicher, 1984; Spears, Doosje, & Ellemers, 1997; Tajfel & Turner, 1979/1986; Turner & Brown, 1978; Turner & Giles, 1981). Tajfel is an especially important model, not only because of his interdisciplinary breadth and command of sociology and political science, but also because he directly linked intergroup relations to societal issues of ideology, social justice, myth, and justification (Tajfel, 1981, 1982, 1984; see also Jost & Major, 2001). By demonstrating that it is possible to conduct controlled, experimental studies on issues of intergroup conflict, competition, and cooperation and to create microcosms of society in the laboratory, Tajfel inspired legions of followers (see Robinson, 1996), including system justification theorists.

A shared commitment to the use of experimental methods, then, in seeking to understand sociostructural effects on human behavior is the first point of convergence between social identification and system justification perspectives (see Jost, 2001, 2004; Kay et al., 2007). That the minimal group paradigm had been used for well over 20 years largely as a way of demonstrating the ubiquity and apparent universality of ethnocentrism and ingroup bias provided a good context in which to apply the perspectivist strategy of standing hypotheses—even widely accepted, seemingly incontrovertible hypotheses—on their head and reconciling them with opposing insights, contrary suppositions, and alternative theories (see Banaji, 2004; Jost, 2004; Jost & Hardin, in press; McGuire, 1989).

A second major influence came from social justice research, and lessons from this topic area seemed to contradict social identity theory and its emphasis on group-serving biases in attribution and social perception (Hewstone, 1989; Hogg & Abrams, 1988). Specifically, work on the "tolerance of injustice" (e.g., Crosby, 1984; Jennings, 1991; Martin, 1986; Tyler & McGraw, 1986) challenged the notion that individuals and groups consistently defend their interests and identities. I am referring here to the oft-noted tendency for victims of deprivation and disadvantage to refrain from seeing their situations as unfair and illegitimate (Jost, 1995; Jost & Hunyady, 2002; Jost & Kay, 2010). A system justification perspective leads one to inquire how and why people are motivated to maintain the "belief in a just world" (Lerner, 1980; see also Jost, Fitzsimons, & Kay, 2004; Kay & Jost, 2003; Kay et al., 2005), especially when it directly conflicts with motives for self-enhancement and group enhancement and the tendency to make ingroup-favoring attributions for failure and disadvantage.

The third influential source, the details of which had been largely set aside by social and even political psychologists but which helped to reconcile inconsistencies between the first two, was the Marxist–feminist analysis of ideology, which aims to understand "the ways in which people may come to invest in their own unhappiness" (Eagleton, 1991, p. xiii; see also Elster, 1982; Gramsci, 1971; Jost, 1995; Jost & van der Toorn, 2011; Lukács, 1971; MacKinnon, 1989). Although phenomena such as outgroup favoritism, internalization of inferiority, and the tolerance of injustice may be baffling to social scientists and others who assume that attitudes and behaviors are driven largely by self-interest, group interest, or needs for personal or collective self-esteem, there is a long tradition of Marxian social theory on the phenomenon of false consciousness, defined as the holding of "false beliefs that sustain one's own oppression" (Cunningham, 1987, p. 255; see also Jost, 1995; Jost & Jost, 2007; MacKinnon, 1989; Runciman, 1969). This work emphasizes the *cognitive* dimensions of oppression and system preservation, building on Marx and Engels's (1846/1970) observation, "The class which has the means of material production at its disposal, has control at the same time over the means of *mental production* [italics added]" (p. 64). The Marxian insight about the nature and function of ideology as an instrument of system justification transformed the methods and goals of social science in the 19th and 20th centuries (e.g., Fromm, 1962; MacKinnon, 1989), and it is present even in critiques of communist systems, such as that of Havel (1991), quoted above.

System justification theory, then, seeks to integrate social identity theory (especially its concern with whether social systems or hierarchies are perceived as legitimate and/or stable), social justice research (especially the phenomena of tolerance of injustice and belief in a just world), and Marxian–feminist theories of ideology and false consciousness (especially the notion that ideas are used to justify and rationalize social inequality). System justification theory posits that people both consciously and unconsciously use attitudes, beliefs, and stereotypes to defend, bolster, and legitimize social systems that affect them (Jost, Banaji, & Nosek, 2004). These social systems can range in size and scope from relationship dyads and family systems to work organizations, governments, institutions, and society as a whole. Blasi and Jost (2006, p. 1124) noted,

> The property of "systematicity" implies that there exists some sustained differentiation or hierarchical clustering of relations among individuals or groups within the social order. [System justification theory] suggests that people are motivated to accept and perpetuate features of existing social arrangements, even if those features were arrived at accidentally, arbitrarily, or unjustly.

Thus, one of the key theoretical assumptions of a system justification perspective is that people tend to use ideas about groups and individuals to justify the way things are, so that existing social arrangements are perceived as legitimate, desirable, and fair, perhaps even natural and inevitable. Consistent with this view, there seems to be a relatively general (but not necessarily universal) bias in favor of the *status quo* (see also O'Brien & Crandall, 2005). To take one particularly nefarious but instructive example, describing torture as a long-standing practice of the U.S. military—that is, an established part of the societal status quo—significantly increases citizens' support for the use of torture (Crandall, Eidelman, Skitka, & Morgan, 2009). Cognition, from a system justification perspective, is deployed in the service of the social system (Jost, 2001), and it may bring both costs and benefits to the individuals and groups who cognize on behalf of the system (Jost & Hunyady, 2002; Jost, Pelham, Sheldon, & Sullivan, 2003).

THE PROBLEM OF OUTGROUP FAVORITISM

The earliest statement of system justification theory sought to account for the consensuality of social stereotypes across group boundaries and the occurrence of *outgroup favoritism*—that is, the tendency for members of disadvantaged groups to hold more favorable attitudes toward members of other, more advantaged groups than they hold about themselves and their own fellow group members (Jost & Banaji, 1994). This phenomenon has been central to the study of social psychology at least since Lewin (1941/1948) wrote about "Jewish self-hatred" and Clark and Clark (1947) observed that African American children frequently described Black dolls as less attractive and less desirable than White dolls. According to system justification theory, members of *both* advantaged and disadvantaged groups engage in thoughts, feelings, and behaviors that reinforce and legitimate existing social systems, and outgroup favoritism is one such example of the legitimation of inequality between groups.

We define outgroup favoritism in cognitive, affective, and behavioral terms (see also Jost, 2001; Jost & Banaji, 1994; Jost, Banaji, & Nosek, 2004; Jost et al., 2002). It refers to the tendency to express an evaluative preference for members of a group to which one does not belong. The argument we are making is not that people are motivated to prefer outgroups simply because they are exotic or different from one's own group. Rather, we regard outgroup favoritism as but one manifestation of the motive to justify the system, insofar as it reflects an acceptance (conscious or unconscious) rather than a rejection of the existing social hierarchy.

Many real-world groups exhibit outgroup favoritism on both implicit and explicit measures and on a wide range of evaluative dimensions (e.g., Ashburn-Nardo, Knowles, & Monteith, 2003; Jost et al., 2002; Lane, Mitchell, & Banaji, 2005; Nosek, Banaji, & Greenwald, 2002; Overbeck, Jost, Mosso, & Flizik, 2004; Rudman, Feinberg, & Fairchild, 2002; Uhlmann, Dasgupta, Elgueta, Greenwald, & Swanson, 2002; Yoshimura & Hardin, 2009). Jost, Banaji, and Nosek (2004) found that as many as 40% to 50% of African Americans harbor implicit biases in favor of European Americans (and against African Americans), and a similar proportion of gay and lesbian respondents harbor implicit biases in favor of heterosexuals (and against homosexuals). They also found that rates of outgroup favoritism on the part of African Americans and gays and lesbians increased as participants became more politically conservative, suggesting that outgroup favoritism is indeed a partly ideological process, as suggested by system justification theory.

The seriousness of the problem of internalized inferiority among members of disadvantaged groups was well appreciated by earlier generations of social psychologists, such as Dollard (1937), Bettelheim (1943), Lewin (1941/1948), Clark and Clark (1947), Allport (1954), and Elkins (1967), but it is frequently minimized or overlooked by social identity theorists and others who stress self-enhancement, social identification, and ingroup favoritism to the point of excluding other processes, including rationalization of the status quo and internalization of inequality (e.g., Leyens & Demoulin, 2009, pp. 203–204). In comparing social identity and system justification theories, Spears, Jetten, and Doosje (2001) noted, "An important contribution of system justification theory is that it has clearly put the phenomenon of outgroup bias back on the agenda, in a way that has certainly been lacking from the main thrust of empirical work within the social identity tradition" (p. 354).

Sidanius (1993), too, critiqued social identity theory for failing to account adequately for the phenomenon of outgroup favoritism among members of disadvantaged groups, as did Hinkle and Brown (1990). Social dominance and system justification theorists, therefore, are in general agreement that social identity theory's primary social psychological mechanisms of category accentuation, self-categorization, social comparison, self-esteem maintenance, and status competition are insufficient to account for the ideological basis of outgroup favoritism (see also Sidanius, 1993; Sidanius & Pratto, 1999), although the issues are complicated and sometimes controversial, as we will see below.

DISTINCTIVENESS OF THE SYSTEM JUSTIFICATION PERSPECTIVE

The point of system justification theory is not simply to assert that outgroup favoritism and the tolerance of injustice exist. Nevertheless, we did call attention to the fact that prevailing theories—which tended to stress self-interested motives and drives to maintain or enhance individual and collective self-esteem—were not well suited to handle these cases, and this was an important first step in staking out the goals for a theory of system justification (Jost, 1995; Jost & Banaji, 1994). Since 1994, we have sought to make a more constructive contribution by empirically investigating the ways in which people suffer from and attempt to cope with and resolve three potentially contradictory needs or motives (see also Jost & Burgess, 2000; Jost, Burgess, & Mosso, 2001; Jost & Hunyady, 2002; Jost & Kay, 2005; Jost & Thompson, 2000; Kay & Jost, 2003).

The first of these we refer to as "ego justification," and it captures the need to develop and maintain a favorable self-image and to feel valid, justified, and legitimate as an individual actor. The second is referred to as "group justification," and this is the primary focus of social identity theory: the desire to develop and maintain favorable images of one's own group and to defend and justify the actions of fellow ingroup members. The third is "system justification," and it captures epistemic, existential, and relational needs to perceive the status quo as fair, legitimate, and justifiable; we focus most of our research efforts on this motive, because it has received so much less attention than the others.

Although Tajfel's erudite writings probably did touch on all three of these functions or levels, social identity theory has contributed far more to our understanding of the first two motives than the third (see also Jost, 2001, 2004; Jost & Banaji, 1994). Social dominance theory, as we will see, addresses the second and third motives, but in such a way that they are frequently conflated with one another (Jost, Banaji, & Nosek, 2004; Jost & Thompson, 2000). Only system justification theory unambiguously addresses the possibilities that (a) there is a *motive* to justify the existing social order and (b) this motive is sometimes, paradoxically, strongest among those who are most disadvantaged by the social order (see also Henry & Saul, 2006; Jost, Pelham, et al., 2003).

System justification theory is in a unique position to capture the shared, collaborative nature of psychological adherence to (vs. rejection of) the status quo (see also Jost, Ledgerwood, & Hardin, 2008). A major difference between a system justification perspective and theories of social identification and social dominance is alluded to in this opening quotation by Vaclav Havel (1991), in which he argued, "The system is not ... a social order imposed by one group upon another" (p. 144). The complete passage from Havel is as follows:

> Position in the power hierarchy determines the degree of responsibility and guilt, but it gives no one unlimited responsibility and guilt, nor does it completely absolve anyone. Thus the conflict between the aims of life and the aims of the system is not a conflict between two socially defined and separate communities; and only a very generalized view (and even that only approximative) permits us to divide society into the rulers and the ruled. ... In the post-totalitarian system [the line of conflict] runs de facto through each person, for everyone in his own way is both a victim and a supporter of the system. What we understand by the system is not, therefore, a social order imposed by one group upon another, but rather something which permeates an entire society and is a factor in shaping it. (Havel, 1991, p. 144)

Of the three theories, system justification theory most clearly conceptualizes the social order in terms of a collaborative process that turns virtually everyone into a victim and supporter of the system. Theories of social identification and social dominance fail to acknowledge the existence and strength of the system justification motive, they reject the theoretical utility of the concept of false consciousness, and they tend to view the social order as something that is imposed by one group on another. These three limitations, it turns out, are related to one another, and they prevent these theories from accounting adequately for counterintuitive findings such as those summarized below concerning the effects of social status on support for the system and its authorities.

Limitations of Theories of Social Identification and Social Dominance

Both social identity and social dominance perspectives are limited because they represent the social order as something that is imposed by one group on other groups. Although we agree that it is true to some (perhaps major) extent that inequality is foisted on others by members of dominant groups, the converse is also true: Social inequality is accepted, justified, and perpetuated even by members of subordinated groups. To the extent that social identity theory locates all social behavior on a continuum ranging from "interpersonal" to "intergroup" behavior (Tajfel, 1981; Tajfel & Turner, 1979/1986), it lacks a solid explanation for the fact that people often support unequal social systems even when an alternative system would serve their own personal and group interests better (e.g., Frank, 2004). In part, this is because people find it difficult to imagine "cognitive alternatives," as Tajfel and Turner (1979/1986) proposed (but did not adequately explain), and in part because people tend to rationalize what they see as inevitable, even if it was initially defined as unattractive (e.g., Gilbert, Pinel, Wilson, Blumberg, & Wheatley, 1998; Kay et al., 2002). Only system justification theory explains why people would actively derogate alternatives to the status quo.

Social dominance theorists are better equipped than social identity theorists to handle issues of ideological consensus (Sidanius, Levin, & Pratto, 1996), mainly because they assume that people are hardwired to display submission as well as dominance (Sidanius & Pratto, 1993). Nevertheless, the bulk of their empirical efforts are devoted to demonstrating that members of advantaged groups hold attitudes that are more supportive of authority figures, legal institutions, and the social order than are members of disadvantaged groups, which is consistent with self-interest and needs for dominance (e.g., Pratto, Sidanius, Stallworth, & Malle, 1994; Sidanius, 1993; Sidanius & Pratto, 1993, 1999; Sidanius, Pratto, & Bobo, 1996). "Hierarchy enhancing" attitudes, they suggest, are more prevalent among members of high-status and powerful groups, because such attitudes satisfy their needs for social dominance. Thus, social dominance theory conceives of hierarchy as something that is imposed by dominant groups on subordinate groups.

The Strong Form of the System Justification Hypothesis

System justification theory recognizes that conflicts between ego, group, and system justification do exist for members of disadvantaged groups more than for members of advantaged groups (e.g., Jost et al., 2001), and this means that when motives for ego justification or group justification are highly salient, members of disadvantaged groups probably will not engage in system justification as strongly as will members of advantaged groups. Nevertheless, an emphasis on the system-serving (rather than self-serving or group-serving) functions of attitudes, beliefs, and ideologies means that preservation of the societal status quo is more of a collaborative process in which, as Havel said, "everyone … is both a victim and a supporter of the system." Or, in the language of Bourdieu (1977/1986), "the task of reproducing the relations of domination is taken over by objective mechanisms, which serve the interests of the dominant group without any conscious effort on the latter's part" (p. 189).

This issue is at the heart of the controversy concerning the concept of false consciousness, which system justification theorists see as a key to understanding the social psychological effects of oppression (e.g., Blasi & Jost, 2006; Jost, 1995; Jost & Banaji, 1994; Jost & Jost, 2007). Social identity theorists (e.g., Haslam, Turner, Oakes, Reynolds, & Doosje, 2002; Spears et al., 2001; Yzerbyt, Rocher, & Schadron, 1997, p. 50), while social dominance theorists (Sidanius & Pratto, 1999, pp. 103–104; Sidanius et al., 2001, pp. 310–311), by contrast, seek to reject and distance themselves from the concept of false consciousness. By retaining the insightful Marxian–feminist notion that people suffer as a result of illusions that sustain their ideological and psychological attachments to the status quo, system justification theorists are in a better position to understand counterintuitive findings in social and political psychology (see also Jost, 1995; Jost, Banaji, & Nosek, 2004; Jost, Fitzsimons, et al., 2004; Jost & Hunyady, 2005).

For example, a system justification perspective helps to understand why people who are economically disadvantaged generally oppose income redistribution (e.g., Frank, 2004; Jost, Blount, Pfeffer, & Hunyady, 2003; Kluegel & Smith, 1986; Lane, 1959/2004), why women accept and internalize certain forms of gender inequality (e.g., Jackman, 1994; Jost & Kay, 2005; Major, 1994), and why at least some members of racial and ethnic minorities reject egalitarian alternatives to the status quo (e.g., Gilens, 1999; Jost & Thompson, 2000). Other theories are well poised to explain self-interested (or group-interested) behavior, but they are ill equipped to deal with these counterintuitive phenomena, largely because they assume that social attitudes and behaviors follow from group identification, party membership, ethnocentrism, dominance needs, and other individual or collective forms of symbolic or material self-interest. For instance, Leyens and Demoulin (2009) write that, "Everybody is accustomed to right wing (conservative) political parties that are supported by the wealthiest people" (p. 202), but they ignore working class conservatism altogether (but see Frank, 2004; Napier & Jost, 2008a).

The strongest form of the system justification hypothesis, which draws also on the logic of cognitive dissonance theory, is that members of disadvantaged groups would be even *more* likely than members of advantaged groups to support the status quo (see Jost, Pelham, et al., 2003). This is a paradoxical effect of the system justification motive. Cognitive dissonance researchers are well-known for having demonstrated that people who are most socially and physically deprived develop the strongest needs to justify their own suffering, in order to reduce dissonance (e.g., Aronson & Mills, 1959; Wicklund & Brehm, 1976). Analogously, if indeed there is indeed a motivation to justify the system in order to reduce ideological dissonance and defend against threats to the system's legitimacy, it follows that those who suffer the most from the system would also have the most to explain, justify, and rationalize. As Elster (1982) noted, "The interest of the upper class is better served by the lower classes spontaneously inventing an ideology justifying their inferior status" (p. 142). Bourdieu's (1977/1986) take is even more explicit:

> Once a system of mechanisms has been constituted capable of objectively ensuring the reproduction of the established order of its own motion ... the dominant class have only to *let the system they dominate take its own course* [italics added] in order to exercise their domination (p. 190)

From a social psychological perspective, it is important to point out that cognitive dissonance theory alone would not predict that members of disadvantaged groups would resolve dissonance in a manner that consistently reinforces rather than challenges their state of disadvantage (see also Blasi & Jost, 2006; Jost, Fitzsimons, et al., 2004; Jost & Hunyady, 2002). This is yet another reason why we need a theory of system justification.

Jost, Pelham, et al. (2003) explored the possibility of enhanced system justification on the part of the disadvantaged in five national survey studies. In the first, they found that low-income respondents and African Americans were significantly more likely than high-income respondents and European Americans to support limitations on the rights of citizens and media representatives to criticize the government. In a second study, low-income Latinos were more likely to trust in government officials and to believe that "the government is run for the benefit of all" than were high-income Latinos, even after adjusting for educational differences and excluding politically conservative Cuban respondents.

A third study addressed meritocratic ideology and found that low-income respondents were more likely than high-income respondents to believe that large differences in pay are necessary to "get people to work hard" and "as an incentive for individual effort." Once again, these effects retained significance after adjusting for education. In the fourth study, African Americans living in the South (compared to African Americans living in the North) possessed lower income levels but professed a stronger belief that the system is meritocratic. In a fifth study, Jost, Pelham, et al. (2003) found that low-income respondents and African Americans were more likely than high-income respondents and European Americans to believe that economic inequality is both legitimate and necessary. The endorsement of meritocratic ideology was associated with greater economic satisfaction for all respondents, whether rich or poor, consistent with the palliative function of system-justifying ideology proposed by Jost and Hunyady (2002; see also Napier & Jost, 2008b).

Henry and Saul (2006) replicated the most distinctive finding from these studies—that members of disadvantaged groups can be the most ardent supporters of the status quo—in the context of extreme poverty in Bolivia. Specifically, they found that children coming from the lowest status ethnic groups in Bolivia (the indigenous groups of Quechuans and Aymarans) were more likely than children coming from middle-status (Mestizo) and high-status (Hispanic) ethnic groups to believe that political dissent should be suppressed and that the Bolivian government adequately meets the needs of the population. The authors noted that these results were even more surprising given that the high-status Hispanic leader President Hugo Banzer Suárez led the government at the time.

We are not proposing that an inverse relationship between social status and support for the system and its authorities will always hold. Presumably, this depends on many factors, including the salience and strength of competing ego and group justification motives (Jost et al., 2001; Jost, Pelham, et al., 2003) and the degree of group permeability or, more precisely, upward mobility that is seen as possible given the rules and constraints of the system (Blair & Jost, 2003; Hogg & Abrams, 1988; Tajfel & Turner, 1979/1986; Wright, 2001). Nonetheless, evidence of enhanced system justification among the disadvantaged directly challenges social identity theory's assumptions that social and political attitudes primarily or exclusively reflect group membership as well as social dominance theory's assumptions that hegemonic groups will always take the ideological lead in enforcing the social order.

Our findings are consistent not only with evidence of "working-class conservatism" (e.g., Frank, 2004; Jost, Glaser, et al., 2003; Lipset, 1960/1981; Napier & Jost, 2008a; Stacey & Green, 1971), but also with many other apparently anomalous findings lacking a theoretical home. Members of low-income groups, for example, tend to score higher than members of high-income groups on right-wing authoritarianism (Altemeyer, 1981), power distance (Hofstede, 1997), and the belief in a just world (Hunt, 2000). Kay and Zanna (2009) proposed that feeling psychologically *dependent* on the social system should increase one's motivation to defend and justify it. Several studies conducted by van der Toorn, Tyler, and Jost (2010) provide evidence that is consistent with this proposition.

The fact that members of disadvantaged groups are (under some circumstances, at least) more likely than others to justify the system is consistent with the notion that they are motivated to reduce ideological dissonance on behalf of the very system that deprives them. The system's needs seem to have become their own; this alludes to a relatively mundane instantiation of the ominous conclusion to George Orwell's novel *1984*: "But it was all right, everything was all right, the struggle was finished. He had won the victory over himself. He loved Big Brother." This is the essence of what is often meant by the term "false consciousness" (see Jost, 1995, for a conceptual and empirical review of work related to this concept), and I suspect that if social scientists were to fully repudiate (rather than refine) the concept of false consciousness—as many writers in the social identity and social dominance traditions have urged—they would need to come up with a similar concept to do the same theoretical work.

Situational and Dispositional Moderators of System Justification Motivation

System justification theory is the first to distinguish clearly among the three motives of ego, group, and system justification. Consequently, it has taken the lead, even over its predecessors, in identifying the social and psychological consequences of supporting the status quo, especially among members of low-status groups (e.g., Haines & Jost, 2000; Henry & Saul, 2006; Jost, 2001; Jost & Burgess, 2000; Jost et al., 2001, 2002; Jost & Thompson, 2000; O'Brien & Major, 2005). Many have criticized system justification theorists for emphasizing the "power" of the status quo, as opposed to the (allegedly equivalent) power of social change motivation (e.g., Désert & Leyens, 2006; Haslam et al., 2002; Reicher, 2004; Spears et al., 2001). On this point, we refer critics to no less an authority on social dynamics than Kurt Lewin (1947): "The study of the conditions for change begins appropriately with an analysis of the conditions for 'no change,' that is for the state of equilibrium" (p. 341).

Work from several independent but related research programs on system justification theory supports the conclusion that for members of advantaged groups, motives for ego justification, group justification, and system justification are consistent and complementary, whereas for members of disadvantaged groups, these motives are often in conflict with one another. Jost and Burgess (2000), for instance, found that members of low-status groups exhibited greater attitudinal ambivalence (or psychological conflict) directed at their own group than did members of high-status groups. Furthermore, we find that increased levels of system justification are associated with increased levels of ambivalence among members of low-status groups as the conflict is made worse but with *decreased* ambivalence among members of high-status groups, for whom these needs are consistent and reinforcing.

There is also evidence that when members of disadvantaged groups do provide ideological support for the status quo, as in the examples mentioned above, it comes at the expense of self-evaluation and ingroup evaluation. Research by Jost and Thompson (2000) showed that economic system justification and generalized opposition to equality are associated with decreased self-esteem, increased neuroticism, and increased outgroup favoritism among African American respondents. These same system-justifying variables were associated with increases in self-esteem and ingroup favoritism and decreases in neuroticism (or guilt) among European Americans. O'Brien and Major (2005) replicated these results, finding that the above pattern held for strongly identified members of disadvantaged groups—who would be expected to have the most intense conflicts between group and system justification motives—but not for weakly identified members, who apparently opted for what was good for themselves (as well as for the perceived legitimacy and stability of the system) over what was good for their own group.

Critics also allege that system justification theory lacks moderating variables to explain variability in the tendency to support the status quo (e.g., Désert & Leyens, 2006; Huddy, 2004; Reicher, 2004; Rubin & Hewstone, 2004). Sidanius et al. (2004, p. 870), for example, stated that system justification theory "relies on a universal cognitive bias to explain why people support systems that work against their own interests" and that the theory "has yet to articulate when people will and will not try to justify the social systems in which they live." Rubin and Hewstone (2004) similarly suggested, "The absence of moderating variables means that there is nothing to prevent the general motive for system justification from causing social systems to come to rest in permanent states of social stability, rather than to fluctuate between stability and change as social identity theory assumes" (p. 835). Most hyperbolically, Désert and Leyens (2006) claimed, "[System justification theory] views the system as a 'fatum,' *as a given forever*" (p. 311, [italics added]).

These allegations are simply untrue and suggest that these critics lack familiarity with the published literature on situational and dispositional variability in system justification motivation (e.g., see Jost, Banaji, & Nosek, 2004; Jost, Blount, et al., 2003; Jost et al., 2001; Jost, Glaser, et al., 2003; Jost & Hunyady, 2002, 2005; Jost, Kivetz, Rubini, Guermandi, & Mosso, 2005; Jost et al., 2003, 2008; Kay et al., 2005, 2007; Kay & Zanna, 2009; Ullrich & Cohrs, 2007). It would be more accurate to say that we, following a perspectivist philosophy of science, resist the temptation to propose that a *single* variable, process, mechanism, and so on could ever account for the full range of variability in a dependent variable as complex and multiply determined as prosystem versus antisystem behavior (Jost & Hardin, in press). For instance, I have already stated that behavioral outcomes should be affected not only by the strength of the system justification motive but also by the strength of ego and group justification motives and whether they are operating in a manner that is consistent or inconsistent with system justification (e.g., Jost & Burgess, 2000; Jost, Ledgerwood & Hardin et al., 2001; Jost & Thompson, 2000).

Our research has also identified a number of other situational and individual difference variables that serve to increase or decrease levels of system justification by virtue of the fact that they increase epistemic, existential, or relational needs to attain certainty, safety, and social validation. For example, we have found that exposure to high- (vs. low-) system threat—that is, information that is potentially threatening to the legitimacy or stability of the social system—leads people to endorse system-justifying stereotypes more enthusiastically (Jost et al., 2005; Kay et al., 2005), to adopt more politically conservative beliefs and opinions (Jost, Glaser, et al., 2003), and to score more highly on direct measures of system justification (Ullrich & Cohrs, 2007). Studies show that being reminded of complementary stereotypes that create an "illusion of equality" also cause people to justify the social system more enthusiastically (Jost & Kay, 2005; Kay & Jost, 2003). And, as mentioned above, feeling psychologically dependent on the system is yet another factor that increases one's satisfaction with the status quo and with institutional authorities (Kay & Zanna, 2009; van der Toorn et al., 2009).

With regard to dispositional moderators of system justification tendencies, we find that individuals who possess heightened needs to reduce uncertainty and threat—as measured in terms of personal needs for order, certainty, structure, and closure and chronic levels of death anxiety—also tend to gravitate toward system-justifying belief systems (Jost, Glaser, et al., 2003; Jost & Hunyady, 2005; Jost, et al., 2007). Furthermore, chronic tendencies to engage in self-deception, as measured with the use of (entirely apolitical) items developed by Paulhus (1984), are positively associated with the endorsement of politically conservative attitudes (Jost et al., 2010, pp. 181–183) and also with the tendency to believe that procedures and outcomes associated with the free market are inherently fair and legitimate (Jost, Blount, et al., 2003). None of these findings would have been anticipated on the basis of social identity or social dominance theories alone, but they do seem to advance our understanding of when people will or will not challenge the status quo.

Some critics cannot understand how a theory could simultaneously suggest that there is a relatively general psychological tendency to preserve the status quo and that there are also individual differences that explain variation in this tendency (e.g., Désert & Leyens, 2006; Huddy, 2004). Huddy wrote, for example, "There is an essential contradiction in the theory between the existence of universal 'social and psychological needs to imbue the status quo with legitimacy' and individual differences (p. 952)." Although this reaction to system justification theory is a surprisingly common one, it makes little sense in light of the history of social-personality psychology (as well as perspectivist philosophy of science). Is it really controversial to suggest that there would be dispositional (as well as situational) sources of variability in such general, even "fundamental," psychological motives as cognitive consistency, self-enhancement, social identification, and other motives?

System justification theory is and always was designed to be an integrative theory (Jost et al., 2001) and a perspectivist one (Jost, 2004; McGuire, 1989, 1997). Thus, the system justification motive was proposed by Jost and Banaji (1994) to work in conjunction with ego and group justification motives; it was not intended to *replace* those other motives in social psychological theorizing. The hope is that a system justification perspective allows one to incorporate and expand on motives and tendencies identified by other theories and to explore the limits and boundary conditions of those motives, tendencies, and theories. The remainder of this chapter is devoted to further clarifying some of the points of convergence and divergence between system justification theory and the other two perspectives. We first address the relationship between social identification and system justification theories and then turn to consider the relationship between social dominance and system justification theories.

RELATIONS BETWEEN SOCIAL IDENTITY AND SYSTEM JUSTIFICATION THEORIES

Social identity theory, as mentioned above, is an extremely important precursor to the theory of system justification. This is largely because it links individual and collective levels of analysis; because it attempts to contextualize interpersonal and intergroup behavior in light of history, culture, and politics; and because it adopts an experimental approach to the study of intergroup relations and social structures (see also Jost, 2001, 2004; Jost & Hunyady, 2002; Jost & Major, 2001).

Areas of Agreement

First, social identity theory brings a social psychological perspective to bear on intergroup relations such that differences in status and power are predicted to affect group members' perceptions of themselves and of their own group and of other groups (Sachdev & Bourhis, 1987, 1991; Tajfel, 1978), and these perceptions are theorized to affect the future course of relations between the groups as well as the viability of the social system itself (Tajfel & Turner, 1979/1986; Wright, Taylor, & Moghaddam, 1990). Thus, in many ways, social identity theory first charted the territory that is now also surveyed by social dominance and system justification theorists.

Second, social identity theory introduced factors such as perceptions of the legitimacy and stability of the status system as potentially relevant to ingroup and outgroup favoritism (Ellemers et al., 1993; Spears et al., 2001; Tajfel & Turner, 1979/1986; Turner & Brown, 1978). What is more accurate, social identity theory was the first psychological theory of intergroup relations to import these and related concepts from sociological works such as Berger and Luckmann's (1967) *The Social Construction of Reality* and Hirschman's (1970) *Exit, Voice, and Loyalty*. That these ideas are central to an understanding of relations between groups that differ in social status and power is an assumption that is shared by social identity, social dominance, and system justification theorists alike.

Third, the notion that social groups invent ideologies that justify their competition against other groups (Tajfel, 1981), when combined with perspectives emphasizing the ideological consent of subordinated groups (Jost, 1995), helps to explain why stereotypes and other ideas that justify social and material inequalities are frequently endorsed even by members of subordinate groups. That is, we agree that a prominent source of system-justifying ideologies in society is the attempt by dominant group members to explain and rationalize their own group's dominance. This is the group justification function identified by Tajfel (1981), namely, the "justification of actions, committed or planned, against outgroups" (p. 156).

Thus, many (but by no means all) examples of system justification are historically traceable to acts of group justification by members of advantaged groups. At the same time, however, we think that Tajfel's (1981) account is incomplete, because it underestimates the power of the system to regulate and determine human behavior, and it ignores the strength of the system justification motive that is present even among members of subordinate groups (see also Jost & Hunyady, 2002, 2005; Jost et al., 2010; Jost, Pelham, et al., 2003). Because people are motivated to believe that the world they inhabit is legitimate, fair, and rational, the (subjective) preservation of the system is a shared, collaborative process that is set into motion by the (objective) structural constraints of the system itself. As Havel (1991) put it, "Individuals confirm the system, fulfill the system, make the system, *are* the system" (p. 136). For this reason, it is at best only partially accurate to "divide society into the rulers and the ruled" (Havel, 1991, p. 144), as both social identity and social dominance perspectives appear to do. The legitimation and stabilization of inequality in the social order must be conceptualized as a systemic process and not merely as the result of conflict, competition, or dominance struggles between groups.

Areas of Disagreement

The limitations of social identity theory make it more of a starting point than an end point for the theory of system justification (see also Jost, 2001, 2004; Jost & Banaji, 1994). For this reason, we think that critics such as Reicher (2004), Désert and Leyens (2006), Rubin and Hewstone (2004), Leyens & Demoulin (2009), and others are wrong when they argue that there is no need for theories of social dominance or system justification because we already have a perfectly good (and more or less complete) theory of social identification. Social identity theory tends to locate all human behavior on a "continuum" that ranges from individual to group identification or from "self-categorization" to "group categorization" or from interpersonal to intergroup behavior (e.g., Tajfel, 1981; Turner, Hogg, Oakes, Reicher, & Wetherell, 1987; see also Stangor & Jost, 1997). This is not to say that social identity theorists have never addressed issues of ideology, myth, or society. We have already mentioned that Tajfel's (1981, 1982, 1984) expansive writings do touch on these themes, and some of his followers have taken them up from time to time as well.

The problem is that the systemic or structural issues are typically approached from the standpoint of group interests and identities and, occasionally, in relation to individual needs and abilities. But the structural, objective consequences of the social system are hard to approach from a subjectivist perspective alone (e.g., Turner, 1982). For instance, the *nonconscious* effects of belonging to a given social, economic, or political system (e.g., Ashburn-Nardo et al., 2003; Jost, Banaji, & Nosek, 2004; Jost et al., 2002; Lane et al., 2005; Rudman et al., 2002; Uhlmann et al., 2002) are not fully captured by a theory that emphasizes the salience of levels of self-categorization as the key explanatory variable, because salient self-categorizations are by definition conscious, explicit, and subjectively acknowledged. It is also necessary to understand the "existence of mechanisms capable of reproducing the political order, independently of any deliberate intervention" (Bourdieu, 1977/1986, p. 189).

Furthermore, it is insufficient to construe the social system simply as a larger or more inclusive group or to say that the system exerts its effects only through processes of subjective identification or self-categorization, as Spears et al. (2001) and Rubin and Hewstone (2004) suggested. The evidence suggests, for example, that nearly all African Americans disavow the legitimacy of racial inequality at a conscious, explicit level, and yet sizeable percentages of African Americans internalize the consequences of the inequality at an unconscious, implicit level (e.g., Ashburn-Nardo et al., 2003; Jost, Banaji, & Nosek, 2004; Livingston, 2002). Furthermore, Jost et al. (2005, Study 3) found that an experimental manipulation of system threat at the national level led Israeli respondents not to band together to defend national unity and to achieve a superordinate group identification—as one might expect on the basis of social identity theory—but rather to emphasize status differences *between* Ashkenazi and Sephardic Jews and to engage in complementary stereotypic differentiation, thereby rationalizing the legitimacy of differences between the two groups and bolstering the unequal status quo (see also Kay et al., 2005; Napier, Mandisodza, Andersen, & Jost, 2006).

For all of these reasons, we think that social identity theory underestimates the psychologically compelling, collaborative nature of system justification processes (against one's subjective wishes and desires, in some cases, and at some risk to self-esteem and to positive evaluations of the ingroup). It also downplays the power of dominant ideology (such as the belief in meritocracy) to capture the imaginations of people whose personal and group interests are not well served by that ideology. Our research suggests that ideology satisfies system justification motives by allowing all (or nearly all) of us to preserve cherished beliefs that the societal status quo is relatively fair, legitimate, justified, and better than most alternatives to it.

Several more specific conclusions follow from these general points concerning social identity theory's neglect of objective psychological consequences of the social system. As we argued in our original formulation of system justification theory (Jost & Banaji, 1994), social identity theory exaggerates the generality of ingroup favoritism and discounts the possibility that system justification is a motivated, goal-directed process. We recognize that some have argued that social identity theory is not primarily a theory of intergroup bias (e.g., Ellemers, Haslam, Platow, & van Knippenberg, 2003; Reicher, 2004; Rubin & Hewstone, 2004; Spears et al., 2001), but if we focus on actual implementations of the theory and the research practice of social identity theorists, it is difficult to avoid the conclusion that it has been used far more to predict, describe, and explain ingroup than outgroup favoritism.

To illustrate the imbalance within social identity theory's own tradition of scholarship, Jost, Banaji, and Nosek (2004) reviewed several books on social identity and intergroup relations and compared the number of index entries for "ingroup bias" and "ingroup favo(u)ritism" to entries for "outgroup bias" and "outgroup favo(u)ritism." For 21 books published between 1981 and 2003, Jost, Banaji, and Nosek (2004) found that there were 300 index entries for "ingroup favoritism," and there were 16 entries for "outgroup favoritism," half of which came from a single chapter by Hinkle and Brown (1990). This lopsidedness is also manifest in major handbook chapters and review articles on social identification and intergroup relations (e.g., Brewer & Brown, 1998; Deaux, 1996; Hewstone, Rubin, & Willis, 2002). Brown (2000b), for instance, did not even mention "outgroup favoritism" in his comprehensive review, "Social Identity Theory: Past Achievements, Current Problems, and Future Challenges," although Hinkle and Brown (1990) seemed to feel that it posed a significant problem for the theory a decade earlier. A recent historical review by Hornsey (2008) similarly sidestepped the issue. Some may see the emphasis on ingroup favoritism (and de-emphasis on outgroup favoritism) as appropriate and warranted, on the grounds that ingroup favoritism is far more prevalent than outgroup favoritism, but this, too, is contradicted by the evidence (e.g., Jost, 2001; Jost & Banaji, 1994; Jost et al., 2002; Uhlmann et al., 2002). As mentioned above, nearly half of African Americans and homosexuals exhibit implicit biases in favor of European Americans and heterosexuals, respectively (Jost, Banaji, & Nosek, 2004). Leyens and Demoulin (2009) concede that the presence of outgroup bias "would have meant that the dominated group accepted the values of the dominant one" (p. 204), as hypothesized by system justification theory, but they seem surprisingly unaware of how much empirical evidence of outgroup favoritism exists.

Our second criticism is that the open-endedness of the theory allows social identity theorists to make exactly opposite predictions in key areas, such as the hypothesized effects of relative group status on ingroup and outgroup favoritism (e.g., Brown & Wade, 1987; Sachdev & Bourhis, 1984). For example, some researchers have hypothesized that minority groups of low status would discriminate *more* than groups of high status (e.g., Branthwaite & Jones, 1975; Brewer, 1979; Sachdev & Bourhis, 1984). Sachdev and Bourhis (1984) reasoned as follows:

> Since minority group membership confers a relatively insecure and negative social identity, *minorities should show more discrimination and less fairness* [italics added] than majorities. Discrimination, according to [social identity theory], serves to achieve (or maintain) a positive social identity. Conversely, since majority group membership confers a comparatively secure and positive social identity, *majorities can afford to be fair towards minorities* [italics added]. (p. 47)

Although this passage seems to confound social status with numerical status (as is often the case in the real world), there are two claims here: (a) People with threatened social identities (such as members of low-status groups) should show an increase in ingroup favoritism, and (b) people with secure social identities (such as members of high-status groups) should show fairness and perhaps even magnanimous outgroup favoritism (see also Brewer, 1979; Mummendey & Simon, 1989; van Knippenberg, 1984). Leach et al. (2003) went so far as to suggest, "Members of actual low-status groups, whose group identity is chronically threatened by their relative inferiority to higher status groups, evaluate out-groups most negatively" (p. 933).

Most studies, however, find precisely the opposite—namely, that low-status groups frequently evaluate higher status outgroups more positively and to evaluate their *own* groups more negatively (for a review, see Jost, Banaji, & Nosek, 2004). Thus, the evidence contradicts some clear derivations from social identity theory and highlights inconsistencies in various theoretical accounts. It seems relevant that Sachdev and Bourhis (1984) used social identity theory to predict a negative relationship between ingroup status and the degree of ingroup bias, whereas Sachdev and Bourhis (1987) used the same theory to predict a positive relationship.

Social identity theory was developed at least in part to account for the initially unexpected finding that "minimal" laboratory groups with no history of interaction displayed ingroup favoritism with regard to social stereotyping, performance evaluation, and resource allocation (Tajfel & Turner, 1979/1986). Drawing extensively on Festinger's (1954) social comparison theory, it was argued that because people need to evaluate themselves favorably and because group memberships are an important constituent of the self-concept, people tend to evaluate their own group more favorably than they evaluate other groups (Tajfel & Turner, 1979/1986; Turner, 1975). Thus, according to at least some versions of social identity theory, there is a general drive to enhance individual and collective self-esteem by making favorable comparisons between the ingroup and relevant outgroups (Hogg & Abrams, 1988; Rubin & Hewstone,

1998; Tajfel & Turner, 1979/1986). Turner (1999) disputed this interpretation vociferously, suggesting that there may no longer be only one version of social identity theory. Nevertheless, Hornsey (2008, pp. 214–215) concluded that "self-esteem has not been written out of the theory" and that social identity theory still assumes "an ongoing process to achieve, maintain, *and protect* a positive self-concept (broadly defined)."

Social identity theorists often invoke the concept of "social reality" to explain why perceptions of legitimacy and stability are so often consensual and why members of disadvantaged groups express outgroup favoritism (e.g., Brewer, 2007; Ellemers, Van Rijswijk, Roefs, & Simons, 1997; Hogg & Abrams, 1988; Rubin & Hewstone, 2004; Spears et al., 2001). However, we think that the theory fails to explain why ideological claims concerning legitimacy and stability would be less open to dispute and less subject to ingroup-favoring biases than other beliefs and representations studied by social identity theorists. It is not clear why social identity theory, which postulates a significant amount of distortion and bias in the attribution process (Cooper & Fazio, 1986; Hewstone, 1990; Hogg & Abrams, 1988; Hornsey, 2008), would lead proponents to rely on a concept like the incontrovertibility of social reality in seeking to explain outgroup favoritism among low-status group members. Along these lines, Brewer (2007, p. 733) wrote,

> Although group members may prefer to see themselves as competent and smart, comparative evaluations on these traits are constrained by reality. Evidence for so-called *outgroup favoritism* [italics added] (Jost, 2001; Jost, Banaji, & Nosek, 2004; Sachdev & Bourhis, 1991) is generally limited to findings that members of lower status groups evaluate high-status outgroups more positively than their ingroup on status-relevant dimensions of evaluation. In effect, they are *simply acknowledging objective differences in status, power, or wealth and resources* [italics added].

The notion that outgroup favoritism on the part of racial and ethnic minorities reflects the acknowledgment of "objective differences" is problematic in several respects, and Brewer (2007) is clearly mistaken about the existing evidence, as are Rubin and Hewstone (2004) and Leyens and Demoulin (2009).[2]

Members of disadvantaged groups do not merely show outgroup favoritism on "status-relevant dimensions of evaluation." Much as the African American children studied by Clark and Clark (1947) believed that the White dolls were prettier and more desirable in general in comparison to the Black dolls, we find that nearly half of African Americans and homosexuals show outgroup favoritism on implicit measures of *liking* or *evaluation* (Jost, Banaji, & Nosek, 2004). That is, they find it easier to associate their own group with *generically* (i.e., not status-specific) *unpleasant* verbal stimuli and to associate the more advantaged outgroup with pleasant verbal stimuli than vice versa.

Outgroup favoritism on the part of members of disadvantaged groups (such as racial or ethnic minorities and women) also manifests itself in terms of consequential behavioral outcomes such as choice of interaction partner and decisions about how to name one's children (Jost et al., 2002). Furthermore, the notion that outgroup favoritism simply reflects "objective differences" and accommodation to "reality constraints" is of no use in explaining why exposure to system threat increases the display of outgroup favoritism among members of disadvantaged groups (Jost & Hunyady, 2002; Jost et al., 2005) or why outgroup favoritism is more prevalent among politically conservative (vs. liberal) members of disadvantaged groups (Jost, Banaji, & Nosek, 2004; Jost et al., 2001)—unless one makes the highly dubious assumptions (in light of other social psychological evidence) that system threat and political conservatism are associated with increased judgmental *accuracy.*

Rubin and Hewstone (2004) risked trivializing the situation faced by members of disadvantaged groups when they compared the situation they confront to a "football match" in which "members of the losing team must admit that they lost the game and that the other team won" (p. 831). They wrote,

> According to social identity theory, the need for a positive identity would motivate members of the losing team to adopt one or more cognitive identity management strategies in order to mitigate the impact of their relatively secure negative social identity. However, if members of the losing team are asked who won the game, the need to maintain an accurate representation of social reality constrains the response that they could give: Although they would like to say, "we won the game" in order to satisfy their need for a positive social identity, this response would be inaccurate, dysfunctional, and maladaptive. Instead, the members of the losing team must admit that they lost the game and that the other team won. System justification theorists would argue that this admission of defeat (i.e., outgroup favoritism) represents an active attempt to support the status inequality between the two football teams. In contrast, social identity theorists offer the more parsimonious explanation that this response is simply the passive reflection of the current status quo, as specified in a socially shared reality. (p. 831)

Setting aside the dubious ideological assumption that society provides a "level playing field" on which everyone is free to compete and the worrisome implications of comparing, say, gays and lesbians to a team that "tried and lost," Rubin and Hewstone are right about one thing: Some cases of system justification are passive (and unconscious) rather than active (and conscious). But they—like Brewer (2007)—are wrong that "admitting defeat" (or "acknowledging objective differences") does not involve some degree of psychological capitulation to the status quo. As Bourdieu (1977/1986) put it, the "most successful ideological effects ... ask no more than complicitous silence" (p. 188).

At minimum, "admitting defeat" involves recognizing the legitimacy of the referees' authority as well as their conduct, the rules of competition, the league itself, and perhaps even the fairness of the other team's behavior. Otherwise, the members of the "losing team" would not simply say, "We lost"; they would say, "They cheated" or "We were robbed." Furthermore, it seems to me that there is a world of difference between "admitting defeat" and developing automatic associations linking one's own racial or ethnic group to words or images that are unpleasant and even disgusting (Ashburn-Nardo et al., 2003; Jost, Banaji, & Nosek, 2004; Jost et al., 2002; Nosek et al., 2002; Overbeck et al., 2004; Rudman et al., 2002; Uhlmann et al., 2002).

The fact that expressions of moral outrage are relatively rare among society's "losers" tells us something important (e.g., Kinder & Sears, 1985). It tells us, among other things, that Simon and Klandermans (2001, p. 324) went too far in their application of social identity theory when they concluded, "Feelings of illegitimate inequality or injustice typically result when social comparisons reveal that one's ingroup is worse off than relevant outgroups." On the contrary, most members of disadvantaged groups *realize* that they are worse off than others, but truly rebellious, system-challenging behavior is hard to come by. Even during periods of relatively widespread discontent and participation in collective action (such as the 1960s), only a relatively small minority of citizens actually fight for social change, and they typically face backlash and condemnation by the majority. As the historian Howard Zinn (1968) noted in one of the most volatile years of the 20th century, "What we should be most concerned about is not some natural tendency towards violent uprising, but rather the inclination of people, faced with an overwhelming environment, to submit to it" (p. 17).

System justification theory seeks to understand why psychological capitulation to the status quo is so common. By stipulating that for epistemic, existential, and relational reasons people are motivated to defend current social, economic, and political arrangements (see also Haines & Jost, 2000; Jost et al., 2005, 2010; Jost, Ledgerwood, & Hardin, 2008; Kay et al., 2002, 2005; Ledgerwood, Mandisodza, Jost, & Pohl, 2008; Ullrich & Cohrs, 2007) and that even members of disadvantaged groups tend to see those arrangements as relatively fair and legitimate (e.g., Henry & Saul, 2006; Jost & Hunyady, 2002, 2005; Jost, Pelham, et al., 2003), system justification theory is in a better position than other theories to account for widespread *resistance* to social change.

It appears that Tajfel (1984) was aware of some of the limitations of social identity theory that we have discussed. For instance, with regard to ingroup and outgroup favoritism he wrote,

> This disymmetry between the "superior" and "inferior" groups has been recognized to some extent in the social identity approach to intergroup relations which has specified the different strategies for achieving distinctiveness that can be adopted by members of groups which differ in status. ... *But this is not enough* [italics added]. (p. 700)

Elsewhere, he noted the significance of justice perceptions in helping to understand when group members will accept and when they will reject the social system:

> [An] important requirement of research on social justice would consist of establishing in detail the *links between social myths and the general acceptance of injustice* [italics added], and research which would attempt to specify the sociopsychological conditions which could be expected to contribute to the dissolution of these patterns of acceptance. (Tajfel, 1982, p. 164)

Here, Tajfel seems to be appealing to social justice researchers to determine when people will engage in system justification and when they will not. His use of the term "myth" alludes to the need for a theory of *false* consciousness such as that provided by a system justification approach. It is curious—given this critical theoretical heritage—that contemporary social identity theorists tend to back away from the concept of false consciousness and assume instead that, as a general rule, members of disadvantaged and advantaged groups are highly responsive to "reality constraints" (e.g., Brewer, 2007; Haslam et al., 2002; Reicher, 2004; Rubin & Hewstone, 2004; Spears et al., 2001; Yzerbyt et al., 1997).

Tajfel's death in 1982 caused a fairly serious setback in making progress on the ambitious theoretical and empirical goals of social identity theory. The influence of the theory has remained strong, but most empirical research since then has addressed issues of personal and collective self-esteem, situational and individual variability in identification with the ingroup, and perceptual and cognitive processes of self-categorization (e.g., Abrams & Hogg, 1990; Brown, 2000a, 2000b; Hornsey, 2008; Oakes, Turner, & Haslam, 1994; Rubin & Hewstone, 1998; Spears, Oakes, Ellemers, & Haslam, 1997; Turner, 1999; Turner et al., 1987). Empirical work on antecedents of the perceived legitimacy and stability of the social system, ideological processes in groups, and "myths" that foster the "acceptance of injustice" has fallen off, and one can ask whether, after nearly 40 years of research, social identity theory has progressed substantially beyond what was outlined by Turner and Brown (1978), Tajfel and Turner (1979/1986), and Tajfel (1981) with respect to these themes. System justification theory aims to pick up where these astute researchers left off.

RELATIONS BETWEEN SOCIAL DOMINANCE AND SYSTEM JUSTIFICATION THEORIES

Social dominance and system justification theorists agree that the social identity perspective does not provide a completely satisfying account of outgroup favoritism among the disadvantaged (e.g., Jost, 2001, 2004; Jost & Banaji, 1994; Sidanius, 1993; Sidanius & Pratto, 1999). Similarly, social dominance and system justification perspectives postulate a great deal of ideological consensus across groups, as a result of the spread of dominant ideology and cultural hegemony, whereas social identity theorists presume a great deal of dissensus arising from intergroup distinctions. Reicher, Hopkins, and Condor's (1997) work on social categorization and political rhetoric exemplifies social identity theory's emphasis on conflict between groups over definitions of reality (see also Reicher, 2004), whereas Sidanius's work in isolating shared and unshared variance in ideological domains indicates that dominant groups are not the only ones who possess beliefs that support the societal status quo (Sidanius et al., 2001; Sidanius, Levin, et al., 1996; see also Jost, Pelham, et al., 2003). This may turn out to be a case of arguing about whether the glass is half full or half empty, but at least the theoretical differences are relatively clear.

Social dominance theory was developed in part to improve upon the inadequacies of social identity theory to deal with outgroup favoritism among groups low in social standing (Sidanius, 1993; Sidanius & Pratto, 1993). Its proponents have described it as a "biopolitical" theory in which inequality between groups is viewed as evolutionarily adaptive. The "most basic assumption" of social dominance theory is that *"all social systems will converge toward the establishment of stable, group-based social hierarchies"* (Sidanius & Pratto, 1993, p. 177; italics in original). Thus, the theory has no problem accounting for the existence of outgroup favoritism among low-status groups—it takes such behavior to reflect the genetic mandate of the human species. From a system justification perspective, which emphasizes the human capacity to rationalize aspects of whatever social system happens to be in place, this assumption is overstated (Jost, Banaji, & Nosek, 2004).

According to social dominance theory, one of the social psychological mechanisms by which the species purportedly maintains unequal relations between groups is the development and transmission of "legitimizing myths"—or what Bourdieu (1977/1986) referred to as "legitimating discourses." These legitimizing myths include racist, sexist, and other xenophobic ideologies that seek to justify the discriminatory treatment of some social groups. Social attitudes may be located on a continuum ranging from "hierarchy enhancing" to "hierarchy attenuating" (Pratto et al., 1994). The legitimizing myths described by social dominance theorists and the notion that some attitudes serve to enhance hierarchies whereas others serve to attenuate them are both extremely congenial to the system justification perspective (see Jost & Sidanius, 2004).

Asymmetrical Effects of Group Attachment and System Support as a Function of Status

It follows from perspectives of social dominance and system justification that group attachment and system support are compatible for high-status groups but relatively incompatible for low-status groups (Jost & Burgess, 2000; Jost & Thompson, 2000). For example, Levin, Sidanius, Rabinowitz, and Federico (1998) demonstrated that endorsement of system-justifying beliefs (such as political conservatism and perceived system legitimacy) was positively related to ethnic ingroup identification among European Americans but negatively related to ingroup identification among Latinos and African Americans. These effects were replicated in a follow-up study involving the high-status group of Ashkenazi Jews in Israel relative to the low-status group of Arabs in Israel. Sinclair, Sidanius, and Levin (1998), too, found that attachment to American society was positively related to ethnic identification and attachment for European Americans, but it was negatively related to these variables for Latinos and African Americans.

Similar patterns of results were obtained in a separate study in which patriotism and national attachment can be seen as representing system justification concerns. For Latinos and African Americans, patriotism and identification with the United States were negatively related to ingroup favoritism, whereas among European Americans a positive relation was observed (Sidanius, Feshbach, Levin, & Pratto, 1997). In Israel, too, nationalism and patriotism were positively related to ingroup identification and ingroup preference among Jews, but they were negatively related for lower status Arabs. All of this evidence is consistent with the notion that group and system justification tendencies are complementary for high-status groups, but they are contradictory for members of low-status groups (Jost et al., 2001). It constitutes an important and well-supported point of convergence between social dominance and system justification theories.

Do Some Assumptions of Social Dominance Theory Function as "Legitimizing Myths"?

Social dominance theory holds that humans have adapted a general preference for group-based hierarchies and that dominant groups are biologically hardwired to defend their position of dominance by developing hierarchy-enhancing attitudes. Désert and Leyens (2006, p. 311) mistakenly attributed this view to system justification theory. By far the strongest empirical evidence obtained in support of social dominance theory concerns sex differences in social behavior. In particular, it has been found that males tend to exhibit more ingroup favoritism, more outgroup hostility, more politically conservative attitudes in at least some domains, and higher scores on measures of social dominance than do females (e.g., Pratto et al., 1994; Sidanius, Pratto, & Rabinowitz, 1994).

It is claimed to be *inevitable* that groups will display ingroup favoritism from above and outgroup favoritism from below, producing ideological and behavioral "asymmetry." The theory is self-consciously pessimistic, significantly more so than is system justification theory. Sidanius (1993), for instance, declared,

> Any efforts designed to alter status boundaries between hegemonic and negative reference groups are doomed to failure. (p. 216)

The aim of system justification theory, by contrast, is to identify social and psychological variables that lead people to accept, defend, bolster, and justify existing forms of social, economic, and political arrangements rather than to reject, challenge, attack, and criticize them. This theoretical endeavor is inspired in part by McGuire's (1983, 1989, 1997) perspectivist philosophy of science, which advocates the reconciliation of opposites, and in part by observations that virtually every historical case of group domination (or systemic inequality) is met with some acceptance and some resistance on the part of subordinated groups. At the same time, the empirical evidence obliges us to acknowledge that the former response is more common than the latter (Kinder & Sears, 1985; Moore, 1978; Zinn, 1968).

One of the key differences between social dominance theory and system justification theory concerns the question of evolutionary origins of ideology and specific forms of intergroup behavior (see also Jost, Banaji, & Nosek, 2004; Sidanius et al., 2004). Thus, Désert and Leyens (2006) are incorrect in stating that system justification theory "supposes that all societies are hierarchical" (p. 311). Whereas social dominance theory is a sociobiological (or biopolitical) theory that holds ethnocentrism and discrimination to be "adaptive," "inevitable," and part of "human nature" (Sidanius, 1993; Sidanius & Pratto, 1993), system justification theory highlights processes of ideological socialization as determinants of stereotypes and other social and political attitudes (e.g., Jost & Banaji, 1994; Jost & Hunyady, 2002; Jost, Ledgerwood, & Hardin, 2008) and the fact that people are motivated to defend and bolster the social status quo, regardless of its specific features (Jost, Banaji, & Nosek, 2004; Jost et al., 2010; Kay et al., 2002).

From the standpoint of system justification theory, the ideas that inequality is inevitable and that egalitarian social systems are doomed to fail risk encouraging a fatalistic view of social and political change (see Jost, 1995). In fact, using evolutionary theory to grant existing forms of social relations a privileged or permanent position may not be substantially different from other legitimizing myths that are analyzed by social dominance theorists. To the list of "paternalistic," "reciprocal," and "sacred" legitimizing myths identified by Sidanius (1993), then, one might add the "naturalistic legitimizing myth" that relations of dominance and subordination are determined by human nature or other biological inevitabilities (see also Jost & Hamilton, 2005).

To investigate whether the evolutionary tenets of social dominance theory function—at least for some people—as a kind of legitimizing myth, we conducted a small study to assess the link between social dominance orientation and endorsement of evolutionary explanations for social inequality (see also Keller, 2005, for a study of the ideological correlates of the belief in genetic determinism). We found that people who scored relatively high on Pratto et al.'s (1994) social dominance orientation (SDO) scale agreed more with scientific claims about the immutability and biological inevitability of status hierarchies (derived from articles on social dominance theory) in comparison with people who scored low on the SDO scale. Specifically, several hundred college students completed the SDO scale, and a subset that scored in either the top tertile or the bottom tertile on the scale was contacted by telephone more than one month later by an experimenter who was unaware of their SDO scores. Respondents were asked to indicate their level of agreement or disagreement with 16 statements that were taken from scientific articles and book chapters written by social dominance theorists (e.g., Pratto et al., 1994; Sidanius, 1993; Sidanius, Levin, et al., 1996; Sidanius & Pratto, 1993; Sidanius, Pratto, & Rabinowitz, 1994).

The scientific statements were ordered into the following four categories according to theoretical and empirical concerns: (a) *inevitability/immutability* (e.g., "All human societies are inherently group-based hierarchies and inherently oppressive" [Sidanius, 1993, p. 196]; "There will always be a negative reference group and that group will always be discriminated against" [Sidanius, 1993, p. 215]; "Any effects designed to alter status boundaries, such as affirmative action, equal housing, and anti-discrimination laws, between high status and low status groups are doomed to failure" [Sidanius, 1993, p. 216]); (b) *evolutionary adaptiveness* (e.g., "All human societies are inherently group-based social hierarchies, hierarchies which have had functional utility for the survival of human species over evolutionary time" [Sidanius, 1993, p. 214]; "Social systems that are hierarchically organized will have a competitive advantage over social systems that are not hierarchically organized" [Sidanius & Pratto, 1993, p. 175]; "Social hierarchy is a survival strategy that has been selected by most if not all species of primates, including *homo sapiens*" [Sidanius & Pratto, 1993, p. 174]); (c) *historical pervasiveness* (e.g., "All human societies throughout recorded history have been hierarchically organized" [Sidanius & Pratto, 1993, p. 174]; "Group conflict and group-based inequality are

TABLE 11.1   Mean Strength of Agreement With the Tenets of Social Dominance Theory (and Standard Deviations) as a Function of Respondent's Level of Social Dominance Orientation (SDO)

	Low SDO (n = 55)	High SDO (n = 48)	t test (df = 101)
Inevitability/immutability	5.01 (1.05)	5.93 (1.17)	4.23°°
Evolutionary adaptiveness	5.68 (1.09)	6.15 (1.29)	2.00°
Historical pervasiveness	6.31 (1.02)	6.47 (1.36)	ns
Status and self-esteem	5.79 (1.38)	5.94 (1.68)	ns
Total score (all items)	5.55 (0.82)	6.02 (1.10)	2.47°

Note: Higher scores indicate stronger agreement with scientific statements made by social dominance theorists; responses were made on a scale ranging from 1 to 10. Significance levels for (two-tailed) independent samples t tests are as follows: $°p <$ .05 and $°°p <$ .001.

pervasive in human existence" [Pratto et al., 1994, p. 741]); and (d) *status and self-esteem* (e.g., "The higher one's social rank, the higher one's self esteem should be" [Sidanius & Pratto, 1993, p. 183]; "One of the immediate benefits that one individual derives from discriminating against another individual is enhanced self esteem" [Sidanius & Pratto, 1993, p. 176]).

Results, which are summarized in Table 11.1, indicate that people who scored relatively high on the SDO scale were more likely than people who scored low on the SDO scale to agree with the tenets of social dominance theory overall and especially with its assumptions concerning the inevitability, immutability, and evolutionary adaptiveness of inequality. Of course, this does not mean that respondents with high SDO scale scores are wrong to endorse these statements, although it does suggest that for at least some people, their endorsement has an ideological basis. Furthermore, the style of reasoning that accompanies some of the assumptions of social dominance theory is itself associated with the kind of ideological beliefs that are critiqued by social dominance theorists in many other contexts (e.g., Pratto et al., 1994; Sidanius, Pratto, et al., 1996).

The evidence from our study reveals that people who scored high on the SDO scale are more likely than others to adopt "naturalistic legitimizing myths" in seeking to explain social inequality among social groups (see also Jost & Hamilton, 2005; Keller, 2005; Yzerbyt et al., 1997). Such myths may well reflect what Bourdieu (1977/1986, pp. 81–85) referred to as a "class *habitus*," that is, a "system of lasting, transposable dispositions" that explain and justify past experiences and present perceptions and that also tend to reproduce the objective social structures they seek to understand. In this context, it may be worth highlighting an observation Bourdieu offered concerning the relationship between the system-justifying belief systems of social scientists and their subjects:

The ideological use many societies make of the lineage model and, more generally, of genealogical representations, in order to justify and legitimate the established order ... would doubtless have become apparent to anthropologists at an earlier date if the theoretical use they themselves make of this theoretical construct had not prevented them from inquiring into the functions of genealogies and *genealogists*. (p. 19; italics in original)

Social Dominance Orientation Conflates Group Justification and System Justification

In recent years, social dominance researchers have focused their efforts on the measurement of individual differences (e.g., Pratto et al., 1994). This research demonstrates that, among other things, people who possess high levels of "social dominance orientation" will be more likely to subscribe to "hierarchy-enhancing legitimizing myths" that provide "moral and intellectual justification for continued and increased levels of hierarchy and inequality among socially constructed groups" (Levin et al., 1998, p. 376). The development and validation of individual difference measures such as "right-wing authoritarianism" and "social dominance orientation" have advanced considerably our understanding of the psychological bases of ideology and intergroup behavior (e.g., Altemeyer, 1998; Jost, Glaser, et al., 2003; Pratto et al., 1994; Whitley, 1999). System justification researchers in particular have benefited from the use of these scales (as well as "belief in a just world" and "Protestant work ethic" scales; e.g., Jost, Blount, et al., 2003; Jost & Burgess, 2000; Jost & Thompson, 2000; Kay & Jost, 2003; Overbeck et al., 2004).

Despite the SDO scale's impressive ability to predict social and political attitudes and even occupational choices, Jost and Thompson (2000) argued that there is an inherent conceptual ambiguity surrounding the definition of social dominance. Specifically, past definitions of SDO have confounded two concepts that system justification theorists seek to distinguish, namely group justification and system justification. At times, SDO is treated as synonymous with the need to express ethnocentrism, ingroup dominance, and ingroup favoritism. Sidanius (1993), for instance, referred to SDO as a "generalized imperial imperative" and a "will to group dominance" whereby "individuals desire social dominance and superiority for themselves and their primordial groups over other groups" (p. 209). Pratto et al. (1994) provided a similar definition of SDO as "the extent to which one desires that one's in-group dominate and be superior to out-groups" (p. 742; see also Sidanius, Pratto, & Mitchell, 1994).

Other investigations of social dominance, however, equate it with preferences for unequal social relations, whether inequality favors the ingroup or not. According to Sidanius, Pratto, and Rabinowitz (1994), SDO is defined as "an individual difference variable expressing very generalized, group-relevant anti-egalitarianism and the desire to establish hierarchical, dominant/subordinate relationships among social groups" (p. 195). The authors concluded, "Those belonging to low-status groups and who have high levels of SDO are likely to display *particularly low levels of ingroup attachment* [italics added]" (p. 210), a statement that is at odds with the above definition of SDO as a desire for ingroup superiority. Research by Levin and Sidanius (1999) supports this conception of SDO as a form of system justification, indicating that among Latinos in the United States and Arabs in Israel, SDO is associated with decreased (rather than increased) ingroup identification and evaluation (see also Overbeck et al., 2004).

A system justification analysis serves as a corrective by helping to disentangle two distinct psychological orientations that are confounded by existing definitions and measurements of social dominance (Jost & Thompson, 2000). The first definition of SDO corresponds to "group-based dominance," insofar as it describes a tendency to maintain or enhance the position of the ingroup relative to other groups. The second conceptualization, "opposition to equality," is akin to system justification, because it describes a tendency to defend and provide ideological reinforcement for the hierarchical social system, regardless of the consequences for the position of the self or the ingroup.

The importance of distinguishing between group and system justification components of SDO becomes clearest when one considers the responses of groups that are relatively low in social or economic status, such as African Americans, compared to other reference groups, such as European Americans. The implications of social dominance theory are fairly clear when it comes to the psychology of high-status group members. Proponents of "White supremacy," such as David Duke, would be expected to hold attitudes that are extremely high in SDO. "Black power" leaders such as the late Malcolm X, however, seem much more difficult to classify from a social dominance perspective. Would Malcolm X score extremely high or extremely low on measures of SDO? If one stresses the (group justification) notion of social dominance as fighting for ingroup goals and values, then one would assume that pro-Black activists such as Malcolm X would score very high on SDO. If, however, one focuses on the (system justification) notion of social dominance as related to the preservation of hierarchical social relationships, then Malcolm X and others like him would be expected to score very low on SDO. To take another example, Clarence Thomas and other politically conservative African Americans would be expected to score high on one aspect of social dominance, but they would be expected to score relatively low on the other. Unless one distinguishes between group and system justification components of social dominance orientation, serious conceptual and methodological ambiguities arise, especially when one considers the attitudes held by members of disadvantaged groups.

We (Jost & Thompson, 2000) found that, as hypothesized, a two-factor solution of the SDO scale fits the data better than a one-factor solution. More important, we found that the two factors predicted different social and psychological outcomes for European Americans than for African Americans. Specifically, "group-based dominance" was positively related to ingroup favoritism for both groups. "Opposition to equality," however, was related positively to self-esteem and ingroup favoritism for European Americans, but it was related *negatively* to ingroup favoritism and self-esteem for African Americans. Thus, we found that the two factors or subscales of the SDO scale have *opposite* effects on self-esteem and ingroup favoritism for members of a relatively disadvantaged group, which is consistent with our analysis of conflicts among ego, group, and system justification motives. Many other researchers have replicated the two-factor structure of the SDO scale, and Eagly, Diekman, Johannesen-Schmidt, and Koenig (2004) put it to especially valuable use in understanding the social and political attitudes of women (see also Kugler, Cooper, & Nosek, 2010 for a review).

CONCLUDING REMARKS

It should be clear from the foregoing that system justification theory probably would not exist in the absence of social identity and social dominance theories, both of which inspired a perspectivist student of intergroup relations (see also Jost, 2001, 2004; Jost & Hunyady, 2002; Jost & van der Toorn, 2011). As Reicher (2004) pointed out, the three theories share many scientific and other commitments, and it would be a mistake to think that these commonalities are cosmetic or trivial. We also concur with Sidanius et al. (2004) that much is gained by integrating the major insights of the three theories.

At the same time, the goal of this chapter has been to emphasize what is unique and distinctive about a system justification perspective and why this perspective helps to shed light on relatively neglected themes in social and political psychology, especially the extent to which the existing social system is maintained—even by those who stand to lose from its continued existence—through conscious and unconscious processes of rationalization and collaboration. What is needed is a sophisticated social psychological understanding of what Bourdieu (1977/1986) characterized as "the dialectical relationship between the objective structures and the cognitive and motivating structures which they produce and which tend to reproduce them" (p. 83). Engaging in open and critical debate concerning issues such as these can only help us, in science and in society, to sharpen the meaning of our inquiries and the contours of our knowledge. This is yet another reason to foster pluralism with regard to theoretical and other systems and to encourage, whenever possible, their constructive and mutual confrontation.

ACKNOWLEDGMENTS

I thank Jeffrey Pfeffer for encouraging me to write this chapter, a very early version of which was presented at the 23rd annual scientific meeting of the International Society for Political Psychology in Seattle, Washington. I am grateful for feedback I received there from, among others, Marilynn Brewer, Jack Citrin, Miles Hewstone, Felicia Pratto, and Tom Tyler. I thank Liza De Angelis, Sarah Quesnell, and Alison Wortman for their work on data collection and Cara Jolly and Tina Schweizer for assistance with manuscript preparation. Finally, Mahzarin Banaji, David Dunning, Peter Glick, Phillip Goff, Elizabeth Haines, Orsi Hunyady, Aaron Kay, Jeffrey Pfeffer, Eliot Smith, Russell Spears, and Cheryl Wakslak provided very helpful comments on previous drafts. The writing of this chapter was supported in part by National Science Foundation Award No. BCS-0617558, titled "Dynamic Cognitive and Motivational Properties of System Justification."

NOTES

1. With regard to both of these goals, it appears that system justification theory has proved useful not only in our own empirical research programs but also in the research programs of many others. See, for example, Ashburn-Nardo, Knowles, and Monteith (2003); Blanton, George, and Crocker (2001); Chen and Tyler (2001); Crandall, Eidelman, Skitka, and Morgan (2009); Glick and Fiske (2001); Goodwin, Operario, and Fiske (1998); Henry and Saul (2006); Ho, Sanbonmatsu, and Akimoto (2002); Kaiser, Dyrenforth, and Hagiwara (2006); Kay and Zanna (2009); Keller (2005); Lane, Mitchell, and Banaji (2005); Lau, Kay, and Spencer (2007); Livingston (2002); Major et al. (2002); Mendes, Blascovich, Hunter, Lickel, and Jost (2007); Nosek, Banaji, and Greenwald (2002); O'Brien and Crandall (2005); O'Brien and Major (2005); Pelham and Hetts (2001); Rudman, Feinberg, and Fairchild (2002); Schimel et al. (1999); Uhlmann, Dasgupta, Elgueta, Greenwald, and Swanson (2002); Ullrich and Cohrs (2007); and Yzerbyt, Rocher, and Schadron (1997).

2. Brewer (2007) also suggested, "Much of the data cited as evidence of out-group bias may actually reflect a form of in-group bias if members of the underprivileged group systematically underestimate the status difference between groups … [by] rating the out-group only slightly higher than the in-group on relevant dimensions" (p. 733). Such a pattern of data is in fact quite consistent with the notion that for members of disadvantaged groups, the effect of system justification motivation is mitigated to at least some degree by countervailing ego and group justification motives. But Brewer's (2007) account neglects other patterns of data that are consistent with the notion that—at least sometimes—members of disadvantaged groups are even more strongly motivated than others to engage in system justification (e.g., Jost, Pelham, Sheldon, & Sullivan, 2003). For instance, data from public opinion surveys reveal that African American respondents not only accepted unfavorable stereotypes of their own group as *lazy, irresponsible,* and *violent* but endorsed these stereotypes about their own group *even more strongly* than European American respondents did (Sniderman & Piazza, 1993).

REFERENCES

Abrams, D., & Hogg, M. (Eds.). (1990). *Social identity theory: Constructive and critical advances*. New York: Springer-Verlag.

Allport, G. W. (1954). The nature of prejudice. Reading, MA: Addison-Wesley.

Altemeyer, R. A. (1981). *Right-wing authoritarianism*. Winnipeg: University of Manitoba Press.

Altemeyer, R. A. (1998). The other "authoritarian personality." *Advances in Experimental Social Psychology, 30,* 48–92.

Aronson, E., & Mills, J. (1959). The effect of severity of initiation on liking for a group. *Journal of Abnormal and Social Psychology, 59,* 177–181.

Ashburn-Nardo, L., Knowles, M. L., & Monteith, M. J. (2003). Black Americans implicit racial associations and their implications for intergroup judgment. *Social Cognition, 21,* 61–87.

Banaji, M. R. (2004). The opposite of a great truth is also true: Homage to koan #7. In J. T. Jost, M. R. Banaji, & D. Prentice (Eds.), *Perspectivism in social psychology: The yin and yang of scientific progress* (pp. 127–140). Washington, DC: APA Press.

Bartels, L. (2006). What's the matter with *What's the matter with Kansas? Quarterly Journal of Political Science, 1,* 201–226.

Berger, P. L., & Luckmann, T. (1967). *The social construction of reality*. Garden City, NY: Anchor Books.

Bettelheim, B. (1943). Individual and mass behavior in extreme situations. *Journal of Abnormal and Social Psychology, 38*, 417–452.

Blair, I., & Jost, J. T. (2003). Exit, loyalty, and collective action among workers in a simulated business environment: Interactive effects of group identification and boundary permeability. *Social Justice Research, 16*, 95–108.

Blanton, H., George, G., & Crocker, J. (2001). Contexts of system justification and system evaluation: Exploring the social comparison strategies of the (not yet) contented female worker. *Group Processes and Intergroup Relations, 4*, 127–138.

Blasi, G., & Jost, J. T. (2006). System justification theory and research: Implications for law, legal advocacy, and social justice. *California Law Review, 94*, 1119–1168.

Bourdieu, P. (1986). *Outline of a theory of practice*. Cambridge, UK: Cambridge University Press. (Original translation published 1977)

Branthwaite, A., & Jones, J. E. (1975). Fairness and discrimination: English versus Welsh. *European Journal of Social Psychology, 5*, 323–338.

Brewer, M. B. (1979). Ingroup bias in the minimal intergroup situation: A cognitive-motivational analysis. *Psychological Bulletin, 86*, 307–324.

Brewer, M. B. (2007). The importance of being we: Human nature and intergroup relations. *American Psychologist, 62*, 728–738.

Brewer, M. B., & Brown, R. J. (1998). Intergroup relations. In D. T. Gilbert, S. T. Fiske, & G. Lindzey (Eds.), *The handbook of social psychology* (Vol. 2, 4th ed., pp. 554–594). Boston: McGraw-Hill.

Brown, R. J. (1988). *Group processes: Dynamics within and between groups*. Oxford, UK: Blackwell.

Brown, R. (2000a). *Group processes: Dynamics within and between groups* (2nd ed.). Oxford, UK: Blackwell.

Brown, R. (2000b). Social identity theory: Past achievements, current problems and future challenges. *European Journal of Social Psychology, 30*, 745–778.

Brown, R. J., & Wade, G. (1987). Superordinate goals and intergroup behaviour: The effect of role ambiguity and status on intergroup attitudes and task performance. *European Journal of Social Psychology, 17*, 131–142.

Chen, E. S., & Tyler, T. R. (2001). Cloaking power: Legitimizing myths and the psychology of the advantaged. In A. Y. Lee-Chai & J. Bargh (Eds.), *The use and abuse of power: Multiple perspectives on the causes of corruption* (pp. 241–261). Philadelphia: Psychology Press.

Clark, K. B., & Clark, M. P. (1947). Racial identification and preference in Negro children. In E. E. Maccoby, T. M. Newcomb, & E. L. Hartley (Eds.), *Readings in social psychology* (pp. 602–611). New York: Holt, Rinehart, and Winston.

Cooper, J., & Fazio, R. H. (1986). The formation and persistence of attitudes that support intergroup conflict. In S. Worchel & W. G. Austin (Eds.), *Psychology of intergroup relations* (pp. 183–195). Chicago: Nelson-Hall.

Crandall, C. S., Eidelman, S., Skitka, L. J., & Morgan, G. S. (2009). Status quo framing increases support for torture. *Social Influence, 4*, 1–10.

Crosby, F. (1984). The denial of personal discrimination. *American Behavioral Scientist, 27*, 371–386.

Cunningham, F. (1987). False consciousness. In *Democratic theory and socialism* (pp. 236–267). Cambridge, UK: Cambridge University Press.

Deaux, K. (1996). Social identification. In E. T. Higgins & A. W. Kruglanski (Eds.), *Social psychology: Handbook of basic principles* (pp. 777–798). New York: Guilford.

Désert, M., & Leyens, J.-P. (2006). Social comparisons across cultures I: Gender stereotypes in high and low power distance cultures. In S. Guimond (Ed.), *Social comparison and social psychology* (pp. 303–317). Cambridge, UK: Cambridge University Press.

Dollard, J. (1937). *Caste and class in a southern town*. New Haven, CT: Yale University Press.

Dovidio, J., & Gaertner, S. (2010). Intergroup bias. In S.T. Fiske, D. Gilbert, & G. Lindzey (Eds.), *Handbook of social psychology* (5th edition, Vol. 2, pp. 1084–1121). Hoboken, NJ: Wiley

Eagleton, T. (1991). *Ideology*. London: Verso.

Eagly, A. H., Diekman, A. B., Johannesen-Schmidt, M. C., & Koenig, A. M. (2004). Gender gaps in sociopolitical attitudes: A social psychological analysis. *Journal of Personality and Social Psychology, 87*, 796–816.

Elkins, S. (1967). Slavery and personality. In R. S. Lazarus & E. M. Opton, Jr. (Eds.), *Personality* (pp. 395–420). Middlesex, UK: Penguin.

Ellemers, N., Haslam, S. A., Platow, M. J., & van Knippenberg, D. (2003). Social identity at work: Developments, debates, directions. In S. A. Haslam, D. van Knippenberg, M. J. Platow, & N. Ellemers (Eds.), *Social identity at work: Developing theory for organizational practice* (pp. 3–26). New York: Psychology Press.

Ellemers, N., Van Rijswijk, W., Roefs, M., & Simons, C. (1997). Bias in intergroup perceptions: Balancing group identity with social reality. *Personality and Social Psychology Bulletin, 23*, 186–198.

Ellemers, N., Wilke, H., & van Knippenberg, A. (1993). Effects of the legitimacy of low group or individual status on individual and collective status-enhancement strategies. *Journal of Personality and Social Psychology, 64*, 766–778.

Elster, J. (1982). Belief, bias, and ideology. In M. Hollis & S. Lukes (Eds.), *Rationality and relativism* (pp. 123–148). Oxford, UK: Blackwell.

Festinger, L. (1954). A theory of social comparison processes. *Human Relations, 7*, 117–140.

Festinger, L. (1957). *A theory of cognitive dissonance*. Stanford, CA: Stanford University Press.

Frank, T. (2004). *What's the matter with Kansas?* New York: Metropolitan Books.

Fromm, E. (1962). *Beyond the chains of illusion: My encounter with Marx and Freud*. New York: Simon & Schuster.

Gelman, A. (2008). *Red state blue state rich state poor state*. Princeton, NJ: Princeton University Press.

Gilbert, D. T., Pinel, E. C., Wilson, T. D., Blumberg, S. J., & Wheatley, T. (1998). Immune neglect: A source of durability bias in affective forecasting. *Journal of Personality and Social Psychology, 75*, 617–638.

Gilens, M. (1999). *Why Americans hate welfare: Race, media, and the politics of antipoverty policy*. Chicago: University of Chicago Press.

Glick, P., & Fiske, S. T. (2001). An ambivalent alliance: Hostile and benevolent sexism as complementary justifications for gender inequality. *American Psychologist, 56*, 109–118.

Goodwin, S. A., Operario, D., & Fiske, S. T. (1998). Situational power and interpersonal dominance facilitate bias and inequality. *Journal of Social Issues, 54*, 677–698.

Gramsci, A. (1971). *Selections from the prison notebooks*. New York: International.

Gurr, T. (1970). *Why men rebel*. Princeton, NJ: Princeton.

Haines, E. L., & Jost, J. T. (2000). Placating the powerless: Effects of legitimate and illegitimate explanation on affect, memory, and stereotyping. *Social Justice Research, 13*, 219–236.

Haslam, S. A., Turner, J. C., Oakes, P. J., Reynolds, K. J., & Doosje, B. (2002). From personal pictures in the head to collective tools in the world: How shared stereotypes allow groups to represent and change social reality. In C. McGarty, V. Yzerbyt, & R. Spears (Eds.), *Stereotypes as explanation: The formation of meaningful beliefs about social groups* (pp. 157–185). Cambridge, UK: Cambridge University Press.

Havel, V. (1991). The power of the powerless. In V. Havel (Ed.), *Open letters* (pp. 125–214). London: Faber & Faber.

Henry, P. J., & Saul, A. (2006). The development of system justification in the developing world. *Social Justice Research, 19*, 365–378.

Hewstone, M. (1989). *Causal attribution*. Oxford, UK: Blackwell.

Hewstone, M. (1990). The "ultimate attribution error"? A review of the literature on intergroup causal attribution. *European Journal of Social Psychology, 20*, 311–335.

Hewstone, M., Rubin, M., & Willis, H. (2002). Intergroup bias. *Annual Review of Psychology, 53*, 575–604.

Hinkle, S., & Brown, R. (1990). Intergroup comparisons and social identity: Some links and lacunae. In D. Abrams & M. A. Hogg (Eds.), *Social identity theory: Constructive and critical advances* (pp. 48–70). New York: Springer-Verlag.

Hirschman, A. O. (1970). *Exit, voice, and loyalty: Responses to decline in firms, organizations, and states*. Cambridge, MA: Harvard University Press.

Ho, E. A., Sanbonmatsu, D. M., & Akimoto S. A. (2002). The effects of comparative status on social stereotypes: How the perceived success of some persons affects the stereotypes of others. *Social Cognition, 20*, 36–57.

Hoffman, A. (1989). *The best of Abbie Hoffman*. New York: Four Walls Eight Windows.

Hofstede, G. H. (1997). *Cultures and organizations: Software of the mind*. New York: McGraw-Hill.

Hogg, M. A., & Abrams, D. (1988). *Social identifications: A social psychology of intergroup relations and group processes*. London: Routledge.

Hornsey, M. J. (2008). Social identity theory and self-categorization theory: A historical review. *Social and Personality Psychology Compass, 2*, 204–222.

Huddy, L. (2004). Contrasting theoretical approaches to intergroup relations. *Political Psychology, 25*, 947–967.

Hunt, M. O. (2000). Status, religion, and the "belief in a just world": Comparing African Americans, Latinos, and Whites. *Social Science Quarterly, 81*, 325–343.

Jackman, M. R. (1994). *The velvet glove: Paternalism and conflict in gender, class, and race relations*. Berkeley: University of California Press.

Jennings, M. K. (1991). Thinking about social injustice. *Political Psychology, 12*, 187–204.

Jost, J. T. (1995). Negative illusions: Conceptual clarification and psychological evidence concerning false consciousness. *Political Psychology, 16*, 397–424.

Jost, J. T. (1997). An experimental replication of the depressed entitlement effect among women. *Psychology of Women Quarterly, 21*, 387–393.

Jost, J. T. (2001). Outgroup favoritism and the theory of system justification: An experimental paradigm for investigating the effects of socio-economic success on stereotype content. In G. Moskowitz (Ed.), *Cognitive social psychology: The Princeton symposium on the legacy and future of social cognition* (pp. 89–102). Hillsdale, NJ: Lawrence Erlbaum.

Jost, J. T. (2004). A perspectivist looks at the past, present, and (perhaps) the future of intergroup relations: A quixotic defense of system justification theory. In J. T. Jost, M. R. Banaji, & D. Prentice (Eds.), *Perspectivism in social psychology: The yin and yang of scientific progress* (pp. 215–230). Washington, DC: APA Press.

Jost, J. T., & Banaji, M. R. (1994). The role of stereotyping in system-justification and the production of false consciousness. *British Journal of Social Psychology, 33*, 1–27.

Jost, J. T., Banaji, M. R., & Nosek, B. A. (2004). A decade of system justification theory: Accumulated evidence of conscious and unconscious bolstering of the status quo. *Political Psychology, 25*, 881–919.

Jost, J. T., Banaji, M. R., & Prentice, D. (Eds.). (2004). *Perspectivism in social psychology: The yin and yang of scientific progress.* Washington, DC: APA Press.

Jost, J. T., Blount, S., Pfeffer, J., & Hunyady, G. (2003). Fair market ideology: Its cognitive-motivational underpinnings. *Research in Organizational Behavior, 25*, 53–91.

Jost, J. T., & Burgess, D. (2000). Attitudinal ambivalence and the conflict between group and system justification motives in low status groups. *Personality and Social Psychology Bulletin, 26*, 293–305.

Jost, J. T., Burgess, D., & Mosso, C. (2001). Conflicts of legitimation among self, group, and system: The integrative potential of system justification theory. In J. T. Jost & B. Major (Eds.), *The psychology of legitimacy: Emerging perspectives on ideology, justice, and intergroup relations* (pp. 363–388). New York: Cambridge University Press.

Jost, J. T., Fitzsimons, G., & Kay, A. C. (2004). The ideological animal: A system justification view. In J. Greenberg, S. L. Koole, & T. Pyszczynski (Eds.), *Handbook of experimental existential psychology* (pp. 263–283). New York: Guilford.

Jost, J. T., Glaser, J., Kruglanski, A. W., & Sulloway, F. (2003). Political conservatism as motivated social cognition. *Psychological Bulletin, 129*, 339–375.

Jost, J. T., & Hamilton, D. L. (2005). Stereotypes in our culture. In J. Dovidio, P. Glick, & L. Rudman (Eds.), *On The Nature of Prejudice: Fifty years after Allport* (pp. 208–224). Oxford, UK: Blackwell.

Jost, J. T., & Hardin, C.D. (in press). On the structure and dynamics of human thought: The legacy of William J. McGuire for social and political psychology. *Political Psychology.*

Jost, J. T., & Hunyady, O. (2002). The psychology of system justification and the palliative function of ideology. *European Review of Social Psychology, 13*, 111–153.

Jost, J. T., & Hunyady, O. (2005). Antecedents and consequences of system-justifying ideologies. *Current Directions in Psychological Science, 14*, 260–265.

Jost, J. T., & Kay, A. C. (2005). Exposure to benevolent sexism and complementary gender stereotypes: Consequences for specific and diffuse forms of system justification. *Journal of Personality and Social Psychology, 88*, 498–509.

Jost, J. T., & Kay, A. C. (2010). Social justice: History, theory, and research. In S.T. Fiske, D. Gilbert, & G. Lindzey (Eds.), *Handbook of social psychology* (5th edition, Vol. 2, pp. 1122–1165). Hoboken, NJ: Wiley.

Jost, J. T., Kivetz, Y., Rubini, M., Guermandi, G., & Mosso, C. (2005). System-justifying functions of complementary regional and ethnic stereotypes: Cross-national evidence. *Social Justice Research, 18*, 305–333.

Jost, J. T., Ledgerwood, A., & Hardin, C. D. (2008). Shared reality, system justification, and the relational basis of ideological beliefs. *Social and Personality Psychology Compass, 2*, 171–186.

Jost, J. T., Liviatan, I., van der Toorn, J., Ledgerwood, A., Mandisodza, A., & Nosek, B. A. (in press). System justification: How do we know it's motivated? In A. C. Kay et al. (Eds.), *The psychology of justice and legitimacy: The Ontario symposium* (Vol. 11). Hillsdale, NJ: Lawrence Erlbaum.

Jost, J. T., & Major, B. (2001). Emerging perspectives on the psychology of legitimacy. In J. T. Jost & B. Major (Eds.), *The psychology of legitimacy: Emerging perspectives on ideology, justice, and intergroup relations* (pp. 3–30). New York: Cambridge University Press.

Jost, J. T., Napier, J. L., Thorisdottir, H., Gosling, S. D., Palfai, T. P., & Ostafin, B. (2007). Are needs to manage uncertainty and threat associated with political conservatism or ideological extremity? *Personality and Social Psychology Bulletin, 33*, 989–1007.

Jost, J. T., Pelham, B. W., & Carvallo, M. (2002). Non-conscious forms of system justification: Cognitive, affective, and behavioral preferences for higher status groups. *Journal of Experimental Social Psychology, 38*, 586–602.

Jost, J. T., Pelham, B. W., Sheldon, O., & Sullivan, B. N. (2003). Social inequality and the reduction of ideological dissonance on behalf of the system: Evidence of enhanced system justification among the disadvantaged. *European Journal of Social Psychology, 33*, 13–36.

Jost, J. T., & Sidanius, J. (2004). Political psychology: An introduction. In J. T. Jost & J. Sidanius (Eds.), *Political psychology: Key readings* (pp. 1–17). New York: Psychology Press.

Jost, J. T., & Thompson, E. P. (2000). Group-based dominance and opposition to equality as independent predictors of self-esteem, ethnocentrism, and social policy attitudes among African Americans and European Americans. *Journal of Experimental Social Psychology, 36*, 209–232.

Jost, J. T., & van der Toorn, J. (2011). System justification theory. In P.A.M. van Lange, A. W. Kruglanski, & E. T. Higgins (Eds.), *Handbook of theories of social psychology*. London: Sage.

Jost, J. T., Wakslak, C., & Tyler, T. R. (2008). System justification theory and the alleviation of emotional distress: Palliative effects of ideology in an arbitrary social hierarchy and in society. In K. Hegtvedt & J. Clay-Warner (Eds.), *Justice: Advances in group processes* (Vol. 25, pp. 181–211). Bingley, UK: JAI/Emerald.

Jost, L. J., & Jost, J. T. (2007). Why Marx left philosophy for social science. *Theory and Psychology, 17*, 297–322.

Kaiser, C. R., Dyrenforth, P. S., & Hagiwara, N. (2006). Why are attributions to discrimination interpersonally costly? A test of system- and group-justifying motivations. *Personality and Social Psychology Bulletin, 32*, 1523–1536.

Kay, A., Jimenez, M. C., & Jost, J. T. (2002). Sour grapes, sweet lemons, and the anticipatory rationalization of the status quo. *Personality and Social Psychology Bulletin, 28*, 1300–1312.

Kay, A. C., & Jost, J. T. (2003). Complementary justice: Effects of "poor but happy" and "poor but honest" stereotype exemplars on system justification and implicit activation of the justice motive. *Journal of Personality and Social Psychology, 85*, 823–837.

Kay, A. C., Jost, J. T., Mandisodza, A. N., Sherman, S. J., Petrocelli, J. V., & Johnson, A. L. (2007). Panglossian ideology in the service of system justification: How complementary stereotypes help us to rationalize inequality. In M. Zanna (Ed.), *Advances in experimental social psychology* (Vol. 39, pp. 305–358). San Diego, CA: Elsevier.

Kay, A. C., Jost, J. T., & Young, S. (2005). Victim derogation and victim enhancement as alternate routes to system justification. *Psychological Science, 16*, 240–246.

Kay, A. C., & Zanna, M. (2009). A contextual analysis of the system justification motive and its societal consequences. In J. T. Jost, A. C. Kay, & H. Thorisdottir (Eds.), *Social and psychological bases of ideology and system justification*. New York: Oxford University Press.

Keller, J. (2005). In genes we trust: The biological component of psychological essentialism and its relationship to mechanisms of motivated social cognition. *Journal of Personality and Social Psychology, 88*, 686–702.

Kinder, D. R., & Sears, D. O. (1985). Public opinion and political action. In G. Lindzey & E. Aronson (Eds.), *Handbook of social psychology* (Vol. II, 3rd ed., pp. 714–726). New York: Random House.

Kluegel, J. R., & Smith, E. R. (1986). *Beliefs about inequality: Americans' views of what is and what ought to be.* New York: Aldine de Gruyter.

Kugler, M., Cooper, J., & Nosek, B. A. (2010). Group-based dominance and opposition to equality correspond to different psychological motives. *Social Justice Research*.

Lane, K. A., Mitchell, J. P., & Banaji, M. R. (2005). Me and my group: Cultural status can disrupt cognitive consistency. *Social Cognition, 23*, 353–386.

Lane, R. E. (2004). The fear of equality. *American Political Science Review, 53*, 35–51. (Original work published 1959) (Reproduced in *Political psychology: Key readings*, by J. T. Jost & J. Sidanius, Eds., New York: Psychology Press)

Lau, G. P., Kay, A. C., & Spencer, S. J. (2007). Loving those who justify inequality: The effects of system threat on attraction to women who embody benevolent sexist ideals. *Psychological Science, 19*, 20–21.

Leach, C. W., Spears, R., Branscombe, N. R., & Doosje, B. (2003). Malicious pleasure: *Schadenfreude* at the suffering of another group. *Journal of Personality and Social Psychology, 84*, 932–943.

Ledgerwood, A., Mandisodza, A., Jost, J. T., & Pohl, M. (in press). Working for the system: Motivated defense of meritocratic beliefs. *Social Cognition*.

Lerner, M. J. (1980). *The belief in a just world: A fundamental delusion*. New York: Plenum.

Levin, S., & Sidanius, J. (1999). Social dominance and social identity in the United States and Israel: Ingroup favoritism or outgroup derogation? *Political Psychology, 20*, 99–126.

Levin, S., Sidanius, J., Rabinowitz, J. L., & Federico, C. (1998). Ethnic identity, legitimizing ideologies, and social status: A matter of ideological asymmetry. *Political Psychology, 19*, 373–404.

Lewin, K. (1947). Group decision and social change. In T. M. Newcomb & E. L. Harley (Eds.), *Readings in social psychology* (pp. 330–344). New York: Holt.

Lewin, K. (1948). Self-hatred among Jews. In K. Lewin (Ed.), *Resolving social conflicts: Selected papers on group dynamics*. New York: Harper & Brothers. (Original work published 1941)

Leyens, J. P., & Demoulin, S. (2009). Hierarchy-based groups: Real inequalities and essential differences. In S. Otten, K. Sassenberg, & T. Kessler (Ed.), *Intergroup relations: The role of motivation and emotion*. New York: Psychology Press.

Lipset, S. M. (1981). Working-class authoritarianism. In S. M. Lipset (Ed.), *Political man: The social bases of politics* (pp. 87–126). Baltimore: Johns Hopkins. (Original work published 1960)

Livingston, R. W. (2002). The role of perceived negativity in the moderation of African Americans' implicit and explicit racial attitudes. *Journal of Experimental Social Psychology, 38*, 405–413.

Lukács, G. (1971). *History and class consciousness*. Cambridge, MA: MIT Press.

Mackie, D. M., & Hamilton, D. L. (Eds.). (1993). *Affect, cognition, and stereotyping: Interactive processes in group perception*. San Diego, CA: Academic Press.

MacKinnon, C. A. (1989). *Towards a feminist theory of state*. Cambridge, MA: Harvard University Press.

Major, B. (1994). From social inequality to personal entitlement: The role of social comparisons, legitimacy appraisals, and group memberships. *Advances in Experimental Social Psychology, 26*, 293–355.

Major, B., Gramzow, R. H., McCoy, S. K., Levin, S., Schmader, T., & Sidanius, J. (2002). Perceiving personal discrimination: The role of group status and legitimizing ideology. *Journal of Personality and Social Psychology, 82*, 269–282.

Martin, J. (1986). The tolerance of injustice. In J. M. Olson, C. P. Herman, & M. P. Zanna (Eds.), *Relative deprivation and social comparison: The Ontario symposium* (Vol. 4, pp. 217–242). Hillsdale, NJ: Lawrence Erlbaum.

Marx, K., & Engels, F. (1970). *The German ideology* (C. J. Arthur, Ed.). New York: International Publishers. (Original work published 1846)

McGuire, W. J. (1983). A contextualist theory of knowledge: Its implications for innovation and reform in psychological research. *Advances in Experimental Social Psychology, 16*, 1–47.

McGuire, W. J. (1989). A perspectivist approach to the strategic planning of programmatic scientific research. In B. Gholson, W. R. Shadish, Jr., R. A. Niemeyer, & A. C. Houts (Eds.), *The psychology of science: Contributions to metascience* (pp. 214–245). New York: Cambridge University Press.

McGuire, W. J. (1997). Creative hypothesis generating in psychology: Some useful heuristics. *Annual Review of Psychology, 48,* 1–30.

Mendes, W. B., Blascovich, J., Hunter, S. B., Lickel, B. & Jost, J. T. (2007). Threatened by the unexpected: Physiological responses during social interactions with expectancy-violating partners. *Journal of Personality and Social Psychology, 92,* 698–716.

Moore, B., Jr. (1978). *Injustice: The social bases of obedience and revolt.* White Plains, NY: M. E. Sharpe.

Mummendey, A., & Simon, B. (1989). Better or different? III: The impact of importance of comparison and relative in-group size upon intergroup discrimination. *British Journal of Social Psychology, 28,* 1–16.

Napier, J. L., & Jost, J. T. (2008a). The "anti-democratic personality" revisited: A cross-national investigation of working class authoritarianism. *Journal of Social Issues, 64,* 595–617.

Napier, J. L., & Jost, J. T. (2008b). Why are conservatives happier than liberals? *Psychological Science, 19,* 565–572.

Napier, J., Mandisodza, A., Andersen, S. M., & Jost, J. T. (2006). System justification in responding to the poor and displaced in the aftermath of Hurricane Katrina. *Analyses of Social Issues and Public Policy, 6,* 57–73.

Nosek, B. A., Banaji, M. R., & Greenwald, A. G. (2002). Harvesting implicit group attitudes and beliefs from a demonstration website. *Group Dynamics, 6,* 101–115.

Oakes, P. J., Turner, J. C., & Haslam, A. (1994). *Stereotyping and social reality.* Cambridge, MA: Blackwell.

O'Brien, L. T., & Crandall, C. S. (2005). Perceiving self-interest: Power, ideology, and maintenance of the status quo. *Social Justice Research, 18,* 1–24.

O'Brien, L. T., & Major, B. (2005). System justifying beliefs and psychological well-being: The roles of group status and identity. *Personality and Social Psychology Bulletin, 31,* 1718–1729.

Overbeck, J., Jost, J. T., Mosso, C., & Flizik, A. (2004). Resistant vs. acquiescent responses to ingroup inferiority as a function of social dominance orientation in the USA and Italy. *Group Processes and Intergroup Relations, 7,* 35–54.

Paulhus, D. L. (1984). Two-component models of socially desirable responding. *Journal of Personality and Social Psychology, 46,* 598–609.

Pelham, B. W., & Hetts, J. J. (2001). Underworked and overpaid: Elevated entitlement in men's self-pay. *Journal of Experimental Social Psychology, 37,* 93–103.

Pratto, F., Sidanius, J., Stallworth, L. M., & Malle, B. F. (1994). Social dominance orientation: A personality variable predicting social and political attitudes. *Journal of Personality and Social Psychology, 67,* 741–763.

Reicher, S. (1984). The St. Paul's riot: An explanation of the limits of crowd action in terms of a social identity model. *European Journal of Social Psychology, 14,* 1–21.

Reicher, S. (2004). The context of social identity: Dominance, resistance, and change. *Political Psychology, 25,* 921–945.

Reicher, S., Hopkins, N., & Condor, S. (1997). Stereotype construction as a strategy of influence. In R. Spears, P. J. Oakes, N. Ellemers, & S. A. Haslam (Eds.), *The social psychology of stereotyping and group life* (pp. 94–118). Oxford, UK: Blackwell.

Robinson, W. P. (Ed.). (1996). *Social groups and identities: Developing the legacy of Henri Tajfel.* Oxford, UK: Butterworth Heinemann.

Rubin, M., & Hewstone, M. (1998). Social identity theory's self-esteem hypothesis: A review and some suggestions for clarification. *Personality and Social Psychology Review, 2,* 40–62.

Rubin, M., & Hewstone, M. (2004). Social identity, system justification, and social dominance: Commentary on Reicher, Jost et al., and Sidanius et al. *Political Psychology, 25*, 823–844.

Rudman, L. A., Feinberg, J., & Fairchild, K. (2002). Minority members' implicit attitudes: Automatic ingroup bias as a function of group status. *Social Cognition, 20*, 294–320.

Runciman, W. (1969). False consciousness. In *Sociology in its place* (pp. 212–223). Cambridge, UK: Cambridge University Press.

Sachdev, I., & Bourhis, R. Y. (1984). Minimal majorities and minorities. *European Journal of Social Psychology, 14*, 35–52.

Sachdev, I., & Bourhis, R. Y. (1987). Status differentials and intergroup behavior. *European Journal of Social Psychology, 17*, 277–294.

Sachdev, I., & Bourhis, R. Y. (1991). Power and status differentials in minority and majority group relations. *European Journal of Social Psychology, 21*, 1–24.

Schimel, J., Simon, L., Greenberg, J., Pyszczynski, T., Solomon, S., Waxmonsky, J., & Arndt, J. (1999). Stereotypes and terror management: Evidence that mortality salience enhances stereotypic thinking and preferences. *Journal of Personality and Social Psychology, 77*, 905–926.

Scott, J. (1990). *Domination and the arts of resistance.* New Haven, CT: Yale University.

Sidanius, J. (1993). The psychology of group conflict and the dynamics of oppression: A social dominance perspective. In S. Iyengar & W. J. McGuire (Eds.), *Explorations in political psychology* (pp. 183–219). Durham, NC: Duke University Press.

Sidanius, J., Feshbach, S., Levin, S., & Pratto, F. (1997). The interface between ethnic and national attachment. *Public Opinion Quarterly, 61*, 103–133.

Sidanius, J., Levin, S., Federico, M., & Pratto, F. (2001). Legitimizing ideologies: The social dominance approach. In J. T. Jost & B. Major (Eds.), *The psychology of legitimacy: Emerging perspectives on ideology, justice, and intergroup relations* (pp. 307–331). New York: Cambridge University Press.

Sidanius, J., Levin, S., & Pratto, F. (1996). Consensual social dominance orientation and its correlates within the hierarchical structure of American society. *International Journal of Intercultural Relations, 20*, 385–408.

Sidanius, J., & Pratto, F. (1993). The inevitability of oppression and the dynamics of social dominance. In P. Sniderman, P. E. Tetlock, & E. G. Carmines (Eds.), *Prejudice, politics, and the American dilemma* (pp. 173–211). Stanford, CA: Stanford University Press.

Sidanius, J., & Pratto, F. (1999). *Social dominance: An intergroup theory of social hierarchy and oppression.* New York: Cambridge University Press.

Sidanius, J., Pratto, F., & Bobo, L. (1996). Racism, conservatism, affirmative action, and intellectual sophistication: A matter of principled conservatism or group dominance? *Journal of Personality and Social Psychology, 70*, 476–490.

Sidanius, J., Pratto, F., & Mitchell, M. (1994). In-group identification, social dominance orientation, and differential intergroup social allocation. *Journal of Social Psychology, 134*, 151–167.

Sidanius, J., Pratto, F., & Rabinowitz, J. L. (1994). Gender, ethnic status, and ideological asymmetry: A social dominance interpretation. *Journal of Cross-Cultural Psychology, 25*, 194–216.

Sidanius, J., Pratto, F., van Laar, C., & Levin, S. (2004). Social dominance theory: Its agenda and method. *Political Psychology, 25*, 845–880.

Simon, B., & Klandermans, B. (2001). Politicized collective identity: A social psychological analysis. *American Psychologist, 56*, 319–331.

Sinclair, S., Sidanius, J., & Levin, S. (1998). The interface between ethnic and social system attachment: The differential effects of hierarchy-enhancing and hierarchy-attenuating environments. *Journal of Social Issues, 54*, 741–757.

Sniderman, P., & Piazza, T. (1993). *The scar of race.* Cambridge, MA: Harvard University Press.

Spears, R., Doosje, B., & Ellemers, N. (1997). Self-stereotyping in the face of threats to group status and distinctiveness: The role of group identification. *Personality and Social Psychology Bulletin, 23,* 538–553.

Spears, R., Jetten, J., & Doosje, B. (2001). The (il)legitimacy of ingroup bias: From social reality to social resistance. In J. T. Jost & B. Major (Eds.), *The psychology of legitimacy: Emerging perspectives on ideology, justice, and intergroup relations* (pp. 332–362). New York: Cambridge University Press.

Spears, R., & Manstead, A. S. R. (1989). The social context of stereotyping and differentiation. *European Journal of Social Psychology, 19,* 101–121.

Spears, R., Oakes, P. J., Ellemers, N., & Haslam, S. A. (Eds.). (1997). *The social psychology of stereotyping and group life.* Oxford, UK: Blackwell.

Stacey, B. G., & Green, R. T. (1971). Working-class conservatism: A review and an empirical study. *British Journal of Social and Clinical Psychology, 10,* 10–26.

Stangor, C., & Jost, J. T. (1997). Individual, group, and system levels of analysis and their relevance for stereotyping and intergroup relations. In R. Spears, P. Oakes, N. Ellemers, & S. A. Haslam (Eds.), *The social psychology of stereotyping and group life* (pp. 336–358). Oxford, UK: Blackwell.

Tajfel, H. (Ed.). (1978). *Differentiation between social groups: Studies in the social psychology of intergroup relations.* London: Academic Press.

Tajfel, H. (1981). *Human groups and social categories.* Cambridge, UK: Cambridge University Press.

Tajfel, H. (1982). Psychological concepts of equity: The present and the future. In P. Fraisse (Ed.), *Psychologie de demain.* Paris: Presses Universitaires de France.

Tajfel, H. (1984). Intergroup relations, social myths and social justice in social psychology. In H. Tajfel (Ed.), *The social dimension: European developments in social psychology* (pp. 695–715). Cambridge, UK: Cambridge University Press.

Tajfel, H., & Turner, J. C. (1986). The social identity theory of intergroup behavior. In S. Worchel & W. G. Austin (Eds.), *The psychology of intergroup relations* (pp. 7–24). Chicago: Nelson-Hall. (Original work published 1979)

Turner, J. C. (1975). Social comparison and social identity: Some prospects for intergroup behaviour. *European Journal of Social Psychology, 5,* 5–34.

Turner, J. C. (1982). Toward a cognitive redefinition of the social group. In H. Tajfel (Ed.), *Social identity and intergroup behavior* (pp. 15–40). Cambridge, UK: Cambridge University Press.

Turner, J. C. (1999). Some current issues in research on social identity and self-categorization theories. In N. Ellemers, R. Spears, & B. Doosje (Eds.), *Social identity: Context, commitment, and content* (pp. 6–34). Oxford, UK: Blackwell.

Turner, J.C. (2006). Tyranny, freedom and social structure: Escaping our theoretical prisons. *British Journal of Social Psychology, 45,* 41–46.

Turner, J. C., & Brown, R. (1978). Social status, cognitive alternatives, and intergroup relations. In H. Tajfel (Ed.), *Differentiation between social groups* (pp. 201–234). London: Academic Press.

Turner, J. C., & Giles, H. (Eds.). (1981). *Intergroup behavior.* Chicago: University of Chicago Press.

Turner, J. C., Hogg, M. A., Oakes, P. J., Reicher, S. D., & Wetherell, M. S. (1987). *Rediscovering the social group: A self-categorization theory.* Oxford, UK: Blackwell.

Tyler, T. R., & McGraw, K. M. (1986). Ideology and the interpretation of personal experience: Procedural justice and political quiescence. *Journal of Social Issues, 42,* 115–128.

Uhlmann, E., Dasgupta, N., Elgueta, A., Greenwald, A. G., & Swanson, J. E. (2002). Subgroup prejudice based on skin color among Hispanics in the United States and Latin America. *Social Cognition, 20,* 198–225.

Ullrich, J., & Cohrs, J. C. (2007). Terrorism salience increases system justification: Experimental evidence. *Social Justice Research, 20,* 117–139.

Van der Toorn, J., Tyler, T. R., & Jost, J. T. (2010). *Justice or justification? The effect of outcome dependence on perceived legitimacy of authority.* Manuscript submitted for publication.

Van Knippenberg, A. (1984). Intergroup differences in group perceptions. In H. Tajfel (Ed.), *The social dimension* (Vol. 2, pp. 560–578). Cambridge, UK: Cambridge University Press.

Wakslak, C., Jost, J. T., Tyler, T. R., & Chen, E. (2007). Moral outrage mediates the dampening effect of system justification on support for redistributive social policies. *Psychological Science, 18,* 267–274.

Whitley, B. E., Jr. (1999). Right-wing authoritarianism, social dominance orientation, and prejudice. *Journal of Personality and Social Psychology, 77,* 126–134.

Wicklund, R., & Brehm, J. (1976). *Perspectives on cognitive dissonance.* Hillsdale, NJ: Lawrence Erlbaum.

Wright, S. C. (2001). Restricted intergroup boundaries: Tokenism, ambiguity, and the tolerance of injustice. In J. T. Jost & B. Major (Eds.), *The psychology of legitimacy: Emerging perspectives on ideology, justice, and intergroup relations* (pp. 223–254). New York: Cambridge University Press.

Wright, S. C., Taylor, D. M., & Moghaddam, F. M. (1990). Responding to membership in a disadvantaged group: From acceptance to collective protest. *Journal of Personality and Social Psychology, 58,* 994–1003.

Yoshimura, K., & Hardin, C. D. (2009). Cognitive salience of subjugation and the ideological justification of U.S. geopolitical dominance in Japan. *Social Justice Research, 22,* 298–311.

Yzerbyt, V., & Demoulin, S. (2010). Intergroup relations. In S. T. Fiske, D. Gilbert, & G. Lindzey (Eds.), *Handbook of social psychology* (5th edition, Vol. 2, pp. 1024–1083). Hoboken, NJ: Wiley.

Yzerbyt, V. Y., Rocher, S. J., & Schadron, G. (1997). Stereotypes as explanations: A subjective essentialistic view of group perception. In R. Spears, P. J. Oakes, N. Ellemers, & S. A. Haslam (Eds.), *The social psychology of stereotyping and group life* (pp. 208–235). Oxford, UK: Blackwell.

Zinn, H. (1968). *Disobedience and democracy: Nine fallacies on law and order.* New York: Vintage.

Author Index

Wheeler, D., 44
White, K. M., 136
Whitley, B. E., Jr., 250
Wicklund, R. A., 109, 233
Wieling, M. B., 25
Wieselquist, J., 153
Wiggin, J. S., 206
Wilbur, C. J., 26
Wilke, H., 108, 226
Williams, K., 50
Williams, K. D., 3, 38, 44, 80, 95, 191
Williams, R., 201
Wills, T. A., 67
Wilson, A. D., 117, 118
Wilson, D. S., 2
Wilson, M., 22
Wilson, R., 156
Wilson, T. D., 83
Wingfield, J. C., 171, 172, 179, 180
Winter, J., 156
Wirth, M., 173, 178
Wirtz, P., 21
Witcher, B. S., 48
Woody, S. R., 16
Woodzicka, J. A., 2
Wrangham, R. W., 19
Wright, S. C., 234
Wu, F. C., 173
Wuehrmann, E., 179

Wujastyk, D., 16
Wynne-Edwards, K. E., 179

Y

Yamagishi, T., 116, 201
Yehuda, R., 201
Yoshimura, K., 229
Young, L. J., 161
Young, S., 224, 225
Yzerbyt, V. Y., 232, 249

Z

Zagoory-Sharon, O., 177
Zahn-Waxler, C., 114
Zajonc, R. B., 85
Zak, P., 177
Zak. P. J., 161
Zanna, A. S., 59, 63, 65
Zanna, M., 234
Zanna, M. P., 59, 63, 65, 198
Zehm, K., 137
Zimbardo, P., 80
Zink, C. K., 80
Zinn, H., 247
Zuckerman, M., 107
Zurriga, R., 25

Subject Index

Made in the USA
Middletown, DE
31 January 2018